SECURITY ANALYSIS ON WALL STREET

WILEY FRONTIERS IN FINANCE

Series Editor: Edward I. Altman, New York University

SECURITY ANALYSIS ON WALL STREET

A COMPREHENSIVE GUIDE TO TODAY'S VALUATION METHODS

University Edition

Jeffrey C. Hooke

JOHN WILEY & SONS, INC.

New York • Chichester • Weinheim • Brisbane • Singapore • Toronto

Published by John Wiley & Sons, Inc.

Published simultaneously in Canada.

Library of Congress Cataloging-in-Publication Data:

Hooke, Jeffrey C.
    Security analysis on Wall Street : a comprehensive guide to
    today's valuation methods / Jeffrey C. Hooke.
        p.   cm. — (Wiley frontiers in finance)
    Includes index.
    ISBN 0-471-36247-6
    1. Investment analysis.   2. Securities—Research.   I. Title.
    II. Series.
    HG4529.H66   1998
    332.63'2—dc21   97-46366

Printed in the United States of America

10 9 8 7 6 5 4 3 2 1

Preface

Fortunes are made and lost on Wall Street based on advice from security analysts. They evaluate the prospects of companies issuing common stock and provide "buy" or "sell" recommendations. Despite this fact, it's been a while since an experienced practitioner explained how Wall Street truly approaches security analysis. For the serious investor, financial executive, or corporate manager, knowing how professionals price securities is important. After all, a common share is only worth what someone will pay for it. Since that someone is typically a full-time analyst, equity trader, or investment fund manager, understanding the evaluative framework of such professionals is a prerequisite for optimizing investment results.

Valuing a common stock properly is one of the most challenging tasks in finance. Theories abound on the appropriate methodology for establishing a valuation, ranging from the quasi-scientific discipline of the "intrinsic value" believer to the emotional ravings of the anticipation investor. Among the serious practitioners of valuation, there are important differences of opinion regarding methodology. Most prominent investors demonstrate an eclectic style in stock picking, basing decisions on a combination of techniques. As a result, the stock market lacks a unifying anchor from which common stock appraisals begin, and participants are hard pressed to say which valuation techniques work and which don't.

These differences result in a healthy competition among investors as they test their respective appraisal methods against each other. An enormous amount of trading activity is represented by one investor betting his conclusions against those of someone else. Who's right? Eventually, the market reaches a consensus and a stock's price moves in line with the majority's conclusions.

WHAT IS SECURITY ANALYSIS?

Security analysis is the body of knowledge directed toward the valuation of securities in a rational, systematic way. It has a key principle: Over the long term, the price of an individual stock reflects the business prospects of the issuing company and its economic environment. Over the short term, however, emotional forces frequently impact share values, so the pricing of a security is often a tug-of-war between the "rational" and "irrational" groups.

Security analysts are professionals, well versed in the principles and methods of assessing common stocks. Typically employed by a mutual fund, pension manager, insurance company, or brokerage firm, they follow the financial markets and study individual securities. Based on the results of their research, they make investment recommendations that are expected to provide superior performance.

EQUITY VALUES REFLECT UNCERTAINTY

The investment value of a security depends on so many highly variable factors—and hence, is subject to such rapid changes—that pinpointing the validity of one analyst's reasoning *a priori* is difficult. Analysts' predictions are confounded by, among other matters, unexpected changes in macroeconomic indicators such as interest rates, unforeseen developments in company-specific matters such as new competitors, and unusual shocks to an industry such as technology advances. All three factors can sharply alter a share price. At other times, a stock's value changes for reasons totally unrelated to the general economy, a company's industry, or its underlying business. For example, distinctive patterns in a stock's trading activity prompt people to buy and sell, strictly on the notion that past trading trends are predictive of future values.

The market price of any stock thus represents a jumble of contradictory expectations and hypotheses, influenced constantly by investors processing new data and evaluating changing circumstances. If this analytical process isn't difficult enough, the careful investor must also consider the human factors that affect financial asset values and react accordingly. From time to time, emotional sentiments envelop either an individual stock or the entire market. A herd psychology takes over and pricing defies rational explanation. Investors seeking an economic justification for the resultant values are best advised to step out of the way of the ensuing stampede.

Since disparate investment styles and unpredictable future events both exercise a major influence on stock prices, it is not surprising that most professional money managers cannot consistently select equities that outperform the general market indices. Indeed, according to a large body of academic theory, "beating the market" on a regular basis is impossible. Because share prices reflect all available information, no amount of study can achieve above-average investment results, and those portfolio managers with superior records are simply beneficiaries of the laws of chance. Sooner or later, the odds catch up with them, and their performance returns to normal. The rapid growth of equity index funds is evidence of the broad acceptance of this theory, and it provides a clear sign of investors' frustration with professional money managers.

THE RATIONALITY CONCEPT

As a field of study, security analysis rejects the idea that equity investors are doomed to earn the market return over time and nothing more. Rather, it dictates that the selection of specific stocks for purchase or sale should be based on a rational analysis of investment values. Applying this philosophy in a disciplined manner over the long term produces superior results. Advanced in a comprehensive way by Benjamin Graham and David Dodd in their seminal work, *Security Analysis*, this "rationality concept" has gained a wide following since the book's publication in 1934, and it has elevated the business of stock picking, or "equity management," from a profession of rank speculation into one akin to economics or law. As the times have changed, practicing security analysts have modified many of the founding principles of Graham and Dodd, and have enhanced the field by developing complementary approaches.

Clouding the analyst's reasoned judgment is the modern emphasis on short-term results. Nowadays, a company's share price is either rewarded or punished every three months, depending on whether the firm's quarterly earnings fulfilled, or fell short of, Wall Street's expectations. To reduce the resultant volatility in share prices, companies are tempted to manage quarterly results, feed influential practitioners hints on anticipated earnings, and employ public relation staffs to "spin" the Street on a continuous basis. Such practices contribute to the underlying tension between corporate issuers, which seek top dollar for their shares, and investors, who want to purchase equities at fair value. The short-term orientation also encompasses portfolio managers. In their attempts to beat the indexes on a quarterly basis, many move in and out of stocks on a rapid-fire basis, hoping to gain a small advantage. They may turn over a portfolio two to three times annually, perhaps holding individual stocks only a few months at a time.

WHY STUDY SECURITY ANALYSIS?

Because the stock market has such a strong impact on investment portfolios, career opportunities, and job prospects, it is surprising that so many investors, businesspeople, and students fail to understand the dynamics behind equity valuation. Indeed, a sizable number consider the stock exchanges to be floating crap games. While speculative elements play a role in the markets, the discipline of security analysis underlies stock pricing and its study warrants the sustained interest of many people.

A knowledge of security analysis is useful to the following four categories of individuals:

1. *Corporate executives* must be sensitive to valuation issues when they draw up their company's strategic plan, as well as when they convey the corporate growth story to potential investors. They must understand how practitioners interpret management actions and translate them into share prices.

2. *Investment professionals* regularly encounter all the evaluative techniques described in this book. In my experience, many fail to appreciate the practical and theoretical underpinnings of the methodologies they employ on a daily basis. A sequential review of the building blocks of security analysis can only contribute to better job performance.

3. *Business students* learn about the emphasis now being placed on enhancing shareholder value, but they graduate with only a superficial knowledge of how the real world translates corporate results into P/E ratios. An appreciation of security analysis is necessary equipment when confronting the harsh realities of business and finance.

4. *Individual investors* who seriously follow common stocks benefit from studying security analysis. Their first reward is a reduced susceptibility to "torpedo stocks," those overpriced speculative issues whose prospects have been hyped by others and whose disastrous price plunges can sink a portfolio's performance. Later, as they gain experience and stick to this book's methodology, they'll be comfortable in making stock selections based on their own research and judgement. A strict adherence to the disciplined approach should provide superior returns.

For convenience, the pronoun "he" has been used throughout this book to refer nonspecifically to analysts and investors; the material herein will be equally useful to both men and women who are evaluating securities in the "real world."

This book does not promise to help you beat the market as an investor or make successful decisions as a corporate executive. No book can honestly claim such results. *Security Analysis on Wall Street* is designed to provide a practical, well-rounded review of the security analysis process. After reading this book, the reader is better prepared to make sound investment decisions and well equipped to confront the stock market's numerous intrigues.

JEFFREY C. HOOKE

Chevy Chase, Maryland
July 1999

Acknowledgments

I want to thank several people who supplied interesting viewpoints: Doug Cannon, Alan Fishbein, Jerome Simonoff, and Paul Siegel. A special thanks to the staff at John Wiley & Sons: Mina Samuels, Mary Daniello, Claudio Campuzano, and Myles Thomson. JoAnn Fullerton, who word-processed the manuscript, deserves my thanks as does Nancy Marcus Land of Publications Development Company of Texas. I also want to express my appreciation to Helmut Paul, Andre Cracco, Karl Voltaire, and George Tannous of the International Finance Corporation. And finally, a heartfelt thanks to my wife, Patty, for her encouragement during the preparation of this book.

J. C. H.

Contents

Introduction

To facilitate the reader's understanding of the subject material, *Security Analysis on Wall Street* is divided into five parts:

- *Part I: The Investing Environment.* Part I provides an overview of the environment in which stocks are issued, researched, bought, and sold. In addition to examining why investors analyze stocks in the first place, we look at the roles of the various players, the rules and regulations of the markets, the activities surrounding an initial public offering, and the sources of investment information.

- *Part II: Performing the Analysis and Writing the Research Report.* The investment merits of a particular stock are evaluated through a methodical approach. Both the *history* and the *prospects* of the issuing company are considered. The sequence of this study and the format of the research report are discussed in Part II.

- *Part III: Valuation and the Investment Decision.* At the conclusion of the research report, the analyst must answer two questions: (1) Is this security fairly valued? and (2) based on the previous answer, should I recommend buying or selling the stock? Part III provides the necessary framework to deliver the answers.

- *Part IV: Special Cases.* The model company for the typical security analysis is an industrial manufacturer or service business with a history of improving sales and earnings. Most publicly traded firms don't fit this model, and Part IV reviews popular special cases. In addition, the analysis of international stocks is considered. These stocks are becoming increasingly popular with U.S. investors.

- *Part V: Summary.* The final chapter of the book summarizes the material contained in the earlier parts and reiterates a few useful maxims.

PART I

The Investing Environment

1

Why Analyze a Security?

This chapter covers the origin and evolution of security analysis. The herd psychology and gamesmanship that are endemic to the securities market are discussed, along with modern valuation approaches.

Some investors analyze securities to reduce the risk and chance aspects of investing. They need the confidence supplied by their own work. Others seek value where others haven't looked. They're on a treasure hunt. Still others have fiduciary reasons. Without documentation to justify an investment decision, clients can sue them for malpractice, should investment performance waver. Many investors analyze shares for the thrill of the game. They enjoy pitting their investment acumen against other professionals.

Security analysis is a field of study for the evaluation of securities in a rational way. By performing a rigorous analysis of the factors affecting a stock's price, security analysts seek to find equities that present a good value relative to other investments. In doing such work, professional analysts refute the efficient market theory, which suggests that a monkey throwing darts at the *Wall Street Journal* will, over time, have a performance record equal to the most experienced money manager. In fact, the proliferation of security analysis techniques as well as advances in regulation and information flow contributes to the market's transparency. Nevertheless, on a regular basis, pricing inefficiencies occur. An astute observer takes advantage of the discrepancies.

THE ORIGINS OF SECURITY ANALYSIS

Benjamin Graham and David Dodd made the business of analyzing investments into a profession. With the publication of their book, *Security Analysis*, in 1934, they offered investors a logical and systematic way to evaluate the many securities competing for investment dollars. Until then, methodical and reasoned analysis was in short supply on Wall Street. The markets were dominated by speculation. Stocks were frequently purchased on the basis of hype and rumor, with little business justification. Even when the company in question was a solid operation with a consistent track record, participants failed to apply quantitative measures to their purchases. General Motors was a *good company* whether its stock was trading at 10× or 30× earnings, but was it a *good investment* at 30× earnings, relative to other equities or the bond market? Investors lacked the skills to answer this question. *Security Analysis* endeavored to provide these skills.

The systematic analysis in place at the time was centered in bond-rating agencies and legal appraisals. Moody's Investors Service and Standard & Poor's began assigning credit ratings to bonds in the early 1900s. The two agencies based their ratings almost entirely on the bond's collateral protection and the issuer's historical track record, giving short shrift to qualitative indicators such as the issuer's future prospects and management depth. Dominated by railroad and utility bonds, the rating agencies' methodology lacked transferability to other industries and the equity markets. In-depth evaluations of corporate shares were found in legal appraisals, which were required for estate tax calculations, complicated reorganization plans, and contested takeover bids. Like credit ratings, these appraisals suffered from an overdependence on historical data at the expense of a careful consideration of future prospects.

Graham and Dodd suggested that certain common stocks were prudent investments, if investors took the time to analyze them properly (see Exhibit 1–1). Many finance professors and businesspeople were surprised at this notion, thinking the two academics were brave to make such a recommendation. Only five years earlier, the stock market had suffered a terrible crash, signaling the beginning of a wrenching economic depression causing massive business failures and huge job losses.

By today's standards, the market drop of 1929 is hard to comprehend. On Monday, October 28, 1929, the Dow Jones Industrial Average fell 12.8 percent and an additional 11.7 percent on Tuesday. The two-day drop of 23 percent followed a decline that began on September 3, when the industrial average peaked at 381.17, and then declined 21.6 percent in the weeks preceding the

EXHIBIT 1–1. Graham and Dodd Approach to Stock Selection

Follow these steps:

1. Study the available facts.
2. Prepare an organized report.
3. Project earnings and related data.
4. Draw valuation conclusions based on established principles and sound logic.
5. Make a decision.

Crash. Although the market staged modest recoveries in 1930 and 1931, the October 1929 drop presaged a gut-wrenching descent in stock prices, which wasn't complete until February 1933. Over the 3½-year period, the Dow dropped by 87 percent. A prolonged rally boosted the average 288 percent (to 194.40) by March 1937, only for stock prices to collapse 47 percent by April 1938. The index didn't reach its 1929 high until November 1954, 25 years later.

At the time of the publication of *Security Analysis,* equity prices had doubled from 1933's terrible bottom, but they were only 26 percent of the 1929 high. Shaken by the volatile performance of equities, the public's view of the stock market in 1934 was still a caricature of the 1920s, when common stocks were speculative. Not only was there a dearth of conservative analysis, but the market was afflicted with insider trading, unethical "story stock" pitches, and unscrupulous brokers. For two educators to promote a scholarly approach was radical indeed.

The publication of *Security Analysis* coincided with the formation of the Securities and Exchange Commission (SEC). Designed to prevent a repeat of the 1920s' abuses, the SEC was given broad regulatory powers over a wide range of market activities. It required corporate issuers to disclose all material information and to provide regular public earnings reports. This new information provided a major impetus to the security analysis profession. Previously, companies were cavalier about providing information to the public. Analysts, as a result, operated from half truths and incomplete data. With the regulators' charge of full disclosure for publicly traded corporations, practitioners had access to more raw material than ever before. Added to the company-specific data was the storehouse of economic, market, and industry material available for study. It soon became clear that successful analysts needed to allocate their time and resources efficiently among various sources of information to produce the best results.

NO PROFIT GUARANTEE

It is important to remember that security analysis doesn't presume an absolute value for a given stock, nor does it guarantee the investor a profit. After undertaking the effort to study a security, an analyst derives a range of value, since the many variables involved reduce the element of uncertainty. After an investigation, suppose the analyst concludes that Random Corp. stock is worth $8 to $10 per share. This conclusion isn't worth much if the stock is trading at $9, but it is certainly valuable if the stock is trading at $4, far below the range, or at $20, which is far above. In such cases, the difference between the conclusion and the market prompts an investment decision, either *buy* or *sell* (see Exhibit 1–2).

If the analyst acts on his conclusion and buys Random Corp. stock at $4 per share, he has no assurance that the price will reach the $8 to $10 range. The broad market might decline without warning or Random Corp. might

EXHIBIT 1–2. Random Corp. Stock

$0		$8	$10		$20
BUY	Buy the stock when its price is way below your appraisal.	Your valuation conclusion is $8 to $10 per share.	Sell the stock when it substantially exceeds your appraisal.		**SELL**

suffer an unexpected business setback. These variables can restrict the stock from reaching appraised value. Over time, however, the analyst believes that betting on such large differences provides superior investment results.

DAY-TO-DAY TRADING AND SECURITY ANALYSIS

For the most part, participants in the stock market behave rationally. Day-to-day trading in most stocks causes few major price changes, and large interday differentials can usually be explained by the introduction of new information. Small price discrepancies are often attributable to a few professionals having a somewhat different interpretation of the same set of facts. An investor may believe a stock's price will change because either (1) the market will conform to his opinion of the stock's value over time, or (2) the future of the underlying business will unfold as he anticipates.

In the first instance, perhaps the investor's research uncovered a hidden real estate value on the company's balance sheet. The general public is unaware of this fact. As soon as others acknowledge the extra value, the stock price should increase. In the second situation, the investor may assume more corporate growth than the market assumes. Should the investor's prediction come true, the stock price should increase accordingly. Perhaps 250,000 people follow the markets full time, so there are plenty of differing views. Even small segments of investors with conflicting opinions can cause significant trading activity in a stock.

It is not unusual that professionals using similar methods of analysis come up with valuations that differ by 10 to 15 percent. These small percentages are sufficiently large to cause active trading. As discussed later, the popular valuation techniques require a certain amount of judgment in sifting information and applying numerical analysis, so reasonable people can easily derive slightly dissimilar values for the same security. As these differences become more profound, the price of a given stock becomes more volatile, and divergent valuations do battle in the marketplace. Today, this price volatility is evident in many high-tech stocks. The prospects of the underlying businesses are hard to appraise, even for experienced professionals.

HERD PSYCHOLOGY AND SECURITY ANALYSIS

Ideally, a security analyst studies the known facts of a business, considers its prospects, and prepares a careful evaluation. From this effort, a buy or sell recommendation is derived for the company's shares. This valuation model, while intrinsically sensible, understates the need to temper a rational study with due regard for the vagaries of the stock market.

At any given time, the price behavior of certain individual stocks and selected market sectors is governed by forces that defy a studied analysis. Key elements influencing equity values in these instances are the emotions of the investors themselves. Market participants are human beings, after all, and are subject to the same impulses as anyone. Many emotions affect their decision-making process, but two sentiments have the most lasting impact: *fear* and *greed*. Investors in general are scared of losing money, and all are anxious to make more profits. These feelings become accentuated in the professional investor community, whose members are caught up in the treadmill of maintaining good short-term performance.

Of the two emotions, fear is by far the stronger, as evidenced by stock prices, which fall faster than they go up. Afraid of losing money, people demonstrate a classic herd psychology on hearing bad news, and rush to sell a stock before the next investor. Stocks can drop 20 to 30 percent in price on a single day, even when the new information is less than striking. In the crash of 1987, the Dow Jones Index fell 23 percent in one day on no real news. Buying frenzies, in contrast, take place over longer stretches of time, such as weeks or months. Exceptions include the shares of takeover candidates and initial public offerings.

True takeover stocks are identified by a definitive offer from a respectable bidder. Because the offers typically involve a substantial control premium, investors rush in to acquire the takeover candidate's shares at a price slightly below the offer, thus immediately boosting the company's market valve. Occurring as frequently as real bids are rumored bids. Speculators act on takeover rumors by inflating a stock's price in anticipation of a premium-priced control offer.

All these factors play a role in the next hard-to-analyze security—the initial public offering (IPO). Many IPOs rise sharply in price during their first few days of trading, such as Etoys, an Internet retailer of children's toys. Etoys went public in May 1999, at $20 per share, and jumped 280 percent to $76 per share on its first day of trading. Within three weeks, the stock was selling for $85. Unlike an existing issue, an IPO has no trading history, so the underwriters setting the offering price make an educated guess as to its value. At times, this guess is conservative and the price rises accordingly. More frequently, the lead underwriters "lowball" the IPO price to ensure that the offering is fully sold, protecting themselves from their moral obligation to buy back shares from unsatisfied investors if the price were to fall steeply.

When underwriters get their publicity machines working and an IPO becomes "hot," the herd psychology infects investors, who then scramble over one another to buy in anticipation of a large price jump. At this point, a dedicated evaluation of the IPO has little merit. For a hot deal, equity buyers operate by game theory—what's the other guy thinking and what's he going to pay for this issue? Others use momentum investing logic: I must buy the stock because others are buying it.

MOMENTUM INVESTORS

Extremely influential in short-term pricing moves, momentum investors predict individual stock values based on trading patterns that have happened repeatedly, either in the relevant stock or in similar situations. Thus, if they notice the beginning of a downward price trend, they sell the stock in anticipation of the pattern reaching completion. Naturally, the selling pattern is a self-fulfilling prophecy as other momentum investors are motivated by the increased activity and follow suit. Often lumped together with emotional investors by the media, momentum players attempt to take advantage of the common belief that stocks move in discernible patterns. Two of Wall Street's oldest expressions, "You can't fight the tape" and "You can't buck the trend," are evidence of the futility of injecting a security analysis bias into any price move driven by emotional and momentum factors. The herd instinct that is set off by such behavior contributed to several market crashes in the past. As a result, the federal government prohibits computerized program trading, which activates on the observance of such trends, if market indices drop too much. Right now, the "circuit breaker" kicks in with a 350-point decline in the Dow Jones Average, as it did on October 27, 1997, when the Dow Industrials Average dropped 554 points.

GAME THEORY AND SECURITY ANALYSIS

The average portfolio manager does not have a controlling position in his shareholdings. Public corporations are owned by numerous equity investors, perhaps numbering in the thousands. With this diversity of ownership, the portfolio manager's return in a given stock, or in the general market, is dependent on the behavior of rival investors. If the manager holds onto a stock because he thinks its a good investment, while others are selling because they think the opposite, he loses in the short run. Future results of the company may bear out his original analysis, but in the present he looks bad. This is a dangerous situation in the investment industry, which tends to measure results quarter by quarter rather than year by year. For this reason, knowing how others think and react to events is critical to success.

As the following examples illustrate, some investors bring this dynamic into the realm of game theory and attempt to influence the market's thought processes:

- *False Takeover.* An investor with a reputation for hostile takeovers acquires a position in a company's shares. He files a public notice or leaks his interest to the rumor mill. As other investors react to a potential takeover, they buy the stock and its price increases. In this case, the takeover artist has no intention of bidding for the company. He sells his shares into the buying activity sparked by his original interest, thus realizing a quick profit from speculative expectations. Clinton Morrison, an analyst at John Kinnard & Co., remarks, "It's called a self-fulfilling prophecy. You advertise your position and then you sell into it."

- *Phony Promotion.* A key market player, such as a large fund manager, indicates his strong interest in a certain industry sector, such as cable television. As other investors follow the fund manager's direction by purchasing cable TV stocks, the manager busily unloads his own holdings into the trading strength. One large fund manager was criticized in 1995 for advocating technology stocks in public, when his fund was selling them in private.

- *Story Stocks.* A professional investor establishes a significant position in a little-known company. Using financial publicists, stock newsletters, and aggressive brokers, he weaves a story behind the scenes about the company's unrecognized earnings potential. Although the analysis is sketchy, the growth story is entertaining. Carlton Lutts, editor of the *Cabot Market Letter,* summarized such game theory dynamics well. "A stock, like love, thrives on romance and dies on statistics." As the drumbeating becomes louder and louder, a cross section of investors takes notice. They buy in and the price climbs. When the professional's profit objective is reached, he bails out of his position and winds down the publicity machine. Shortly thereafter, the stock price collapses. This strategy is most effective with early-stage companies and technology firms. Their business prospects are difficult to analyze, making fanciful forecasts hard to dispute. Sometimes, just the rumor of an important investor is enough. In December 1996, Zitel Corp. shares rose from $22-⅞ per share to $72-⅞ per share on rumors that George Soros was amassing a position. When his firm publicly denied the reports on December 30, Zitel's stock price dropped 43 percent, or 31 points, in minutes.

In each of the preceding situations, the outcome of a competitive move by one investor depends on the reactions of his rivals, much like a good chess game. A seemingly irrational reaction by competitors may make a fine strategy unsuccessful. What happens if a professional feeds the takeover rumor mill and no one buys? The risk of the game is that his competitors won't act as expected. This risk decreases if he commands a visible leadership role in the market and has a strong public relations operation. Former Goldman, Sachs strategist, Leon Cooperman, for example, has the qualifications to be a top game player at his new firm, Omega Advisors. Of course, selection of the target stock must be made carefully. Competitors may see through a promoter's strategy or simply ignore the new information presented to them.

THE PREMISE OF SECURITY ANALYSIS

Practicing security analysts acknowledge the impact of human emotions, herd behavior, and game theory on stock prices, and they factor these elements into their investment conclusions. Generally, these are short-term influences, and sooner or later, most share prices reflect a rational view of underlying economic values. This rational view is far from absolute. Investment evaluation is not an exact science, and reasonable people examining the same facts are bound to have differences. Over the long haul, an analytical approach toward stock selection offers superior results, as occasional instances of price irrationality provide obvious opportunities. Maintaining a valuation discipline in emotional markets is one of the analyst's hardest challenges. Few people want to face the ridicule of going against the crowd by sticking to accepted standards, even though equity investors invariably return to normal measures of determining value after periodic infatuations with untested themes. These notions of rationality and consistency form the bedrock of the security analysis profession.

A large part of a stock's price is set by expectations of its future growth in earnings. While a competent study of the past frequently provides the basis for an earnings projection, even the most talented analyst has a limited ability to predict the growth rate of a given company for years ahead. This implies that a major portion of any analyst's valuation is the product of educated guessing. As with similar vocations, many conclusions look terribly wrong with 20–20 hindsight. Sometimes the actual earnings of a company come in substantially lower than forecast data, and the stock price drops accordingly. An analyst who recommended the stock has made a mistake, but level-headed investors, realizing the field's limitations, don't demand perfection. Rather, excellence can be achieved by partial success. In baseball, a .300 hitter "fails" 7 out of 10 times at bat, yet he is among the best. For security analysts, the grading process is more complicated than baseball, but a professional who is right 60 to 70 percent of the time is considered exceptional. Luck plays a role in compiling this kind of track record, but over time the importance of chance diminishes in favor of analytical skill.

Graham and Dodd summarized the analyst's requirements many years ago in *Security Analysis:*

To do these jobs credibly the analyst needs a wide equipment. He must understand security forms, corporate accounting, the basic elements that make for the success or failure of various kinds of businesses, the general workings not only of our total economy but also of its major segments, and finally the characteristic fluctuations of our security markets. He must be able to dig for facts, to evaluate them critically, and to apply his conclusions with good judgment and a fair amount of imagination. He must be able to resist human nature itself sufficiently to mistrust his own feelings when they are part of mass psychology. He must have courage commensurate with his competence.

SCIENTIFIC METHOD

According to serious practitioners, security analysis is a quasi-science, like medicine or economics. Its systematized knowledge has been derived from the observance of decades of stock market data and the application of common sense. The field's basic tenets have thus been tested by the use of the scientific method, which calls for carrying out three basic steps to reach a conclusion. Exhibit 1–3 summarizes the scientific method alongside its application in the securities market.

Two supermarket stocks can serve as an example. Suppose the respective shares of Safeway and Kroger, two national chains, have the key financial characteristics shown in Exhibit 1–4. Safeway's stock is trading at 15 times earnings. Given the similarity, what should be the P/E multiple of Kroger's stock? All things being equal, Kroger shares should have a 15 P/E multiple, meaning a $30 price (i.e., 15 P/E × $2 EPS = $30). If the Kroger shares are trading at $25, the stock is a buy because it should eventually reach the $30 price. In practice, analysts take this $30 theoretical value as a

EXHIBIT 1–3. Scientific Method Applied to the Securities Market

Scientific Method	Securities Market Example
Step 1: Formulate a hypothesis.	Two similar stocks should have similar prices.
Step 2: Collect data, make observations and test hypothesis.	Observe historical price performance of two similar stocks. Determine whether their prices converge over time.
Step 3: Conclude the validity or predictive ability of the hypothesis.	Sooner or later, two similar stocks will have similar prices. By following this conclusion, an investor looks for two similar stocks with *different* prices. He predicts that the cheaper of the two stocks will rise in price. He acts on his prediction by buying the cheaper stock.

EXHIBIT 1–4. Similar Stock Hypothesis—Two Supermarket Stocks

	Safeway	Kroger
Financial Data		
Five-year compound annual growth in earnings per share	12%	12%
Expected annual growth rate in earnings per share	11%	11%
Debt-to-equity ratio	20%	20%
Earnings per share (EPS)	$1	$2
Share Data		
Price-to-EPS ratio (P/E)	15×	—
Share price	$15	—

Note. The earnings growth rates and debt to equity ratios are identical. The P/E ratios should be similar, all things being equal.

starting point. They then study the future prospects of each company. Certain factors may justify the $25 value, despite the apparent similarities.

Although the "similar stock/similar price" supposition is easy to describe and makes sense, proving this theory and other basic tenets of security analysis in a scientific manner is difficult. In a true science such as physics, observations are repeated in a laboratory environment to verify their accuracy (e.g., a ball is dropped in a vacuum 100 times to confirm the pull of gravity). Security analysis theories, in contrast, are subject to the vagaries of the stock market, which has far too many uncontrolled variables to provide the appropriate conditions for a truly scientific test.

Even the "similar supermarket" example is hard to prove scientifically. Finding two publicly traded supermarket chains with identical financial results is impossible, and most chains have significant differences in market conditions, business operations, and managerial styles. Even with two firms that resemble each other in financial and business attributes, the scientific method is problematic. Much of a company's value is represented by its future potential to generate earnings, as opposed to its present condition and past history. Determining a consensus view of a company's future is accurately described as educated guesswork, rather than scientific deduction.

Despite the drawback of injecting scientific methods into the stock market, investors and finance professors keep trying. Certain of their theories have been proven academically, while others have a commonsense appeal that heightens their acceptance. For example, most professionals consider the next two hypotheses to be valid:

True   Companies with low interest coverage ratios go bankrupt more frequently than those with high interest coverage ratios.

True   Companies with high P/E ratios have better growth records than those with low P/E ratios.

A combination of academic proofs, commonsense ideas, and intuitive beliefs supports these and other notions of security analysis. The systematic application of these concepts has evolved into a rational discipline, which one studies like other quasi-scientific fields such as medicine, economics, or sociology.

SECURITY ANALYSIS TECHNIQUES

As discussed earlier, emotions and trend followers influence the values of companies, but an underlying discipline governs share prices. Over time, this discipline, which is founded in security analysis, tends to correct stock market excesses. Thus, if a "hot" stock such as Ionica Group, the telephone service provider, goes public at a valuation of $900 million although the company has few revenues and no earnings, inevitably the stock price come back to earth, as investors lose their fervor and evaluate the business in terms of its risk-adjusted potential. Elder Beerman was a good company but a speculative stock in 1998, when its initial public offering sold at $22 per share. One year later, it was still a good firm but a better equity value at $7 per share, which was more in line with the company's future prospects. Frequently, the life cycle of pricing excesses begins with a security being bid up to an irrational price by anticipation investors and momentum players, who are then battled by scientifically inclined investors. The latter argue for a realistic valuation based on time-honored value anchors, derived from the four valuation approaches set forth in Exhibit 1–5.

BASIC VALUATION APPROACHES

Of the four principal approaches to security analysis, the first three—intrinsic value, relative value, and acquisition value—lend themselves to the scientific method. All three approaches forecast stock prices on the basis of historical economic, capital market, industry, and corporate statistics, which are then used to establish predictive trends for corporate operating

EXHIBIT 1–5. Common Valuation Approaches of Security Analysts

1. *Intrinsic Value.* The worth of a business equals the net present value of its future dividends.
2. *Relative Value.* Determine a company's value by comparing it to similar companies' values.
3. *Acquisition Value.* Calculate a company's share price by determining its worth to a third party acquirer, such as another operating business, a leveraged buyout firm, or a liquidator.
4. *Technical Value.* A share price can be predicted by examining its historical trading pattern and applying it to the future.

results and share prices. The principal decision variables are earnings projections and comparable company values.

Under the intrinsic value method, future dividends are derived from earnings forecasts and then discounted to the present, thereby establishing a present value for the stock. If the stock is trading at a price lower than this calculation, it is a "buy"; if the market price is higher then the intrinsic value, the stock is a "sell."

For most businesspeople, the intrinsic value approach (discounted cash flow) is their first introduction to security analysis since it is the approach emphasized by business schools and most valuation books. The intrinsic value concept makes economic sense and is theoretically sound, but in the real world its applicability is limited. No professional investor places much weight on projections extending past two or three years, and dividend discount rates are hard to pinpoint. Furthermore, even devoted advocates of this technique are hesitant to promote its use for analyses involving (1) growth companies that don't pay dividends; (2) established companies that are consistent money losers; and (3) complex companies that are liquidation or restructuring candidates.

The relative value approach considers intrinsic values too difficult to determine, owing to the arguments over hard-to-make projections and controversial discount rates. Instead, various valuation parameters of a given publicly traded stock, such as its P/E, price/book and price/sales ratios, are compared with the stocks of companies in the same industry. If the value ratio of the stock being evaluated is substantially lower than its peer group, and if there is no justifiable reason for the discrepancy, the relative value approach views the stock as a buy. Stock valuations are therefore made in a manner similar to many other asset appraisals. In real estate, the value of a house is established by comparing the target house to nearby houses that have sold recently. The relative value approach is attractive to analysts because it takes most of the guesswork out of relying on future projections and discount rates. Its weaknesses stem from three factors. First, few publicly traded companies have exact comparables, leaving a lot of room for subjectivity in the appraisal. Second, investors are in the market to make money in absolute terms, whereas the relative value method focuses on *relative* performance. Suppose an entire industry is the subject of speculative interest, and its share prices crash when expected operating results fail to materialize. The relative value picks fall 20 percent, but the industry's decline is 30 percent. The successful relative value investor is losing less money than other investors committed to the industry, but he's still losing money. Third, relative value places a heavy emphasis on contrasting the historical operating results of similar businesses, when future prospects are critical. "Driving by looking in the rearview mirror" is a perilous investment tactic.

The acquisition value approach suggests that a publicly traded stock should never trade at less than 70 to 75 percent of its worth to a sophisticated and well-financed third party. The analyst evaluates industry acquisition prices compared with the relevant company, and he tests its feasibility as a leveraged buyout or liquidation candidate. If the stock trades at less than 70 percent of its acquisition value, it is probably a buy. By relying on "comparable company" data, the acquisition value approach suffers from the same weaknesses as the relative value method, with the further proviso that comparable public mergers and acquisitions (M&A) deals are rare in many situations. The leveraged buyout (LBO) and liquidation techniques are dependable, but they apply only to a select group of manufacturing and service industries.

The fourth approach, technical analysis, has a wide following but it lacks the broad institutional acceptance of the first three approaches. Often referred to as Wall Street's version of "voodoo economics," technical analysis is concerned solely with the price and volume trading patterns of a stock. This valuation technique does not consider a company's operating history, its earning potential, or other microeconomic factors as relevant to the valuation process. Rather, the technician believes that trading patterns reflect all logical and emotional forces affecting a stock price. An analysis of these patterns, usually in conjunction with industry and market trading indicators, provides predictive trends that enable the technician to forecast stock prices.

Suppose a stock price fluctuates in a small range over a period of months, after it has made a big upward move. This behavior is called a "consolidation" pattern because the stock is consolidating its previous gain. If the stock price breaks through the top end of this range, this is a buy signal, because technical theory says it is poised for another run-up, after which the price will stabilize again (see Exhibit 1–6). Numerous investors and academics have tested this and other technical theories and concluded that there is no evidence to support these claims. Nevertheless, Wall Street is one place where perception easily becomes reality. Since thousands of investors believe in technical analysis, market participants are sensitive to technical opinions in evaluating stock prices. Reports of security analysts often include charts outlining the trading activity of the stock in question, and I have observed that most professional money managers use such charts as one ingredient in buy/sell decisions.

OTHER VALUATION APPROACHES

Technical analysis represents a systemized body of knowledge and numerous books review its procedures. Nevertheless, it straddles the line between rational inquiry and educated speculation. Two common stock-picking approaches that fall into the speculative category are "momentum investing" and "market anticipation" (see Exhibit 1–7).

Both approaches require a sophisticated knowledge of the market's inner workings and an experienced hand in equity trading. They are best employed by professional traders and stock promoters, who participate in the securities

EXHIBIT 1–6. Technical Analysis—Consolidation Pattern

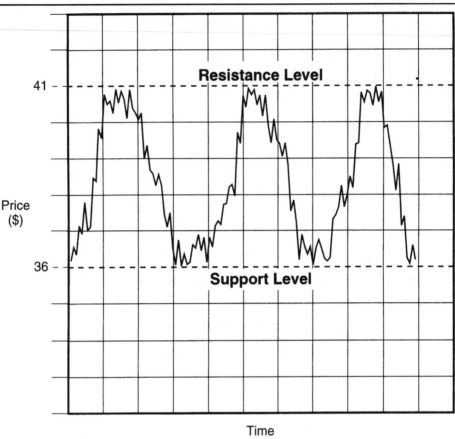

Time

markets on a full-time basis and are thus in a position to react quickly to the sharp price movements endemic to these investment strategies.

Conventional security analysis is sometimes characterized as the art of "buying low, and selling high." Momentum investing, in contrast, is frequently referred to as "buying high, and selling higher," because its adherents look to buy shares which are rising quickly in price. Momentum investors pay close attention to trading trends and give short shrift to the underlying company's sales or earnings; and thus, they represent a subset

EXHIBIT 1–7. Stock-Picking Alternatives to Security Analysis and Technical Analysis

- *Momentum Investing.* Momentum investors attempt to follow buying binges for individual stocks, regardless of the economic rationale behind the price move.
- *Market Anticipation.* Valuation parameters change precipitously among industries and companies. Anticipation investors try to predict dramatic changes before the market consensus.

of the technical community. Having played a major role in many share price run-ups, they are a key source of market volatility, often through automated program trading. Such trading is initiated by a series of signals such as an upward 90-day moving price average, a large positive net cash flow into a stock, or a big jump in trading volume.

The market anticipation approach acknowledges that most stocks are fairly valued by security analysts using the intrinsic value, relative value, and acquisition value methods. At some future point, however, the consensus view on any given stock's earnings power or business risk changes, providing impetus to a higher (or lower) stock price. A typical pronouncement from a market anticipation analyst might be, "The Starbucks shares will increase in value as the market realizes the reduced volatility of the company's earning stream." Such conclusions carry little analytical weight and are most effective when repeated loudly and continually, thus echoing "the squeaky wheel gets the grease" tactic used by promoters in any business. Despite the speculative nature of this approach, even the most rigorous disciples of security analysis are cognizant of the sometimes relentless drumbeating of "market anticipation" investors, who are trying desperately to influence the consensus decision on a stock's value. Their influence has been strong in certain cases and has been observed in the rise and fall of numerous "high flyer" stocks, the peak prices of which defy rational explanation. How else does one explain the rocketlike rise of Amazon.com from $40 per share to $180 in nine months in 1998, the precipitous drop of Dispatch Management from $30 to $3 in the first four months of 1999, or the lightning round trip of Books-a-Million, which rose from $2½ in August 1998 to $46 in October 1998, and then declined to $7 by June 1999?

SUMMARY

Security analysis is a field of study that maintains stocks can be valued in a methodical and sensible way. While acknowledging the stock market's periodic spasms of emotion and irrationality, it suggests that, sooner or later, the price of a security approaches its economic value, as determined by a reasonable person with the requisite background in business operations, economics, finance, and accounting. This value cannot be pinpointed definitively because security analysis is not a science. Its results depend on the surrounding environment, which constantly changes with new information regarding developments of the business in question. As a quasi-science, security analysis has its limitations yet it provides a reasonable framework for comparing and contrasting investment opportunities. As a result, security analysis is widely accepted in the institutional community and it is the primary means for justifying investment decisions.

Despite its lack of exactitude, security analysis provides careful investors with sufficient tools to recognize pricing anomalies in the market, and then to benefit from them by making the appropriate buy/sell decision. These evaluation tools provide the pricing anchors from which a rational decision can be reached, and they include the intrinsic value, relative value, and acquisition value methods. Technical analysis, a popular stock-picking technique based on trading patterns, is often used as a complement to these approaches.

Because so much of a typical share's value is based on hard-to-predict future results, the stock market is fertile ground for unscrupulous promoters who exaggerate the prospects of investments in which they have a financial interest. The rumor mongering and tub thumping of these players sometimes has the desired effect of inflating the price of a stock. This impact is transitory, and share prices generally return to a modest valuation range in which reasonable people achieve a consensus. Within this band, however, investors still face uncertainty, and so investment selection remains a challenging activity.

QUESTIONS AND SHORT PROBLEMS

1. How does the principal objective of security analysis (i.e., finding superior investment values) contradict the "efficient market" theory?

2. How can a solid company with a strong operating record be a poor investment choice when compared to competing alternatives, such as other stocks or bonds? Why might companies with less stellar records represent better investment choices?

3. A security analyst determines that Incel Corp. stock is worth $20 per share. The current market price is now $15 per share, indicating a likely "buy" decision. Is the analyst guaranteed an eventual $5 per share profit? Why or why not?

4. Name the two emotions that have the most lasting impact on stock prices.

5. Why do underwriters like to price initial public offerings below the value dictated by their supply-and-demand estimates?

6. Which of the following expressions summarizes momentum trading:
    a. Buy high, sell low.
    b. You can't buck the trend.
    c. You have to do your homework.
    d. Stocks thrive on love and die on statistics.

7. The "story stock" technique is often used by promoters for high-tech issues. Why are high-tech companies suitable for this technique?

8. Which statements are relevant to security analysis? Circle all that apply:
    a. Emotions are short-to-intermediate term influences on stock prices.
    b. Over the long-term, security analysis offers above-average investment returns.

c. Security analysis is a science, like chemistry or physics.

d. Security analysis depends on rational behavior over the long-term.

9. Why is security analysis likened to "educated guesswork," even by its practitioners?

10. All things being equal, which of the two chemical stocks shown below should trade at the higher P/E multiple?

	Allchem, Inc.	Tychem Co.
10-year compound annual growth in EPS	12%	9%
Debt-to-equity ratio	20	35
Expected annual EPS growth rate	14	11
P/E multiple	?	?

11. List the four principal approaches to security analysis.

12. Which of the four approaches is almost totally dependent on the analyst's assessment of a company's future earnings potential?

13. Why do "real life" practitioners tend to favor the "relative value" approach?

14. Is "momentum investing" similar to technical analysis?

Adopt-a-Company Exercises

A. To learn security analysis concepts in a practical way, each student (or a group of students) selects a company to follow during the semester. To ease the learning process, students select companies that are relatively easy to understand. The best companies for this purpose are companies that:

- Have a five-year history of sales and positive earnings;
- Offer a low-tech product or service;
- Have a debt to equity ratio of 1:1 or less;
- Are engaged in one industry only; and
- Have completed an IPO within the last five years.

B. Students have two weeks to identify their company for adoption. The instructor will approve the selections that meet the criteria, or provide alternative companies.

2

Who Is Practicing
Security Analysis?

*In this chapter, we discuss the firms and the professionals that
employ security analysis techniques. The role of the analyst differs,
depending on the institutional context.*

Many thousands of people earn their living from working in the securities markets, but only a small percentage are full-time security analysts. About 30,000 can be classified as practitioners. Perhaps 60 percent of them work for institutional money managers such as mutual funds, pension funds, and insurance companies. These institutions invest their cash flows through the purchase of securities, so the trade refers to them as the "buy side." Approximately 30 percent of analysts work for securities firms, publishing research reports that are provided free of charge to institutional and individual clients. These reports purport to sell an analyst's investment ideas to an investor in exchange for fee-generating brokerage business. Securities firms are called the "sell side." If an analyst issues a recommendation on a stock and the investor chooses to follow this advice, the analyst encourages the investor to execute the order through the trading department of the analyst's firm. A smaller group of analysts, perhaps numbering a few thousand, labor for credit rating agencies, market letters, and independent research firms. These enterprises market security analysis opinions either for flat fees or shared brokerage commissions. Regulators such as the Securities and Exchange Commission (SEC) and the New York Stock Exchange (NYSE) also employ dozens of analysts.

The commitment of a firm to employ analysts is a function of its size, style, and activity. Fidelity, the mutual fund giant with $350 billion under management, is an active stock picker and has over 200 analysts on staff. In contrast, Berkshire Hathaway, Warren Buffett's investment vehicle, manages $45 billion with only two analysts, Mr. Buffett and Charles Munger, a close associate. Vanguard Index 500, a $35 billion index fund, uses no analysts. Its portfolio deliberately mirrors the composition of the S&P 500, so stock pickers need not apply. Employing a full-time analyst is uneconomic if a fund's size is less than $50 million. With this relatively small portfolio, the portfolio manager can generate his own research or use the sell-side reports provided to him in exchange for brokerage commissions.

Like buy-side institutions, securities firms show a broad range in their commitment to security analysis. Merrill Lynch, the largest brokerage house, employs over 250 analysts. Its principal competitors show staffs of a similar magnitude. Small regional firms and specialized brokerages employ only a few analysts. Sometimes, their securities salespeople double as analysts to develop investment ideas.

The stock market includes thousands of separate participants, but the vast majority of analysts work for three types of employers:

1. Securities firms.
2. Major institutional investors with $1 billion + under management.
3. Small money management firms.

SECURITIES FIRMS AND THEIR ANALYSTS

Often referred to as "investment banks" or "brokerage houses," securities firms are in the business of creating, marketing, and trading stocks, bonds, and other securities. Many realize substantial revenue from ancillary businesses such as investment banking, merchant banking, and asset management. For the 10 to 15 firms that own the lion's share of the equity marketing business, a research department full of security analysts is critical to maintaining the firm's credibility with buy-side institutions and investment banking clients.

A security analyst's job requirements include:

- Writing research reports on specific companies.
- Reviewing companies and investment ideas with institutional clients.
- Working with the investment banking department.

Most research analysts specialize in one industry—for example, mining, electric utilities, or health care—and monitor 20 to 30 companies in that industry. A narrow focus enables the analyst to become an expert in his industry. This specialization is important to preparing quality reports and impressing institutional clients. Studying the industry, visiting its companies, and reading corporate financial statements support these endeavors.

The sell-side analyst is a storehouse of industry information for the securities firm and its clients, but his primary responsibility is the publication of regular written reports covering the investment attributes of specific companies. These research reports have several functions. First, they review new corporate information such as earnings announcements and management changes. Second, they suggest investment ideas for stocks in the analyst's industry, based, in part, on the new information. Third, they provide written earnings projections to the reader and present formal buy/sell recommendations to the firm's clients. As a supplement to his report writing, the analyst often assists his employer's investment banking department in the solicitation of new advisory assignments in the analyst's industry. Depending on the firm, about 40 percent of the analyst's time involves talking with institutional investors and working with investment bankers. The remainder, 60 percent, is spent writing research reports that are distributed to institutional and individual investors. Most reports are quite short—only 2 to 3 pages—but others, particularly those describing new investment ideas, are 30 to 40 pages long. Making accurate earnings projections and good stock recommendations are important, but surprisingly few institutions keep track of the analyst's predictions. Due to this lack of accountability, the sell-side profession is still referred to as a "page business," meaning the analyst's productivity is often measured in terms of writing volume, rather than results.

Equity research departments help investment bankers obtain financial advisory assignments. Many times, when a corporation plans a public offering, it examines a securities firm's ability to generate quality research reports on its shares. If a brokerage firm employs an analyst who covers the company's industry well, the firm is apt to be rewarded with the transaction's implementation. Following the placement of the offering, favorable research reports support the share price, publicize the issuer's business, and foster trading interest in its stock. In October 1996, Peter Oakes, a top-ranked analyst at Merrill Lynch, the nation's largest brokerage firm, issued a favorable report on McDonald's, which was weathering a tough introduction for its "Arch Deluxe" sandwich. The report refuted Arch Deluxe critics and reaffirmed the buy recommendation on McDonald's stock. Coincidentally, Merrill Lynch investment bankers managed a $200 million preferred stock financing for McDonald's 10 days later.

Generating Trading Revenues with Security Analysis

While corporate advisory fees are important for the big investment banks, trading activity is a larger source of revenue for the average securities firm. When buy-side institutions purchase or sell securities, they do so through a broker, who realizes a commission for executing the trade, collects a small spread on the order, or receives revenue from another broker that actually fills the institution's request. Since most trades usually have an institutional buyer indirectly connected to an institutional seller, one order eventually results in two commissions. Sizable trading volumes thus lead to significant commissions and spread revenues for brokerage firms. Institutions reward quality research by placing buy and sell orders with the analyst's employer. A reputable security analyst who captures this institutional order flow for his firm is therefore a valuable employee.

In addition, the firm's trading department takes short-term positions in a given security, either to fulfill its commitment as a "market maker" or to speculate on an expected price movement. Referred to as "principal" trading, because the firm's own capital is at risk, this activity sometimes involves a consultation with the relevant security analyst, who serves as an information resource for the traders. The security analyst's responsibility thus extends beyond his research and investment banking responsibilities.

The Chinese Wall

According to industry guidelines, the research department of a brokerage firm operates independently of the investment banking and trading departments—it is surrounded by an imaginary "Chinese Wall." Only in this manner can investment clients be assured that the analyst's conclusions are free of conflicts of interest. In practice, this ideal is unworkable and an analyst's opinions are frequently compromised. Many earn more money by bringing in investment banking deals than by writing research reports; thus, they are reluctant to annoy corporate banking clients by issuing sell reports on their respective shares. As a result, most analyst's recommendations are buys, which make investment banking clients happy. Companies that generate a lot of investment banking business often have 20 buy recommendations for every sell, despite the inherent uncertainties regarding corporate performance. A recent study by Mathew Hayward and Warren Boeker of the Columbia Business School proved the obvious: after reviewing 8,000 stock evaluations by securities firms, they found 93 percent of analysts working for firms that do investment banking work for issuers rated the stock higher than analysts at firms that didn't work for the stock issuer.

In the end, the securities firm practitioner is a good source of information and new ideas, but he cannot be considered a totally objective observer. Brokerage firms are primarily in the business of generating banking fees, commissions, and trading profits. Providing unbiased research to investors ranks low on their priority list. This fact was made all too clear in August 1997, when it became obvious that sell-side experts had been completely wrong in recommending the purchase of Southeast Asian stocks. Following a 60 percent drop in these stock prices due to the various devaluations, not one Wall Street analyst was fired for giving bad advice, even though U.S. investors lost billions.

MAJOR INSTITUTIONAL INVESTORS

A major institutional equity investor has $1 billion or more under management. Sizable mutual funds, money management firms, in-house corporate and government pension funds, bank trust departments, and large insurance companies fall into this category. For the most part, these institutions invest someone else's money on a fee-for-service basis. Representative clients are individuals, endowments, corporate retirement plans, and government pension funds lacking the expertise and resources to make their own investment decisions. Professional money managers typically charge annual fees that are a fixed percentage of the market value of the assets under management, usually in the range of 0.5 to 1.0 percent annually. Clients pay these fees whether their investment funds realize profits, make losses, or break even, although consistently poor performance usually results in a client withdrawing its funds from a given manager. Under the standard management arrangement, institutional money managers have no direct participation in the profits (or losses) realized by their investment decisions. Rather, the rewards of above-average performance are indirect. A good track record results in an expanding client base, which means more management fee income. Likewise, the portfolio managers actually selecting investments have no direct participation in portfolio gains or losses. They receive salaries and bonuses. Consistently superior performance on their part results in better pay and improved job prospects.

By virtue of their substantial revenue bases, such organizations can afford to hire a full-time staff of practicing analysts. The size and sophistication of this staff depends on the institutional commitment to in-house evaluation, as opposed to the use of Wall Street research. Portfolio managers work with the in-house analysts to evaluate ideas, investigate companies, and compile research reports on specific stocks. In most institutions, the stock selection process is channeled through a formal investment committee composed of senior executives. The committee considers research reports that provide both (1) a valuation range and (2) a buy or sell suggestion for a particular stock. After their review of a report, the committee decides what to do with the analyst's advice.

In most firms, the committee rubber stamps the portfolio manager's opinion. The portfolio manager is an influential executive and frequently instigates the research report in the first place. If the committee agrees to buy (or sell) a stock, the portfolio manager may be required to take action. In many institutions, however, the portfolio manager has considerable latitude in determining whether to follow the committee's decision. In fact, some progressive funds have eliminated such committees, believing they encourage mediocrity and hamstring the portfolio manager.

Besides assisting in the stock selection process, the analytical staff is a storehouse of knowledge for the portfolio manager. Large money managers own hundreds of different stocks, and their respective portfolio managers are preoccupied with strategy, allocation, and buy/sell decisions. As a result, the managers don't have the time to be familiar with the detailed developments of specific companies in their portfolios. Questions such as "what do you hear about Ford Motor, what's new with Kimberly-Clark, or what do you think of Bay Networks?" are directed to in-house analysts, who are constantly monitoring individual companies and industries. The portfolio manager supplements this in-house feedback with Wall Street opinions and fee-for-service research.

A DYING ART?

In many large institutions, individual stock picking is a dying art because the classic "buy and hold" style is out of touch with the times. The traditional analyst's forte is finding an undervalued situation, investing in the stock and then waiting for others to realize the stock's unrecognized potential. This process requires a medium- to long-term horizon, but portfolio managers today are under pressure to produce superior results every three months. Moreover, the increasing sophistication of the money management industry means that finding bargains is more difficult than it was 20 years ago.

The two quasi-scientific approaches to investment—intrinsic and relative value—are well known and widely accepted. The intrinsic value method pioneered by Graham and Dodd tells the analyst to find a stock so intrinsically cheap that it has little chance of declining. Sooner or later, its price must go up. The relative value approach says find stocks with (1) solid growth prospects and (2) reasonable prices relative to competing stocks in the same industry. Over time, these stocks outperform the others. The disadvantage of the intrinsic value approach is that everyone believes it; virtually all shares meeting the criteria have been bid up in price. The problem of relative value is its reliance on questionable comparisons and uncertain future earnings. Either approach requires a thoughtful, time-consuming analysis of a company, along with a constant monitoring of the investment. Exhibit 2–1 lists the reasons most of today's portfolio managers can't afford to follow this classic style.

As the principal institutional investors grow larger and larger, they diversify their stock selections accordingly, and any one share investment

EXHIBIT 2–1. Institutional Reasons for Deemphasizing Security Analysis

Security analysis doesn't provide immediate results.

Bargain investments are hard to find.

Analytical process is expensive and time consuming.

Huge asset bases of institutions reduce individual stock importance.

Sector rotation, market timing, macro finance, and quantitative investment styles are in fashion.

represents a correspondingly smaller impact on overall investment results. Substantial holdings are concentrated in the widely followed Fortune 100, where valuation discrepancies are hard to find. Not surprisingly, many institutions deemphasize the search for bargain stocks, with the exception of a few special situations, and focus instead on alternative investment styles such as sector rotation, market timing, macro finance, and quantitative analysis.

Sector Rotation

Rather than looking for individual stock bargains by meeting corporate management teams and scrutinizing financial statements, the "sector rotator" portfolio manager looks for a specific industry that he perceives as inexpensive relative to other industries. Once the search is complete, the manager divests his share holdings in the overvalued industry and "rotates" the proceeds into the shares of companies participating in the undervalued industry. The security analyst plays a secondary role by setting up an "approved list" of stock selections within the industry groupings. The key decision points are sector shifts; corporate shares are purchased from the approved list with little follow-up study. In a way, this style is reminiscent of the relative value approach, and the sector rotator can be found saying things such as "Pharmaceutical stocks are cheap relative to hi-tech stocks" or "cyclical industries look like a good play compared to growth industries." Jeff Vinik, formerly of Fidelity's Magellan Fund, was a good sector rotator. Exhibit 2–2 illustrates the pattern followed in sector rotation.

Market Timing

Share prices of companies move in tandem with the broad market. Thus, if the market indices are going down, most stocks follow the trend, as

EXHIBIT 2–2. Sector Rotation

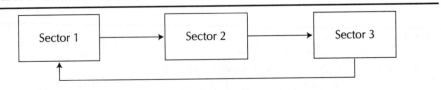

Step 1: Invest in Sector 1.
Step 2: Sector 2 offers better value. Sell Sector 1 and buy Sector 2.
Step 3: Dump Sector 2 stocks when Sector 3 looks better.
Step 4: Sector 1 prices fall. Portfolio manager sells Sector 3 shares and enters Sector 1 again.

macroeconomic factors such as interest rates, currency volatility, or oil prices overwhelm positive company-specific indicators such as higher earnings. Many portfolio managers combine stock picking and sector rotation techniques with a forecast of major market movements. If they think that stock prices will rise, they become 100 percent invested in equities. Anticipating a downward movement, they reduce their equity exposure and place a portion of the portfolio in cash. If managers think market timing is more important than stock selection, this lessens the security analyst's role in the decision process.

Strong Discovery Fund learned the downside of market timing in 1996. Richard Strong, who favored growth stocks and aggressive tactics, ran the Fund. By late 1995, he predicted that an upcoming U.S. recession would cause interest rates to fall, and thus, increase bond prices. Accordingly, the $500 million fund moved 40 percent of its assets out of stocks and into bonds. Instead, interest rates increased and bond prices declined. In 1996, stock prices climbed and the Strong was whipsawed. Other growth funds recorded 14 to 15 percent gains, but Discovery had a 3 percent loss.

Macro Finance

Macro finance investors select individual stocks and industry groupings on the basis of global themes. If U.S. interest rates are supposed to fall, they buy utility stocks, which tend to rise in price during periods of lower interest rates. Political problems in the Mideast might prompt the acquisition of domestic oil company shares. Frequently, the purchase or sale of company-specific securities is done with little knowledge of the underlying business. The in-house analyst's role is thus diminished, and the approved stock list is derived primarily from Wall Street research. George Soros of the Quantum Fund is the best known macro finance manager.

Quantitative Analysis

The 1990s have seen an explosion in the use of "derivatives." Derivatives are investments that draw their value from an underlying security (a stock, bond, or index). Popular derivatives include convertible bonds, put/call options, and futures contracts. Quantitative managers use convertibles, options, and futures to exploit brief discrepancies in value between the derivative and the underlying security. The profits on a given trade are typically a fraction of a percentage point, but the trading position only lasts a day or two, giving the manager the opportunity to turn his capital over quickly. As an example, if you make only 0.1 percent per day on your trading, your annual return on investment is over 40 percent. Quantitative analysis relies heavily on sophisticated computer programs that ferret out these price discrepancies in real time.

Many determinants of the sector rotation, market timing, macro finance, and quantitative styles have short lives. Institutions using these styles have a high turnover, perhaps trading the value of their portfolios two or three times per year, so the average stock is held for less than six months. This frenzied activity leaves little time for the security analyst to monitor companies effectively and write research summaries.

All of the preceding approaches are called "active management" strategies because the portfolio manager is making definite investment decisions based on his philosophy of investment. Despite the immense time and money that institutions dedicate to this exercise, most portfolio managers are unable to outperform the broad market indices, such as the S&P 500 Index, on a consistent basis. Even the best managers of large funds exceed market results by only 2 or 3 percentage points annually. While there are some sensible explanations for this situation, it remains problematic for customers who place funds with these managers. With most institutions offering returns that are less than the market indices, clients are turning increasingly to the passively managed index funds.

INDEX FUNDS

Index funds attempt to mirror the performance of a stock index by owning a representative sample of the stocks that make up the index. Once the sample is established, there is no need to manage actively the portfolio since it tracks the index's movements. Existing funds copy dozens of indexes ranging from a broad index such as the S&P 500, a high-tech index like the NASDAQ computer index, or a foreign index such as the IFC Emerging Markets index. About 10 percent of U.S. equity funds under management are placed in index funds. The nation's largest index fund, Vanguard Index 500, had $35 billion in assets as of May 1999 and it ranked as the third largest fund in the country, trailing only the $61 billion Fidelity Magellan Fund and the $33 billion Investment Co. of America Fund.

Index funds represent a victory for the efficient market theory, which contends that stock prices reflect all available information. The analyst's search for an undervalued security is therefore futile, since its attributes have been fully appraised by others. The growth of index funds also signals the investor's frustration with security analysts and portfolio managers. Indeed, "The S&P 500 has been beating about 80 percent of all mutual funds for the past 10 years," according to a *Barron's* study. Index funds are now major institutional players.

SMALL MONEY MANAGEMENT FIRMS

Because of their size, management limitations, and diversification requirements, large institutional investors fully invested in equities tend to have performance results that closely track the broad market indices. Smaller firms, with less than $1 billion under management, retain considerably more flexibility in designing a strategy that beats the market. They can search out value among the many companies too small for large institutional investment. Small cap stocks far outnumber big name equities like Coca-Cola and Ford Motor, and pricing inefficiencies are more prevalent. Simply defining a "small cap" universe as stocks with a value between $25 million and $500 million creates over 5,000 potential names for study. Exhibit 2–3 provides a list of advantages for small investment funds.

With a limited asset base, the portfolio manager of a $1 billion fund can make meaningful commitments to individual stocks without unduly influencing their prices. Large institutions can't do this. To gain a significant position in a small cap stock, their own buying efforts upset the normal price behavior. Accordingly, second-tier institutions can afford to be research intensive, scouting the market for cheap stocks and spending substantial time analyzing special situations. A stronger orientation toward security analysis is also found among the smaller funds that focus on just one industry. A bio-tech fund, for example, needs only one or two security analysts to cover the principal public companies in the industry, thus providing fundwide analysis in a cost-effective manner. Other small institutional investors emphasize a single theme such as buying "growth stocks" or "value stocks." The firm's analysts do not cling to a specific industry focus, believing that growth companies exhibit certain characteristics which are common among all fast-growing businesses. Likewise, a "value analyst" sees repeated patterns in the evaluation of shares trading below their intrinsic worth.

In a small fund, portfolio managers and security analysts both generate investment ideas, which are forwarded to an investment committee. Like the committees of larger institutions, small fund committees rely heavily on the portfolio manager's guidance. In certain small institutions, such as hedge funds, the governance structure is looser, and portfolio managers operate without formal investment committees.

Most of the smaller mutual funds, asset managers, and bank trust departments charge clients a fixed annual service fee based on a percentage of the market value of assets under management. Like the larger institutions, these money managers charge fees whether or not the client makes money. They typically pay their portfolio managers and security analysts a salary

EXHIBIT 2–3. Security Analysis for Small Investment Funds

Specific stock selections can make a difference in overall portfolio returns.

A small fund can make a major commitment to an attractive "small cap" stock.

Analysis of complex situations such as distressed securities is more easily accomplished.

A small fund can focus on one industry group and take advantage of specialized analytical knowledge of that industry.

---

plus a variable bonus. A limited number are set up as investment partnerships, whereby the manager receives a percentage of the profits. The portfolio manager and his key analysts are the general partners, and the clients contributing most of the money are the limited partners. A common arrangement is for the general partners to put up 1 percent of the capital in exchange for 20 percent of the profits, although more and more partnerships now require the fund to earn a minimum return, such as 8 percent annually, before the general partner's "carried interest" applies.

Any fund that provides the managers with a 20 percent cut of the partnership profits is referred to as a "hedge fund." This term originated many years ago with groups of investors who pooled large sums for buying stocks they thought would rise in price, at the same time selling shares they thought would decline. In this way, they profited from both a general rise or fall in share prices. The potential for losses was lessened by the counterbalancing bets (the "hedge"). In the old-time hedge funds, the general partner received 20 percent of the profits, and the nickname stuck to subsequent equity partnerships involving a large management carry. Today's hedge funds, in contrast, trade stocks in a wide-open fashion, and very little is hedged. In fact, hedge fund managers pride themselves on making large bets on narrow investment themes.

Because a hedge fund manager multiplies his 1 percent capital investment by a factor of 20:1, security analysts relish the opportunity to join hedge funds and actually pick stocks, rather than just recommending them. Many successful analysts make the transition to lucrative hedge fund positions.

INDIVIDUAL INVESTORS: A SPECIAL CATEGORY

The vast majority of individual investors lack the time, training, and experience to analyze intensively their equity investments. Most avoid the pain of specific stock selection by purchasing mutual funds. Others indulge in the occasional equity speculation based on a broker's suggestion, a friend's advice, or a news item. A small minority apply the tools in this book to evaluate share prices.

As noted earlier, information is the lifeblood of the stock market. In this regard, the individual investor operates at a significant disadvantage relative to securities firms and prominent institutions. The majority of corporate information is distributed in an even-handed fashion, but frequently word of a significant event leaks out to key market players, who are then in a position for a short time to make a profit. Besides access to leaks, institutions and securities firms have greater access to corporate management in getting questions answered. On Wall Street, the individual hears information last. For example, a number of sell-side analysts move stock prices when issuing recommendations to buy or sell, as investors quickly follow their advice. At most securities firms, such recommendations are first telephoned to the biggest buy-side institutions, then faxed to secondary buy-side customers, and finally mailed to individual account holders. Institutions receive favored treatment because they represent the most profitable commission volume.

Professional traders, who hunch over computer screens for eight hours a day, also have advantages over individuals in profiting on new information. Other than day traders, few individuals spend their time tracking stock prices and following news reports on a minute-to-minute basis, yet data coming over the computerized Dow Jones Tape is read immediately by at least 100,000 professionals. Printed information in the *Wall Street Journal*, while only 12 hours old, is thus already discounted by practitioners. As a result, the typical individual works off stale information that is days or weeks old. Only superior analytical effort overcomes this disadvantage.

The high commissions charged by many brokerage firms compound the information problem for the average investor. A $20,000 stock order can easily result in a $200 commission, which is 1 percent of the trade's value. (On-line brokers are cutting these costs by 80%.) Furthermore, most individuals lack access to real-time trading data. The brokerage firms take advantage of this fact by failing to execute the trades for the client's maximum benefit, thus providing the firm and its trading affiliates with added profit while reducing the individual's returns. Such deception sometimes takes place in an institutional context. For example, as a World Bank executive, I sold 300,000 shares of a Mexican company through a U.S. securities firm. Not aware that I had access to real-time Mexican trading data, the firm informed me that the shares had been sold for $7.52 each. In fact, I observed the trades on a Bloomberg system and saw the shares being sold in large lots at $7.57 to $7.62 per share. Only after I presented the firm's sales director with this evidence did the trader admit his "mistake," which would have cost the World Bank $25,000. Robbing a bank of $25,000 is a serious crime, but cheating customers for a few pennies a share is a widely accepted practice at many brokerage firms.

Despite these obstacles, some investors apply security analysis techniques to their investment activities and realize superior performance. In my experience, the most successful players fall into two groups: (1) those with prior financial experience, which enables them to perform their own analysis; and (2) those with a strong industry expertise, which allows them to foresee developments impacting stock prices in that one industry.

Although the odds are stacked against individual investors, the situation is far from hopeless. There are thousands of publicly traded stocks, and the vast institutional and brokerage communities can't monitor every company on a continual basis. Valuation anomalies occur regularly because the tens of thousands of daily tape watchers don't maintain complete coverage. As individuals search for discrepancies, they can also practice common sense in the selection of widely followed stocks. Full-time players inevitably get caught up in Wall Street's herd mentality, which frequently produces outlandish valuations for the "stock of the month." Inevitably, prices of these businesses return to earth after practitioners face their excesses, so an occasional "short sale" by an knowledgeable individual is appropriate. Likewise, common sense sometimes triggers a contrarian approach on the buy side, as someone purchases selected stocks that have fallen from grace.

The 1999 run-up in Internet stocks was a good example of institutions going overboard in betting on the financial prospects of Internet services. Over a 12-month period, the share price of Marketing Services Group shot up from $2 to $60, only to decline sharply in June 1999 to $16.

SUMMARY

Many thousands of people participate in the equity markets on a regular basis, but there are only 30,000 full-time security analysts. Most of these professionals work in three settings: security firms, major institutions, and small institutions.

Securities firms have the greatest concentration of analysts, with the larger firms employing dozens of professionals specializing in distinct industries. In addition to following specific companies and publishing research reports, these analysts work with institutional clients to figure investment choices and interact with the firm's bankers to generate advisory fees.

On the institutional buy side, the analyst's role is closer to that of a pure stock picker. As the in-house industry expert and resident numbers guru, he works closely with portfolio managers in establishing a rational basis for investment selection. The analyst's status is magnified in smaller institutions, which can make meaningful commitments to his investment recommendations, but his impact becomes less in the large institutional environment. A big mutual fund company has multiple funds covering hundreds of stocks, and few specific shares are individually important to overall results. By virtue of their size, large institutions rely frequently on sector rotation, market timing, macro finance, and quantitative investment techniques. These methods deemphasize security analysis in favor of broader investment themes.

QUESTIONS AND SHORT PROBLEMS

1. What's the difference between the "sell side" and the "buy side" in the securities markets?

2. List the duties of a security analyst at an investment bank. Why is the report writing aspect of the job sometimes referred to as a "page business"? Name the three functions of a research report.

3. What is the purported "Chinese Wall" of the typical brokerage firm? How does the protective function of the wall come to be routinely compromised?

4. The typical mutual fund is paid in which of the following ways:
   a. The fund annually receives a fixed percentage fee, based on the market value of assets under management.
   b. The fund receives a variable fee, based on relative investment performance and portfolio size.
   c. The fund receives a fixed fee, plus a bonus based on achieving performance targets.
   d. The fund receives a fixed percentage of profits on assets under management.

5. How does the security analyst employed at a large institutional investor contribute to the investment decision process at his employer?

6. Why is individual stock selection becoming de-emphasized at the very large institutional investors?

7. How does rapid portfolio turnover reduce the analyst's importance at major "buy side" institutions?

8. Which of the following is the action of a "sector rotator"?
   a. Sell Japanese utilities when Japanese interest rates rise.
   b. Sell computer stocks and buy software stocks.
   c. Sell oil stocks on news of an OPEC meeting.
   d. Decrease equity percentage of portfolio on learning of P/E multiple revisions.

9. How does the security analyst play a more important role as a small money manager than at a large firm?

10. After one year, the XYZ Hedge Fund has earned 15 percent on its $100 million portfolio. Assuming the standard fee arrangement, how much compensation have the fund managers earned?

11. Name a few disadvantages (vis-à-vis the professional trader) that represent problems for the average retail investor.

Adopt-a-Company

Students continue searching for companies meeting the criteria set forth at the end of Chapter 1.

3

Seeking a Level Playing Field

How level is the playing field? The stock market provides partici-
pants with a reasonably fair chance of matching the other guy's suc-
cess. Nevertheless, certain players either have inherent advantages in
playing the market or exploit weaknesses in the regulatory system. In
this chapter, we examine the system's safeguards and look at their
impact on an initial public offering.

The stock selection process employed by brokerage firms, institutions, and individual investors is heavily reliant on informed trading. The convergence of a security's market value to its rational value doesn't depend merely on the coincidental meeting of supply and demand. Rather, the more important consideration is the quality of information on which investors' decisions are based. Thus, before issuing a buy or sell recommendation, the analyst needs to know, first, the present and future earnings prospects of different investment opportunities and, second, the fair prices of securities competing for the investment dollar. This requirement emphasizes the importance of correct and reliable information on corporate activities, and on open and honest trading in the markets.

Besides enhancing the securities analysis process, good information and orderly markets facilitate the rational allocation of investment funds. In an ideal situation, the share prices arrived at through supply and demand reflect the collective opinion of technically trained investors, who intently study the long-term investment prospects of industries (and companies within a given industry) before making a decision. The long-term expectations of each investment are considered relative to others, and the decision is finalized after an exhaustive comparison of each investment's relative price and risk. While intelligent speculation plays a role in this ideal setup, the exacting decision process ensures that capital flows to those companies demonstrating the best potential for economic success.

Correspondingly, the rigorous analysis diminishes the money-raising ability of those firms with less justification for development.

The foregoing is a perfect system. It is referred to as an "efficient market" in academic parlance. The real-world market, as noted earlier, deviates substantially from this ideal, but it comes closer with better corporate information and improved order execution. In fact, the federal government recognizes an efficient stock market as a legitimate social goal. After all, the economic well-being of the United States requires moving capital into the most deserving industries and ensuring that investors receive fair value. For this reason, the authorities push numerous regulatory initiatives that steer the securities market closer to the efficient model. The government also encourages the stock exchanges to pursue a strong self-regulatory regime.

While the securities market still exhibits many weaknesses, the corporate disclosure and trading standards imposed by the government and the exchanges are largely successful, and most widely followed shares trade at prices that are justifiable based on a studied review of their earnings prospects. Despite these successes, ill practices continue to hamper the market's ability to price shares properly. Dubious exercises include:

- The release of misleading information by companies issuing securities, filing quarterly statements or participating in merger and acquisition activity.

- The manipulation of a stock by either the issuer or by investment bankers, syndicates, or individuals interested in the stock.

- The purchase or sale of a stock based on inside information.

- The use of high pressure sales tactics and false rumors to attract the investing public.

- The utilization of excessive leverage either to acquire shares as a principal or to broker stocks as an agent.

Regulators are enormously influential in reducing the frequency of such abuses, but it is essential to appreciate the limitations under which they operate. The markets represent hundreds of thousands of brokers, institutions, and individuals executing millions of transactions in thousands of securities each day. Even with multimillion dollar budgets, high-speed computers, and dedicated employees, the regulators are outnumbered and outgunned many times over by the major corporations, large securities firms, and professional investors who dominate the stock market. Even when a crooked participant is caught red-handed, the regulators face difficulties. Resolving the most egregious violations of securities laws often requires years of litigation, so unscrupulous participants have a motivation to bend the rules. Professionals realize that the regulators are the investor's friends, but caveat emptor reigns supreme. There is no substitute for a comprehensive analysis before an investment decision is made.

BRIEF HISTORY OF SECURITIES REGULATION

Abuses have occurred throughout the stock market's history, but they became highly visible in the 1920s. This was the first decade when the general public played a large role in buying and selling stocks, and during this time, stock prices advanced rapidly. Many unsophisticated investors, seeing the profits being made, decided to place a portion of their savings into the equity markets. By the late 1920s, over 10 million individual investors held the majority of publicly issued shares, a sharp contrast to earlier days. For many years, the stock markets had been the province of full-time traders and speculators. Established institutions, such as insurance companies and bank trust departments avoided common stocks as being too risky and displayed a marked preference for conservative government and corporate bonds. The entry of the individual investor on a broad scale was positive, since it broadened the number of participants and introduced more capital, but it also provided unscrupulous practitioners with additional opportunities to take advantage of unknowing players.

While important to American finance, the stock markets of the 1920s were speculative. A key contributor to this situation was the lack of information supplied to investors by the issuing companies. Even on the New York Stock Exchange, where many of the larger firms traded, companies provided public stockholders with little more than an abbreviated income statement and balance sheet on an annual basis. Information requirements at the exchanges and for over-the-counter issues often failed to meet this bare minimum. For example, a Sloan and Standard study in 1929 showed that 257 of the 323 leading public companies refused to report annual sales to the public. Quarterly income statements were frequently absent and executives often withheld information about corporate activities, while positioning themselves to take advantage of changing stock prices when the news became public. Also, accounting standards varied widely among companies, and such disparities made a comparative analysis of corporate income statements and balance sheets very difficult. Investors decried their inability to obtain relevant data, but the companies resisted for, among other reasons, fear of alerting competitors to their progress. The exchanges backed up the issuers, although many investment bankers began to realize the unsustainability of minimal disclosure. Serious analysts lacked the requisite information on which to make a rational investment decision, although they were pressed to make commitments as equity prices boomed.

As stock prices spiraled upward, the quality of new issues declined. Investment banks and commercial banks rushed to fill the distribution pipeline with product, without paying sufficient attention to the issuers' long-term earnings prospects. This phenomenon, which is played out in almost every bull market, saw underwriters making marketing decisions without the careful analysis that prudence required. Prices of these low-quality and overvalued securities gyrated widely and thus contributed to the market's shaky underpinnings.

Compounding the problem of scant information and speculative issues were other complications. Unsavory investment practices such as outright fraud, price manipulation, insider trading, secret investment pools, and bear raids were a constant presence behind the scenes. At the same time, many dishonest securities firms, referred to as "bucket shops" or "boiler rooms," were using high-pressure sales tactics to separate inexperienced investors from their money. And finally, commercial banks and brokerage firms greased the trading wheels by supplying customers with liberal credit. Loan-to-value ratios for stocks went as high as 90 percent in the 1920s, versus 50 percent for individuals today. The provision of easy money only accentuated the casino atmosphere of the markets and further distorted the realistic values for equities.

In the absence of meaningful oversight of these activities at the federal level, many states passed laws designed to regulate the in-state sale of securities by out-of-state issuers. Set up to protect local investors, the laws were called "blue sky" regulations since the selling of highly speculative securities was like "selling a piece of the blue sky." Because few states coordinated their efforts, the blue sky restrictions were different from state to state, representing a patchwork of vague and ill-defined regulations. Furthermore, state securities departments were typically poorly trained, understaffed, and underfunded. They were no match for the shenanigans crafted by Wall Street operators.

Supervision by the exchanges over their members was tantamount to inmates running the asylum. Few regulations existed at the exchanges and those on the books were only enforced if the violator blatantly repeated abuses in the face of warnings. Over-the-counter trading was wide-open.

Federal regulation of the 1930s grew out of the notion that dishonest behavior and speculative excesses played a key role in the disastrous Crash of 1929, when stock prices dropped an average of 23 percent in two days. Besides dramatically reducing investors' wealth on paper overnight, the crash paralyzed the nation's financial system and contributed with other economic events to the ensuing Great Depression. As the Hoover administration and the exchanges dragged their feet on implementing stronger protective measures, abuses continued making headlines in the newspapers, resulting in a Senate investigation that justified forceful oversight. Within six months of Roosevelt's election, the Securities Act of 1933 was passed. By 1934, the Securities Exchange Act dictated the formation of the Securities and Exchange Commission (SEC), a separate agency devoted to protecting investors and maintaining fair and orderly markets. A separate piece of legislation, the Glass-Steagall Act, divorced commercial banks from the securities business.

THE CHIEF REGULATOR—THE SECURITIES AND EXCHANGE COMMISSION

The SEC's purpose was to supervise the appropriate flow of information between the issuing corporations and investors, and it quickly gained the reputation of being a "disclosure agency." Before issuing securities trading on national exchanges, companies needed to submit for SEC approval lengthy registration statements, describing the securities and the company's business, financial history, and likely prospects. (Later, in 1964, Congress extended the regulations to over-the-counter issues.) Regular filings with the agency continued thereafter and all such documentation was made available for public dissemination. Companies were required to disclose many other matters of relevance to shareholders, such as details on takeover inquiries, significant business changes, and management compensation. A public company also needed to have its annual financial statements audited by an independent accounting firm, thereby transforming the accounting business into one of the growth industries of the 1930s. While the availability of this level of corporate information is taken for granted today, its appearance following the SEC legislation spawned the growth of corporate information gathering and security analysis businesses. No longer would investors be operating from spotty data, half-truths, and misinformation.

Prior to the SEC, security offering materials were designed as marketing devices rather than disclosure documents. The offering prospectus contained bits and prices of information that hardly provided the raw material for an independent assessment. The guiding principle of the prospectus was inducing the potential investor to buy, so many prospectuses provided inadequate disclosure, extravagant promises, and outright misstatements. Consider the claims of Texas Eagle Oil Company in a 1919 offering announcement. With only a six-month operating history and no record of sales or earnings, the firm announced:

> . . . With the claws of an eagle we have gripped the oil fields of Mid-Texas. Only 10,000 shares open to public subscription.
>
> This company is as sound as a bank. Insured profits, verified accounts, open books. No secrets.
>
> Deposit your money [i.e., buy shares—author's addition] with us with the same confidence that you have in your bank.

The SEC regulates by information. For new issues, companies furnish a sufficient amount of information so that a "reasonable person" can make an informed investment decision. At the same time, the sponsoring investment banks are required to make an investigation of each issue before it is brought to market. The issuers and other responsible parties are liable in court for any important misstatement or omission of fact that contributes to investors buying an issue and subsequently losing money. As Auerbach and Hayes have put it, the SEC tries to reverse caveat emptor by making "the seller beware." The SEC has a staff of experienced accountants, attorneys, and financial analysts for new issue evaluation, but it relies on the information supplied in the filing process. It has neither the staff nor resources to conduct its own inspection of the companies behind the issues. As a result, the disclosure system depends on the combined self-regulatory actions of the issuers, investment bankers, attorneys, and accountants involved with a transaction. They are the investors' line of defense against outright fraud or unintentional misrepresentation in the written materials provided for public consumption.

The disclosure system works pretty well, but it has important flaws. Perhaps the most prominent of these is the manner in which corporate disclosure documents are written. To reduce the chances of their issuer client being sued by an investor, lawyers take over the entire descriptive process. The result of their efforts is that the review of the issuer's business and prospects is set forth in a dry and stilted fashion that is comprehensible only to professionals. The average investor is turned off by the documentation, fails to study it, and is therefore easy pickings for unscrupulous promoters, particularly for new offerings that haven't been tested in the market. Being on a number of brokerage calling lists, I receive solicitations from bucket-shop brokers, who end their sales pitches quickly when I ask pointed questions or request a prospectus.

The disclosure system often fails in laying out the major risks of an issue. I have seen companies, lawyers, and bankers do their best to obfuscate important business risks by burying them in legal mumbo jumbo. The following sentence from Template Software's 1997 initial public offering prospectus is illustrative:

> The Company's revenues have been attributable to a limited number of products and related services. As a result, factors adversely affecting the pricing of or demand for such products and services could have a material adverse effect on the Company's business, operating results and financial condition.

Why not just simply say the truth?

> The company is a one-product business. Any negative change in the demand or pricing for this product will result in a substantial loss of your investment.

Lastly, a corporate security derives its value from the company's prospective performance—not its past history. Why can't a prospective issuer disclose management's latest projections for the business? The corporation can provide this information—and the SEC encourages the practice—but the issuer's lawyers always advise against distributing projections to the public. Our legal system is to blame. Even with cautionary warnings included in a prospectus, the issuer can be successfully sued by investors should they lose money on the deal. Similarly, prospectuses don't contain "comparable company" data. This information is an integral part of a security analysis, yet it never appears in a prospectus.

The SEC admits that its "truth in securities" laws don't prohibit the sale of speculative securities and overpriced stocks, nor do they ensure that investors receive a fair return on their investments. This is an odd position to maintain, considering the government insists on restricting less apparent

EXHIBIT 3–1. The Regulatory Role of the Securities and Exchange Commission

---

Information for new issues.

Maintenance of information flow for existing public companies.

Fair trading and sales practices by securities firms.

Registration of exchanges with SEC oversight on self-supervision activities.

Registration of securities firms and supervision of honest business practices.

Regulations governing investment companies and investment advisers such as mutual funds, bank trust departments, and insurance companies.

---

financial abuses, such as hidden interest charges in leases and misleading insurance marketing practices. Nonetheless, the SEC regulations try to provide investors—and security analysts—with sufficient information on which to make an intelligent decision. Thus, the market makes the ultimate judgment on what a security is worth, not the government. Exhibit 3–1 lists aspects of the SEC's regulatory role.

SALES AND TRADING PRACTICES

Besides requiring adequate and accurate information from public corporations, the SEC administers laws that seek to maintain fair and orderly markets. These laws give the SEC broad authority to supervise the activities of the principal players in the stock market—the stock exchanges, securities firms, and money managers (and their employees)—and to regulate unfair trading practices such as insider trading, undisclosed investment pools, and price manipulation. Like the disclosure rules, sales and trading regulations are essentially carried out by self-regulatory mechanisms. The New York Stock Exchange, American Stock Exchange, NASDAQ (National Association of Securities Dealers Automated Quotations), and various regional exchanges have rules that members are supposed to follow to protect investors, and these organizations operate monitoring and enforcement departments to find and punish violators (Exhibit 3–2). Thus, a poorly capitalized securities firm or a renegade stockbroker should be caught first by the industry's regulatory bodies, rather than by the SEC.

If the exchanges discover a dishonest action by someone *outside* the industry's regulatory scheme, the violation is referred to the government. Brokerage firms are on guard to look for customer insider trading, to deny their facilities for stock price manipulation, and to restrict speculative excesses by in-house brokers and account holders, but the system is far from perfect. Many securities firms look the other way when they see improper behavior, and the SEC fosters this complacency by regulating in a reactive manner, waiting for someone to complain before investigating problems.

Based on my own experiences in the investment banking business, I conclude that the self-regulatory system is effective in halting most egregious

EXHIBIT 3–2. The Investment Game and Regulatory Framework of the Securities and Exchange Commission

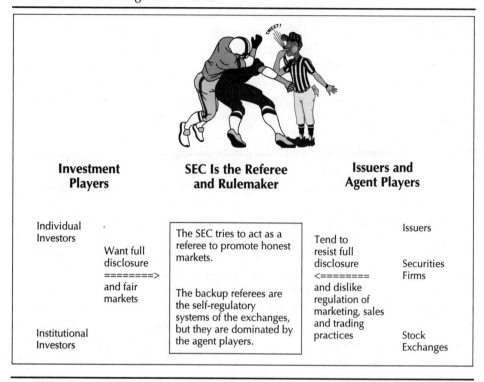

Investment Players	SEC Is the Referee and Rulemaker	Issuers and Agent Players
Individual Investors		Issuers
Want full disclosure ========> and fair markets	The SEC tries to act as a referee to promote honest markets.	Tend to resist full disclosure <======== and dislike regulation of marketing, sales and trading practices	Securities Firms
	The backup referees are the self-regulatory systems of the exchanges, but they are dominated by the agent players.	
Institutional Investors		Stock Exchanges

abuses, but it falters consistently around the margins. Instances abound of shoddy marketing practices directed at unsophisticated investors, poor brokerage firm execution practices that cheat customers, and insider trades that go undetected. For example, in August 1996 the SEC censured the National Association of Securities Dealers (NASD) for failing to police wrongdoing in the NASDAQ Stock Market. NASDAQ is the national over-the-counter market featuring hundreds of well-known companies such as Microsoft, Intel, and Apple Computer. Like other U.S. stock markets, the NASDAQ is self-regulated, and the NASD is the primary enforcer of trading rules. Yet, for many years, NASD turned a blind eye to habitual rule breaking by its members. The securities firms that dominated NASDAQ trading often cheated customers for a few pennies per share by executing their trades improperly. The recent reorganization of NASD hopefully will change its half-hearted attempts to regulate its members. According to one NASD regulator, "We have the evidence (on abuses) but NASD management doesn't want to go and kick ass. They just want to answer the mail and send lawyers and spin doctors to Capitol Hill, saying what a great stock market we've got."

Insider trading is another activity that hurts the market's credibility. The illegal insider trading of Barnett Bank's stock in August 1997, just before a $15 billion takeover bid was announced, upset Barnett Bank's share price for 48 hours. Afterward, the news was widely available, so the manipulation was of short duration. Nevertheless, the integrity of Barnett Bank's price was damaged for several days. Almost every takeover stock goes up before the official announcement, yet the authorities rarely go after the perpetrators.

Furthermore, the SEC does nothing to eliminate the conflict of interest inherent in the respective jobs of individual stockbroker and institutional securities salesperson. Inevitably, the compensation of these individuals is directly related to the amount of trading activity they generate from their customers. As a result, they are under constant pressure to do more business, even if increased portfolio turnover is not to the customer's benefit. Likewise, permitting securities firms to direct "order flow" to corporate affiliates or other sweetheart arrangements is a conflict that should be addressed.

The system of an elite group of specialists is an area of frequent abuses. Specialist firms are small firms assigned to maintain an orderly progression of prices in selected exchange listed stocks. They match, buy, and sell orders brought to them by brokers. To keep the market orderly, they are responsible to buy for their own account when there are more sellers than buyers and to sell from their holdings when there is an excess of buyers. The specialist firm has an advantage because it has the "order book" in a given stock, and from this it knows the market position of the stock at any moment—bids below market, offers above, as well as any stop-loss orders. Since it is permitted to act as broker and also to trade its own account, the firm has powerful inside information versus those who trade with it. The firm's interests as a trader are in conflict with its duties as a broker, and the evidence shows that few specialists truly enhance liquidity in the stocks they cover. Most huge block trades are handled by large security firms—away from the thinly-capitalized specialists; and the specialist system failed completely in the Crash of 1987 when many specialists, to avoid the slightest loss, set unrealistically low prices for stocks in which they traded—thus encouraging the price decline rather than forestalling it.

The problem of control of the stock markets is thus a difficult one. It involves not only the regulation of the thousands of corporations whose securities are publicly traded and the markets and dealers in these securities, but also the control and suppression of an endless variety of stock promotion and trading schemes. An increase in the SEC's budget, an expansion of the Justice Department's efforts against securities fraud, and a federal takeover of the self-regulatory mechanisms of the exchanges would improve the environment dramatically.

For the most part, abuses don't amount to large amounts of money compared with a typical day's trading volume, and, with few exceptions, they tend not to affect a security's economic value for a long period. If left unchecked, however, these actions have a cumulative impact by undermining investor confidence. Unless investors and issuers sense that they are treated fairly, the markets don't function properly and can't ensure an adequate supply of capital for economic growth.

MARGIN REGULATION

The control of speculation is assisted by the government's regulation of margin buying. Margin is the use of credit to buy securities. Liberal credit contributes to unrestrained bull markets by increasing equity investment monies. In an effort to reduce speculation on borrowed funds, the government, through the Federal Reserve, sets the maximum loan-to-value ratio for common stocks. This ratio has been set at 50 percent for many years. Brokers also monitor cases of excess stock margin credit on an individual basis.

THE LIFE CYCLE OF A SECURITY ISSUE

As set forth in Exhibit 3–3, the regulatory machinery follows a publicly issued security through its creation; sees that relevant information flows to the investment community; oversees the buying, selling, and marketing of the issue as it becomes seasoned in the aftermarket; and requires proper disclosure when it is delisted, by repurchase, takeover, merger, or bankruptcy.

The SEC review is at its most intense during a security's initial public offering (IPO), but most trading volume is accounted for by seasoned issues beyond the IPO stage. This daily buying, selling, and marketing of aftermarket issues is dominated by the self-regulatory system, with the SEC interfering when obvious violations occur or when someone reports illicit activity. Signifying the end of one security and perhaps the expansion of another, mergers and acquisitions are closely reviewed by the SEC to ensure fair dealing. Mergers and acquisitions (M&A) represent billions of investor dollars and tend to be complicated, so the potential for unscrupulous behavior is enhanced. Similarly, the SEC evaluates Chapter 11 reorganizations, which involve a level of analysis far above that possessed by most professionals.

Case Study: Eagle Publishing Company.   A case study is helpful in tracing the regulatory scheme. Eagle Publishing Company ("Eagle" or the "Company"), reviews its capital budget for 2000 and decides it needs $25 million in additional equity capital. After evaluating its financing options, the Company concludes that an initial public offering of common stock represents the optimal strategy. This decision sets in motion a five-step process culminating in the Company's shares trading in the aftermarket, as shown in Exhibit 3–4.

EXHIBIT 3–3. Regulation through the Security Life Cycle

Phase of Life Cycle	Regulatory Framework
1. Initial public offering takes place.	Ensure proper disclosure. Meet exchange listing requirements. Underwriters conduct due diligence investigation.
2. The IPO becomes a seasoned issue, bought and sold in the aftermarket.	Company (issuer) must supply financial reports and other relevant data regularly. SEC supervises stock exchanges and securities firms in their self-regulatory efforts to prevent abuses in trading, buying, selling, and marketing of the stock. SEC and exchanges monitor capital adequacy of securities firms dealing in the issue. SEC looks for price manipulation, insider trading, and other illegal actions outside the exchange system.
3. Issue is delisted.	SEC requires full disclosure on takeovers and mergers of public companies. To protect public investor interests, the SEC can participate in the bankruptcy proceedings of public companies. Exchanges remove companies that fail to meet listing requirements.

EXHIBIT 3–4. Eagle Publishing Company—Steps in the Initial Public Offering Process

1. Eagle selects an investment bank.
2. Eagle, its banker, and other advisors prepare a prospectus for the SEC.
3. The marketing process for Eagle's IPO begins.
4. Eagle's shares are priced and sold into the market. The Company receives its needed capital.
5. Eagle's shares trade in the aftermarket.

Step 1. Selecting an Investment Bank

Based on previous banking relationships or associates' recommendations, a typical prospective issuer invites several investment banks to study the issuer's business, provide an equity valuation, and promote their respective abilities to carry out an IPO. Depending on the complexity of the issuer's business, the state of its financial and operating records, and the reputation of its management, this preliminary activity lasts from a few weeks to several months.

In Eagle's case, the evaluation process goes quickly because the Company presents no difficult valuation issues. As a publisher of specialty trade magazines, Eagle is in a low-tech business with a low fashion content. It has audited financial statements, which are important, and the results indicate steady growth in sales and earnings. The Company's management information system (MIS) and record-keeping system are up-to-date and allow the potential underwriters to access operating data readily. Finally, the management team is experienced and well respected, eliminating the need for lengthy background checks. Preliminary information about the company is shown in Exhibit 3–5. Financial data appear in Exhibit 3–6.

Three investment banks study the Company's business for several weeks, prepare financial projections, and compare these results with existing publicly held magazine publishers. Afterwards, each bank meets separately with Eagle's owners and managers to discuss an expected price for the Company's shares and to review a marketing plan for the offering. As is common in these situations, the three investment banks—Castle Stone & Company, Branch Day, Inc., and Levy Brothers—have well-honed presentations and show price estimates for Eagle's shares that are reasonably similar. Describing the process of having his company valued by New York investment bankers, Drew Peslar, co-owner of Automotive Moulding Co., once remarked, "I felt like a kid in wonderland." The Eagle information is shown in Exhibit 3–7.

Although Branch Day's net pricing of $13.25 per share is slightly higher (even after its costly commission structure) than the others, Eagle selects Castle Stone & Co. as its investment banker. The firm's key selling point is its experience with publishing concerns. In concert with this new financial

EXHIBIT 3–5. Eagle Publishing Company

Objective	To raise $25 million via an initial public offering of common stock.
Use of Proceeds	The net proceeds will be used in the Company's capital expenditure program.
Business	Eagle publishes a group of specialty trade magazines targeted at niche industries.
Financial Summary	Selected financial results are set forth in Exhibit 3–6.

EXHIBIT 3–6. Eagle Publishing Company Summary—Financial Data—
Year Ended December 31

(In Millions)	1996	1997	1998
Income Statement Data			
Sales	$115.0	$130.0	$150.0
Gross profit	40.0	46.0	53.0
Earning before interest and taxes	10.0	12.0	15.0
Net earnings	4.0	5.3	7.0
Balance Sheet Data			
Working capital	21.0	24.0	22.0
Total assets	99.0	108.0	116.0
Total debt	20.0	25.0	30.0
Stockholders' equity	36.0	40.0	45.0
Per Share Data (10 Million Shares)			
Earnings per share	0.40	0.53	0.70
Book value per share	3.60	4.00	4.50

Note. Eagle's track record is good and its balance sheet is solid.

advisor, Eagle commences the preparation of an offering prospectus for its
shares.

Step 2. Preparing the Prospectus

The prospectus is the principal disclosure statement for Eagle's financing.
Like most such documents, this prospectus is going to be lengthy—probably
90 to 100 pages including audited financial data. Ensuring that the prospectus contains accurate and adequate information requires the efforts of a large
team of professionals (see Exhibit 3–8).

EXHIBIT 3–7. Eagle Publishing Company—Proposed Initial Public Offering

	Castle Stone & Co.	Branch Day, Inc.	Levy Brothers
Gross proceeds	$25.0MM	$25.0MM	$25.0MM
Commissions and expenses (as a percentage)	7.0%	8.0%	7.0%
Net proceeds	$23.3MM	$23.0MM	$23.3MM
Number of shares	2.0MM	1.9MM	2.1MM
Expected price per share	$12.50	$13.25	$11.75
P/E Ratio	18×	19×	17×
Percentage ownership represented by IPO	17%	16%	17%

Note. Branch Day's proposal has the highest price, but also the highest commissions.

EXHIBIT 3–8. Eagle Publishing Company—Initial Public Offering Prospectus Preparation Team

---

From Eagle Publishing

Eagle executives including finance, legal, accounting, and operations personnel.

Eagle's outside legal counsel.

Eagle's independent accounting firm.

From Castle Stone

Three to five investment bankers.

The firm's research analyst for publishing companies.

Castle Stone's outside counsel.

An outside publishing expert.

Working off prospectus models from previous publishing deals, the team puts in long hours constructing a document that describes fully the Company and the securities being offered. Most of the descriptive drafting is done by Eagle's chief financial officer, two or three junior bankers, and senior associates from the two law firms. Financial data is provided by the Company and its independent accountants. The accountants also check the veracity of Eagle's operating statistics, such as number of magazine titles, lists of subscribers, and volumes of ad pages. All the prospectus language corresponds to the dry legal style which is de rigueur for SEC documents; and, as a result, the team has a tough time putting a marketing spin in the document. Eagle's prospectus is representative of an initial public offering; it contains the sections required by the SEC, as listed in the Table of Contents shown in Exhibit 3–9.

As Exhibit 3–9 indicates, the majority of the prospectus is descriptive, relaying facts to the investor, who then forms an opinion from this data and related information, such as industry conditions, comparable stock prices, and general economic expectations. A full description of a large business could run into hundreds of pages, but Eagle, like most companies, doesn't provide a surplus of data for competitive reasons. The prospectus authors judge what's important from an investor's standpoint and what's not, hopeful that the SEC's requirements are met. Although Eagle's executives, bankers, and attorneys form a consensus on which facts should be included to inform investors, certain disclosure items become a topic of debate. Subscriber cancellation statistics and advertiser renewal rates head the list. Are they necessary? Do they make a meaningful difference in the investor's decision process? Due diligence by the bankers reveals substantial volatility in subscriber cancellations, and Castle Stone's lawyers insist on public disclosure. Management protests this suggestion, but the lawyers win the argument through the tactic of casting the specter of future litigation over the deal.

As the drafting continues in stops and starts, the investment bank continues its investigation of Eagle's business. The bankers collect and analyze

EXHIBIT 3–9. Eagle Publishing Company—Initial Public Offering Prospectus

Table of Contents

Prospectus Summary
Certain Risk Factors
Use of Proceeds
Capitalization
Selected Consolidated Financial Data
Management's Discussion and Analysis of Financial Condition and Results of Operation
Business Description
  Overview
  Product Line
  Research and Development
  Distribution and Significant Customers
  Marketing and Customer Support
  Manufacturing and Suppliers
  Competition
  Trademarks
  Litigation
  Personnel
  Properties
Management
Principal Stockholders
Underwriting of the Common Stock
Legal Opinions
Consolidated Financial Statements

financial and operating data, question Eagle's management, interview its lawyers and accountants, and visit selected operating sites. Supplementing this due diligence is a wealth of outside data developed by Castle Stone on the magazine publishing industry. As the process unfolds, the bankers obtain a thorough understanding of Eagle's business from a financial point of view and develop a mental list of the Company's strengths and weaknesses. Two of the bankers, having worked on previous publishing financings, bring helpful industry comparisons into their evaluation efforts. After several weeks of study, Castle Stone concludes that its first impressions of Eagle's business were accurate and the bank's underwriting committee authorizes the firm to continue the transaction.

Most of the legal team focuses on the prospectus drafting, but two lawyers concentrate on legal due diligence. This task begins with a review of Eagle's legal status as a corporation. It then proceeds to a review of the Company's bylaws and all minutes of meetings of shareholders and directors to determine whether they were conducted appropriately. All books and records relating to share ownership and voting control are studied. Additional legal due diligence consists of a review of Eagle's trademarks, significant contracts, litigation, leases, and other relevant issues. The SEC mandates disclosure on many such items, and the attorneys make special note to highlight one important lease and one significant lawsuit.

With the drafting nearly complete, the Company's chief financial officer and the investment banks renew their request to eliminate the "Certain Risk Factors" section from the prospectus. In describing several business risks of the company, the section attaches a speculative element to the offering, lowering the share price and complicating the marketing effort. Undue risk isn't the case, in their opinion, since Eagle is a strong company with a good track record. A Certain Risk Factors section, therefore, is inappropriate. Even though Eagle is more established than most first-time issuers, the lawyers resist the notion of dropping the section, maintaining that Eagle is untested as a public company and lacks the resources of larger publishers. The description of risks stays in the document, but the lawyers water down the section's warnings.

In my experience, the Certain Risk Factors section of a prospectus hides the truth while covering the issuer's backside from legal liability. These sections are filled with generalities, yet they largely ignore the specific risks of an issuer's business. Explicit concerns, meanwhile, are papered over with incomprehensible legal jargon. Exhibit 3–10 provides examples of risks described in IPO prospectuses, against my translation in plain English. As the exhibit indicates, SEC risk disclosure is "disclosure" in name only. Security analysts must diligently make their own evaluations.

Eagle's IPO prospectus outlines 15 risks, which is slightly below average for an IPO. Most contain 20 to 25 risks, of which 70 to 80 percent are boilerplate items found in every IPO prospectus. The first prize for most risk factors in my experience goes to the Hambrecht & Quist Group deal, which had 48 separate risks. This surplus of caution obscured H&Q's key survival issues, making the investor's analysis more difficult.

Along with numerous exhibits that the public never sees, the completed Eagle prospectus is sent to the SEC's Washington-based corporate finance department for review. At the same time, the offering is forwarded to the NASD, which must approve Eagle's share listing on NASDAQ. The deal is placed in the queue at SEC headquarters and Eagle's attorneys are told to expect a response within four weeks. During the first week, a corporate finance analyst is assigned to the proposed transaction. Trained to look for possible omissions or misstatements in the prospectus, he has available to assist him a variety of in-house experts and databanks. Because of the experience of the Eagle team and the solid operating history of the Company, the analyst finds only a few items requiring further clarification. Consulting with his colleagues, he sends the SEC's comments in a letter, which is forwarded to the Company's attorneys. Although the letter covers multiple disclosure items, the attorneys need to review just a few comments in conversations with the SEC analyst. Three topics are annual subscriber cancellation rates, year-to-year ad page growth,

EXHIBIT 3–10. Initial Public Offerings Selected "Risk Factors" Language

Risk Factors from Actual IPOs	Author's Translation
Limited Operating History The Company commenced operations in May 1997 and has a limited operating history upon which investors may evaluate the Company's performance.	This boilerplate means the issuer is a start-up operation, which is highly speculative. The deal rightfully should be sold only to sophisticated venture capital firms.
Recent Losses The Company has incurred significant operating losses to date and there can be no assurance that the Company will be profitable in the future.	Boilerplate. The Company is a speculative operation; it's selling stock without a decent operating history.
Competition: Ease of Entry The Company's industry is intensely competitive. There are many well-established competitors with greater resources than this issuer.	About 95% of prospectuses contain this generality. Most documents fail to specify those factors that ensure the issuer's survival. Few outline the select competitors that can destroy the issuer's business. For example, on February 26, 1997, Microsoft announced it was going to compete with Citrix Systems. The next day, Citrix stock fell 59%.
Rapid Expansion The Company intends to expand rapidly. There can be no assurance that the Company will be able to achieve its goals.	There are no guarantees, so the boilerplate states the obvious. Incredibly, this passes for disclosure in today's marketplace.
Reliance on Major Clients A significant portion of the Company revenues will be derived from relatively few clients.	If the Company loses a major customer, it will go broke. How does an investor gauge the strength of customer relationships? The prospectus remains silent on this matter.
Risks Associated with Acquisitions The Company intends to pursue strategic acquisitions to pursue growth. Acquisitions involve a number of special risks, including . . .	The Company may "roll the dice" on a large acquisition. You've been given fair warning.
Reliance of Key Personnel The Company is dependent to a large extent upon the efforts of a few senior management personnel, including. . .	The Company has no management depth. Investors are betting on one or two individuals.
Reliance of Technology The Company may not be successful in anticipating technological change or in developing new technology on a timely basis.	The Company is successful in hi-tech now, but it's not sure how long the success can last. Time for the owners to cash out!

EXHIBIT 3–10. *(Continued)*

Risk Factors from Actual IPOs	Author's Translation
Pro Forma Deficit to Fixed Charges The Company had a deficit of earnings to fixed charges last year.	The Company is having troubles servicing its debts. Equity is needed to strengthen the balance sheet.
Concentration of Product Line The Company's revenues are almost entirely dependent on sales of one product.	If the market changes in this product, the Company will fail.
Government Regulation The regulatory environment is subject to change, which could adversely affect the Company.	This is a popular boilerplate warning. Few specifics are offered to investors.
Amortization of Intangible Assets Approximately 70% of the Company's assets consist of goodwill arising from acquisitions.	The issuer is alerting you that you're paying for thin air, rather than hard assets, such as inventory, plant, and equipment.
Dilution After giving effect to this offering, the new investors will experience substantial dilution in the net tangible book value of their shares.	The insiders and venture firms that founded the company paid $3 per share two years ago. You, the public investor, are paying $20 for shares that will have a tangible book value of $4. You must hope that earnings growth continues for a long time, because there's a lot of room between $4 and $20.
Antitakeover Provisions The Company's bylaws make it difficult for a third party to acquire the Company (i.e., without management permission).	Even though the IPO is a "hot issue," management disenfranchises stockholders by limiting their voice in takeover matters. This arrangement is universal in new IPOs.

Other Common Provisions
   Absence of Prior Market for Common Stock.
   Shares Eligible for Future Sale.
   Potential Conflicts of Interest (i.e., between management and investors).
   Possible Volatility of Stock Price.
   Possible Need for Additional Financing.
   Absence of Dividends.
	Typical boilerplate that states the obvious for new and untested issues.

and long-term distribution contracts. The SEC also objects to exaggerations of the Company's future prospects in the document.

For a first offering, the SEC's suggestions on the Eagle document were less than average. After a discussion of the SEC's requirements, the Eagle team redrafts accordingly and sends the prospectus to the SEC for final approval. The cover page of this document appears as Exhibit 3–11.

Step 3. The Marketing Process

Confident that the prospectus (or registration statement) will receive the SEC's green light, the investment bankers commence their marketing effort in earnest. Castle Stone orders hundreds of copies of the preliminary prospectus to be sent to clients who have an interest in the transaction, and its bankers write a two-page "crib sheet" for retail brokers and institutional salespeople, outlining the principal attractions of Eagle and justifying the asking price for the shares. For large institutional clients, the bankers schedule a series of meetings in key investment centers—New York, Boston, Chicago, Minneapolis, San Francisco, and London—where management gives slide show presentations and takes investors' questions (this series of meetings is referred to as a "road show"). Institutions with a keen interest and a deep pocket receive one-on-one discussions with Eagle management between the road show presentations.

A big part of the marketing effort is generating enthusiasm among Castle Stone's salespeople. Eagle's management visits the New York offices of Castle Stone to charge up the sales force, and the Castle Stone's sales manager stresses two key facts: in-house allotments are large and IPO commissions are 10 times the size of normal commissions. As the road show meetings continue, the pumped up sales force sings the praises of Eagle Publishing.

During these marketing sessions, analysts and investors focus on the Company's growth prospects. Few look at its balance sheet or object to paying 3.5× the book value for the shares. With many investor inquiries directed at projections (which are not available in the widely distributed prospectus), Eagle managers respond to questions like "Will you earn $0.85 this year?" with vague answers like "maybe," or "there's a good chance of this." Definitive answers such as "yes, we project $0.90 per share" heighten the possibility of later lawsuits if they are made in a public forum. Behind closed doors, bankers and managers get more specific with projections.

Fortunately, the stock market climbs during the road show, and investors are inclined to buy. The Company has a good story to tell and the price talk is in line with similar publishing stocks. As a result, Castle Stone receives numerous orders for Eagle shares over the two-week marketing period. By the end of the road show, Castle Stone's order book appears solid, as shown in Exhibit 3–12.

EXHIBIT 3–11. Eagle Publishing Company Prospectus

PRELIMINARY PROSPECTUS DATED JULY 10, 1999
2,000,000 Shares

Eagle Publishing Company
Common Stock

All the shares offered hereby are being issued and sold by Eagle Publishing Company (the "Company"). Prior to the Offering, there has been no public market for the Common Stock. See "Underwriting" for information relating to the factors considered in determining the initial public offering price. The shares of Common Stock have been approved for quotation on The Nasdaq National Market under the symbol "EPCC." The expected offering price is $11 to $13 per share.

See "Risk Factors" beginning on page 10 of this Prospectus for a discussion of risk factors that should be considered by prospective purchasers of the shares of Common Stock offered hereby.

THESE SECURITIES HAVE NOT BEEN APPROVED OR DISAPPROVED
BY THE SECURITIES AND EXCHANGE COMMISSION OR
ANY STATE SECURITIES COMMISSION NOR HAS THE SECURITIES
AND EXCHANGE COMMISSION OR ANY STATE SECURITIES
COMMISSION PASSED UPON THE ACCURACY OR ADEQUACY
OF THIS PROSPECTUS. ANY REPRESENTATION TO THE
CONTRARY IS A CRIMINAL OFFENSE.

	Price to Public	Underwriting Discounts and Commissions (1)	Proceeds to Company (2)
Per Share			
Total (3)			

(1) The Company has agreed to indemnify the U.S. Underwriters and the Managers against certain liabilities, including liabilities under the Securities Act of 1933, as amended. See "Underwriting."

(2) Before deducting estimated expenses of $600,000, all of which will be paid by the Company.

(3) The Company has granted the U.S. Underwriters and the Managers a 30-day option to purchase up to an additional 300,000 shares of Common Stock on the same terms as set forth above solely to cover over-allotments, if any. See "Underwriting." If all such shares are purchased, the total Price to Public, Underwriting Discounts and Commissions and Proceeds to Company will be $_____, $_____, and $_____, respectively. See "Underwriting."

The shares of Common Stock are being offered by the several U.S. Underwriters and the several Managers named herein, subject to prior sale, when, as and if received and accepted by them and subject to certain conditions. It is expected that certificates for shares of Common Stock will be available for delivery on or about July _____, 1999 at the offices of Castle Stone & Co., 700 Wall Street, New York, New York 10001.

Castle Stone & Co.

EXHIBIT 3–12. Eagle Publishing Company—Initial Public Offering of Two Million Shares—Investment Banker's Order Book

Volume of Buy Orders in Shares	Maximum Price Tolerance per Share
1,800,000	$13.50
2,500,000	13.25
4,000,000	13.00
5,000,000	12.75
6,000,000	12.50
5,500,000	12.25
7,000,000	12.00

· Like any seller of merchandise, Castle Stone receives more buy orders as the offering price decreases. The book stands at 7 million shares at $12, versus 1.8 million shares at $13.50.

Step 4. Pricing the Deal

With clearances from the SEC and NASD on the latest registration statement, Castle Stone is ready to underwrite and sell Eagle's shares.

As the syndicate manager examines the order book, he indicates a preference for a $12.75 offering price. At this level demand is 5 million shares, even though Eagle is selling only 2 million shares. This smaller amount appears to be fully salable at $13.25 per share, but Castle Stone, like most investment banks, prefers to sell a deal at the price where shares are heavily oversubscribed. Although this practice tends to shortchange corporate issuers, it helps the bank in two ways. First, sensing a popular offering, many of Castle Stone's clients expand their orders in anticipation of Castle Stone allotting them 50 percent or less of their original request. If the firm filled all orders completely, thousands of shares would be dumped into the market, leaving the underwriters with the moral obligation to support the share price by purchasing the excess supply. With clients playing games, the syndicate manager is unsure of the deal's true demand and he uses an IPO "rule of thumb" which dictates that his order book should be 2 to 2½ times the size of the offering. Two and one-half times 2 million is 5 million shares. Second, the bank has substantial flexibility in setting the IPO price, so it can almost guarantee a short-term capital gain to the first investors. Accordingly, Castle Stone has an incentive to price the shares slightly below the market value. By allocating shares carefully, the firm rewards favored institutional clients which do a lot of commission business.

Multex.com's 1999 IPO, for example, was priced at $14. After the first day of trading, the stock price was $33⅝. Investors who bought the offering before the first trade were 140 percent ahead of the game.

As Castle Stone's syndicate managers and bankers reveal their $12.75 pricing suggestion to Eagle, they concurrently recruit a group of securities firms to participate in underwriting the deal. The 15 to 20 firms that act as co-underwriters receive small allotments of Eagle shares to sell (along with a small underwriting fee) in exchange for bearing the risk that the deal falls apart after its pricing. The underwriting group (or syndicate) has a life of one month and assumes the moral responsibility for maintaining the market for Eagle shares by repurchasing shares that are offered below the IPO price.

Records are kept of institutions that buy Eagle shares only to dump them on the syndicate later. Because Castle Stone has orders for 5 million shares and only 2 million are available, the likelihood of a price collapse in Eagle's shares is remote. Even then, the syndicate may support the price for just a few days, limiting its losses.

Listening to the banker say that "A deal that goes up in price is a good deal, because everyone makes money," Eagle agrees to the $12.75 price. After brokerage commissions, underwriting fees, and expenses, this figure nets out to $11.86 per share. A final prospectus, with the price now included, is sent to the SEC that same day. With little new information to evaluate—and no authority to judge the fairness of the price—the SEC's analyst rubber-stamps the deal, and the Company releases the offering for sale the next day. As the investors remit their money to Castle Stone for distribution to Eagle, the IPO process ends and aftermarket trading begins. Exhibit 3–13 illustrates the distribution of Eagle's initial public offering.

EXHIBIT 3–13. Distribution of Eagle's Initial Public Offering

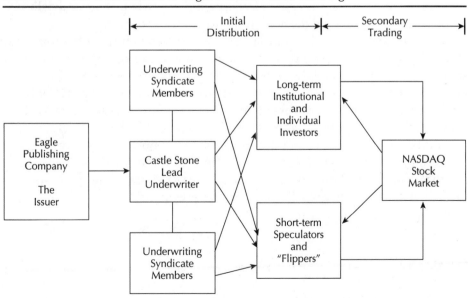

Step 5. Eagle Shares in the Aftermarket

With excess demand built into the market, the bidding for Eagle's shares climbs rapidly to $13.50 per share—representing a 6 percent gain in two days for those lucky institutions that received allotments from Castle Stone and the other underwriters. Despite telling the salespeople that they wanted to hold the shares as long-term investments, many institutions succumb to the temptation to make a quick profit, and "flip" the shares to others at the higher price. Over the first two days of trading, one million Eagle shares change hands, and many of the trading commissions so generated go into Castle Stone's accounts.

A few weeks later, trading in Eagle stock settles down to 20,000 shares per day. Several sell-side analysts find the Company to be an interesting growth story and write research reports. At the same time, newsletters, stock information services, and business periodicals place Eagle in their respective databases, and the SEC and NASD establish the Company's reporting schedules. In three months, Eagle's first quarterly statement is due at SEC headquarters. The stock becomes a seasoned issue.

With the issue becoming seasoned in the aftermarket, the SEC and NASD settle down to monitoring the stock's trading rhythm and the Company's ongoing developments. Having just started life as an IPO, the stock remains especially susceptible to being touted by professional investors or traders who have an interest in spreading rumors because they hold a position in the shares. Observing trading patterns primarily via computer, regulators try to guard against shrewd traders who "paint the tape" of Eagle's new shares by buying and selling the stock among themselves in the hope that artificial activity will lure momentum investors. They look for an increase in volume prior to corporate press releases, which is evidence of insider-derived activity. And they examine purchases by large buyers to see that no disclosure guidelines are violated by those accumulating large positions.

From time to time, the regulators receive complaints stemming from abuses that go undetected by their monitoring systems. For example, two small institutions complain about the aftermarket sales practices of two brokerage firms, whose salespeople claimed the stock price "could only go up." A professional trader protests the failure of four market maker brokerages to honor their publicized bids for Eagle shares. With no evidence (such as taped conversations or computer records) to support their grievances, the three complainants receive little satisfaction from the regulators, who realize that abuses are hard to prove without a paper trail. The protests and investigative materials are filed and may later establish a pattern of poor behavior by the offending firms.

SUMMARY

The SEC and the self-regulatory system govern the relations between the issuers, security markets, and investors. Of critical importance to maintaining the fairness of markets is ensuring that the prospective purchaser of a security receives accurate and adequate information on which to make a sensible judgment. The Securities and Exchange Commission, an agency of the U.S. government, has the responsibility of ensuring that appropriate disclosure takes place, and the United States has the most successful disclosure program in the world. The SEC also promotes honest and orderly behavior in the marketing, buying, and selling of stocks among the stock exchanges and numerous securities firms. Due to its small size relative to the vastness of the markets, the SEC delegates most of its supervision function to a self-regulatory scheme, whereby the exchanges and firms try to prevent themselves and others from engaging in illegal and unethical behavior. While the incidence of abuses is less in the United States than in other markets, the self-regulatory scheme is lacking in many respects. Security analysts are thus advised of the need to redouble their investigatory efforts.

QUESTIONS AND SHORT PROBLEMS

1. Why is reliable information critical to the stock selection process?
2. How is reliable and available information critical to the proper operation of an effective securities market?
3. List three dubious practices that are still common in the U.S. stock market.
4. What's the principal reason that securities regulators are unable to catch the many market professionals who break securities laws?
5. What prompted the establishment of the Securities and Exchange Commission (SEC)?
6. Why is the SEC known as a disclosure agency? Does it exercise power to regulate share prices?
7. Which is the principal flaw of the SEC disclosure system?
    a. SEC doesn't verify the facts contained in the issuer's prospectus.
    b. SEC fails to encourage a sufficient level of marketing materials in the issuer's prospectus.
    c. SEC regulations do not cover over-the-counter issues.
    d. Issuer disclosure documents are written in legalistic jargon.
8. Management projections of a company's future performance are critical tools for securities valuation. Nevertheless, prospective investors rarely see projections in prospectuses. Select the principal reasons:
    a. SEC regulations prohibit the publication of projections because they are not factual.
    b. Brokerage firms underwriting the deals discourage issuers from releasing projections.
    c. Lawyers representing the issuers discourage the issuers from releasing projections.

    d. Corporate managements are afraid they will not achieve the projections.

    e. All of the above.

9. Under the framework of disclosure, describe the underlying tension between (a) the corporate issuer of securities and (b) the likely purchaser of those securities.

10. How has the specialist system frequently failed at the stock exchanges?

11. Describe the principal conflict of interest in the commission-driven job of retail stockbroker.

12. Name the five steps of an initial public offering (IPO).

13. Why is Eagle Publishing an attractive company for an IPO?

    a. It has audited financial statements.

    b. It has a solid operating record.

    c. It has a good management team.

    d. All of the above.

14. What determines whether unfavorable information should be included in an issuer's IPO prospectus?

15. How have issuers and their bankers and attorneys diminished the interpretive value of the "Certain Risk Factors" section of the IPO prospectus?

16. Consult *Barron's* or a similar financial newspaper and select a recent IPO of a young high-tech company. Telephone the prospectus department of the brokerage firm that led the underwriting syndicate. Ask the firm to send you a copy of the IPO prospectus (which, by law, they have to do). Compare the risk factors in Exhibit 3–10 with the risk factors in the prospectus.

17. What is an IPO road show? What happens during a road show?

18. For its IPO, Swan Mfg. Co. hired an investment banking syndicate to sell 5 million shares. After canvassing many investors, the syndicate's order book appeared as follows:

Number of Buy Orders in Shares	Investors' Maximum Price Tolerance
3,000,000	$25
5,000,000	23
8,000,000	21
13,000,000	19
20,000,000	17

What will be the likely price charged by the syndicate? Why?

19. What is the fundamental purpose behind the SEC requiring a stock issuer to publish a prospectus that is then distributed to potential investors?

Adopt-a-Company

By using the SEC's Edgar System, accessing another Internet provider, or calling your adopted company's headquarters, obtain a copy of the company's IPO prospectus. Read the prospectus. Examine the risk factors section, if any. Consider business risks found in the section.

4

Other Sources of Information

This chapter reviews the sources of information that provide the practitioner with the raw material for an analysis. The strengths and weaknesses of the sources are described clearly.

The SEC mandates adequate and accurate disclosure by public corporations, but SEC reports are not the only source of information. The interpretation of corporate information depends on the concurrent analysis of many disparate facts and opinions. Interestingly, the sources of original data are surprisingly few. They consist, on the one hand, of official reports and press releases of the issuer, same-industry firms, and related enterprises, together with the occasional corporate meeting for investors and management to discuss matters. On the other hand are the reports of general business conditions provided by trade associations, trade journals, consulting firms, state and federal governments, and banks and securities firms. All this data is processed by numerous organizations and individuals who purport to be recorders and analysts of the issuer's industry, with some of them having an interest in advising on investments. With so many "experts" analyzing the same data, the need for hands-on investigative work by the securities analyst becomes apparent. In the case of Eagle, field trips to publishing representatives, magazine distributors, printers, and retailers are a necessary part of the security analyst's job.

THE BUSINESS MEDIA

The United States is a media-oriented society and the media—newspapers, magazines, television, movies, radio, and other forms of communication—have a sizable impact on business. This influence naturally extends to general stock price levels and to individual corporate share values. Unlike official corporate reports and press releases, the material published by the media is unregulated by the SEC or the stock exchanges, so the public is exposed to whatever news, opinion, or "spin" the media feels is appropriate to disseminate. The majority of institutional investors that dominate the stock market pursue a rational approach to investment decisions, but the executives devising these strategies are human beings. They read the newspapers and watch television like everyone else. Their minds respond to media interpretation of everyday events and enter this data into the mass of information justifying a portfolio move.

For the general public, which represents an important source of trading activity, the part played by the financial media is pronounced. Only a small percentage of individual investors ever read a SEC prospectus, because they are written in a style that discourages the average person. Nor do most people refer to other original sources of corporate, industry, or macroeconomic information. Relatively few have access to or bother to consult independent financial services such as Standard & Poor's, Moody's, Value Line, or Multex.com. On some occasions, a stockbroker sends an individual client an in-house research report, but this action tends to be the exception rather than the rule. Even the typical stockbroker (and many an institutional equity salesperson) relies heavily on the business media for corporate news and promising investment ideas. Thus, a large proportion of the investing public looks to the media for the basic information on which to make investment decisions.

Only a handful of media sources present company-specific news with the kind of depth that contributes to a serious security analysis. Television and radio, for example, limit their daily financial coverage to a few items on overall business conditions and whether the stock market went up or down that particular day. A couple of cable TV channels focus on individual companies from time to time, but in the grand tradition of television, the presentation is usually simplified to such an extent that the analysis is worthless. Business magazines with a wide circulation are few in number. *Fortune, Business Week, Forbes,* and *Barron's* lead this media group. The latter two magazines devote a lot of space to analyzing individual companies and market trends, while *Fortune* and *Business Week* focus on stories of overall business interest, often including general reviews of companies and industries. Company-specific news articles in business magazines tend to be brief, perhaps 1 to 3 pages of text, with most of the subject matter stripped of the technicalities that are necessary for an informed judgment. Written for the busy executive, these articles provide an interesting piece of information or twist of fact, thereby inviting the executive to explore the company further if he so desires.

The daily business press is dominated by the *Wall Street Journal,* which has an extremely wide following among security analysts. Many businesspeople rely on the *Journal* for day-to-day information concerning business conditions and for a reliable interpretation of what is going on. Of the general interest daily papers, only the *New York Times* makes a serious effort at publishing a business section. Most dailies consider business and finance to be boring and overly complex, and thus unsuitable for a general newspaper, even though the economic well-being of many Americans is tied to the securities markets. As a result, the business sections of many newspapers are filled with meaningless filler from the Dow Jones tape, AP wires, and corporate press releases, items that cost little or nothing for the newspaper to produce. Typical business reporting for a local paper includes local executive promotions, local corporate earnings reports, stock market performance statistics, and share price quotes by the thousands.

The lack of resources dedicated to business reporting means that many news items generated by corporations, their public relations firms, and stock promoters go unchallenged. A critical review of this material requires the media to provide time, money, and training to investigatory reporters. The low priority given to business by media sources signifies few dollars to such an effort, and the majority of business reporters lack extensive backgrounds in business or finance. Even at the *Wall Street Journal,* the doyenne of U.S. business reporting, less than one-third of the reporters have degrees in business or economics. The situation is similar at *Forbes,* one of the better business magazines. Under pressure to produce interesting copy in a short time, business reporters are targets for the vast publicity machines surrounding the securities markets, and many hundreds of thousands of dollars are spent by interested parties trying to garner legitimate publicity for a favored stock. Besides the imprimatur of respectability attached to a CNN report or a *Wall Street Journal* article, the best thing about such stories, if favorable, is that their content is unscreened by the SEC. Exaggerations, omissions of fact, and misstatements can sometimes slip through, even when an able reporter covers the story. The security analyst has to balance such reporting against his own assessment of the facts.

CORPORATION MANUALS, STOCK GUIDES, AND ADVISORY NEWSLETTERS

If a news article or TV show stirs an interest in a particular stock, the investor's next stop is a corporation manual, stock guide, advisory newsletter, or Internet service. All these media provide basic descriptive and financial data on thousands of issuers, with varying levels of editorial comment included. Most offer statistical histories of the issuer's stock price and trading volume, and most furnish data either on-line or through a computer disk format, enabling the customer to manipulate the data mathematically and to compare the issuer to similar investments simultaneously.

- *Corporation Manuals.* Examples include Standard & Poor's, Moody's, and Bloomberg Information Services. These provide a summary of SEC documents, business descriptions, and operating and investment histories. The information is updated regularly. Another function is the compilation of general business, trade, banking, and other economic data.

- *Stock Guides.* Standard & Poor's, Moody's, and Value Line publish the most popular stock guides. These provide a very short abstract of a stock's financial and investment characteristics, which is also included in the corporation manuals.

- *Internet Services.* Most free Internet portals provide basic information—similar to stock guides—along with related news articles and opinions. Pay-for-service sites offer professional analyst reports and software that assists in the analytical process.

- *Advisory Newsletters.* There are hundreds of advisory newsletters, offering advice to long-term investors and short-term speculators. In reviewing the merits of a particular security, they are apt to provide a business description and financial summary—derived from SEC documents—along with an appraisal of the security and a recommendation of "buy or sell."

The corporation manuals, stock guides, and most Internet services are simply renditions of fact, with little interpretive weight put behind the data. The newsletters, on the other hand, purport to offer advice on the future price of a security or the next movement in the market. Their evaluation of a security can have a wide range. It can be as thorough as the best security analyst's report or as simple as a broker's "inside scoop," with most newsletters falling in between. How good is the advice in these newsletters? The studies which have been done suggest that picking stocks at random is better than selecting equities based on newsletter recommendations. Many publications dispute such claims, but they offer little hard evidence to the contrary.

With newsletters having a mixed record, they are unable to charge heavily for their services. The result is that many cannot afford the staff time needed to research carefully the investment values of securities. For example, *Value Line,* which provides a combination corporation manual/advisory newsletter, is one of the more respectable organizations in this field, yet for cost reasons it prohibits its analysts from making field trips to see companies and managements. How insightful can research be without an occasional out-of-office visit?

TRADE ASSOCIATIONS, CONSULTING FIRMS, GOVERNMENT PUBLICATIONS, AND FINANCIAL ORGANIZATIONS

In the selection of stocks, the analyst must combine his own specialized analysis with an effort to evaluate the effects of broader industry, social, political, and economic factors on a company's fortunes. For example, the ability of a clothing design firm to increase sales in an otherwise soft season for women's apparel may be an indicator of future fashion trends. A social and political drive to reduce smoking could impact the earnings prospects of cigarette firms. An anticipated decline in interest rates could boost revenue for home builders. An appraisal of the larger factors is facilitated by the use of publications produced by trade associations, consulting firms, governments and financial organizations. These are available through subscriptions, libraries, data services, and the Internet.

CREDIT RATING COMPANIES

In addition to publishing corporation manuals and stock guides, Standard & Poor's and Moody's each provide credit rating services that place publicly issued bonds into a rating system comprised of various grades purporting to show an issuer's ability to repay its debts. Most notable are the two broad categories into which gradings are segregated—"investment grade bonds" and "junk bonds" (i.e., below investment grade). Companies pay these firms a fee to obtain bond ratings, which are of great assistance in the marketing process. A few other companies, such as Dun & Bradstreet, Duff & Phelps, Best's Review, and Fitch Investor Services, offer credit rating systems for the debt of corporations. Ratings are distributed publicly, but they attract attention only in the financial trade press or in the publications of the rating companies.

Like most investment analysts, rating agencies are outsiders looking in. They are reliant on management supplying them with information and they make little or no attempt to verify the raw data (including the audited numbers). Standard & Poor's spokesperson, Glen Goldberg, warns investors as much by saying "Rating agencies are not auditors, regulators or police officers of issuer conduct." Individual ratings are reviewed annually by the agencies.

Bond rating analysts are full-fledged members of the security analyst profession and their work resembles that of security analysts functioning as stock pickers. Several firms are copying the bond rating convention by assigning grades to equities, but this practice hasn't caught on with investors. Consequently, there is no "gold standard" for equity ratings such as that maintained by Standard & Poor's and Moody's, which together control 90 percent of the market for bond ratings. Both firms are expanding their products in the equity research area, and Standard & Poor's now offers compendiums of Wall Street research on over 5,000 stocks.

SECURITIES FIRM RESEARCH

Professional analysts read each other's reports, particularly those published by sell-side analysts. In fact, few practitioners write an investment recommendation before consulting what other analysts say about a company or an industry. Although brokerage firms attempt to limit the circulation of their analysts' reports to paying clients, inevitably such research is distributed within the financial community, and it is important for both buy- and sell-side analysts to see the spin that others are placing on a given investment opportunity. Reading competitors' reports is of great importance to an analyst covering a large capitalization stock. Twenty or more sell-side analysts, each considering more or less the same raw information, already have opinions, so there's substantial background data available to consider. For a small cap stock, the analyst's coverage is minimal or infrequent, so the consensus opinion has less influence on the share price. Correspondingly, a fresh analysis of the stock places less weight on competing views.

As noted earlier, brokerage research reports are a good resource. They contain basic information and provide financial projections, along with a reasonably cogent rationale for buying or selling a specific stock. The industry knowledge displayed in these reports is generally impressive, and the authors demonstrate, in many cases, a keen understanding of the potential pitfalls awaiting a business. Nevertheless, in reading this material, the serious investor must be aware of the sell-side analyst's nettlesome proclivities: (1) to generate commissions for his employer; (2) to protect his employer's investment banking business by withholding sell recommendations; (3) to cover his backside with vague recommendations that cannot be definitively linked to a result; and (4) to avoid being left alone, especially when the consensus is recommending something else. Such advice, to say the least, is hardly disinterested, but the analyst's financial review can be insightful and semiobjective. No matter, much of the sell-side research is said today and forgotten tomorrow. That part that remains a permanent record is usually too hedged with reservations to pin down the analyst's record in picking winners. Thus, as a source of advice concerning equities, publicly available research reports have obvious limitations. As a source of information on how others approach an analysis and what the market is thinking, the research literature is a useful tool for one's own investigation.

NEWS TICKERS

Much of the daily business news originates on one of the news ticker tapes. The leading ticker service, the Dow Jones, is operated by the same company that publishes the *Wall Street Journal* and *Barron's*. Other important tickers are Bloomberg and Reuters. Originally, such news was disseminated on rolls of narrow paper running through a clattering machine (hence the name "ticker tape"), but such services now operate electronically, distributing news through tens of thousands of remote computer terminals. Virtually every brokerage firm, institutional investor, and substantial individual investor subscribes to one or more of these tickers, and a visit to a modern-day brokerage firm reveals a sea of computer screens flashing newsworthy items. In addition to financial professionals, the subscribers include every significant media outlet, public relations firm, government, and trade organization having to do with business.

Much of what the tickers present as news are routine corporate press releases on earnings, financings, or similar developments, but they also cover news stories having a broader scope that can influence the markets in general. All of this is accomplished in a crisp, abbreviated writing style that enables the service to alert its subscribers to dozens of fresh items on a minute-to-minute basis. In general, the ticker editorial staffs publish news in a no-nonsense manner with little editorial spin, although they quote the opinions of selected market players on a regular basis.

In addition to covering all kinds of news relevant to business, the tickers are critical sources of real-time market information, covering a huge expanse of price and volume data in any number of domestic and foreign stock, bond, currency, and commodity markets. The speed and accuracy with which they work in this regard is remarkable, and it has made them an indispensable part of the speculative trader's toolbox. For the security analyst, who must necessarily take a longer view, the ticker is of less use, since the deliberate search for value requires an extended investigation rather than a minute-to-minute historical record.

INTERNET

SEC reports are available on the Internet, and many companies operate Web pages that provide information. General reports on the economy, industries, and markets are also present on the Internet. A variety of brokerage firms and Internet companies offer services to assist investors in obtaining corporate information and making decisions. The Internet's use as a vehicle for publicizing and marketing investment opportunities is growing quickly, and the Web has gained a 15 percent share of individual brokerage accounts.

SUMMARY

The key to any successful security analysis is information. Information is the lifeblood of the stock market, and the ability to gather and analyze data correctly is highly prized in the investment business. After an analyst has made the decision to evaluate a particular stock, the foundation of his study is the data contained in the issuer's filings with the SEC. Supporting this work is a comparative analysis of similar firms, as derived from their respective SEC documents. With this effort as a base, the analyst consults sources of information that complement the SEC materials. Some of these sources provide original data, while others offer news interpretations, opinions, or compilations of fact.

Principal Sources of Information

- Business media, such as magazines, newspapers, and television.
- Corporation manuals, stock guides, and advisory newsletters.

- Trade associations, consulting firms, government publications, and financial organizations.
- Credit rating companies.
- Securities firm research reports.
- Electronic news tickers.
- The Internet.

With multiple resources at hand, the security analyst needs to pick and choose his sources carefully, or risk being inundated with data. Zeroing in on the right information is an important skill for the novice analyst to develop.

QUESTIONS AND SHORT PROBLEMS

1. What is original source data for a security analysis? Do investors today rely principally on original source data in making an investment decision?

2. Individual investors buy billions of dollars worth of corporate shares. Why do most individuals fail to consult the prospectuses relating to the issuance of such securities?

3. Why don't daily newspapers provide extensive coverage of business news?

4. What are the differences between stock guides and advisory newsletters?

5. How many "sell side" analyses are likely to cover a prominent stock such as IBM?
   a. 5 to 10.
   b. 10 to 15.
   c. 15 to 20.
   d. More than 20.

6. What factors contribute to the reduced objectivity of "sell side" analyses? Circle the one best answer.
   a. Desire to conform, need to generate commissions.
   b. Desire to conform, need to generate commissions, protect employer's investment banking business.
   c. Desire to maintain high accuracy in corporate earning projections and need to predict turning points.
   d. Need to avoid litigation in IPOs, desire to recruit new clients.

7. Download the latest Form 10-Q from the Internet for a company in the Dow Jones 30 Industrials. Download the company's latest press release from its Web site.

8. Using the Internet, Value Line or a similar service, obtain a list of companies that are comparable to the company selected in Question 7. Compare the companies' stock prices, P/E ratio, and earnings growth records.

Adopt-a-Company

Review news stories over the past three months for the company you selected in Chapter 1.

PART II

Performing the Analysis and Writing the Research Report

The investment merits of a particular stock are evaluated through a methodical approach. Both the history and prospects of the issuing company are considered. The sequence of this study and the format of the research report are discussed in Part II.

5

Starting the Analysis

Chapter 5 describes the format that is used to perform a security analysis. A written report is prepared by the analyst, who examines the prospects of issuers in a methodical top-down manner. Current Wall Street practice is compared with this model.

The material covered in the first few chapters makes it evident that the pricing of securities is a rational process. Most prices reflect the reasoned judgment of hundreds—perhaps thousands—of seasoned professionals who have access to substantial information regarding economic expectations, capital markets, industrial performance, company-specific operations, and comparable company valuations. This rational process is frequently tempered by emotional and speculative excesses that affect individual securities as well as general pricing levels. Contributing to these occasional excesses are the conscious actions of a revolving list of sharp players; they seek to profit by directing the analytical process away from the efficient market envisioned by the academic community. Instead, they want to replace studied evaluation with rumors, misstatements, and price manipulations. The resulting misperception of a stock's value can become reality. Injecting a sense of order and fairness into this dynamic marketplace are several regulatory bodies, notably the Securities and Exchange Commission and the stock exchanges.

With this review of the real world in hand, Chapter 5 introduces the structured format of security analyses. It emphasizes the discipline needed by the analyst to succeed in this charged environment. After these two topics, the chapter outlines the widely accepted *top-down* approach.

Under the top-down approach, the consideration of a corporate investment begins with a study of the principal economies in which the corporation operates. If the relevant economies appear promising, the analyst proceeds to evaluate the prospects for the capital market in which the

EXHIBIT 5–1. Top-Down Approach for Campbell Soup Shares

Macroeconomic Prospects	With most of Campbell Soup's earnings originating in the United States, the analyst inquires about the future health of the U.S. economy.
↓	
Capital Markets	Will the U.S. stock market increase in price over the long term? Even given strong individual corporate performance, Campbell Soup's stock price is heavily dependent on general market conditions.
↓	
Packaged Food Industry	Demand and pricing trends in the U.S. packaged food industry affect Campbell Soup's operations.
	Are more competitors entering the business?
↓	Are more people opting to use restaurants, instead of cooking at home?
Campbell Soup • Business analysis • Financial analysis	A thorough analysis of Campbell Soup's business, management, and financial condition is required to predict earnings and value sensibly.

corporation's stock trades, the outlook for its industry, and, finally, the status of the company's financial position and the basis for its earnings potential. A top-down study of Campbell Soup shares, for example, might proceed as shown in Exhibit 5–1. Using the information gained from his top-down analysis, the analyst prepares judgments regarding the likely value of Campbell Soup's stock over the intermediate to long term.

THE SECURITY ANALYSIS PROCESS

A competent security analyst follows a methodology that has changed little over the past 20 years. Each step of the evaluation imposes a discipline on the analyst, and the structured format prohibits cutting corners that might lead to faulty conclusions. The finished product, referred to as a research report, is designed to be user-friendly. Thus, a properly written document is comprehensible not only to the analyst/author, but also to other investment professionals. Buy-side reports produced for in-house consumption are used by the analyst's colleagues (portfolio managers, stock traders, and other analysts), and they must be easy to read and concise. Sell-side reports, authored by brokerage firm analysts, place even more emphasis on clear writing since these documents receive a far greater distribution than the buy-side product.

The analyst's challenge, therefore, is twofold. One, he must investigate the specific investment situation in a disciplined way, covering all the requisite intellectual bases; this is the only means of reaching an investment decision that is convincing to himself and others. Two, the tone and style of his report must appeal to fellow professionals. Otherwise, no one will listen to his ideas. The successful analyst is usually one with a cogent writing ability, enabling him to interest readers while getting his point across. And, since most members of his audience lack his expertise, the thoughtful analyst explains and simplifies the technicalities and jargon endemic to operating industries. Complicated investment themes are boiled down to key decision points, and the analyst and his readers can then communicate effectively with each other.

The model research report begins with a short description of the company that has issued the common stock under evaluation, and a summary recommendation for investment action. Included in the introductory paragraph are the company's product lines, its areas of operation, and its annual sales and profits. A second paragraph might characterize the company according to its place in the industry life cycle (e.g., "growth company" or "cash cow") and summarize its three- to five-year historical trends in sales and earnings, along with a prognosis on future prospects. The third paragraph reviews recent significant developments in the company's business (e.g., new product or acquisition), industry (e.g., more competition from imports), or country operations (e.g., recession in Mexico, which accounts for 20 percent of sales). This section closes with the analyst's rationale for his recommended investment decision. For example, *sell* the stock because earnings growth will decline. The introduction encourages the reader to proceed to the body of the report. A table of contents for a model research report is set forth in Exhibit 5–2 on page 74.

MODEL RESEARCH REPORT

Following the introduction and recommendation, the research report follows the top-down model. The report begins with an economic analysis, assessing the state of the economy and its likely impact on future stock prices and industry earnings growth. A healthy economy often translates into higher stock values and is positive for most industries. For a food company such as Campbell Soup, a growing U.S. economy means sales increases as more people select high-value-added convenience foods. For companies operating in the United States, the economic analysis focuses on the course of the business cycle and on key indicators such as interest rates. The underlying assumption is long-term growth. For less-developed nations, such as Mexico or Thailand, the economic analysis is more involved since the economies are inherently unstable and pose more risk for the investor. Once the report concludes that the economy supports equity investment, it moves on to a study of the capital market.

EXHIBIT 5–2. Model Research Report

Table of Contents

Section	Topic
1.	Introduction
2.	Macroeconomic Review
3.	Relevant Stock Market Prospects
4.	Review of the Company and Its Business
	Industry analysis
	Company specific analysis
	Future prospects
	Financial summary
5.	Financial Analysis
	Historical evaluation
	Current earnings power estimate
	Review of accounting methods
	Adjustments to historical financial data
6.	Financial Projections
	Listing of principal assumptions
	Projected data
7.	Application of Valuation Methodologies
8.	Recommendation
	Comparison of analyst's valuation to market price of the stock
	Recommended investment decision

As noted earlier, the influence of market movements on individual stock prices is considerable. Even when the earnings per share of a given stock are advancing quickly, its share price can decline if broad market indices are performing badly. Likewise, even companies with poor earnings prospects may see their shares' prices rise during bull markets. A thorough research report addresses the important question: Is the general market going up? Or down? How does this affect the share price of the company under study? Making an accurate prediction of the short- to intermediate-term direction of a stock market is difficult, and few people have proved to be adept market timers. Nevertheless, a complete research report presents an opinion on where the market is heading. There is little to be gained by buying a "good" stock in a down market. Inevitably, its price will be dragged down with those of other stocks.

In the United States, where the stock market has been trending upward for 25 years, analysts shrug off this concern by asking investors to look beyond short-term market movements. In less-developed countries, the stock markets are far more volatile, and general price indices can easily decrease (or increase) by 30 to 40 percent per year. In the first half of 1999, for example, the stock market of Portugal dropped by 55 percent. The Hong Kong market rose by 59 percent. Both movements diminished the impact of company-specific effects, like higher earnings, on individual share prices.

THE ANALYST'S RESPONSIBILITY

Few investment firms expect the security analyst to be economic forecaster, market timer, industry expert, and company analyst at the same time. The job would be impossible. Instead, the sections of the model research report are divided among three separate executives: the economist, the market strategist, and the security analyst (see Exhibit 5–3).

A full-time in-house economist or an outside consulting firm supplies the macroeconomic overlay for the analyst's research report. Variables such as future gross national product (GNP) growth, interest rates, and foreign exchange rates are left out of the analyst's hands. Thus, if the economist predicts sharply higher interest rates, the analyst may have a hard time recommending housing stocks, which have lower earnings in times of high interest rates. The investment firm's market strategist takes responsibility for defining the market's direction. His view is synthesized into a recommended portfolio allocation. If the brokerage house believes the stock market is going up, it recommends a portfolio weighting toward common stocks, such as 65 percent stocks, 25 percent bonds, and 10 percent cash. If the firm anticipates a bear market, the suggested stock allocation is smaller, such as 35 percent stocks, 50 percent bonds, 15 percent cash. For reasons of being prudent and hedging bets, few strategists recommend 100 percent stock weightings (or 100 percent bonds); their record of success is too erratic to justify full commitments.

If the economic analysis and capital markets forecast are taken out of the analyst's hands, what is left? A lot. Even after these two top-down evaluations are provided, the analyst has considerable work ahead. First, he must present a studied outlook on the industry in which the company operates. Not only must the report explain the factors driving the demand for the industry's products, but it must also keep the reader abreast of significant developments. What new product lines are being introduced? Is the price/cost structure changing? Which competitors are profiting at the expense of others? A thorough grounding in a company's industry is a prerequisite to an individual company analysis, and this is why professional analysts limit their work to one or two industries.

EXHIBIT 5–3. Dividing Responsibility for Top-Down Analysis

Economic Prospects	An economist assists the analyst by providing a macroeconomic forecast.
Capital Markets	The market strategist supplies an opinion on likely market movements.
Industry Outlook	The security analyst is responsible for studying the industry and evaluating the company, taking into account economic forecasts.
Company-Specific Evaluation	A critical analyst function is predicting corporate earnings reliably.

EXHIBIT 5–4. Constructing a Research Report—Important Building Blocks

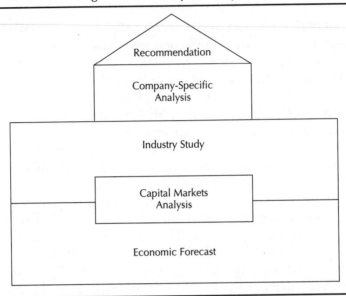

By assembling an economic review, a capital markets forecast, and an industry study, the analyst lays the foundation for his company analysis (see Exhibit 5–4), which provides an understanding of the subject business and an in-depth look at its operating results. Of critical importance are determining the sustainability of the issuer's earnings stream and reaching a conclusion on the likelihood of future growth. Accomplishing these objectives require the analyst to synthesize his knowledge of the company and industry into an earnings projection. In deriving this forecast, the company section covers the disciplines of economics, marketing, business strategy, financial analysis, valuation, and management.

THE CASCADE OF PROJECTIONS

Any corporate earnings forecast is conditional on many variables. The top-down approach isolates the critical macroeconomic, capital market, and industry elements that affect a company's performance. It then establishes a predictive relationship between those variables and the company's earnings. For example, every +1 percent increase in U.S. gross national product tends to produce a 1.5 percent rise in cement sales. A cement company with a constant market share expects to see unit sales gains of 4.5 percent if GNP rises 3 percent.

The job of the analyst is to identify the most influential variables out of the hundreds available. Optimally, he ties in the relationships with statistical links such as positive regressions. Once the connections are made, the economic forecast provides a basis for the capital markets forecast which

EXHIBIT 5–5. Cascade of Forecasts—Homebuilding Company

Top-Down Analysis	Sample Forecast for Homebuilder
Economy	GNP will increase 3 percent ↓
Capital Markets	Interest rates will decline ↓
Industry	Housing starts to increase ↓
Homebuilding Company	Homebuilding Company to gain market share, so its sales will rise 15% instead of the 10% industry average. Steady profit margins signify a 15% earnings increase.

influences the industry forecast. Finally, the forecasts reach the individual company level. The cascading of forecasts is shown in Exhibit 5–5 for a home builder.

Developing a chain of forecasts with real predictive ability is difficult. Any projection of economic or business indicators is inherently uncertain, so each forecast has a margin of error, which becomes magnified as you move from the top economy level to the bottom company section. This is particularly apparent with longer horizons, and the accuracy of analysts' forecasts drops dramatically as the period lengthens.

This inexactitude is understandable when one considers just a few of the top-down variables that influence the average company. Consider a soft drink producer such as Coca-Cola, whose earnings are conditional on many factors, as set forth in Exhibit 5–6.

SELECTING STOCKS FOR STUDY: TOP-DOWN VERSUS BOTTOMS-UP

As discussed in Chapter 2, most of the investment styles that portfolio managers use to select stocks for purchase or sale are predicated on the top-down format. The prospective investor develops a general outlook for the economy and capital market, selects those industries that he expects to prosper within that framework, and focuses on specific companies operating within the chosen industries. As portfolio managers and security analysts find themselves measured in relative terms (e.g., they perform *relatively* well when their stocks decline 10 percent in price as the market drops 15 percent) they place greater emphasis on the bottoms-up approach to identify good investment opportunities. Worrying about a broad market move becomes less of an issue.

EXHIBIT 5–6. Top-Down Analysis—Selected Factors to Study Coca-Cola

Economy
GNP growth in the United States.
Timing of business cycle.
GNP growth in principal foreign markets of Coca-Cola.
Inflation.
Relationship between GNP and soft drink consumption.
Demographics: Young people drink more soft drinks than older people.
Fashion trends: Are soft drinks being replaced by fruit juices, iced teas, or bottled water?
U.S. and foreign income tax rates.
U.S. currency value versus foreign currencies: Valuation affects exports and foreign currency translation.

Capital Markets
Interest rates: Higher rates impact Coca-Cola financing costs.
Stock market: Higher share prices could lessen financing costs and spur acquisitions.

Soft Drink Industry
Demand trends: Is cola consumption rising?
New products: Is the company keeping up with new products and brand names?
Competitors: Is the competition expanding production capacity and advertising?
Government: Will government regulation hurt the industry?
Raw materials: What are the anticipated prices of sugar and corn syrup, two principal raw materials?

Company-Specific Factors
Causes of past and present profitability.
Growth expectations.
Predicted profit margins.
Product mix and new products.
Acquisition: Will acquisitions contribute to growth?
Management changes: Can new management carry out the plan?
Balance sheet issues: What's leverage going to be? Are share repurchases a possibility?
Dividend policy.

With a bottoms-up methodology, a portfolio manager selects shares for study by examining financial ratios that indicate a bargain relative to similar offerings. For example, a common screening technique is investigating all manufacturers that (1) are profitable, (2) record consistent sales growth, and (3) have market price/book value ratios of less than 2.0× (or some equivalent benchmark). A computer search might produce 50 candidates meeting these criteria and representing several industries. The portfolio manager then parcels out these investment possibilities to analysts covering

EXHIBIT 5–7. Top-Down versus Bottoms-Up

Top-Down	Bottoms-Up
Macroeconomy	Screens for Relative Value on Financial Ratios
↓	↓
Capital Markets	Macroeconomy
↓	↓
Industry	Industry
↓	↓
Company-Business Analysis	Company-Business Analysis
↓	↓
Financial Analysis	Financial Analysis

the respective industries. Peter Lynch, the legendary manager of Fidelity's Magellan Fund, was a prominent bottoms-up investor.

Similarly, an analyst covering a group of stocks in the same industry inevitably looks first at those firms in the group that have a low P/E ratio (or other low valuation benchmark). This could be the sign of a potential bargain, if the consensus opinion is unduly penalizing the stock or underestimating its potential. Thus, the stock may represent a *relatively* good value compared with its peer group. (The risk here is that the group's price level is already high.) In any group setting, there are individual issues that appear attractive in contrast to the inflated value of similar stocks. On identifying a relative bargain, the analyst prepares a "top-down" report justifying a recommendation.

At the extreme end of the bottoms-up style are strict value investors. They screen for stocks that appear cheap on an intrinsic basis. Sample screening criteria target firms whose market value is less than accounting book value. Usually, bargains in this respect have serious flaws. The company participates in a dead-end industry or has serious financial problems. A thorough top-down analysis is then required to justify the investment. Exhibit 5–7 provides a comparison of the top-down and bottoms-up styles.

LIMITED TIME AND RESOURCES

As the partial listing for Coca-Cola illustrates, analysts are confronted with a vast amount of information from which they can construct an analysis. To avoid being drowned in a sea of facts and statistics, intelligent practitioners pick and choose data that make a meaningful contribution to their reports and projections. Likewise, analysts are responsible for producing reports in real time; they can't afford to study a security forever. In most cases, they provide conclusions on incomplete information and rely on their judgment and experience to advance opinions.

This information-sifting function varies with the industry. Different industries require different predictive factors. Economic developments influencing the tobacco industry will not have the same effect on the chemical business. The same can be said for industry factors at the individual company level. Certain chemical industry changes may play a greater role in the performance of Dow Chemical than DuPont. Selectivity of information is instrumental to the analyst's performance.

Obtaining information is time consuming and expensive. Similarly, establishing quantitative formulas linking economic indicators, industry variables, and company-specific results is a long, laborious, and costly task. Many times, regressions have negligible predictive value, so the time and money goes for naught. Professionals recognize this situation and learn to live with imprecise valuations. To preserve the validity of their work in a world of unscientific estimates, analysts rely heavily on the notion of the "margin of safety."

THE MARGIN OF SAFETY

The margin of safety principle is a linchpin of security analysis, for Graham and Dodd recognized early on that economic and financial forecasts were inherently uncertain. As a defensive measure, they encouraged analysts to refrain from a purchase recommendation unless the related research report provided a protective cushion between the market's price and the analyst's indicated value (see Exhibit 5–8). A reasonable cushion in today's market is 15 percent. Thus, if your research report concludes that Enron Corp.'s shares are worth $35 each, and the market price is $30, then Enron is a buy because the estimated value is at least 15 percent higher than the market price (i.e., $35/$30 = 117%). The logic works similarly for sale decisions and short-sale recommendations. If your research report shows a Mobil share value of $85 to $90 when the stock is trading at $120, you should recommend that Mobil shares be sold.

The margin of safety principle applies to all valuation approaches covered in this book: intrinsic value, relative value, acquisition value, leveraged buyout value, and liquidation value. Since these methods are less than exact, a 15 percent cushion provides a reasonable degree of assurance that an investment recommendation is correct. Nonetheless, applying a margin of safety is no guarantee against losses. It just reduces the probability of loss in favor of increasing the chances of profit. Consider it to be the equivalent of an insurance policy.

Going hand in hand with the margin of safety principle are sensible economic and financial projections. There's little sense in providing yourself with a protective cushion on the investment recommendation when your forecasts are unrealistic. Most analysts err on the side of optimism. They have trouble foreseeing economic recessions and industry turning points. For example, few analysts anticipated the problems of nuclear

EXHIBIT 5–8. The Margin of Safety Principle—Subject Shares Trading at $100

Analyst's Independent Valuation and Related Action

Sell	No Recommendation			Buy
$0	$85	$100	$115	

Margin of
Safety Area

Current Share
Price = $100

0	$85	$100	$115

Market Price of Subject Shares is $100

power, which damaged the electric utility industry. And many professionals become "captured" by the companies they cover, since they are so reliant on them for information. This closeness diminishes the analyst's objectivity, and the company's public relations hype can flow through to the projections. Given this possibility and the future's uncertainty, a conservative bias in forecasting is an important complement to the margin of safety principle.

SUMMARY

The typical equity research report evaluates stocks in the following way: A stock is reviewed and researched under the top-down approach. The top-down approach utilizes what is called the "chain of projections" first made popular by Graham and Dodd. Analyses are completed and projections are performed at five critical levels in the evaluation. The top of the analysis is a review of macroeconomic trends for the country in which the subject company's operations are based. Subsequent analysis is then focused on descending subject areas, beginning with an analysis of the capital markets and followed in succession by an industry analysis, a company analysis (i.e., a microeconomic analysis) and a financial-statement analysis. Macroeconomic, capital market, industry, company, and financial data are projected from these analyses. Because the dominant variables in many of these projections are macroeconomic, the key projection assumptions lie in the

EXHIBIT 5–9. Model Research Report

1. Introduction
2. Macroeconomic Review
3. Relevant Stock Market Prospects
4. Review of the Company and Its Business
5. Financial Analysis
6. Financial Projections
7. Application of Valuation Methodologies
8. Recommendation

---

macroeconomic analysis. Dependent variables then cascade from the top assumptions.

Consider, for example, apparel retailing companies: the number of clothes that an average store sells in a given year is going to be largely dependent on the strength of the overall U.S. economy. Obvious independent variables might be new apparel fashion trends and the store's advertising expenditure. The model research report (see Exhibit 5–9) presents the information in an organized way.

The vast majority of analysts begin their reports with industry trends as their top theme. Macroeconomic and capital-market predictors of corporate performance are left to their employers' in-house economists and market strategists, and these views are incorporated by the security analyst into his company report. A key objective of the research report is to provide the reader with an accurate estimate of the company's earnings for the next three years, along with a basic understanding of its business prospects. Long-term projections are then derived from these short-term estimates.

With financial projections in hand, the security analyst prepares his valuation of the company's shares. After comparing this valuation to the market price of the shares, he makes an investment recommendation. If the valuation is lower than the current stock price, the recommendation is a sell. If the valuation is higher than the stock price, the recommendation is a buy.

QUESTIONS AND SHORT PROBLEMS

1. Suppose that Maytag Corporation is preparing to spin off its dishwasher business through an initial public offering. The business sells dishwashers to residential homeowners in the United States, and most people tend to buy a new dishwasher when they buy a new home. Show an outline for a top-down analysis of the prospective

security and indicate the important factors to consider at each level of study.

2. What's the importance of following a strict methodology in preparing a research report?
    a. Institutional investors demand a set format.
    b. The methodology provides a discipline that reduces the chances of a faulty conclusion.
    c. A consensus report must adhere to a prepackaged outline.

3. Why is the preparation of an equity research report akin to building a house from the ground up? Which sections of the report represent the foundation?

4. Which of the following research report sections are not the responsibility of the security analyst?
    a. Company business analysis.
    b. Macroeconomic forecasts.
    c. Stock market prospects.
    d. Review of the company's historical results.
    e. Application of valuation methodologies.

5. For every 10 percent decline in gasoline prices, car mileage increases by 5 percent. For every 1 percent increase in car mileage, auto parts demand grows by 0.8 percent. Tellab Auto Parts, Inc. has a 10 percent market share when gasoline prices decline by 20 percent. What is its expected sales growth? If Tellab makes an acquisition that increases its market share from 12 percent to 14 percent, what will be its sales growth (including the growth from the first part of the question)?

6. Outline the fundamental differences between the "top down" approach to security analysis, and the "bottoms up" approach.

7. All things being equal, which of the following four comparable forms would be the initial candidate of a "bottoms up" investor?

	P/E Ratio	Price/Book Value Ratio
Firm A	18.1	2.3
Firm B	18.6	2.7
Firm C	22.1	2.6
Firm D	19.0	3.0

8. Matti Corp. shares are trading at $66 per share. After an extensive study, a security analysis concludes that the fair value per share is $72, indicating the market undervalues Matti Corp. If the analyst follows the margin of safety principle, does he recommend buying the stock?

9. Telephone the investor relations (IR) officer of a publicly traded company. Select a company that has annual sales between $250 million and $1 billion and a one industry focus. Ask the IR officer if the company's

information package includes brokerage firm research reports. If the answer is yes, request the package. If the answer is no, continue trying until you find a company that distributes its research reports to interested parties.

Adopt-a-Company

Repeat Assignment 9 for your company.

6

Industry Analysis

*The industry analysis is an important part of the research report.
The proper organization of this analysis, the five principal themes of
such a study and the common pitfalls of an industry evaluation are
discussed herein.*

In developing investment recommendations, the typical analyst begins serious research at the industry level. As noted in Chapter 5, the analyst receives "top-down" economic and capital market forecasts from others. The initial responsibility is tying these macro parameters into an industry outlook, thus laying the groundwork for judging the prospects of selected participants. The fortunes of an individual company are closely intertwined with those of the industry in which it operates. An in-depth industry study is thus a prerequisite for a proper security analysis. A thorough understanding of the industry facilitates the evaluation process, and for this reason, many practitioners limit themselves to one or two industries. This chapter reviews preparing an industry analysis, which is covered under Section 4 of the model research report (Exhibit 6–1).

BACKGROUND

Whatever outlook an analyst develops for a particular industry, not all companies have prospects mirroring the broader view. Some perform better than the general expectation; others worse. Consider the waste disposal industry in December 1996. The principal companies were mired in the industry's image of operating problems, poor economics in recycling, and a glut of landfill space. As a result, their P/E ratios suffered. Meanwhile, three young enterprises carried premium P/E ratios, as the market showed interest in their strong acquisition programs (see Exhibit 6–2).

EXHIBIT 6–1. Model Research Report

1. Introduction
2. Macroeconomic Review
3. Relevant Stock Market Prospects
4. Review of the Company and Its Business✓
   Industry Analysis✓
5. Financial Analysis
6. Financial Projections
7. Application of Valuation Methodologies
8. Recommendation

The dual track status of waste disposal firms is duplicated in other industries. Wal-Mart, for example, has enjoyed far higher valuation ratios than other general merchandise retailers, such as Sears, although many of these competitors make money. The big difference has been Wal-Mart's higher growth rate.

As a general rule, institutional investors want analysts to stick to industries with a positive outlook. Even the best buggy whip manufacturer was a poor bet at the turn of the 20th century. Similarly, the most attractive CB radio producer turned out to be a loser in the 1980s. The chosen industries don't have to be stellar performers; they just require a reasonable justification for investment.

Broad Industry Trends

While the competent analyst has a broad knowledge of the industry he covers, his research reports have a narrow focus, limiting reviews of industry trends to those that affect a specific company's future performance. Contributing to the reader's understanding of the industry requires comparisons. For example, analysts covering the early years of the VCR compared it with the introduction of the television. Original themes are important.

EXHIBIT 6–2. Snapshot of the Waste Disposal Industry

Established Companies	P/E Ratio
Laidlaw	23
WMX Technologies	25
Browning-Ferris	18

New Acquisitive Players	
Allied Waste	56
USA Waste Services	26
Republic Industries	72

Rehashing widely available data is of little use to the reader, unless it sets the stage for company-specific projections. These forecasts appear toward the end of the research report, after a groundwork has been laid.

As the subject company grows larger, the industry analysis becomes complicated. Major corporations today have multiple lines, many of which are not comparable. General Electric has 13 separate divisions producing products as dissimilar as gas turbines and home appliances. For those firms with disparate businesses, the industry analysis evolves into an *industries* analysis, as each distinct segment is valued separately as a part of a larger whole. See Chapter 16, "Break-Up Analysis," for a full description of this technique.

Contrary Opinions

Of particular interest to investors are contrarian opinions. Research analysts are reluctant to stick their necks out. They follow the herd, and as a result, their reports are disappointingly similar. For the most part, analysts work around the edges of the consensus view on an industry's prospects and a company's forecasts. When a practitioner reaches a strikingly different conclusion from that of everyone else, he tends to couch it in vague terms. Then, if he ends up wrong, his error is less obvious. The depressing outcome of this environment is that many analysts, particularly those on the sell side, are reduced to arguing about a company's next quarterly earnings report. Will earnings be 46 cents per share or 45 cents? When a respected analyst goes against the grain and replies that earnings will be 15 cents instead of 45 cents, institutional investors sit up and take notice.

Few analysts predict reversals of trends that have been long accepted on Wall Street, despite the frequency of such occurrences, so a fresh look at the status quo is real news. One important industry reversal happened in June 1996. After years of raising prices for their brand-name products, Kellogg Co., General Mills, and Ralcorp.—the three principal U.S. cereal makers— cut prices by 20 percent in response to declining demand for their products. In a few days, cereal prices dropped to the levels of the late 1980s. Some observers had noticed increasing consumer resistance to high cereal prices, but few analysts predicted this change, which caused cereal company share prices to decline as earnings projections fell.

ORGANIZING AN INDUSTRY ANALYSIS

An industry analysis can take various forms, but the outline set forth in Exhibit 6–3 is customary. The industry analysis begins with positioning the specific industry within its life cycle. Defining a sector in this way is important on Wall Street. Investors place a premium on simple investment themes. Thus, the faster the analyst pigeonholes an industry into the "life cycle" chart, the better.

EXHIBIT 6-3. Model of an Industry Analysis

Industry classification:
 Life cycle position
 Business cycle

External factors:
 Technology
 Government
 Social
 Demographic
 Foreign

Demand analysis:
 End users
 Real and nominal growth
 Trends and cyclical variation around trends

Supply analysis:
 Degree of concentration
 Ease of entry
 Industry capacity

Profitability:
 Supply/demand analysis
 Cost factors
 Pricing

International competition and markets

Source. Association for Investment Management and Research. Note how the industry analysis is broken down into its key components.

INDUSTRY CLASSIFICATION

Classification by Industrial Life Cycle

In general conversation, industries are described by the product they produce or the service they provide. Hospital chains, HMOs, and physician health groups are "medical service" industries. Newspaper firms, magazine publishers, and book companies fall in the "publishing" category. Sporting goods manufacturers, recorded music distributors, and toy producers are lumped into the "recreation" sector. Security analysis uses these descriptions, while further classifying industries by certain economic characteristics.

The most popular segmentation tool is the industrial life cycle, which reflects the vitality of an industry over time. A staple of business textbooks and management consulting firms, the life cycle theory outlines four phases that mark the beginning to end of an industry: the *pioneer, growth, mature,* and *decline* phases (see Exhibit 6-4).

EXHIBIT 6–4. Industry Classification: The Industrial Life Cycle

Life Cycle Phase	Description
Pioneer	Product acceptance is questionable and implementation of business strategy is unclear. There is high risk and many failures.
Growth	Product acceptance is established. Roll-out begins and growth accelerates in sales and earnings. Proper execution of strategy remains an issue.
Mature	Industry trend line corresponds to the general economy. Participants compete for share in a stable industry.
Decline	Shifting tastes or technologies have overtaken the industry, and demand for its products steadily decreases.

As its name implies, the pioneer phase is the riskiest point of corporate life. The industry is struggling to establish a market for its products. Cash needs for working capital and fixed assets are substantial, yet the industry is losing money or is marginally profitable. Its potential for success attracts equity investors, who are prepared to take a total loss on their investment and know that. Seven out of 10 start-up businesses fail to survive. During overheated stock markets, speculative ventures often go public and become fodder for the security analyst community.

The second stage is the growth phase. Here, practitioners acknowledge the industry's product acceptance and have a brief historical framework for estimating future demand. The big questions are: How far, and how fast? So-called growth industries occupy a large amount of analysts' time, because they sometimes provide excellent returns. Of particular interest to analysts is identifying a growth industry at the ground floor, before everyone jumps on the bandwagon and boosts the stock price.

A classic growth industry spurs demand for a product that the consumer (or the industrial client) didn't know he needed. The best example is a new technology; cellular advances, for example, sparked a demand for car phones, which few people realized they needed beforehand. Another growth story is the better mousetrap. Before Office Depot, few people realized they needed an office supply superstore; most shopped at local stationers and department stores for these items. The total market for office supplies is stagnant, but office superstores represent a legitimate growth industry within the larger market. Growth companies prosper independent of the business cycle.

Besides experiencing rapidly increasing sales, growth industries frequently enjoy fat profit margins. This happy situation continues until new competitors, attracted to the high returns, enter the industry. As competition stabilizes and market penetration reaches practical limits, the industry progresses to the *mature* phase.

If growth industries have above-average increases in sales and earnings, mature industries produce "average" results. Unit sales gains follow economic growth. Thus, if the economy improves by 3 percent in one year, an analyst expects a mature industry's unit sales to rise by 3 percent. Adding a 5 percent inflation factor means the industry's sales increase by 8 percent annually. Mature industries usually provide a staple product or service. Examples include the food, auto, and furniture industries.

Within a mature industry may be one or more *growth companies.* Typically, such firms achieve above-average growth in one of two ways. First, they gain market share by offering an improved quality or service (i.e., the better mousetrap). American Greetings' market share in the mature greeting card industry has increased from 33 to 35 percent over the past five years. Consumers like its products better than those of the competition. Alternatively, a company grows in a mature industry by gobbling up others. Since 1991, Service Corporation International has increased its market share in the funeral business from 5 to 10 percent, by acquiring over 200 competitors. Sales in its industry advanced 8 percent annually over that time, but Service Corporation's gains averaged 31 percent each year.

The last stage in the life cycle is the decline phase. Demand for the industry's products decreases and the remaining participants fight over shares of a smaller market. With no new capacity needs and diminished profit margins, the industry attracts little capital and established firms begin to exit the sector. As demand dries up, companies fail and the remaining participants consolidate. The better-managed survivors anticipate this fate and avoid it by using cash flow to diversify into promising industries. Westinghouse's takeover of CBS exemplified such diversification.

Classification by Business Cycle Reaction

In addition to the industry life cycle, Wall Street characterizes industries by the way in which they react to the business cycle. Market economies do not grow in a straight line. They expand, go into a recession where growth slows or stops, and then enter a recovery, which leads into the next expansion (see Exhibit 6–5). The duration of a U.S. business cycle can be 5 to 10 years. Certain industries prosper more than others during different phases of the business cycle. Industry's behavior places it into one of three categories: *growth, defensive,* or *cyclical* (see Exhibit 6–6).

A growth industry achieves an above-normal rate of expansion, independent of the business cycle. Even if the economy is in a recession, the growth industry's sales and earnings rise. New technology and products are the hallmarks of a growth industry. The computer software industry sailed through the 1990–1991 recession with higher revenues.

Defensive industries exhibit stable performance through the business cycle. Sales and earnings proceed in an upward direction. Strong growth is apparent during an economic upturn, but there is a slight dip in profitability

EXHIBIT 6–5. U.S. Business Cycles 1976 to 1996

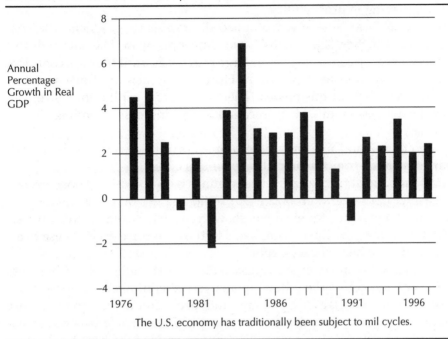

Annual Percentage Growth in Real GDP

The U.S. economy has traditionally been subject to mil cycles.

during recession years. Defensive industries usually fall into the mature category. Examples include (1) electric and gas utilities since people require heat and light in their homes regardless of economic conditions; (2) food, cigarette, and beer companies since demand for their products remains inelastic (although consumers may shift to lower-priced brands); and (3) government contractors since governments tend to spend whether or not the economy expands.

Cyclical industries are those whose earnings track the cycle. Their profits benefit from economic upturns, but suffer in a downturn. The earnings movement is exaggerated. Boom times are followed by "bust times." Thus, when economic growth rates only move a few percentage points, cyclicals go from substantial losses to huge profits. General Motors' operating loss in

EXHIBIT 6–6. Industry Classification by Business Cycle Behavior

Behavior Pattern	Description
Growth	Above-normal expansion in sales and profits occurs independent of the business cycle.
Defensive	Stable performance during both ups and downs of business cycle.
Cyclical	Profitability tracks the business cycle, often in an exaggerated manner.

1991 was $2.8 billion; its 1996 operating profit topped $4 billion, representing a huge swing in profitability.

Classic cyclical businesses produce discretionary products, the consumption of which is dependent on economic optimism. The auto industry is cyclical, because consumers defer large purchases until they are confident of the economy's positive direction. Heavy equipment and machine tool producers are cyclical businesses. Their customers, capital-intensive concerns, defer investment during recessions and increase spending during recoveries.

Exhibits 6–7 and 6–8 provide examples of three firms and how their earnings changed over the preceding business cycle.

Certain cyclical firms experience earnings patterns that do not correlate well against the general economy, but trend against other economic variables. Brokerage firms, for example, show cyclicality based on stock prices. Agricultural firms exhibit earnings tied to the crop price cycle. These firms are lumped into the cyclical category.

The characterization of an industry through the life cycle or business cycle techniques colors the follow-up analysis. Practitioners compare those industries with similar designations and draw inferences about future revenue, earnings performance, and valuation. In such side-by-side evaluations, industry-specific nuances are ignored in favor of the broader theme.

A second problem associated with industry classification is self-deception. Once an analyst labels an industry as a growth industry, he (and

EXHIBIT 6–7. Business Cycle Earnings Comparison—Gross National Product (GNP) versus Earnings per Share (EPS)

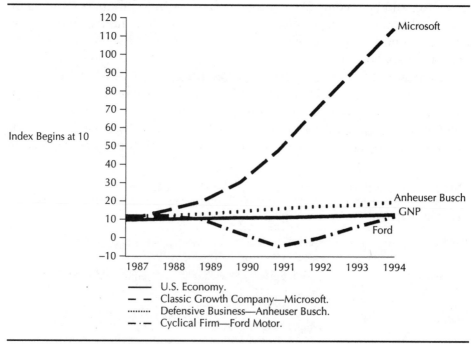

───── U.S. Economy.
─ ─   Classic Growth Company—Microsoft.
······· Defensive Business—Anheuser Busch.
─ · ─ Cyclical Firm—Ford Motor.

EXHIBIT 6–8. Business Cycle Earnings Comparison—GNP Changes versus EPS Changes

		1987	1988	1989	1990	1991	1992	1993	1994
Real GDP	% Chg	2.9	3.8	3.4	1.3	−1.0	2.7	2.3	3.5
Growth Company—	EPS	0.16	0.25	0.34	0.52	0.82	1.21	1.58	1.98
Microsoft	% Chg	77.8	56.3	36.0	52.9	57.7	47.6	30.6	25.3
Defensive Business—	EPS	1.02	1.23	1.34	1.48	1.63	1.73	1.78	1.94
Anheuser Busch	% Chg	20.0	20.6	8.9	10.4	10.1	6.1	2.9	9.0
Cyclical Firm— Ford Motor	EPS	4.53	5.48	4.57	0.93	−2.40	−0.73	2.28	4.97
	% Chg	47.1	21.0	−16.6	−79.6	Neg.	Neg.	—	218.0

Note. The recession began in 1990 and extended through 1991. The cyclical behavior of Ford Motor is evident.

his audience) is tempted to place subsequent facts that come to light within the growth framework. Pigeonholing an industry helps in telling the investment story, but the experienced analyst doesn't let labels prejudge developments that don't fit the model.

As one illustration, consider the Internet service industry in 1996. Many early investors compared this industry with cable TV in the late 1970s. Both Internet and cable TV were hooked into the home by wire and both required monthly subscription charges. As analysts monitored the Internet services industry more closely, however, they noticed a significant difference. Internet service was not a quasi-monopoly like cable TV, and customers switched suppliers more frequently than cable TV subscribers. The Internet industry fell into the growth classification, but practitioners needed a fresh look at its economics. Internet stock prices dropped accordingly in late 1996.

Likewise, the bagel chain industry attracts comparisons with the formerly fast food business. Dennis Lombardi, who heads a restaurant consulting practice, repeated a familiar premise, "There's an awful lot of room for more bagel shops. All you have to do is contrast it to the hamburger chains." With 11,000 restaurants, McDonald's has several times the total number of bagel shops, but the differences are compelling. Hamburgers are viewed as all-American lunch and dinner food. In contrast, bagels occupy the breakfast segment and have an ethnic tradition.

A common error with industry classification occurs when the analyst paints all industry participants with the same brush. Inevitably, not all companies in a *mature* industry are *mature* companies. Beer brewing is a mature industry, yet small microbrewers are considered growth companies. Steel is a cyclical industry, but Nucor's stability defies this classification. Industry analysis thus complements the company analysis described in Chapters 7 to 11.

The process of placing an industry into its life cycle and business cycle categories involves performing the work outlined in Exhibit 6–3. By studying the industry's external influences, demand trends, supply factors, profitability and competition, an analyst forms opinions about its prospects and suitability for investment.

EXTERNAL FACTORS

No industry operates in a vacuum. Each is subject to numerous outside influences that significantly impact sales and earnings. The first stage of the top-down analysis considers the economic variables that affect industry performance, and the life cycle and business cycle techniques provide direction in this regard. As the industry study unfolds, however, the practitioner examines external factors that aren't purely economic (see Exhibit 6–9).

External issues fall into five broad categories: technology, government, social changes, demographics, and foreign influences. For each of these categories, there are "big picture" themes that affect a particular industry, and the analyst's job is twofold. One, he avoids the temptation to fall into the role

EXHIBIT 6–9. Industry Analysis—External Factors Affecting Sales and Profitability

Technology	For established industries, the question is: Does the industry face obsolescence from competing technologies? (Typewriters were quickly replaced by word processors in the early 1980s). Infant industries introducing new technologies pose a different question: Will the market accept innovation?
Government	Government plays a large role in many industries. New regulations, or changes to old laws, can impact an industry's sales and earnings. In certain cases, government policies create new industries (e.g., the automobile protective safety bag industry).
Social Changes	Changes in lifestyle spark many industries. The rise of two-earner families fueled growth in the convenience food and restaurant industries. Concern over animal rights hurt the fur retailing industry.
Demographics	Demographic shifts are watched by analysts. The "greying" of America supports nursing home stocks. It is also a factor in the rebound of the golf equipment industry, as baby boomers reduce strenuous activity in their later years.
Foreign Influences	The United States is the largest economy, but its industries are subject to foreign influences. Overseas textile firms decimated the U.S. textile industry. Higher income levels in developing nations, meanwhile, contributed to huge overseas demand for U.S. movies and musical recordings.

of futuristic visionary. Instead, he concentrates on trends that can demonstrably affect the industry over a three- to five-year period. Two, he addresses the impact of these trends in quantifiable form. It is not enough to say "advances in satellite technology and capacity will fuel the global pager business"; investors want to know the percentage gains in industry sales from these factors. A numerical forecast is better than a vague pronouncement.

In the majority of research reports, the basic assumption regarding the industry's external environment is that history will repeat itself. Past trends continue into the future, and thus, most industry sales projections are based on time series analysis. Projecting the sales of new industries is more tricky, but 99 percent of public companies are beyond the start-up stage, so analysts extrapolate brief historical results into a forecast. Unless there is a firm basis for a contrary opinion, this rearview-mirror approach is reasonable. As noted earlier, this method encourages complacency, and the analyst relying on it can miss important reversals. Nonetheless, a historical grounding in an industry is a prerequisite for an evaluation of external influences. Exhibit 6–10 provides an example of the effects of external factors on an industry.

Technology

The initial analysis of technology focuses on *survival*. Will the industry's product offerings fend off perceived substitutes derived from newer technology? The eyeglass industry, for example, has prospered for years against

EXHIBIT 6–10. Sample External Factors Affecting Health Care Industry Sales

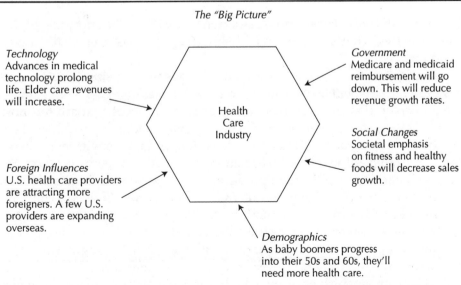

several contact lens technologies. The record player industry, in contrast, became obsolete with the introduction of the CD player.

In many cases, an outside technological idea enhances an industry. Gains in the biotechnology area were eventually transferred to the agricultural industry, where they contributed to higher crop yields. Improvements in civil aviation technology led directly to a travel boom, which lifted tourist industry revenues. VCRs represented 100 percent of electric appliance sales growth in the mid-1980s. Current pundits believe digital technology will spur growth in digital TV sales.

Sometimes, a new technology is a blessing and a curse. Nuclear power originated in the defense industry. Transferred to electric utilities, nuclear power was quickly accepted in the 1970s because its variable costs were lower than conventional technologies, such as coal and oil generation. Unforeseen problems in safety and the environment tainted nuclear power in the 1980s, and the related expenses crippled many utilities.

In the case of a new competing technology, the established industry usually has several years to prepare a defense. A common strategic response is either:

1. Copy the competition, as Wal-Mart did in the wholesale club industry with Sam's Wholesale Club (a virtual clone of Price Club).
2. Buy the competition, as IBM's software division did when it acquired Lotus Development Corporation.

Competent managements recognize technological trends and adjust their companies accordingly.

Government

Government taxes, laws, and regulations impact every industry in the United States. That's one reason Washington, DC, has over 50,000 registered lobbyists.

The federal tax code serves a legitimate revenue raising function, but it's loaded with loopholes designed to serve special interests. For example, the oil exploration industry has depreciation allowances that are far more favorable than those available to the average manufacturing industry. Federal quotas on imported goods provide certain industries with extra benefits. For example, the quota levied on Japanese auto imports protects the sales and earnings of domestic producers. A negative shift in the political fortunes of either the oil exploration industry or the auto industry could result in unfavorable government actions, leading to lower earnings. The analyst's projections would be modified accordingly.

Business organizations complain about regulation, but regulations play a valuable role in promoting worker safety, consumer protection, and fair play. Government influence cuts both ways. Some government agencies practice regulatory overkill that harms industry unnecessarily, but it is a fact that multiple businesses were founded on new government initiatives or rely on government regulation to prosper. If you're a business, what better way to avoid risk than to have the government require a minimum price for your products, set up barriers to foreign imports, or allow you to merge with the competition? Regulation "creep" has continued in Republican and Democratic administrations, and the analysts of the 1990s monitor government developments much more closely than did their 1960s' counterparts.

A recent example of a negative external influence is the government assault on the tobacco industry. By declaring tobacco a drug and placing it under FDA jurisdiction, the government clearly seeks to diminish the industry's prospects. Alternatively, the federal emphasis on environment enforcement is a boon to the environmental services sector. One relatively new industry that received a huge leg up from the government was the cellular phone industry. Rather than sell cellular monopolies to the highest bidder, the government gave the rights away via lottery in the 1980s, saving the operators billions of dollars. State deregulation is sweeping through the electric utilities, and this turning point means dramatic changes for this staid industry.

Consider Paxson Communications Corp., a network of 46 UHF stations that run half-hour informercials most of the day. Faced with limited capacity, many cable TV systems declined to carry these broadcasts, but in March 1997 the U.S. Supreme Court upheld the government's "must carry" rules, requiring cable companies to show any and all local broadcast channels, even Paxson's low-rent UHF programs. On the day of the ruling, the company's share price jumped 30 percent, illustrating the effect of government.

Federal, state, and local government spending accounts for 35 percent of gross national product. Any shifts in the spending patterns of these organizations influence the affected industries. Declines in the defense budget during the 1990s prompted a wave of consolidations among defense contractors. At the local level, the privatization of municipal waste services contributed to revenue gains among waste management firms. Imagine the shift in dollars if the government privatized just a small portion of the public education system!

External factors relating to government play a significant role in the analysis of foreign stocks. Most countries have more restrictive trade regimes than the United States, and local producers get complacent after years of protection. A dramatic liberalization in tariff policy can destroy a local industry that is uncompetitive with the global multinationals. Similarly, nations set up artificial barriers to protect favored industries (and companies) from outside threats. Japan, for example, has a maze of bizarre regulations that limit U.S. agricultural imports, thereby assisting Japanese farmers. Brazil's "local content" rules forestall the importation of cars and ensure the survival of the inefficient local auto industry. Argentina has a special tax on cola drinks, designed to punish Coke and Pepsi bottlers in favor of local fruit drink producers.

Social Changes

Social factors boil down to lifestyle and fashion changes. In either case, the analyst is ready to evaluate their impacts on the relevant industry.

Of the two social influences, fashion is the more unpredictable, and this complicates the job of researching fashion-oriented industries. The women's fashion cycle, for example, is quite short, and a hot clothing item may only have a shelf life of one, maybe two years, before it is replaced by another style. Baseline sales for the industry trend upward, but fashion changes impact short-term projections. Similar phenomena occur in the toy, recreation, and film industries.

Analysts can mistake a short-term fashion cycle for a long-term trend. In one of my financings, an analyst projected a steady upward move in leather coat sales, despite evidence that demand for such garments historically went through up and down cycles. Three years after the transaction, leather coat sales had dropped by over 20 percent.

Lifestyle changes, in contrast, take place over long periods of time. An increase in health consciousness, for example, resulted in a per capita decline in hard liquor consumption. Given fair warning, several spirits producers, such as Seagram's, responded by diversifying into the production of wine, which increased in popularity over the same time span. The gradual shift of women into the workforce, from 41 percent in 1965 to 58 percent in 1995, and the increasing suburbanization of society, acutely affected the auto industry. Besides spawning a need for two cars per family, these changes prompted the minivan boom, as suburban parents juggled responsibilities for ferrying children to after-school activities.

Demographics

Demography is the science that studies the vital statistics of population, such as distribution, age, and income. By observing trends in these statistics, analysts develop investment themes regarding various industries. In the United States for example, the age shift of the baby boomers into their 40s and 50s has sparked a strong interest in retirement planning. The result has been higher revenues for money management firms as the boomers put savings into stocks and bonds. In Malaysia, about 50 percent of the population is under the age of 21, and analysts tout local brewing stocks, in anticipation of a large increase in the beer-drinking population. In Indonesia, rising per capita incomes push a demand for electric appliances, giving analysts reason to be optimistic about the future growth of local utilities.

Demographic trends unfold over long periods of time, and they are thus easier to identify and track than other external factors. This circumstance doesn't lead to absolute certainty. Analysts frequently agree on the existence of a trend (e.g., the rising percentage of single-parent families) but disagreement occurs in sizing up it's impact on relevant industries.

Foreign Influences

As global trade expands, industries become sensitive to foreign influences. For example, the U.S. economy's health is heavily dependent on imported oil. Overseas disruptions in the supply/demand dynamic of this resource ripple through several industries, including the oil, chemical, and leisure sectors. Other U.S. industries are under assault from foreign competitors: automobile parts, apparel, and electronics are three of the more popular targets. At the same time, U.S. exports have never been stronger, reflecting the economic liberalization of nations previously keeping out U.S. products.

Reflecting this liberalization theme, analysts evaluate selected industries on a global basis. Demand projections are aggregated by country, and the external influences referred to herein are considered from a global perspective. This approach is appropriate for worldwide commodity businesses such as oil, metals, and agricultural products, although it is applied at times to categories such as defense, semiconductors, and airlines.

Keeping Your Focus

Big-picture trends are interesting to study, but undisciplined research does little to advance an equity evaluation. Isolating the critical elements in an external analysis is difficult and most research reports fail in this regard. The reports often present outside factors that resemble a jumble of competing influences, and the identifiable opportunities for an industry seem canceled out by the emerging threats. The end result: analysts extrapolate the past into the future, and fail to uncover compelling changes that can move an industry's sales off historical trends. As noted earlier, this rearview-mirror method is appropriate for many industries, but an incisive effort is required either to unlock an industry's potential or to spot its incumbent weakness.

Two external reviews are set forth in the following case studies.

Case Study: Cable TV Industry.   The cable TV industry is a latter stage growth business. It is a defensive industry in terms of the business cycle, with growth aspects. Most U.S. homes have been wired for cable TV, but the industry is still grabbing advertising dollars away from the broadcast networks. Cable TV is fundamentally a regulated monopoly, and regulators generally allow monthly subscriber charges to track inflation.

May 1999 research reports emphasized the influence of technology and government in the industry's future, as shown in Exhibit 6–11.

The external factors were largely positive in 1999, and analysts concluded that the cable TV industry's above-average revenue growth rate would continue. Higher pay-TV revenues and increased channel availability would enable the industry to garner a growing share of ad revenues, while docile regulators would rubber-stamp inflation-driven subscriber

EXHIBIT 6–11. Cable TV Industry External Factors and Related Threats

---

Technology

Opportunities

Improved pay TV technology increases revenues.

More compression means more channels *and* more revenues.

New technology permits phone and Internet service over cable lines.

Threats

Improved technology enhances the direct broadcast satellite (DBS) industry's ability to attract customers.

Technology is available for phone companies to send TV programming through telephone wires.

Government

Opportunities

There is no political will to cut the industry's monthly subscriber rates.

Liberal regulatory policies expand cable merger options to phone companies and software providers.

Many recent mergers as telecommunications, cable TV, and Internet providers combine.

Threats

Regulators can change their minds on subscriber fees.

New law allows phone companies to compete in cable TV. These companies are larger and have more resources than most cable firms.

Social Changes

Opportunities

No significant opportunities were gleaned from existing social trends.

Threats

American television viewing on a per capita basis is up 5% from 1990 to 1998, but it may be reaching a saturation point at 4.3 hours per day.

Demographics

No significant opportunities or threats are apparent from underlying demographic changes.

Foreign Influences

The industry's customers and principal suppliers are located in the United States. Foreign influences are practically nil.

---

rates. Direct broadcast satellite service, an obvious cable TV substitute was a minor threat. It had just a 3 percent market share in TV homes and its premium service (and rates) were acceptable to only high-end consumers. The likelihood of driving Internet and telephone products through the wires boosted cable TV values.

Case Study: Trucking Industry.   The trucking industry is divided into two sectors, the long-haul business, whereby a full truckload is shipped long distances over several days; and the short-haul business, which consists primarily of less than full loads shipped within a 200-mile radius. Trucking is a cyclical industry, and its volumes are directly correlated to industrial production. The industry also follows a capacity cycle. The industry over-expands during good times, and new trucks may be running half empty when the economy is prospering. Labor costs are 60 percent of sales and qualified drivers are hard to find. This capacity problem and labor issue can lead to rate cuts in good economic times and lower profits. The primary competitors are railroads in the long-haul segment and air freight companies in the short-haul business. Exhibit 6–12 lists external factors affecting the trucking industry.

No external factors threaten the industry's survival. Trucking is going to be with us for a long time, but serious issues involve new competition and a driver shortage, with few counterbalancing opportunities. External factors contribute to the consensus belief that trucking industry revenues will grow slower than the general economy. Future profitability will be below average.

DEMAND ANALYSIS

The ultimate purpose of preparing an economic analysis, industry life cycle placement, and external factor review is an assessment of future demand for the industry's products. Applying such study to numerical forecasts is accomplished differently, as discussed below:

1. *Top-Down Economic Analysis.* We look for specific macroeconomic variables that affect an industry's sales. An ideal situation is when revenues correlate strongly to one economic statistic, thus reducing the need for multiple forecast inputs. Cement demand growth in Mexico, for example, is historically 1.7×GNP growth. Analysts, as a result, rely on GNP forecasts to project cement unit volume.

2. *Industry Life Cycle.* Categorizing the industry within its life cycle position (or its business cycle sensitivity) provides a framework for demand forecasts. The U.S. food industry is "mature," so unit sales should track GNP and population growth. The Internet industry is "growing," and this characterization provides a guide to above-normal sales increases.

3. *External Factors.* Many outside factors are fairly stable, and their impact on an industry are easily predictable. Others are highly variable, and thus bring an element of uncertainty into the analysis. Including these items, items into a sales forecast is a qualitative exercise, requiring judgment.

By considering the preceding three major themes, the analyst establishes a future sales line for the industry. Most times, this sales trend turns out to be an extrapolation of past history, as suggested by the trend line for

EXHIBIT 6–12. Trucking Industry External Factors and Related Threats

Technology

Opportunities

Growing use of on-board computers and satellite tracking improve delivery times for truckers.

Just-in-time-inventory acceptance is helping truckers vis-à-vis railroads.

Threats

Railroads' introduction of *Roadrailer* (a trailer equipped with highway and rail wheels) and the *Iron Highway* (a flexible train that facilitates truck trailer hauling) brings new competitive threats to the short-haul market.

Government

Opportunities

No significance.

Threats

The federal government is permitting large railroad mergers, which will increase pressure on the long-haul segment.

New safety regulations tighten the driver licensing process, acerbating a shortage of drivers.

Government is cutting back its loan program to truck driving schools, thus contributing to the driver shortage.

Social Changes

Opportunities

Increasing acceptance of women and minorities as truck drivers could relieve driver shortage.

Threats

Desire to spend more time at home reduces pool of applicants, as people choose alternative professions.

Demographics

Opportunities

No special issues.

Threats

Truck driving is a younger person's profession. The baby boom years (1946–1964) were followed by a birth decline, so there's a smaller pool of eligible drivers.

Foreign Influences

The trucking industry's customers and principal suppliers are located in the United States, except for oil, which is 50% imported. Gasoline costs account for 15% to 20% of revenues, but gas prices are reasonably stable.

EXHIBIT 6–13. Established Industry—Common Extrapolation for Annual Sales Results

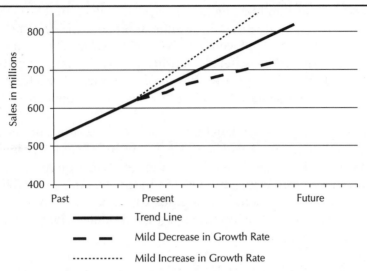

the established industry in Exhibit 6–13, but not always. Sometimes, careful study reveals the likelihood of a turning point that affects the industry's fortunes dramatically. Even an extrapolation result provides useful insights. For example, the water service industry has shown a 7 percent growth rate. Suppose your analysis indicates a continuation of the trend, but only at 5 percent. The 2 percent difference leads you to believe the industry's prospects are overblown, and you sell your shareholdings while prices are still high. In Exhibit 6–13, a mild decrease in the growth rate produces 10 percent lower sales in the future.

Once a trend has been forecast, the analyst's next step is studying the industry's customers. Where does the demand originate? Who's buying and why?

Customer Study

A forecast of aggregate demand is helpful, but a full understanding of what drives an industry's revenue is achieved through learning the customers. Since a typical industry serves thousands of clients, evaluating them individually is impossible. Segmenting the customers into submarkets, on the other hand, enables the analyst to study a smaller number of factors that contribute to demand. As he sequentially studies each submarket, he builds an aggregate demand profile, submarket by submarket.

For example, the demand forecast for the Mexican cement market relied heavily on GNP trends. As a backup to this methodology, I subdivided the market into five segments and considered demand in each segment to verify the accuracy of the GNP multiplier. Both methods revealed a likely demand around 31 million tons, including exports (see Exhibit 6–14).

In Exhibit 6–14, I categorized the submarkets by usage: homebuilding, infrastructure projects, and commercial construction. But demand segments can be classified by different definitions. David Aaker, a noted business strategist, divides segments between customer characteristics and product-related approaches. Exhibit 6–15 shows samples from the U.S. market.

A careful analyst studies demand on the basis of several submarket classifications. Following Dr. Aaker's advice, I examined Mexican cement forecasts on a geographic basis. I divided Mexico into five regions and looked at individual market need (see Exhibit 6–16). In this instance, the GNP, usage, and geographic methods delivered aggregate forecasts that were highly correlated. Utilizing multiple approaches is a good double check for any sales forecast.

Established Industries. For established industries, the analyst should contact long-time customers to figure what drives demand in each submarket. What guides the customer's buying decisions? How does it differ by submarket? What changes are occurring in the customer's motivation? What implication will they have on industry revenues? Discussions with customers and a study of buying habits indicate whether prior trends continue.

For example, VCRs captured 70 percent of the U.S. housing market after ten years. Unit growth dropped in the 1990s. Personal computers represent

EXHIBIT 6–14. Mexican Cement Market—Building Aggregate Demand by Submarket

Submarket	Estimated Demand (MM Tons)
Residential	10.5
Commercial	8.2
Infrastructure	7.3
Transformers[1]	2.2
Export	3.0
Total Submarket Demand	**31.2**
GNP-Based Demand	30.4

[1] Manufacturing of concrete block, concrete pipe, and so on.

EXHIBIT 6–15. Approaches to Defining Demand Segments

Customer Characteristics	Demand Segment
Geographic	Southern region as a market for trendy clothing versus the West Coast
Type of business	Computer needs of restaurants versus manufacturing firms versus banks versus retailers
Size of firm	Large hospital versus midsize versus small
Lifestyle	Tendency of Jaguar buyers to be more adventurous, less conservative than buyers of Mercedes-Benz
Sex	The Virginia Slims cigarettes for women
Age	Cereals for children versus adults
Occupation	The paper copier needs of lawyers versus dentists

Product-Related Approaches	Demand Segment
User type	Appliance buyer—home builder, homeowner, small business
Usage	The heavy potato users—the fast-food outlets
Benefits sought	Dessert eaters—those who are calorie-conscious versus those who are more concerned with convenience
Price sensitivity	Price-sensitive Honda Civic buyer versus the luxury Mercedes-Benz buyer
Competitor	Those computer users now committed to IBM
Application	Professional users of chain saws versus the homeowner
Brand loyalty	Those committed to IBM versus others

Source. Developing Business Strategies by David Aaker (New York: John Wiley & Sons, Inc., 1995).

a newer appliance. They appear in 32 percent of U.S. homes but are concentrated in the higher income households. This low penetration (relative to VCR's) promotes a high growth rate until computer saturation occurs in all income segments (see Exhibit 6–17).

Growth Industries.   A growth industry has yet to penetrate all its future submarkets. In addition to researching the existing customer base, the analyst considers new outlets for the industry's products. The pager business, for example, was confined to businesspeople. In recent years, it has expanded to personal use. Fast-food chains were selling to the lunch and dinner market. In the 1980s, they attracted the breakfast segment. Identifying a

EXHIBIT 6–16. Mexican Cement Market—Building Aggregate Demand by Submarket—Geographic Basis

Geographic Market	Estimated Demand (MM Tons)
Central Mexico	11.2
Northern Gulf	5.9
South Mexico	5.2
Central Pacific	3.2
North Pacific	2.2
Export	3.0
Total Geographic Market Demand	30.7
Submarket Based Demand	31.2
GNP-Based Demand	30.4

new use or user group is important to confirming a growth industry's upward movement.

Untested Industries.   Some publicly-traded companies furnish a truly new product or service. Given a minimal level of product acceptance, these firms have little or no track record from which the analyst can build a sales forecast. Although the risk profile of these stocks is higher than most, the decision process is not entirely speculative.

A first step is determining whether the new industry fulfills a need that (1) exists, and (2) isn't being met by another industry. The managed care industry was founded in response to the urgent need of corporations to cut employee medical costs. Assuming a need is verified, analysts typically forecast new industry sales based on the experience of a similar industry.

EXHIBIT 6–17. Comparable Household Penetration—Two Electronic Products

	1980	1985	1990
VCR	2%	37%	70%
	1985	**1990**	**1995**
Personal Computers	10%	23%	32%

One illustration is the office products superstore industry, as typified by Office Depot and Staples. No sooner did these two companies go public than analysts settled into a comparison with discount warehouse clubs, such as Price Club and Costco. Market share and saturation levels for Office Depot and Staples were calculated on models similar to the warehouse club experience. For every 250,000 people in a metropolitan market, for example, analysts figured one warehouse club could succeed. After some observation, they used similar logic in quantifying 25,000 white collar workers and 100,000 people per office products superstore.

Input/Output and Industry Demand Forecasts

Input-output analysis observes the flow of goods and services through the production process, including intermediate steps as the goods proceed raw-material to finished product. A rising consumption of the finished product boosts demand for industries supplying the intermediate steps. For example, the personal computer boom elevates the demand for the semiconductor, an important PC component.

EXHIBIT 6–18. Demand Analysis Model for the Hotel Furniture Market

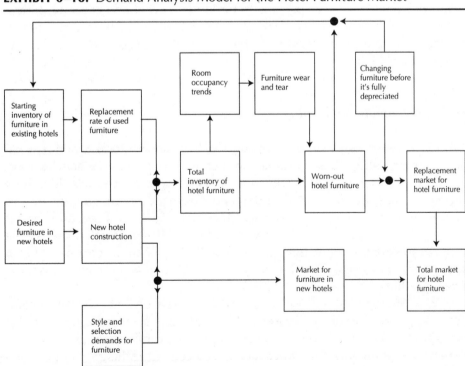

If one industry is a major customer of another, an analyst uses input-output analysis to derive partial demand for the latter's products. Alternatively, the higher consumption of one industry's offerings sparks demand for complementary products. The wide-scale introduction of the VCR boosted the video rental business. In the 1980s, analysts calculated video demand through algebraic formulas based on VCR purchases. A typical formula was that one VCR purchase meant three video rentals per month. The demand models can be complex and contain many variables. Exhibit 6–18 on page 101 shows one rendition for the hotel furniture market.

SUPPLY ANALYSIS IN THE INDUSTRY STUDY

In reviewing industries, analysts spend most of their time studying *demand* trends. They usually assume the supply side of the equation takes care of itself. If industry revenues are rising, more investment pours in. If revenues are declining, existing capacity services the falling demand. This model is valid in the long term, but its applicability over the short to intermediate term varies by industry.

The temporary help industry fits the classic model well. With its emphasis on low-skilled workers, the industry can find new employees quickly, thus ramping up capacity in a short time. In contrast, supply that is dependent on capital intensive producers is a different story. Steel and packaging require three- to five-year periods to build plants that add capacity. Industries that use highly skilled workers, such as software, can face short-term capacity constraints as they wait for training programs to provide new employees.

Projecting Supply Availability

Supply is a function of unused capacity and the ability to bring on new capacity. Interpreting these variables well enough to make a reasonable forecast is complicated. That's why few analysts attempt the job. Ideally, a supply forecast dovetails with a demand forecast, and the analyst has an idea about future market equilibrium. If future supply and demand are out of balance, prices for the industry's products will be affected unless the suppliers change their behavior in time. The ideal research report has a supply/demand graph like the one shown in Exhibit 6–19. In this case, the graph predicts a future capacity problem.

The supply projection is easiest when the industry has only a few competitors, generating output at a discrete number of sizable facilities. It also helps if the industry's economics make imports prohibitively expensive, so the analyst can ignore foreign capacity. The cement industry is a good example of this model. First, only large plants, with long construction lead times, make cement. Second, the low value per ton makes transportation

EXHIBIT 6–19. Demand/Supply Graph—Hypothetical Industry

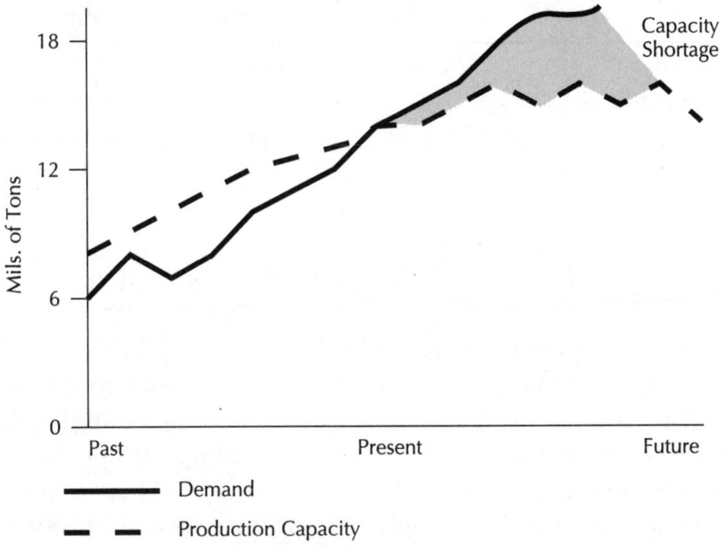

Note. There's a capacity shortage in the future. This could mean higher product prices.

uneconomical beyond a 250-mile radius from the plant. Thus, it's a simple matter to forecast available supply: An analyst counts nearby capacity and adds expansions planned for the next three to five years.

In Mexico, for example, this process is straightforward. The cement market is dominated by two companies operating just 29 plants, and their expansion plans are public knowledge. All plants have ample reserves of raw materials. An illustrative calculation for supply appears in Exhibit 6–20.

The forecast demand for cement is matched against the supply trend, as shown in Exhibit 6–21. The chart shows capacity utilization rates exceeding 88 percent from 1996 to 1999, which is considered *high* for the industry. The projection suggests that additional capacity be initiated.

EXHIBIT 6–20. 1996 Mexican Cement Market—Availability of Supply Calculation (Millions of Tons per Year)

	1996	**1997**	**1998**	**1999**
1996 capacity	36.0	36.0	36.0	36.0
1997 additions, net	—	1.0	1.0	1.0
1998 additions, net	—	—	3.7	3.7
1999 additions, net	—	—	—	1.3
Total Estimated Capacity	36.0	37.0	40.7	42.0

Note. Additions are net of closures.

EXHIBIT 6–21. 1996 Supply/Demand Forecast—Mexican Cement Industry

	1996	1997	1998	1999
Available capacity	36.0	37.0	40.7	42.0
Expected demand	31.0	33.0	35.5	38.0
Capacity utilization	86%	89%	87%	90.5%

PROFITABILITY, PRICING, AND THE INDUSTRY STUDY

A security analyst wants to select profitable industries. What's the point of investing in growth industries if sales go up, but profits go down? A supply/demand forecast gives an indication of future profitability. If supply appears to be in line with demand, industry earnings will probably stay on their trend line. Indeed, profitability is vital for industries to make the investment needed to increase supply. A projected oversupply will retard investment since it augurs lower prices. A 1997 study by Lehman Brothers predicted sharply lower prices for copper (from 110¢/lb. to 60¢/lb.), resulting from prospective increases in mining capacity.

Factors contributing to *pricing* include:

- Product segmentation.
- Degree of industry concentration.
- Ease of industry entry.
- Price changes in key supply inputs.

To begin, most industries effectively segment their product offerings by brand name, reputation, or service, even when the products are quite similar. Over-the-counter medicines are one example. The ingredients of the store brand and the name-brand are typically identical, yet the name-brand product has a 40 percent price premium.

An industry with a high degree of concentration inhibits price movements. Assuming that demand and supply are in reasonable balance, the major players have an incentive to engage in monopolistic behavior. Artificially high prices can be sustained by price signaling, confidential agreements, and other means. Outsiders have problems breaking into the inner circle to learn what's going on. In Mexico's cement market, for example, the two major producers control 85 percent of the market, and they barely hide the fact that collusion exists. In several U.S. industries, similar behavior occurs, but it's kept behind closed doors.

Monopolies promote artificial pricing, and an industry's ease of entry is a key variable in holding prices to the free market model. Semiconductor production poses an obvious problem; the entry ticket—a new plant—costs $1 billion. The specialty retailing industry, in contrast, is wide-open. An entrepreneur can rent store space, lease fixtures, and stock inventory for less than $75,000.

Certain industries rely heavily on one or two inputs. Price changes in these inputs affect products costs and profitability. Sometimes, the industry can pass through increased costs in the form of higher prices. At other times, competitive pressures stand in the way. In 1996, for example, the price of corn, a key chicken feed, reached historical highs. Poultry producers, such as Tyson Foods and WLR Corp., were unable to raise prices enough to compensate and their profitability fell.

Industry Profitability Is Important

Supply/demand analysis, cost factors, and pricing flexibility are critical elements in determining future industry profitability. Without earnings, an industry can't finance the commitment to personnel, plant, and research and development that is needed to prosper. An industry with a poor profit outlook is an unlikely investment candidate indeed.

INTERNATIONAL COMPETITION AND MARKETS

Competition

Competitive analysis is the topic of many books. Michael Porter of the Harvard Business School, is a leader in the field, and approaches competition from multiple directions, as set forth in Exhibit 6–22. Security analysis synthesizes the work of experts like Dr. Porter, and this section provides a brief treatment of the subject.

A first step in the competitive analysis is defining the industry. While this task was discussed earlier, it is helpful to remember that some analysts cover the chemical industry; some follow the chemical fertilizer industry; and still others research the specialty chemical industry. Industries are segmented into smaller industries. *Institutional Investor* magazine divides the computer industry into seven subindustries: computer services, data networking, the Internet, PC hardware, PC software, server and enterprise hardware, and server and enterprise software. Placing your company into its subindustry and identifying its competitors becomes the second step in your competitive analysis.

For each competitor, the analyst develops an appreciation of its business strategy and its effects on the company under study. For example, in the managed care business, Aetna pursues a national program. Physician Health Services focuses on the Southeast region. Managed Care Solutions sticks to Medicaid managed care. If Aetna shifted to Medicaid contracts, it would harm Managed Care Solutions' prospects.

Finally, the analyst is advised to outline the strengths and weaknesses of industry participants. Exhibit 6–23 illustrates many of the items considered

EXHIBIT 6–22. Five Competitive Forces That Determine Industry Profitability

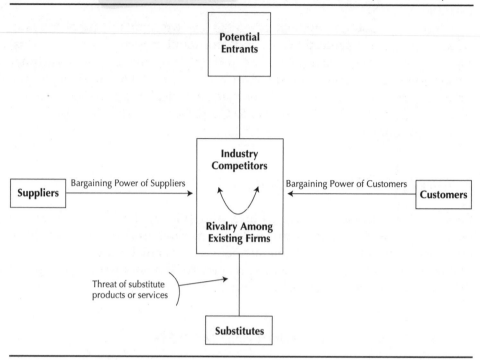

Source. Competitive Advantage by Michael E. Porter (New York: The Free Press, 1985).

in such an outline. Financial track record and balance sheet strength are priorities for analysts, but a review of other factors reveals whether better results can be achieved by the competition, perhaps at the expense of the subject company. Similarly, if the subject company's strengths dominate areas where the competition is weak, a higher degree of confidence is gained for your forecasts.

Each industry has a few dominant success factors that can be drawn from Exhibit 6–23. Analysts (and corporate strategists) inventory these items and the relative positions of competitors. Exhibit 6–24 presents this comparative analysis in tabular form.

A firm's ability to sustain its sales and earnings is highly dependent on the status of the competition. Does the subject company have the ability to be aggressive—take the offense? Or, does it have to protect market share and husband financial resources—play defense? The competitor profile facilitates game theory for the practitioner.

International Competition

The world is becoming a smaller place and industries increasingly reflect a globalization theme. This characterization is most advanced with commodity

EXHIBIT 6–23. Competitive Analysis: Analysis of Strengths and Weaknesses of Each Industry Participant

Innovation	Management
Technical product or service superiority	Quality of top and middle management
New product capability	Knowledge of business
Research & Development	Culture
Technologies	Strategic goals and plans
Patents	Entrepreneurial thrust
	Planning/operation system
	Loyalty—turnover
	Quality of strategic decision making

Manufacturing	Marketing
Cost structure	Product quality reputation
Flexible production operations	Product characteristics/differentiation
Equipment	Brand-name recognition
Access to raw material	Breadth of product line—systems
Vertical integration	capability
Workforce attitude and motivation	Customer orientation
Capacity	Segmentation/focus
	Distribution
	Retailer relationship
	Advertising/promotion skills
	Sales force
	Customer service/product support

Finance—Access to Capital	Customer Base
From operations	Size and loyalty
From cash on hand	Market share
Ability to use debt and equity financing	Growth of segments served

Source. Developing Business Strategies by David Aaker (New York: John Wiley & Sons, Inc., 1995).

industries such as oil, metals, and basic foodstuffs, but it also dominates intermediate sectors such as textiles, semiconductors, and chemicals. Indeed, about 40 percent of the S&P 500's earnings are connected to international activities.

The United States is the leading economy, has the greatest number of publicly traded securities, and operates the most developed financial markets. For these reasons, the security analysis profession has made great strides here. The downside of this situation has been a nearsightedness on the part of many United States practitioners. Even though industries extend globally, Wall Street research often stops at the U.S. border, and analysts frequently give short shrift to corporate foreign operations and international trends. As institutions emphasize global research, more work will be dedicated to this important area.

EXHIBIT 6–24. Sample Competitor Analysis for a Research Report

Competition Indicators	Major Competitors			
	A	B	C	D
Market position	Vulnerable	Prevalent	Strong	Vulnerable
Profitability	Low	Average	Average	Average
Financial strength	Low	High	Unknown	Low
Product mix	Narrow	Broad	Narrow	Narrow
Technological capability	Average	Strong	Average	Weak
Product quality	Minimum	Good	Satisfactory	Minimum

Source. *Management Policy, Strategy and Plans* by Milton Leontiades (New York: Little, Brown & Company, 1982).

SUMMARY

The industry analysis is a continuation of the top-down approach. By studying the industry, its external environment, demand and supply balance, likely profitability and competitive situation, the security analyst confirms whether the industry is appropriate for investment. The written research report only presents a limited amount of information and practitioners highlight a few key factors in reviewing an industry. Frequently, their audience prefers a one-word summary in the industry review, such as *growth, mature,* or *decline.* With a knowledge of the industry terrain, the analyst proceeds to a specific stock selection. Which of the participants are the winners? Which are the losers? Company-specific analysis and valuation are covered in the next few chapters.

QUESTIONS AND SHORT PROBLEMS

1. Using the research reports obtained in Question 9 of Chapter 5, compare and contrast these professional reports with the model research report outlined in Exhibit 6–1. (Adopt-a-Company reports may be used for comparison.)

2. Why are investors keenly interested in research reports that provide contrary opinions on a particular stock?

3. Why is Ford Motor Company in the mature phase of its industrial life cycle? Consult the *Wall Street Journal* and select two companies in the growth and decline phases.

4. With the help of library sources, trace the life cycle of the CB radio industry. CB radios were popular in automobiles 15 to 20 years ago.

5. The greeting card industry is mature, with sales growing 5 percent to 8 percent annually. How does a greeting card firm become a growth company in this mature industry? Circle all that apply:
   a. Expand market share by offering better products and services.
   b. Acquire competing firms.
   c. (a) and (b)
   d. Expand advertising expenditures.
   e. Complete new public offering to boost financial reserves.

6. Many investors classify companies according to the manner in which the companies' sales and earnings react to the business cycle. If GNP increases by 4 percent in a given year (and inflation is 3 percent), what might be the sales performance of a typical cyclical company?

7. Which stock has the most defensive characteristics?
   a. Campbell Soup.
   b. Merrill Lynch.
   c. Ford Motor Company.
   d. Sears Roebuck.

8. Which stock is the most cyclical?
   a. NationsBank.
   b. Ryland Homes.
   c. Federated Department Stores.
   d. Amazon.com.

9. An analyst immediately labels a company as a growth business. How might this opinion influence his follow-up study?

10. Consult the historical results of Ford Motor Company through the library, SEC, or Internet. Explain briefly what factors prompted earnings to decline dramatically from 1990 to 1992.

11. Should an analyst define a company as a defensive company before completing his report?

12. Explain which two of the following external factors are most important to the sales growth of the U.S. defense industry?
   a. Technology.
   b. Government.
   c. Social changes.
   d. Demographics.
   e. Foreign influences.

13. Why do many research reports project historical factors into the future?

14. The CD industry made the record player industry obsolete. List three industries made obsolete in the last 20 years by new technologies.

15. U.S. businesses often complain about government regulation and interference. How do restrictions on sugar imports help the domestic sugar producers?

16. How did the U.S. government encourage the growth of the cellular phone industry in the 1980s?

17. As the average age of the U.S. population advances, what industries benefit from this demographic shift?
    a. Nursing homes.
    b. Pharmaceutical.
    c. Leisure.
    d. Travel.
    e. All of the above.

18. In Exhibit 6–11, DBS is described as a threat to conventional cable TV. How real is the DBS threat at this time?

19. Determine which of the following statements are true or false:
    a. Trucking industry is defensive.
    b. Trucking industry is a growth industry.
    c. Trucking is cyclical.
    d. Trucking is labor intensive.
    e. Trucking has a surplus of drivers.
    f. Government involvement can grow the trucking industry significantly.

20. Exhibits 6–14 and 6–16 provide two means of calculating aggregate demand for an industry. What's the point of using two or more approaches to build a demand forecast? What's wrong with using just one approach?

21. The table below shows the household penetration of two products, VCRs and PCs. How would you complete the Internet line?

Electronic Products	Comparable Penetration		
	1980	**1985**	**1990**
VCR	2%	37%	70%
	1985	**1990**	**1995**
Personal Computers	10%	23%	32%
	1990	**1995**	**2000**
Internet	?	?	?

Should the use of the Internet track prior PC demand growth?

22. Complete a demand analysis model—similar to Exhibit 6–18—for the high school graduation ring market.

23. Forecasting the potential supply of cement over a three-year period is straight forward in many markets. How is projecting the supply of clothing available to retailers a more difficult exercise over the same time period?

24. A company's survival depends, in part, on the level of competition. Why is it important for the analyst to define *distinctly* a company's position in its industry?

25. Compare and contrast the U.S. industry positions of Budweiser and Corona beer. Compare and contrast the customers, pricing, and brand loyalty.

26. Complete the table (see Exhibit 6–24) for the following companies in 1999:

Competition Indicators	Burlington Coat	Ross Stores	Dress Barn
Market position			
Profitability			
Financial strength			
Product mix			

27. Outline the key strengths and weaknesses of Ford Motor Company in the following areas:

____ Innovation

____ Management

____ Manufacturing

____ Marketing

____ Financial

____ Customer Base

Consult appropriate research sources. Use Exhibit 6–23 as a guide.

Adopt-a-Company

Complete Question 26 for your company and its principal competitors. Complete Question 27 for your company.

7

Company-Specific Analysis

*Having covered macroeconomic, capital market, and industry factors
affecting the subject company, the analyst proceeds to study the
firm's operations and finances. In this chapter, we outline the steps
involved in structuring a company-specific analysis.*

For many practitioners, company-specific analysis is where the fun starts. At this level, the stock selection process begins in earnest. The foundation of economic forecasting, capital markets analysis, and industry study is in place (see Exhibit 7–2), and their research now focuses on the attributes of a single stock.

The first step of the analysis begins with a written review of the company's business, included under Section 4 of the research report (see Exhibit 7–1). This review is *descriptive* and *analytical*. Its purpose is twofold: (1) to ensure that the practitioner follows the discipline of placing relevant information on paper; and (2) to convey to the reader the analyst's

EXHIBIT 7–1. Model Research Report

1. Introduction
2. Macroeconomic Review
3. Relevant Stock Market Prospects
4. Review of the Company and Its Business✓
   Industry Analysis
   Company-Specific Analysis✓
5. Financial Analysis
6. Financial Projections
7. Application of Valuation Methodologies
8. Recommendation

EXHIBIT 7–2. The Components of a Research Report

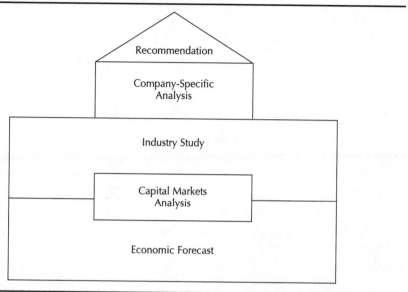

Note how the company-specific analysis rests on the foundation of industry study, capital markets analysis, and economic forecast.

understanding of the company's business and operating environment. The business review, along with the historical financial analysis, provides the basis on which financial projections are made. Financial projections, of course, are a key determinant of valuation.

OUTLINE OF A BUSINESS ANALYSIS

The business outline set forth in Exhibit 7–3 covers many of the topics required in a prospectus. Unlike a prospectus, the research report includes the analyst's *interpretation* of the facts and trends, along with whatever additional data the analyst believes is relevant. Furthermore, the research report places the appropriate emphasis on matters meriting special attention, whereas, the business review of a prospectus fails to highlight the factors on which a valuation should rely.

SYSTEMATIC APPROACH AND COMPETITIVE ADVANTAGE

The review is systematic. In a step-by-step fashion, the analyst plows through each element of a company's business. Along the way, he (and the reader) are forced to focus on the company's abilities in each aspect of its operations. Is the product line good enough to garner new customers? Is the distribution system better than the competition's? Examining these

EXHIBIT 7–3. Business Review Outline for a Research Report

General Information
  Overview and Business Description
  Corporate Strategy
  Life Cycle
  Financial Summary

Products and Markets
  Product Line and New Products
  Market for the Company's Products
  Marketing Strategy and Customer Support
  Significant Customers

Production and Distribution
  Manufacturing Process and Costs
  Distribution
  Suppliers and Raw Materials

Competition
  Competitive Environment
  Comparative Analysis of Competition

Other Topics
  Research and Development
  Foreign Sales and Earnings
  Government Regulation
  Personnel
  Properties
  Management

areas separately enables the analyst to piece together that combination of assets, skills, and innovation that enable the firm to prosper.

The previous chapter focused on how the industry makes money. Now the analyst determines how the firm accrues sales and earns profits. Business strategists call this exercise a search for the firm's "sustained competitive advantage (SCA)." Without an SCA, a company's customers are ready for the taking. Competitors close in and the firm's ultimate survival is in question. The business review zeros in on the elements supporting an SCA.

Business scholars ascribe sustainable competitive advantages to three basic strategies:

1. *Low Costs.* The firm's cost of producing its goods and services is lower than the competition. Battle Mountain's low-cost Golden Giant mine, for example, gives it a leg up on competing gold-mining firms.

2. *Differentiation.* The customer perceives that the firm offers something that is unique (Template Software offers unique cost-cutting techniques in software development).

3. *Focus.* The firm selects a narrow customer base that is underserved by the industry. Wal-Mart started by building stores in small rural towns that Sears and Kmart avoided.

These advantages occur in various parts of a profitable operation, encouraging the practicing analyst to pursue the segmented study outlined in Exhibit 7–3. In his book, *Competitive Advantage* (New York: Free Press, 1985), Michael Porter echoes a similar approach:

> Competitive advantage cannot be understood by looking at a firm as a whole. It stems from the many discrete activities a firm performs in designing, producing, marketing, delivering, and supporting its product. Each of these activities can contribute to a firm's relative cost position and create a basis for differentiation. A cost advantage, for example, may stem from such disparate sources as a low-cost physical distribution system, a highly efficient assembly process, or superior sales force utilization. Differentiation can stem from similarly diverse factors, including the procurement of high quality raw materials, a responsive order entry system, or a superior product design.

Individual investors would be surprised at the number of times professionals buy a stock, yet fail to pinpoint the company's competitive advantages. Dozens of fast-food chains have gone public, but only a handful prosper under the continuing onslaught of McDonald's and a few other major players. In 1989, 56 companies made disk drives in the United States; by 1997, only 11 survived. Breaking into an established market is difficult. Take the breakfast cereal market. The latest brand to make the top 10 was Honey Nut Cheerios in 1979, almost 20 years ago.

Sometimes the ability to beat the competition is referred to as a company's "franchise value." A study by Morgan Stanley & Co. ranked prominent firms' franchises in terms of expected duration, absent major improvements. Strong consumer brands and images like Coke and Disney topped the list. Technology firms had shorter durations. A partial list appears in Exhibit 7–4.

Maintaining a competitive advantage is essential to the corporation's survival, but it shouldn't be an end in itself. If developing new products or

EXHIBIT 7–4. Franchise Values of Major Corporations

Company	Perceived Life of Competitive Advantage
Coca-Cola	Over 20 years
Disney	Over 20 years
Budweiser	10 years
Dun & Bradstreet	10 years
Intel	4 to 6 years
Netscape	2 to 3 years

holding onto market share is too expensive, for example, the corporation damages its equity value by building up an SCA. For example, J.M. Smucker, a regional producer of jams, is losing share and store shelf space to food conglomerates. Running a major ad campaign and renting sufficient shelf space to reverse this trend would bankrupt this medium-size business.

The following sections examine the Business Review Outline in greater detail.

GENERAL INFORMATION

Overview and Business Description

To begin a business review, the analyst provides a brief history of the company and a summary description of its operations. Ownership and corporate structure are briefly outlined, and the analyst relates key features of the investment theme supporting the company shares.

Corporate Strategy

Although many analysts are content to extrapolate a company's historical sales into the future, enterprising practitioners examine a company's business plan to determine what drives revenues in the long term. The credibility of a plan rests on management matching corporate advantages and resources against likely competitor moves.

In some industries, the strategy appears simplistic. The Rainforest Cafe model was straightforward. Revenues from a base of four restaurants were expected to grow by 8 percent annually. With existing managerial and financial resources, 20 restaurants, providing $160 million in annual revenues, were to be added in 1997 and 1998. The plan was not fully implemented as base sales declined. Exhibit 7–5 summarizes Rainforest's initial expansion strategy.

In other industries, the process is infinitely more complicated. Pharmaceutical drug companies, for example, typically own a catalog of drugs. As technology advances and new drugs predominate, the sales of drugs in the catalog decline. Similarly, when an established drug goes "off patent," corporate sales of the drug decrease in the face of generic competition. Management estimates the rate of lost sales and plans new drug innovations to replace sales lost from the off-patent products. The large Swedish drug firm, Astra AB, faces this dilemma. It is highly dependent on sales of the ulcer drug Losec, the world's biggest selling prescription medicine, whose patent expires in 2001. Because 45 percent of Astra's $5 billion in sales are from Losec, revenues will plunge when Losec's patent expires.

In reviewing a drug company's plans, the pharmaceutical analyst has to convince himself that the firm has the ability to maintain a pipeline of new products. He must also be assured that catalog revenue declines follow management's plan, rather than a more negative scenario. Exhibit 7–6

EXHIBIT 7–5. Rainforest Cafe—Initial Expansion Strategy (in millions, except for restaurants)

	Year Ending December 31		
	1996	**1997**	**1998**
Number of Restaurants			
Existing restaurants	2	6	15
New restaurants	4	9	11
Total	6	15	26
$5 million capital expenditure per new restaurant			
Capital expenditures	$20.0	$ 45.0	$ 55.0
Projected Sales			
Existing restaurant-full year	$25.0	$ 70.0	$225.0
New restaurant-partial year	15.0	72.0	88.0
Total projected sales	$40.0	$142.0	$313.0

Source. Rainforest SEC reports, Rainforest Cafe, and research reports.
Note. Rainforest's restaurant opening program provided higher sales.

shows a sample business plan. Note how overall sales jump from $700 million to $900 million, even as 1998 catalog revenues drop.

Other companies are "one trick" ponies. Information Management Resources, a pricey tech stock, derived 50 percent of its 1996 revenues from year 2000 projects. Such activity involved converting computer software to accommodate more than two-digit entries for years (e.g., 1997 is read as "97"). Since many computers read 2000 and 1900 as the same, IMR's stock was trading at 100x earnings in 1997—greater than the P/E multiples of the hi-tech sector at the time—only to decline sharply in 1998.

EXHIBIT 7–6. Pharmaceutical Drug Company—Sample Business Plan (in millions)

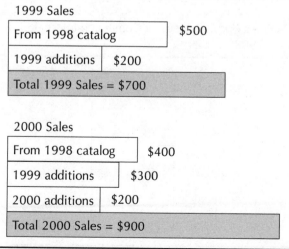

Note that older drug revenues are replaced by new product additions.

Many companies combine internal growth and acquisitions. At Danaher Corp., a manufacturer of hardware products, baseline sales have increased an average of 8 percent annually since 1994. By carrying out a successful program of acquisitions, management has boosted total sales growth to 18 percent annually. Danaher now has yearly sales exceeding $2.9 billion. Finding sizable deals, which meaningfully increase revenues, has become more difficult. In 1999, the analyst must decide if this strategy can be continued without the firm paying unreasonable acquisition prices (see Exhibit 7–7).

Within multiline companies, the strategic framework incorporates a "portfolio approach." For example, Akso Nobel describes its operations as a portfolio. It participates in four different industry segments: *chemicals, coatings, fibers,* and *pharmaceuticals.* Under this discipline, the disparate operating businesses of a corporation are nothing more than a collection of assets. Any business units having similar operational characteristics are combined, leaving little operating synergy between the divisions, which act more or less independently. The holding company acts as the repository of excess cash generated at the divisional level, and it dispenses finance, legal advice, personnel regulations, and accounting services to the divisions. In most cases, the holding company is the divisional bank, and the division managers must apply to the bank to obtain new capital. New business ideas are appraised by the bank, which considers whether the divisional applicant has researched its request properly and whether it has the skills to use the capital efficiently.

Besides evaluating the *business strategies* of the various divisions, the analyst must consider the *allocation process* of the divisional bank. Is it placing money into the most deserving operations? Regularly, security analysts consult the famous Boston Consulting Group growth/share matrix (see Exhibit 7–8) to gain insights.

The growth/share matrix enables holding company managers (and security analysts) to classify each "division," each "business," or each "asset" into a quadrant. The manager then considers whether to implement the

EXHIBIT 7–7. Danaher Corp. Strategy of Combining Internal Growth and Acquisitions (1994–1998)

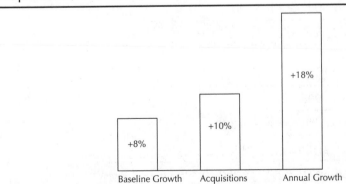

EXHIBIT 7–8. How to Define an Operating Division by the BCG Growth/Share Matrix

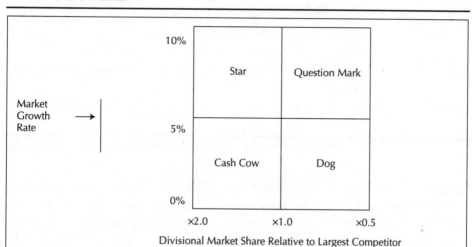

recommended strategy for divisions falling into that respective quadrant. According to the strategy, the cash thrown off by divisions with strong market shares in low-growth markets (cash cows) is reinvested in "stars" to support their growth and market share objectives. Alternatively, the cash is siphoned off to "question marks" to assist in their push to become stars. "Dogs" (mature divisions with small market shares in low-growth markets) receive little capital, even if they are profitable. They are candidates for divestiture, as a means to generate more cash for the question marks and stars. The BCG framework is simple, but effective, and it has influenced a generation of corporations, and correspondingly, stock analysts.

The growth/share matrix approach prompts practitioners to suggest that companies spin off dogs and question marks. The remaining operations are thus easier to pigeonhole as a growth stock or a mature business. Witness AT&T's spin-off of NCR, a perennial drag on growth.

Life Cycle

The corporate life cycle provides an easy way to label a stock. At the company level, there are four stages, which mirror the definitions covered in the industry discussion in Chapter 6. Exhibit 7–9 summarizes the cycle.

Individual companies can proceed through the entire cycle while the industry remains in one stage. I see this phenomenon with numerous growth stocks.

One memorable round-trip was Victor Technology, one of many personal computer manufacturers founded in the early 1980s. Victor began in 1980 and perfected its computer in 1981. By 1982, the company registered

EXHIBIT 7–9. Corporate Life Cycle

Stages	Expected Sales Performance
Pioneer	Unpredictable and volatile sales movements.
Growth	Steady growth in sales as product acceptance widens.
Stable	Moderate sales increases as the market for the company's product matures.
Decline	Sales decrease as customers are attracted to newer, innovative products.

$65 million in annual sales and sported a $120 million market value. It was a growth company in a growth industry, competing with the likes of Apple and IBM. In 1983, the shakeout began, and by early 1984, Victor declared bankruptcy, just as the personal computer industry started its long growth phase. David Taft, a Victor marketing executive who hadn't experienced Wall Street hype, invested in the stock. After his shares became worthless, he wryly remarked, "I got a million dollar education at Victor!"

Financial Summary

Reports provide a summary income statement and balance sheet in the beginning section, with details supplied in a later segment. For diversified companies, this information is broken down by line of business. Statistical data on unit sales, capacity utilization, and similar operating items may be listed here.

PRODUCTS AND MARKETS

Product Line and New Products

In this section, the analyst identifies the products and/or services that the company sells. Bear in mind that many product-oriented firms have a heavy service component. Gateway 2000 manufactures a reputable line of personal computers, but the clincher is often the company's postpurchase service contracts. Perhaps, the subject company is selling status in addition to products. Johnnie Walker Red is a fine scotch, but is it worth 50 percent more than its quality competitors? Besides a simple description of the product line, this section should provide the reader with an understanding of why the company's products are well received by its customers.

If available, statistics related to sales volume by product line (dollar and unit volume) are presented here. Estimated gross margins by product line are included. Three to five years of such data show trend lines and complement the analyst's interpretation of the information. Increasing dependence on one product line or declining margins are warning signals. For example, Stride Rite Corporation, the children's shoe manufacturer, receives 60 percent of its income from one brand, *Keds*.

New products and services are usually extensions of established offerings, but, true innovations should be mentioned if they have the potential to impact results. A market rationale for the new product and evidence of satisfactory test studies provide added credibility to these discussions. Pharmaceutical firms provide details in this regard and software companies do the same. Similarly, retailers sometimes release the results of new store concepts to investors. For example, in 1995 and 1996, Toys 'Я' Us publicized the test results of a copy-cat concept, Babies 'Я' Us. Wall Street liked the idea and Toys 'Я' Us opened additional outlets. In late 1996, the company expanded its commitment and bought Baby Superstores, a competitor of the new operation, for $376 million.

Firms segment their larger markets into submarkets, by virtue of a cost differentiation strategy. Optimally, the analyst knows dollar sales and unit sales by submarket, and the firm's relative position. Does it have a leading share? Is it the #2 player? Are certain submarkets growing faster than the industry? Answers to these questions enable the analyst to judge the company's business plan.

In evaluating airline securities, Standard & Poor's places market share and position at the top of the list. See Exhibit 7–10.

Marketing Strategy and Customer Support

The analyst's report describes the company's marketing strategy and presents the tactics that make the selling effort effective. Tactical areas include:

- Price.
- Service.
- Reputation.
- Geographic coverage.
- Product warranties.
- Credit terms.
- Return policy.

Pricing policy goes hand-in-hand with the marketing strategy, but it involves large corporate objectives. Does the company hold down price to increase share, or does it boost prices to lift margins? The analyst needs to understand the "how" and "why" of pricing by product line.

Advertising is sometimes an important facet of marketing strategy. At the high end, Estee Lauder, a cosmetic company, spends a remarkable 29

EXHIBIT 7–10. Company-Specific Analysis Example—Standard & Poor's Important Rating Factors for Airlines

---

Market Share

Share of industry traffic, measured by revenue passenger miles or revenue ton miles for airlines with significant freight operations

Share of industry capacity, measured by available seat miles or available ton miles

Trend of overall market share

Market share among travel agencies of computerized reservation system (CRS) owned by or shared by airline (Travel agencies tend to book a disproportionate number of tickets on airlines whose CRS they use.)

Position in Specific Markets

Geographic position of airline's hubs for handling major traffic flows; position of competing hubs of other airlines

Share of enplanements and flights at hubs

Share at major origination and destination markets; economic and demographic growth prospects of those markets

Strength of competition at hubs and in major markets served

Barriers to entry/infrastructure constraints
    Gates
    Terminal space and other ground facilities
    Air traffic control; takeoff and landing slot restrictions

Position in international markets
    Growth prospects of markets
    Treaty and regulatory barriers to entry
    Strength of foreign and U.S. competition

Revenue Generation

Utilization of capacity, measured by "load factor" (revenue passenger miles divided by available seat miles)

Pricing
    Yield (passenger revenue divided by revenue passenger miles)
    Yield adjusted for average trip length (Airlines with shorter average trips tend to have higher yields.)

Unit revenues, measured by passenger revenue per available seat mile (yield times load factor)

Effectiveness of revenue management—maximizing revenues by managing trade-off between pricing and utilization

Service reputation; ranking in measures of customer satisfaction

Productivity, measured by revenues or revenue passenger miles per employee or per dollar of assets

Cost Control

Operating cost per available seat mile
    Adjusted for average trip length
    Adjusted for use of operating leases and differing depreciation accounting

Labor
    Labor cost per available seat mile
    Structure of labor contracts; existence and nature of any "B-scales" (lower pay scales for recent hires)
    Flexibility of work rules; effect on productivity
    "Scope clauses" limits on outsourcing
    Status of union contracts and negotiations; possibility of strikes
    Labor relations and morale

Fuel costs and impact of potential fuel price hikes, given fuel efficiency of fleet and nature of routes flown

Commissions, marketing, and other operating expenses

Aircraft Fleet

Number and type of aircraft in relation to current and projected needs

Status of fleet modernization program
    Average age fleet; age weighted by seats
    Proportion of aircraft meeting "Stage III" noise requirements
    Fuel efficiency of fleet
    Aircraft orders and options for future deliveries

cents out of each sales dollar on advertising. Caterpillar, a heavy machinery manufacturer, spends less than 1 percent. For companies where advertising expense is a significant expense, this section shows advertising costs for the preceding three years and estimates the advertising budget for the coming year. If a business is spending more ad dollars yet not generating sales, there is a problem.

Customer support is tied to product and service offerings. How many sales end the minute the customer walks out the door or receives delivery? Follow-up service, warranties, repair, and return policies are critical parts of the product selling package. Auto manufacturers, such as Ford Motor Company, now offer "cradle to grave" service. After purchasing a Ford, the customer receives warranty protection, and the car's service calls are recorded in a dealer's computer system. Software producers attach regular service calls to their product sales, and the accounting period for a sale extends several years, reflecting the ongoing service obligation. Wartsila Diesel's support system is global. Clients that need help with their power plants can have Wartsila technicians fly in on 48 hours' notice, even to remote areas such as Uzbekistan, Malawi, or Honduras.

After describing the customer support component of the company's business, the analyst identifies its competitive advantages in this regard. A follow-up step is measuring the company's support structure against the competition.

Significant Customers

A company's market position is clarified by its customers. If a company sells services to Texaco and Exxon, investors perceive it as a stronger business than one selling to Murphy Oil and Triton Energy. Prestigious customers lend a sense of strength to an operation, giving it instant credibility on Wall Street. Of course, big corporations have better bargaining power than smaller firms, so blue chip business is sometimes a loss leader for companies. Suppliers of Wal-Mart, a tough client, can attest to this fact.

A diversified customer base is an asset because it diminishes the impact of losing any one customer. Practitioners get nervous when one source represents more than 10 percent of sales. Creditworthy customers are a plus also. Gibson Greetings, the greeting card company, incurred a large loss when Phar-Mor, a major customer, went bankrupt and defaulted on its receivables.

PRODUCTION AND DISTRIBUTION

Manufacturing Process and Costs

The principal determinants of product cost are explained here and bottlenecks in the production process are exposed. For example, natural gas is the principal raw material of a methanol producer, amounting to 20 percent of variable cost. This fact is useful to mention in a methanol research report. Likewise, a bottleneck in the methanol process is pipeline throughput and cracker capacity.

Remember, service companies follow repetitive processes to deliver "products" to their customers. For service businesses, the analyst should understand the stages of this production variant and the costs attached thereto.

An examination of the manufacturing process enables the analyst to discover whether the company can fulfill the production side of its business plan. If more facilities are needed, or the existing plants require upgrading, the related cash investment must be factored into the financial analysis.

As Exhibit 7–11 illustrates, the competitive ability of a pulp and paper producer is dependent on its manufacturing cost position. That's why Standard & Poor's devotes significant emphasis to production costs at the mill level.

Distribution

Certain industries emphasize the distribution function so the research report explores this topic. According to conventional wisdom, a company should control its distribution network once a given sales volume is achieved. The rise of specialized distribution firms and integrated logistics providers has changed this notion. A thorough research report considers the merits of the company's distribution choices.

Suppliers and Raw Materials

The analyst's investigation into suppliers and raw materials is basically a search for weakness. A company with access to different suppliers is less of a risk than a firm that relies on one or two. If the production process involves just a few inputs, this dependency raises a red flag, particularly if the price of one of the inputs is volatile. A newspaper publisher, for example, buys huge amounts of newsprint, which has a wide price cycle. Publishing margins drop when newsprint prices jump dramatically, because ad rates and newsstand prices can't be increased enough to make up the difference.

COMPETITION

Competitive Environment

With competition covered by the industry study, a general treatment is unnecessary in the company section. An appropriate use of this section is to present a discussion of competitive tactics in the company's submarkets.

EXHIBIT 7–11. Company-Specific Analysis—Standard & Poor's Important Rating Factors for the Pulp and Paper Industry

Manufacturing
Cost Position

Low-cost status
  Operating margins
  Return on assets
  Mill margins
  Mill cash cost/ton
  Mill total cost/ton
  Man hours/ton

Modern efficient asset base
  Capital expenditures as a percent of net fixed assets over last 10 years
  Repair and maintenance expenditures as a percent of net fixed assets over last 10 years
  Ratio of capital expenditures to inflation-adjusted depreciation
  Are facilities "built-out" or is there room for additions?
  Are facilities integrated (on-site pulping)?
  Are machines new, in good running order?
  Mill site configuration and layout
  Process control and computer utilization

Mill location
  Closeness to growth markets
  Closeness to major metropolitan regions
  Closeness to deep seaports for export
  Freight advantages
  Harvest costs

Labor Relations
  Union vs. nonunion mills
  History of labor disruptions
  Advantageous wage rates and work-rule flexibility
  Union contract expiration schedules

Customer Satisfaction

Quality, service, customer loyalty
  Independent surveys

Evaluation by commercial printers and publishers, and customers

Product Mix
  Value-added vs. commodity grades
  Sales revenue per product ton
  Diversity of mix
  Breadth of products: full line or one-product supplier?
  Consumer vs. nonconsumer end markets
  Relative pricing sensitivity in key grades

Self-Sufficiency

Fiber self-sufficiency and long-term adequacy
  Fiber sources: internal sources vs. long-term private cutting contracts vs. government contracts vs. outside market purchases
  Fiber mix: softwood vs. hardwood vs. recycled paper
  Reforestation programs

Energy mix and self-sufficiency
  Fuel mix: internal sources vs. oil vs. coal vs. gas
  Cogeneration, hydropower
  Ability to quickly convert or change to alternative energy source

Marketing Prowess
  Gain or loss of market share
  Distribution channels
  Ratio of advertising cost to sales
  New product introductions
  Degree of influence on pricing

Forward integration
  Percent of in-house paper used by converting facilities
  Wholesale and retail distribution

When Southwest Airlines entered the East Coast market, research reports focused on the reactions of USAir and American Airlines. A review of the strengths and weaknesses of Southwest's tactics—and the probable outcomes—represented a large portion of these reports.

Anticipating competitive moves is helpful. For example, the market value of 3Com Corp fell $2 billion in February 1997 after Intel announced a move into the networking business.

Comparative Analysis of Competition

Because companies do not operate in vacuums, their operating performance—sales growth, profit margin, asset turnover, and so on—is judged in comparison with similar firms. At some point in a research report, a practitioner includes side-by-side statistical tables summarizing these comparisons. A 1996 review of five telephone companies appears in Exhibit 7–12.

From data such as that shown in Exhibit 7–12, the analyst reaches conclusions on the comparative ability of the subject company in financial and operating performance. For example, Ameritech has the best ranking in investment per line and lines per employee. Inevitably, such relative measures impact the valuations of the underlying equities, as discussed in later chapters.

OTHER TOPICS INCLUDED IN THE BUSINESS REVIEW

Research and Development

As pointed out in the Corporate Strategy section, earlier in this chapter, corporate growth relies on a steady stream of product extensions and innovations. Some new products are obtained through acquisitions, but the lion's share of innovation is realized through internal research and development.

EXHIBIT 7–12. Comparative Analysis—1996

	Financial Results		Operating Data		
	Sales Growth (%)	Profit Margin (%)	Fixed Asset Turnover	Investment per Line	Lines per Employee
Ameritech	11.0	14.1	1.1×	$713	351
Bell Atlantic	(2.3)	14.3	0.8×	803	333
Bell South	5.1	13.2	0.9	998	308
NYNEX	0.1	11.2	0.8	995	274
Pacific Telesis	5.0	11.7	0.8	724	322

Note. NYNEX scores lower than its peers with these statistics.

The amount of effort devoted to R&D is situational. Hi-tech companies like Amdahl and Applied Magnetics deserve more attention than low-tech businesses such as Bassett Furniture and Detroit Diesel.

R&D trends explain a company's emphasis on developing new revenue sources (although R&D is also used for cost-saving ideas). A rapid decline in R&D expense may signify the firm is robbing future growth to prop up current earnings.

Foreign Sales and Earnings

Public companies report sales and earnings on a consolidated basis. Foreign sales and earnings are not segregated in the financial statements, but relevant information appears in the footnotes. The analyst provides a service to the reader by publishing details on foreign operations.

Foreign sales fall into two categories: (1) exports, and (2) local operations. Exports represent products and services created in the United States and sold abroad. Sales proceeds arrive in the United States and are denominated in dollars. A local operation, in contrast, has its infrastructure in a foreign country, including inventory, accounts receivable, and plant and equipment. To illustrate, Colgate-Palmolive's subsidiary in Brazil is a self-contained business. Its local assets and related sales are denominated in reals, and then translated into U.S. dollars for financial statement consolidation.

A foreign presence is considered a healthy sign. It demonstrates an outward looking company with a global sophistication. Furthermore, in many industries, foreign markets are growing faster than the U.S. market, so an international presence is another vehicle for increasing sales. McDonald's, the quintessential American company, now derives more growth overseas than in the United States. The problem with foreign earnings is the lower degree of certainty compared with domestic income, leading investors to place a reduced value on companies with a heavy reliance on foreign activities.

This "foreign discount" arises from several factors. First, the information on foreign markets is less forthcoming than the U.S. counterpart. The analyst hedges because he has fewer facts from which to draw conclusions, both on exports and local sales. Second, many of the related economies experience volatile swings, heightening the uncertainty of operating results. Third, foreign assets expose the subject firm to exchange rate fluctuations, which have a negative impact when the local currency devalues against the U.S. dollar. Finally, outside the 15 to 20 most developed countries, U.S. foreign subsidiaries run substantial political risks. Local government policies on taxes, tariffs, and worker benefits, for example, can turn on a dime when new administrations assume power. In severe circumstances, the local authorities prohibit the subsidiary from exchanging local currency into dollars and cash dividends to the U.S. parent cease.

AES Corp., an independent power producer, historically built its generating facilities in the United States. In recent years, it has expanded into

Pakistan, Brazil, China, Kazakhstan, and Hungary. Over time, Wall Street analysts have shifted their risk assessment of AES stock accordingly.

Government Regulation

Although government influence is covered in the industry study, some businesses have unique aspects that involve specific government oversights. For example, Long Island Lighting's Shoreham nuclear-powered electric generation facility was declared operational by the federal government, but state authorities blocked its start-up. Eventually, LILCO had to write off the $5 billion investment.

Personnel

A typical corporate executive talks about employees being "his firm's greatest resource," but security analysts downplay the "people" side of the value equation. Often, this is done for good reason. Despite their talk of "valued employees," most firms have high annual turnover rates; 20 to 25 percent is not uncommon. And Wall Street applauds downsizing, despite the outward flow of experience and knowledge.

In the research report, the personnel section discloses the number of employees and the proportion in hourly, commission, or salaried jobs. It may include the percentage of employees represented by a union. Wall Street figures a low union percentage is good and a high percentage is bad. A description of recent work stoppages is appropriate here.

For certain companies, the compensation system merits discussion. A novel employee ownership plan, profit-sharing system, or bonus scheme represents a competitive edge. Likewise, if the corporate culture is unusual, it is pointed out in this section. For example, in *The Microsoft Way*, Randall Stross, a business professor, concludes, "The deliberate way in which (Chairman Bill) Gates has fashioned an organization that prizes smart people is the single most important, and most deliberately overlooked, aspect of Microsoft's success."

Properties

The properties section is relevant for industries that maintain a large asset base relative to sales and earnings. Dozens of firms require this category, including utilities (phone, electricity, gas), petrochemicals, building materials, and autos. Because the company's plant and equipment are vital to its progress, the section reviews the age and efficiency of existing plant, the state of production technology, and the annual cost of maintenance. The emphasis on fixed assets of the pulp and paper industry shown in Exhibit 7–11, exemplifies this attitude. From a financial point of view, the practitioner considers the adequacy of historical maintenance expenses and annual depreciation charges. Are these costs large enough to support the production base? Field visits by the analyst are useful in answering this question.

For companies with a real estate or natural resources bent, the properties section is renamed "income earning assets" or "reserves." It then takes a front and center position. With such businesses, the cultivation and harvesting of the physical asset is the primary contributor to income. Oil companies pump oil out of the ground, real estate firms lease buildings, and so on.

Again, there's nothing wrong with the analyst doing some personal "tire kicking" to make sure the properties reflect balance sheet values. If possible, a field visit should be conducted *without* management's assistance to develop a true picture. Even the pros get tripped up in their due diligent efforts; as evidenced by Donaldson, Lufkin & Jenrette's legal complaint against a major investment banking client whose deal collapsed: ". . . (the client) sought to deceive DLJ representatives during physical inspection of the properties by sending fake work crews to the properties prior to such inspection, thereby creating the illusion that monies were being spent to properly maintain and repair the properties." Jacqueline Doherty, a skilled reporter at *Barron's*, which publicized the story, compared DLJ's due diligence to a trip to a Potemkin village.

Management

In evaluating management, the analyst must answer the following question: *Can the executives do what they say they're going to do?*

The management of a public company speaks in optimistic platitudes: "We're going to grow this company," "Sales and earnings should improve over last year," "This management team is turning the company around!" Yet talk is cheap and poor investment choices are expensive. For this reason, practitioners are keen to know personally the top managers of the companies they cover. They need to know how these executives distill information, how they anticipate strategic moves, and how they implement decisions. While the grading of a manager is subjective—given the complex operating environment of most businesses—experienced industry watchers can separate the wheat from the chaff. Over time, an analyst learns to distinguish between executives with realistic agendas versus those with wishful approaches.

Management teams earn credibility with the investor community, and analysts compare one management group versus another. Sometimes the choice appears easy. For example, most investors would select Lou Gerstner (IBM, American Express) over Donald Trump (Trump Hotels & Casinos) for the CEO post of a large business. Jack Welch of General Electric would be preferable to Carl Icahn of TWA. At times, the Street takes these differences to extreme lengths. On the day Al "Chainsaw" Dunlop was appointed Sunbeam's new CEO, the company's market value rose $800 million (Dunlop was instrumental in enhancing Scott Paper's shareholder returns).

Management depth is important. A large, established company like Sara Lee could lose its top 10 managers, and I suspect it would keep operating like a well-oiled machine. Meanwhile, a company dominated by one person, such as Rupert Murdoch at News Corp., would suffer repercussions if the executive left suddenly.

The small company often has a thin management team. Such firms have several other risks related to size. Almost by definition, a small firm lacks customer, product, and market diversification. In addition, because optimal financing cost is achieved through size, smaller companies suffer from financing handicaps vis-à-vis their larger competitors.

Many small to medium-size companies are family controlled. Since family succession can be a higher priority than professional management at these concerns, family control is a negative for outside shareholders. Furthermore, "keeping the business in the family" stifles a firm's growth potential, as the equity financing needed for new projects is rejected due to family worries over ownership dilution.

The analyst makes judgments about management's integrity. Selfdealing, lavish perks, and huge cash salaries are not evidence of a management whose interests are aligned with those of the shareholders. For investors, prior legal problems of executives are a tip-off in the integrity area.

Occasionally, the composition of the board of directors is reviewed in the management section. For most companies, the board is not worth mentioning because the average director has so little input into the business. The primary qualification of the director is being one of the CEO's golfing buddies, and the chief responsibility is rubber-stamping his initiatives. However, board evaluation plays a role in investment selection in two situations: (1) a speculative stock; and (2) a distressed company. In the first instance, a prominent director lends a patina of respectability to the stock, giving the analyst another reason to lend his own confidence. In the distressed company, the directors play a true watchdog role. In some instances, they fire the CEO and bring in a replacement. Experienced and independent directors are an obvious asset to a troubled business.

SUMMARY

The proper evaluation of a corporate investment requires a thorough assessment of the business fundamentals, and conventional security analysis provides a methodical, step-by-step framework promoting this objective. For each principal aspect of the company's operations, the practitioner gathers data, furnishes a description, and forms a judgment about the company's sustained competitive advantage (SCA). The basis for industry success helps determine which factors are emphasized for a particular company.

For any given company, one or more factors can hold special significance, even if that factor is not common to the industry. For example, a strong market share in a specific geographic hub is a huge asset in the airline industry. In other sectors, such as paper and pulp, below-average production costs at one or two facilities can spell the difference between superior profitability and mediocre results. Reliance on one product is fine when product demand is hot, but the business needs a replacement pipeline for the inevitable cooling-off period. Similarly, a focus on one customer is a vulnerability since relationships can change through no fault of the company.

While many segments of the business review have a subjective element, the evaluation of strategy and management is particularly judgmental. Business environments constantly change and companies continually adjust tactics, yet the analyst is asked to opine on the strategy's general effectiveness over time. Assessing management talent is also difficult. When an executive's track record is identifiable, the analyst must decide if the results were attributable to the manager's skills. Strong subordinates, competitors' mistakes, and plain luck play a large role in an executive's success. To the extent possible, the practitioner's opinion of management reflects reality, rather than wishful thinking.

The business review is a tool for understanding the company and identifying its operational strengths and weaknesses. From the review's multiple parts, we form a composite picture of the firm's prospects and loosely categorize its business as pioneer, growth, mature, or declining. Many sections are grounded in historical fact, but the analysis also relies on judgment as the practitioner gauges those forces that will guide future sales and earnings. Combined with the industry study, the business review provides the analyst (and his audience) with the proper foundation from which to begin the financial analysis.

QUESTIONS AND SHORT PROBLEMS

1. An SEC prospectus regarding a corporate issuer will cover many of the same topics as the analyst's research reports. What is the principal difference in approach between the two documents?

2. The systematic approach outlined in Exhibit 7–3 is widely accepted in the investment industry. Why? Circle all that apply:
   a. It ensures that valuation is closely tied to a business' prospects.
   b. It forces the analyst to study all factors influencing a company's competitive advantage.
   c. It requires a "comparative company" analysis to include equity pricing as well as financial forecasts.
   d. All of the above.

3. In your opinion, which of the following firms has the competitive advantage with the longest life? Why?
   a. Amazon.com.
   b. Ford Motor Company.
   c. Anheuser Busch.
   d. The Limited.

4. You are evaluating the sales growth prospects of Foodwell, Inc., a food retailer. When Foodwell opens a new store, the store starts off with sales of $2 million in the first year, followed by annual sales of $3 million, $5 million, and $5 million thereafter. All of the company's 22 stores are more than four years old, and its expansion plan appears below. Inflation is nil. What is the sales forecast for the third year?

	Year			
	0	**1**	**2**	**3**
Existing sales (in millions)	$132	?	?	?
Number of new stores	0	4	6	5
New store sales (in millions)	0	?	?	?
Total sales	$132	?	?	?

5. How does a holding company with multiple industry segments, such as General Electric, operate under the portfolio approach?

6. A holding company owns three businesses:
   a. A prominent auto parts business with steady growth;
   b. A small property and casualty insurer with cyclical performance; and
   c. A young Internet service provider.

   If the holding company utilizes the BCG growth/share matrix, which business is likely the cash cow providing funds to another division? Which division receives the cash?

7. For a gasoline station operator such as Exxon, which *one* of the following four areas of marketing strategy is likely most important?
   a. Pricing.
   b. Service.
   c. Geographic coverage.
   d. Return policy.

8. Companies should try to achieve a diversified list of customers, with no one customer representing more than 10 percent of sales. Why?

9. Which company has higher advertising expenses as a percentage of sales—Revlon or your local gas utility? Why?

10. A jewelry wholesaler closely follows the price of two commodities because price changes affect the wholesaler's bottom line. What are these two commodities likely to be?

11. If Microsoft decided to go into the theme park business, how might investors react to Walt Disney stock?

12. Operating statistics for four electric power generating firms are:

| Company | Financial Results | | Operating Data | |
	Sales Growth (%)	Profit Margin (%)	Fuel Efficiency (%)	Capacity Utilization (%)
CL Power	6	14	62	72
COCO Power	8	12	57	69
Powertek	10	13	64	72
YT Power	7	16	55	70

On a relative basis, which company should be ranked the highest?

13. What contributes to the lower P/E ratios given to some U.S. companies with a heavy foreign exposure? Circle all that apply:
   a. Foreign economies are often more volatile than the U.S. economy.
   b. Risk of foreign currency devaluing against US$.
   c. Unions are stronger outside of the United States.
   d. Foreign governments might expropriate U.S.-owned facilities.
   e. Foreign accounts of U.S. firms are difficult to audit.

14. Why is the evaluation of management more crucial at a small firm than a big company, such as IBM?

15. How did Donaldson Lufkin & Jenrette get fooled during a client due diligence visit?

Adopt-a-Company

A. Classify your company in its business life cycle phase.

B. Is your company a cyclical business?

C. What's the perceived length of your company's franchise value?

D. List principal new products of the company. What are the major vehicles for new sales?

E. List the principal competitors. Provide a brief comparison of financial results. Include sales and net income growth, profit margin, asset turnover and debt/equity ratio.

F. Is your company dependent on a few customers?

G. What's the percentage of sales represented by foreign operations?

8

Financial Statement Analysis of an Established Business

With the business knowledge gained from the company-specific review, the practitioner is ready to commence a financial statement analysis. This chapter discusses the mechanics of real-life financial statements, and provides numerous examples. Ratios and "comparable company" statistics are used in the estimate of a firm's base earnings power.

For the sophisticated investor, the stock selection process involves a large component of expectations. This investor is usually a student of the "intrinsic value" and the "relative value" schools, which incorporate projections routinely into stock evaluations. To form a reasonable basis for predicting corporate performance, the investor must understand the company's historical financial results. The business review set forth in Chapter 7, enables the practitioner to connect product innovations, competitive struggles, and other qualitative items to sales and earnings movements. As the numerical complement to this review, the financial analysis provides a statistical summary of the past—by reducing it to the common denominator of all profit-seeking enterprises—dollars and cents. (We are now covering Section 5 of the Model Research Report [Exhibit 8–1].)

As another reminder, a substantial minority of investors place minimal emphasis on corporate business and financial analysis. They adhere to the technical, the momentum, and the market anticipation approaches to equity valuation. Included in their ranks from time to time are market timers, sector rotators, and macro finance managers.

EXHIBIT 8–1. Model Research Report

1. Introduction
2. Macroeconomic Review
3. Relevant Stock Market Prospects
4. Review of the Company and Its Business
5. Financial Analysis✓
6. Financial Projections
7. Application of Valuation Methodologies
8. Recommendation

A LOST ART

To a large extent, financial statement analysis is a lost art. Few business schools stress the topic, and MBA students who major in finance graduate with only a rudimentary knowledge of accounting, the nuts and bolts of financial statement analysis. Meanwhile, Wall Street and the institutional community deemphasize a careful study of prior financial results. Research departments are preoccupied with predicting future earnings and they don't take time to scrutinize past accounting data. As a result, investors are routinely "burned" by highly touted companies whose executives use ill-advised accounting policies or simply cook the books.

An example of the former was America Online (AOL), the Internet provider whose stock melted down in 1996, diving from $73 to $25 in six short months. The coup d'grâce was delivered on November 13, when the company took a $350 million charge, and three years of earnings disappeared into thin air. AOL decided to expense the marketing costs needed to attract new customers, rather than continuing to capitalize these costs and depreciate them over time similar to plant and equipment.

BEGINNING THE INVESTIGATION

The financial statement analysis is the beginning of an investigation, and I liken it to detective work. Why did sales go up? or down? Why did profit margins change? Is there a reason for the increase in the inventory-to-sales ratio? The answers to these questions are put to practical use when the analyst prepares the financial projections.

A financial statement analysis of a company begins with the assumption that the statements are not misleading or fraudulent. The risk of material misstatement is small if the statements are audited by a certified public accounting firm—a requirement for publicly traded firms. Even under the supervision of certified public accountants (CPAs), however, firms have flexibility in their use of accounting methods, which may, at times, promote

EXHIBIT 8-2. Holland Corp. (US$ millions)

| | Year Ended December 31 | | | |
| | Actual | | | Projected |
	1997	1998	1999	2000
Sales	$362	$374	$381	$390
Net income[1]	19	21	20	20

[1] Adjusted to eliminate unusual items.

earnings inflation. By permitting liberal techniques when the conservative approach is justified, CPAs risk exaggerations in audited data.

Even though they police fraudulent reporting, CPAs are occasionally fooled by crafty clients. Indeed, the stock market is replete with investors suffering the effects of inaccurate financial statements certified by accountants unable to detect faulty ledgers. The best protection against this problem is a thorough study of the company's financial trends and accounting policies, which can provide evidence of problems. Details on accounting policy are left out of the footnotes to the financial statements, so this research involves telephone calls to the firm's finance department and investor relations personnel.

Having accepted the possibility of inaccurate financial data, the analyst studying the historical statements aims at preparing an estimate of current earnings power. This estimate is used as the platform for future earnings projections. For example, suppose the analyst concludes that Holland Corp. earned $20 million per year in each of the preceding three years, after stripping out all extraordinary items and asset sales during the period. If the business review presented nothing unusual, and all factors were equal, he'd have a logical basis for assuming that $20 million is a reasonable earnings objective in *2000*, as indicated in Exhibit 8-2.

Basing earnings forecasts solely on past performance is akin to driving your car by looking in the rearview mirror. Many investors fall into this trap and pay dearly for their mistake, but a total separation of the future from the past is illogical. Most businesses have a number of fairly stable elements that are readily predictable, so the present and immediate past are good first steps in departing for the future.

THE RAW MATERIALS OF AN ANALYSIS

What are the raw materials from which a historical financial analysis is created? Start with the three financial statements and the attached footnotes:

1. The Income Statement.
2. The Balance Sheet.

3. Statement of Cash Flows.

4. Notes to Financial Statement.

The data from these statements provide a wealth of information for discerning certain trends and patterns. The four primary tools for evaluating corporate performance are:

1. Absolute amount changes.

2. Percentage changes in growth.

3. Common size percentage statements.

4. Financial ratios.

These tools are applied over a three- to five-year period, since interyear comparisons are the best means of facilitating the discovery of trends, patterns, or anomalies. But, be forewarned. This sort of analysis is a lot of work. Exhibit 8–3 shows that if you apply the preceding four analytical tools to each of the three financial statements for a one-year period, you have 12 snapshots of the company's finances for that year. This means plenty of number crunching.

Luckily, the advances of technology reduce the effort involved in preparing raw data. Off-the-shelf analysis software packages assist in the process, or the practitioner can customize an analytical program with Lotus or similar products.

EVOLUTION OF THE APPROACH TO FINANCIAL STATEMENTS

Most analysts begin with the income statement because it provides the best indicator of profitability. Generating profits is the key to a firm's survival, enabling it to attract the resources, client base, and management talent needed to prosper.

In the early days, the balance sheet, rather than the income statement, was the focus of the security analysts. Remembering the Great Crash, they brought a defensive posture to stock selection. Serious investors avoided

EXHIBIT 8–3. Financial Statement Analysis—Matrix of Accounting Data and Analytical Tools

	Absolute Amounts	Percentage Changes	Common Size	Ratios
Income Statement	1	2	3	4
Balance Sheet	5	6	7	8
Source and Uses of Funds	9	10	11	12

EXHIBIT 8–4. Modern Security Analysis

Deemphasizing the Balance Sheet

Inflation. Years of inflation upset the relationship between the historical accounting value and the respective market value of tangible assets. The "depreciation" account is misleading in many financial statements.

Technology. The rise in technology firms, whose businesses are reliant on intellectual capital, has undercut balance sheet based valuations in the 1990s.

Mergers and Acquisitions. Most acquisition prices exceed book value, giving the buyers large goodwill accounts. If operating earnings continue to grow, economic goodwill increases in value, rendering the noncash amortization expenses meaningless.

Intangible Recognition. Savvy investors accept the notion that intangible assets are no less valuable than tangible ones.

shares at prices in excess of book value. They were cautious about leverage and looked closely at the number of times assets covered liabilities. Since the 1960s, the balance sheet landscape has changed entirely (see Exhibit 8–4). Years of inflation, rapid changes in technology, a huge jump in mergers and acquisitions, and an increased recognition of the value of intangible assets have diminished the interpretive worth of accounting-based balance sheet data, which focuses heavily on tangible assets such as accounts receivables, inventory, and plant and equipment. Nowadays, the stock market places high values on intangible as well as tangible values, as long as they generate income. For example, the Dow Jones Industrials traded at 6× book value at May 1999.

Consider the following. An intangible license to operate a cellular phone system can have the same value as the millions of copper pipes, telephone poles, and switching stations owned by a hard-line phone company. A famous brand name such as Chanel No. 5 can have more value than all the manufacturing facilities used to make the product. As a result, balance sheet analysis in the 1990s tends to focus on liquidity and leverage concerns. When are debts coming due? What has been the behavior of the current accounts and their effect on cash flow?

Free cash flow is seen by some analysts as a better measurement of corporate performance than reported earnings in certain industries and high-leverage situations. Although there is usually a strong relationship between profitability and cash flow, many accounting entries affect one and not the other. Thus, an analysis of the statement of cash flows can reveal a level of corporate performance that is either stronger or weaker than might be apparent from earnings. Indeed, some valuation consultants tell investors to forget earnings per share entirely—use price/cash flow ratios instead of price/earnings data. And importantly, large lenders show an eagerness to loan against cash flow rather than just hard assets.

The statement of cash flows is a helpful summary of where the company's cash is going, and it indicates how much cash investment is needed to produce new sales and earnings. Furthermore, along with the income statement, it provides insights into the firm's debt-carrying capacity through the calculation of debt service coverage ratios.

ILLUSTRATION OF THE BASIC APPROACH

As an illustration of the recommended approach to financial analysis, consider Payless Cashways, Inc.'s, results for the three years ended November 30, 1987. Payless was a full-line building materials specialty retailer serving the home improvement, maintenance, and repair market. As of November 1987, the Kansas City-based company operated 193 stores in 26 states. Sales for fiscal year 1987 totaled just under $1.8 billion. It is a useful case study because management published projections in 1988 that we

EXHIBIT 8–5. Payless Cashways, Inc.—Summary Financial Data (in millions)

	Fiscal Year Ended November 30		
	1985	**1986**	**1987**
Income Statement Data			
Net sales	$1390	$1528	$1770
Cost of goods sold	972	1059	1251
Selling, general, and administrative expense	307	343	390
Depreciation	25	29	36
Special charges[1]	—	—	24
Earnings before interest and taxes	86	97	69
Interest on debt	18	15	17
Earnings before taxes	68	82	52
Provision for income taxes	30	40	24
Net income	$38	$42	$28
Earnings per share	$1.12	$1.22	$0.81

[1] To reflect expenses associated with store closings, interest rate swap termination, and transfer of private-label credit card operation.

Balance Sheet Data			
Working capital	$128	$132	$123
Total assets	606	708	813
Long-term debt, less current maturities	120	132	180
Shareholders' equity	333	370	379

Note. Sales were increasing, but earnings were uneven. Balance sheet results were stable.

will compare with actual results. Summary income statement and balance sheet data are shown in Exhibit 8–5.

A cursory glance at this information enables the reader to reach the following conclusions: (1) Payless was profitable and growing; (2) its principal expense was cost of goods sold, which is expected for a retailer that resells products made by others; (3) the company was conservatively leveraged; and (4) 1987's earnings before interest and taxes (EBIT) was reduced sharply by special charges totaling $24 million. This item needs to be considered before proceeding. Management was characterizing the multiple store closings, the interest rate swap termination, and the transfer of private credit card operation as "one-time" items, which would not be repeated. That's why the related costs were designated as "Special Charges" and footnoted in Exhibit 8–6. A review of Payless Cashway's results over the preceding five years indicates that these events were aberrations. Thus, from an analyst's viewpoint in 1988, these developments obscured the normal earnings power of Payless and so should not have adversely affected earnings in future years. In keeping with this interpretation of the facts, our analysis of the Company's "earnings power" eliminates 1987's $24 million of Special Charges, so as to normalize 1987's data. As a result, Payless's normalized EBIT exhibited a consistent trend over the three-year period.

Having modified the data to reflect an improved perception of future potential, the analyst proceeds to the next step, which is a review of the changes in each item expressed of absolute dollar amounts. Most practitioners

EXHIBIT 8–6. Payless Cashways, Inc.—Normalized Income Statement Data (in millions)

	Fiscal Year Ended November 30		
	1985	1986	1987
Original EBIT	$86	$97	$69
Add back: Special charges	—	—	24
Normalized EBIT	86	97	93
Interest on debt	18	15	17
Normalized earnings before taxes	68	82	76
Provision for income taxes	30	40	35[1]
Normalized net income	$38	$42	$41[2]
Normalized earnings per share	$1.12	$1.22	$1.19[2]

[1] Income taxes are assumed to increase proportionally to the higher normalized earnings before taxes (EBIT).

[2] Normalized data shows that the earnings decrease is not so drastic as indicated earlier.

"eyeball" such changes, rather than make the calculations, which appear in the next exhibit.

Absolute Amount Analysis

The big jump in 1987 sales (+242) arose from the acquisition of a 10-store chain, whose results were fully included in the year. Operating income (EBIT) declined slightly in 1987 as expenses were slightly higher than the gain in sales. The large additions to total assets in each year (+52, +102, and +105) illustrated the incremental asset base needed to support sales growth (see Exhibit 8–7).

Percentage Changes

Security analysts make extensive use of year-to-year percentage changes in financial results. As discussed earlier, percentage growth statistics in net income and dividends are key drivers in establishing stock prices. The analyst's ability to predict earnings with confidence is heavily influenced by

EXHIBIT 8–7. Payless Cashways, Inc.—Normalized Financial Data—Absolute Amount Changes (in millions)

	Fiscal Year Ended November 30		
	1985	1986	1987
Income Statement Data			
Net sales	+214	+138	+242
Cost of goods sold	+145	+87	+192
Selling, general, and administrative expense	+55	+36	+47
Depreciation	+8	+4	+7
Earnings before interest and taxes	+7	+11	−4
Interest on debt	+6	−3	+2
Earnings before taxes	+1	+14	−6
Provision for income taxes	—	+10	−5
Net income	+1	+4	−1
Earnings per share	+.03	+.11	−.03
Balance Sheet Data			
Working capital	−9	+4	−9
Total assets	+52	+102	+105
Long-term debt, less current maturities	−41	+12	+48
Shareholders' equity	+76	+37	+9

Note. The gains in sales didn't translate into higher earnings. Total assets steadily increased.

EXHIBIT 8–8. Payless Cashways, Inc.—Normalized Financial Data—
Percentage Changes

	Fiscal Year Ended November 30		
	1985	1986	1987
Income Statement Data			
Net sales	+18%	+10%	+16%
Cost of goods sold	+18	+9	+18
Selling, general, and administrative expense	+22	+12	+14
Depreciation	+47	+16	+24
Earnings before interest and taxes	+8	+13	−4
Interest on debt	+46	−17	+13
Earnings before taxes	+1	+21	−7
Provision for income taxes	−1	+33	−12
Net income	+3%	+11%	−2%
Earnings per share	−3%	+9%	+7%
Balance Sheet Data			
Working capital	−8%	+3%	−7%
Total assets	+9	+17	+15
Long-term debt, less current maturities	−26	+10	+36
Shareholders' equity	+30	+11	+2

his ability to determine relationships between sales, expenses, and the investment required to sustain growth. Financial statements expressed in terms of percentage changes are helpful in making these determinations. The related information for Payless Cashways appears in Exhibit 8–8.

Considering that inflation was 5 percent annually over the 1985–1987 period, Payless appears to be a growth company since it recorded annual sales changes of 18, 10, and 16 percent. EBIT and net income increases were less consistent, however, and EPS advances failed to keep pace with the sales gains. The data shows that the growth in several expense categories exceeded the growth in sales. This suggests that obtaining new sales dollars was an expensive proposition and raises a red flag regarding the company's expansion strategy.

Common Size Analysis

A popular tool in financial analysis is the common size statement. In this presentation, income statement and balance sheet items are expressed as a percentage of sales and total assets, respectively. Since accounting results are reduced to percentages of the same line item, the data arranged in this

EXHIBIT 8–9. Payless Cashways, Inc.—Normalized Common Size Data

	Fiscal Year Ended November 30		
	1985	**1986**	**1987**
Income Statement Data			
Net sales	100.0%	100.0%	100.0%
Cost of goods sold	69.9	69.2	70.7
Selling, general, and administrative expense	22.1	22.4	22.0
Depreciation	1.8	1.9	2.0
Earnings before interest and taxes	6.2	6.5	5.3
Interest on debt	1.3	1.0	1.0
Earnings before taxes	4.9	5.3	4.3
Provision for income taxes	2.2	2.6	2.0
Net income	2.7%	2.8%	2.3%
Earnings per share	—	—	—
Balance Sheet Data			
Working capital	21.1%	18.6%	15.1%
Total assets	100.0	100.0	100.0
Long-term debt, less current maturities	19.8	18.6	22.1
Shareholders' equity	55.0	52.3	46.6

Note. A higher cost of goods sold decreased 1987 earnings; equity declined as a percentage of assets.

way is referred to as "common size." Information for Payless Cashways appears in Exhibit 8–9.

The common size data facilitate comparisons of operating results between years. The exhibit shows that profitability declined as a percentage of sales. EBIT decreased from 6.2 percent to 5.3 percent while net income dropped from 2.7 percent to 2.3 percent. A primary contributor to the decrease was cost of goods sold, which rose from 69.9 percent to 70.7 percent. Other income statement items were stable. The balance sheet data indicates a decline in liquidity and an increase in leverage. Working capital, as a percentage of assets, shrank from 21.1 percent to 15.1 percent, and equity decreased to 46.6 percent from 55.0 percent.

Statements of Cash Flows

The statement of cash flows is a blueprint for seeing how cash is generated and where it goes. Because it has no common size items like "net sales" or "total assets," the statement of cash flows is interpreted with different techniques than the income statement and balance sheet. Furthermore, a number of the accounts have no true baseline from which to measure year-to-year changes. As a result, it confirms (or denies) opinions reached through the analysis of the first two statements.

The statement is divided into three sections:

1. *Cash Flows from Operating Activities.* This section summarizes the net cash generated from selling the firm's product or service, including the effects of changes in working capital needed to support the business.

2. *Cash Flows from Investing Activities.* This reviews the new investment in (or disposition of) fixed assets and acquisitions.

3. *Cash Flows from Financing Activities.* The finance function is separated from the day-to-day operations of the business. This section indicates the methods by which the business is funded, or in certain cases, how excess funds are utilized. For Payless Cashways, the statement of cash flows (Exhibit 8–10) illustrates that the company is a net user of outside financing. Funds from operations do not cover the requisite capital expenditures.

A negative cash flow is not an automatic danger signal. In the 1985 to 1987 time frame, Payless sales grew and it made investments in new stores and an acquisition (while inventory increases stayed in line). Many growing companies exhibit thin or negative cash flow because investment is needed to support growth. Alternatively, mature and declining companies may have positive cash flow, but the analyst must weigh whether this situation is sustainable in the face of competitive threats. In either case, the additional investment in the business should produce an acceptable rate of return. For the $265 million that Payless invested in its business over the three-year period, sales rose only 27 percent and net income (normalized) remained flat—clearly a cause for concern.

Practitioners promote the use of "free cash flow" (FCF) measures that, depending on the methodology, integrate items from the funds from operations, investment activities, and financing sections. These measures are of best use in three- to five-year moving-average computations. Over a one- or two-year period, large differences in working capital accounts, major investments, and specific financings diminish the usefulness of FCF, as demonstrated by the variation in Payless's cash flow data.

EXHIBIT 8–10. Payless Cashways, Inc.—Summary Statement of Cash Flows (in millions)

	Fiscal Year Ended November 30		
	1985	**1986**	**1987**
Net cash provided by operations	$94	$71	$ 48
Net cash used in investing activities	(79)	(81)	(105)
	15	(10)	(57)
Net cash provided by financing	—	10	53
Net increase (decrease) in cash	$15	$ —	$ (4)

At a minimum, the cash flow analysis showed (1) Payless's growth required substantial investment, (2) working capital needs were under control, and (3) the company had the ability to finance its needs on a long-term basis (see Exhibit 8–11).

Ratio Analysis

Ratio analysis relates income statement, balance sheet, and cash flow statement items to one another. Like the other forms of analysis reviewed herein, ratio analysis provides clues in evaluating a firm's current position and in spotting trends toward future performance. Ratios fall into four broad categories:

1. *Profitability Ratios.* Measure return on assets and equity investments. Profit margins, expressed as a percentage of sales in the common size income statement, are defined as profitability ratios.

2. *Activity Ratios.* Measure the efficiency with which the firm manages its assets.

3. *Credit Ratios.* Measure the firm's ability to repay its obligations, its existing leverage situation, and its resultant financial risk.

4. *Growth Ratios.* Measure the firm's performance in expanding its business, a key criterion in valuation.

If one is familiar with the normal proportions that expenses bear to sales in a specific industry, that assets have to sales, and that assets bear to liabilities, it becomes evident through ratio analysis when normal relations go out of sync. The causes for disproportions or extreme variations in the subject company's ratios then become the focus of further study. John Myer, an accounting professor, described a four-step methodology 50 years ago that is still in use today:

Investigating Changes in a Financial Ratio

1. Compare subject company ratios with industry standards and historical norms.
2. Examine the ratio's past trend.
3. Analyze the performance of the components of the ratio.
4. Look at qualitative changes in the underlying business that impact the components.

For example, Exhibit 8–12 shows three firms that experienced a decrease in the ratio of sales to receivables, from 6.0× in 1996 to 5.0× in 1997. In each case, the ratio changed, but for different reasons.

Suppose the industry norm for the sales/receivables ratio is 5.5×. The analyst may be curious about the 6.0× ratio in 1996 for the three companies,

EXHIBIT 8–11. Payless Cashways, Inc.—Statement of Cash Flows (in millions)

	Fiscal Year Ended November 30		
	1985	1986	1987
Cash Flows from Operations			
Net income	$38	$42	$28
Adjustment to reconcile net income to net cash provided by operations:			
Depreciation	25	29	36
Special charges	—	—	24
Deferred taxes	5	—	(7)
Other, net	2	1	2
Net income plus noncash charges	70	72	83
Changes in current accounts, excluding acquisition/ divestitures:			
(Increase) in receivables	(1)	(1)	(4)
Decrease (increase) in inventory	14	(24)	(35)
Increase (decrease) in payables	(2)	24	(1)
Other, net	13	—	5
(1) Net cash provided by operations	94	71	48
Cash Flows from Investing Activities			
Investment in fixed assets (land, buildings, and equipment)	(84)	(62)	(110)
Sale of fixed assets	9	6	6
Other investments	(4)	(2)	(1)
Cash payment for acquisition	—	(23)	—
(2) Net cash used in investing activities	(79)	(81)	(105)
Cash Flows from Financing Activities			
Long-term borrowings	28	15	50
Repayment of long-term borrowings	(69)	(4)	(7)
Net short-term debt incurrence	4	5	36
Sale of common stock	43	—	—
Repurchase of common stock	—	—	(13)
Cash dividends on common stock	(5)	(5)	(5)
Other	(1)	(1)	(8)
(3) Net cash provided from financing activities	—	10	53
(1)+(2)+(3) = Net increase (decrease) in cash	15	—	(4)
Cash at beginning of year	—	15	15
Cash at end of year	$15	$15	$11

Note. Cash flow from operations was reinvested in the business, prompting a need for external financing.

EXHIBIT 8–12. Three Firms with a Decrease in Sales/Receivables Ratio (in millions, except for ratios and percentages)

	Sales	Receivables	Sales/Receivables
Growth Company			
1996	$600	$100	6.0×
1997	700	140	5.0×
1996 Index = 100%	100%	100%	
1997	117	140	
Mature Company			
1996	$600	$100	6.0×
1997	590	118	5.0×
1996 Index = 100%	100%	100%	
1997	98	118	
Declining Company			
1996	$600	$100	6.0×
1997	500	100	5.0×
1996 Index = 100%	100%	100%	
1997	83	100	

as well as the 1997 drop to 5.0×. That is Step 1: a quick comparison to standards. The next step is observing changes. Step 2 reveals the negative trend in the ratio from 1996 to 1997. Finally, in Step 3, the analyst figures out the statistical rationale for the changes:

Growth Company: There was a rise in both sales and receivables, but the receivables rose at a higher rate.

Mature Company: There was a decline in sales but a rise in receivables.

Decline Company: There was a decline in both sales and receivables, but sales declined faster.

The ratio analysis then passes to the business reasons behind the differences. By this time, both the industry analysis and company-specific review have outlined the causes for revenue changes—differences in unit volume and/or prices—and the qualificative elements contributing to sales movements. The cause for variations in receivables requires inquiry into two areas: (1) external factors such as the customers' ability to pay, or (2) internal factors such as changes in collection policy or more liberal credit terms. Answering these questions represents Step 4.

From this illustration, we see that ratio analysis is more than the compilation of statistics over historical periods. The computations provide evidence of the manner in which the business is administered, and significant variations to trends and the norm require study.

Payless Ratio Analysis

Exhibit 8–13 provides selected Payless ratios, segmented into the four categories: profitability, activity, credit, and growth.

A review of the financial ratios paints a picture of a company that was, at best, a mediocre performer. The EBIT/Assets ratio declined from 14 percent in 1985 to 11 percent in 1987. The net profit/stockholders' equity ratio was mired at 11 percent, far lower than the 15 to 20 percent expected by investors in publicly traded stocks. Indeed, "AA" corporate bonds yielded

EXHIBIT 8–13. Payless Cashways, Inc.—Selected Financial Ratios

| | Year Ended November 30 | | | |
	1985	1986	1987	Trend
Profitability Ratios				
$\dfrac{\text{Earnings before Interest and Taxes}}{\text{Total Assets}} =$	14%	14%	11%	Down
$\dfrac{\text{Net Profit}}{\text{Stockholders' Equity}} =$	11%	11%	11%	Stable
Activity Ratios				
$\text{Asset Turnover} = \dfrac{\text{Sales}}{\text{Assets}} =$	2.3×	2.2×	2.2×	Stable
$\text{Inventory Turnover} = \dfrac{\text{Sales}}{\text{Average Inventory}} =$	3.7×	4.0×	4.2×	Up
Credit Ratios				
$\text{Current Ratio} = \dfrac{\text{Current Assets}}{\text{Current Liabilities}} =$	2.0	1.7	1.5	Down
$\dfrac{\text{Long-Term Debt}}{\text{Stockholders' Equity}} =$	0.4	0.4	0.5	Stable
$\dfrac{\text{EBIT}}{\text{Interest}} =$	4.8×	6.5×	5.5×	Up

Growth Ratios
Five-year compound annual growth ratios, using normalized data, are set forth below:

	1982–1987	Trend
Sales	12.0%	Up
EBIT	2.3%	Up
Earnings before taxes	(0.1)%	Down
Net income	(0.2)%	Down
Earnings per share	(1.1)%	Down

Note. With the exception of earnings growth, ratio trends were primarily stable to up. The problem for Payless stock price was that investors placed the greatest weight on earnings growth.

9 percent at the time, indicating that these blue-chip investments provided a handsome return compared with Payless Cashway's business, which carried substantially more risk. The activity ratios indicated some progress in boosting inventory turnover, an important element of a retailing operation, but, at the same time, the credit ratios showed a deterioration of financial strength. The current ratio declined from 2.0 to 1.5 over the three-year period and the long term-to-equity ratio increased from 0.4 to 0.5. Perhaps the growth ratios demonstrated the real failure. Sales grew at a 12 percent compound annual rate, but Payless was unable to bring this growth to the bottom line. EBIT, net income, and earnings per share were flat over the 1982–1987 period. The ratio analysis does not provide a flattering portrait of Payless Cashways.

Management ascribed these negative developments to a weak economy in several geographic areas where the company had a concentration of stores. Consider the following quote from David Stanley, Chairman, in the 1987 Annual Report, "The farm economy, which has affected our performance for several years, showed modest signs of improvement. Of even greater importance to us, the oil patch economy appears to have bottomed out and may indeed be recovering." The final bit of optimism may have spurred hostile takeover inquiries. Prior to such interest the investing public was noncommittal, as the common stock price declined from 1982 to 1987.

Industry-Specific Indicators

In the preceding financial analysis, we reached a few tentative conclusions through standard ratios and the evaluation of financial data arranged in various ways, but it cannot be overemphasized that each situation is unique. Part of the art of analyzing corporate financial performance is selecting which data should be the focus of an investigation. Which ratios are meaningful? What trends are important? What are the best comparative indicators? How reliable are past results in predicting future performance? A sober consideration of these questions prior to the start of any detailed analysis represents a huge time saver for the analyst.

Notwithstanding the importance of financial statement analysis, the interpretation of a company's results extends past the information contained in audited data. Most companies record certain industry statistics that over time have proven to be useful performance indicators. The home-improvement retailing industry is no exception. Exhibit 8–14 lists selected industry-specific data calculated by Payless Cashways over the 1985–1987 time period.

Because retailers can increase sales easily by opening new stores, practitioners use a statistic that isolates the sales growth accruing from established properties from the sales resulting from new stores. This statistic is termed the growth in "same store" sales. An examination of this statistic

EXHIBIT 8–14. Industry-Specific Statistics for Payless Cashways, Inc.

	Fiscal Year Ended November 30		
	1985	1986	1987
Growth in "same store" sales	5.0%	4.4%	2.9%
Growth from acquisitions or new stores	13.2%	5.5%	13.0%
Sales per store (in millions)	$8.1	$8.8	$9.1
Sales per square foot of selling area	$301	$312	$324
Sales per employee (in thousands)	$105	$117	$117

shows the strength of a retailer's underlying growth, without the capital expense of new stores. For Payless Cashways over the 1985–1987 period, same-store sales growth was less than the inflation rate, auguring poor growth prospects for the firm's base business. Recognizing shareholder concerns, management responded to the low 2.9 percent same-store sales growth number in 1987 with the following commentary: "Sales for comparable stores (those open a year or more) increased 2.9 percent. Approximately one-third of our stores operate in the oil-affected states of Texas, Oklahoma, and Colorado. Comparable sales in stores outside of those states increased 7.8 percent."

Same-stores sales data enable an analyst to separate the sales growth from acquisitions. In the case of Payless, this separation was important because acquisitions provided the bulk of sales improvements. Sales efficiency—measured by sales per store, sales per square foot of selling area, and sales per employee—is also a monitor of performance. If inflationary effects are excluded from the data, Payless showed few positive advances.

Comparable Company Performance

Historical financial analysis of a company cannot be conducted in a vacuum. Statistics, ratios, and profit margins are not meaningful numbers in and of themselves; they must be compared with something before they become useful. Much depends on the industry involved. For example, a brokerage firm, with a preponderance of liquid assets, operates with a higher degree of leverage than a home improvement retailer, whose primary assets are real estate and merchandise inventories. Evaluated within the same industry grouping, however, single-company financial data take on new meaning, as the basis for comparisons and the facilitator of analytical conclusions. For this reason, the tools used to evaluate performance are compared with identical data for companies in the same industry. The business that is the object of study is then measured against its peer group. Has it done better or worse than the competition? Do its financial yardsticks meet industry averages? Are its results trending with the industry? The answers to these questions are useful in appraising the relative merits of a business.

In 1987, Payless Cashways had two major competitors whose financial results were publicly available: The Home Depot, Inc. and Lowe's Companies, Inc. A short description of each company follows:

- *The Home Depot, Inc.* Home Depot operated 75 retail warehouse stores that sold a wide variety of building supplies and home improvement products. Sales and net income for the fiscal year ending January 31, 1988, were $1.5 billion and $54 million, respectively.
- *Lowe's Companies, Inc.* Lowe's operated 295 retail stores selling building supplies and home improvement products. Sales and net income for the fiscal year ended January 31, 1988 were $2.4 billion and $61 million, respectively.

Payless's sales and net income for its fiscal year ended November 30, 1987, were $1.8 billion, and $41 million, respectively.

Because the three companies were not identical in size, comparable analyses were evaluated in the context of common size percentages and ratios. Common size data is a typical starting point in a comparative financial analysis, and set forth in Exhibit 8–15 is relevant information from the income statement and balance sheet.

EXHIBIT 8–15. Comparable Common Size Data—Normalized Financial Results

	Payless Cashways	Home Depot	Lowe's Companies
Income Statement Data			
Net sales	100.0%	100.0%	100.0%
Cost of goods sold	71.6	72.2	76.1
Selling, general, and administrative expense	22.0	20.3	17.4
Depreciation	2.0	0.7	1.6
Earnings before interest and taxes	5.3	6.7	4.9
Interest on debt	1.0	0.2	0.8
Earnings before taxes	4.3	6.5	4.1
Provision for income taxes	2.0	2.8	1.5
Net income	2.3%	3.7%	2.6%
Balance Sheet Data			
Working capital	15.1%	20.8%	31.2%
Total assets	100.0	100.0	100.0
Long-term debt, less current maturities	22.1	9.8	18.1
Shareholders' equity	46.6	60.6	56.7

Note. Payless's net margins were lower than the competition, and its balance sheet was more leveraged.

Referring to the income statement data, Payless ranked in the middle of its two competitors in terms of the EBIT/sales ratio. Cost of goods sold for Payless was the lowest at 71.6 percent, but the benefits of this number were overshadowed by the Company's relatively high SG&A expense. Bottom-line performance for Payless, as summarized in the net income/sales ratio, was the smallest of the group, owing to its relatively higher interest costs, a direct result of its increasing debt as shown in the earlier ratio analysis. Payless was more leveraged than its companion companies, both of which had lower working capital/assets and debt/assets ratios and commensurately higher equity/assets ratios.

Comparable ratio analysis indicates that Payless ranked third in financial performance (see Exhibit 8–16).

EXHIBIT 8–16. Comparable Financial Ratios—Normalized Data

	Payless Cashways	Home Depot	Lowe's Companies
Profitability Ratios			
$\dfrac{\text{Earnings before Interest and Taxes}}{\text{Total Assets}} =$	11%	19%	12%
$\dfrac{\text{Net Profit}}{\text{Stockholders' Equity}} =$	11%	10%	11%
Activity Ratios			
$\text{Asset Turnover} = \dfrac{\text{Sales}}{\text{Assets}} =$	2.2×	2.8×	2.4×
$\text{Inventory Turnover} = \dfrac{\text{Average Inventory}}{\text{Costs of Good Sold}} =$	4.2×	5.6×	5.0×
Credit Ratios			
$\text{Current Ratio} = \dfrac{\text{Current Assets}}{\text{Current Liabilities}} =$	1.5	1.7	2.4
$\dfrac{\text{Long-Term Debt}}{\text{Stockholders' Equity}} =$	0.5	0.2	0.3
$\dfrac{\text{EBIT}}{\text{Interest}} =$	5.5×	29.1×	6.2×
Selected Growth Statistics—Latest Five Years			
Sales	12.0%	54.3%	18.8%
EBIT	2.3	50.1	14.4
Earnings before taxes	(0.1)	49.9	16.2
Net income	(0.2)	51.7	19.8
Earnings per share	(1.1)%	41.7	15.8

Note. Payless is slightly below the competition in profitability, activity and credit ratios, and it is a woeful underperformer in the growth category.

EXHIBIT 8–17. Industry-Specific Statistics

	Latest Fiscal Year—1987		
	Payless Cashways	Home Depot	Lowe's Companies
Growth in "same store" sales	2.9%	18.0%	4.0%
Growth from acquisitions or new stores	13.0	36.3	3.0
Sales per store (in millions)	8.1	19.9	8.0
Sales per square foot of selling area	301	265	289

In virtually every ratio category, Payless was at the bottom of its peer group. Profitability and activity ratios were below the competition, and the credit ratios indicated a higher use of leverage. The five-year growth statistics were probably the most worrisome from the standpoint of an equity investor. EBIT growth for Payless stood at an anemic 2.3 percent, compared with the impressive statistics turned in by Home Depot, 50.1 percent, and Lowe's, 14.4 percent. Net income and EPS growth for Payless, correspondingly, were much lower than for the other two retailers.

The industry-specific data was less conclusive in pinpointing Payless as the underperformer. Summary data for the 1987 fiscal year appear in Exhibit 8–17.

Interpreting this data in a meaningful way required a knowledge of the workings of the do-it-yourself (DIY) retailing industry in 1987. Home Depot's stellar performance in "same store" growth was the result of a large proportion of its stores being relatively new compared with the competition. New stores have an accelerated ramp-up in sales during the first three or four years after start-up. By the fourth or fifth year of operation, the stores become mature and experience less frenetic growth. Home Depot was also in the middle of an extensive rollout of its warehouse store program, a concept that both Payless and Lowe's were attempting to copy. A Wall Street darling, Home Depot raised enormous sums to finance this rapid buildup, shown by the 36.3 percent growth in sales from new stores. The lower sales per store recorded by Payless and Lowe's indicated that they were operating smaller units relative to Home Depot.

REVIEW OF PAYLESS FINANCIAL ANALYSIS

Comparable analysis suffers from the fact that no two companies are totally homogeneous in their activities and characteristics. Another drawback lies in the different accounting practices used by companies in the same industry. Finally, past performance is only a guide to future success. Historical financial analysis is only the base from which financial projections and corporate valuations are determined, not the *end-all* for the practitioner.

The financial analysis for Payless Cashways reached the following conclusions:

- *Sales growth* was overly dependent on acquisitions, as many existing stores were located in economically depressed areas.
- *Earnings growth* was nonexistent.
- *Liquidity and credit ratios* were strong, but showed signs of deterioration.
- *Comparable analysis* placed Payless behind two key competitors.

The evidence indicated that Payless was not an outstanding performer. Reflecting this fact, its stock price languished in early 1988 at $11 per share. At this price, the shares traded at only 9.2× normalized earnings and 1.0× book value. Compare these multiples with Home Depot's 16.8× and 2.6×, and Lowe's 10.9× and 1.3×.

MANAGEMENT'S PROJECTIONS

As an example of the interplay between historical analysis and projections, we examine projections furnished by Payless management after a leveraged buyout completed in 1988. Post-buyout, the "new" Payless Cashways had a debt-to-equity ratio of 10:1, demonstrating lenders' willingness to loan against intangible assets and future cash flow. A key element of the $1.1 billion debt financing was a $335 million junk bond issue. In a prospectus furnished to bond investors, Payless provided financial forecasts prepared "to the best of management's knowledge and belief" (see Exhibit 8–18). The forecasts exemplify the optimism found in the vast majority of Wall Street projections: sales continually go up, operating profit margins increase, and working capital needs shrink relative to sales volume. Neither recession nor a new competitor is contemplated, and the business review uncovers no threats to the company's competitive advantages.

The sustained competitive advantages of Payless remained the same: (1) a good, established reputation in its markets; (2) valuable retail locations acquired at low cost; (3) a large, national presence in a fragmented, growing industry; and (4) an emphasis on markets located outside Home Depot's and Lowe's principal trading regions.

Several assumptions used in preparing the projections seemed at odds with the past history of Payless, as shown in the following excerpts from the prospectus.

Forecast Assumption: Sales

The overall annual sales growth rates forecast by Payless are 8% in 1988, 11% in 1989, 11% in 1990, 10% in 1991, 8% in 1992 and 7% in 1993. At the beginning

EXHIBIT 8–18. Payless Cashways, Inc.— Condensed Forecast Financial Data[1]
(in millions)

| | For the Fiscal Year Ended November 30 | | | | | | |
| | Actual | Estimated | Forecast | | | | |
	1987	1988[2]	1989	1990	1991	1992	1993
Income Statement							
Sales	1,770	1,911	2,102	2,543	3,077	3,384	3,723
Gross margin	520	566	644	716	782	851	911
Selling, general, and administrative	(390)	(425)	(455)	(495)	(531)	(560)	(584)
Depreciation and amortization	(36)	n.a.	(62)	(59)	(56)	(53)	(51)
Earnings before interest and taxes	93	n.a.	127	161	196	237	276
Interest	(17)	n.a.	(158)	(158)	(159)	(157)	(153)
Earnings (loss) before taxes	76	n.a.	(31)	3	37	81	122
Income taxes (benefit)	(35)	n.a.	(7)	(6)	(19)	(36)	(52)
Net income (loss)	41	n.a.	(24)	(3)	18	45	70
Balance Sheet							
Working capital	123	120	90	92	61	76	94
Total assets	813	1,522	1,480	1,461	1,466	1,471	1,502
Long-term debt, less current maturities	180	1,086	1,052	1,023	961	917	856
Shareholders' equity	379	98	73	70	69	79	115

Note. The forecast shows uninterrupted growth in sales and earnings. This is typical of 99% of management projections.

[1] Prepared on October 14, 1988, by Payless management.

[2] Not applicable items for 1988 cannot be estimated because of accounting adjustments due to July 1988 leveraged buyout of Payless.

> *of the forecast period Do-It-Yourself customers sales are estimated to comprise approximately 70% of total sales and Professional Contractor (Pro) sales are estimated to comprise approximately 30%. Payless forecasts that by the end of the forecast period Pro sales will represent approximately 40–50% of total sales. Payless believes that the Pro market offers greater growth opportunities than the DIY market where Payless was principally focused in the past.*

This sales assumption does not withstand close scrutiny. Payless planned to achieve this 8–11 percent annual sales growth with minimal new store openings—only four in 1988 and one each in 1989 through 1993—so the revenue increases were totally reliant on same-stores sales growth, which averaged less than 5 percent historically. By way of explanation, management pointed to a new strategy focusing on the Pro market, although the effectiveness of the proposed strategy was untested.

Forecast Assumption: Gross Margins

Payless forecasts gross margins as a percentage of sales to remain relatively constant during the forecast period: 29.3% in 1988 (four months), 30.5% in 1989 and 1990, 30.2% in 1991, 30.3% in 1992 and 30.4% in 1993.

The Company's optimism flowed through to profit margins. The gross margin was projected to climb 1.1 percent over the period, from 29.3 percent to 30.4 percent. No justification was offered for the increase, although the historical record showed gross margin dropping from 30.2 percent in 1983 to 29.4 percent in 1987.

Forecast Assumption: Selling, General and Administrative Expense

The forecast includes annual increases in selling, general and administrative expense of 4.0% in 1989, 8.9% in 1990, 7.2% in 1991, 5.6% in 1992 and 4.2% in 1993. [Author's note—these increases are less than sales gains.] Selling, general and administrative expense as a percentage of sales are forecast to be approximately 21.0% in 1988 (four months) 21.6% in 1989, 21.1% in 1990, 20.5% in 1991, 20.0% in 1992 and 19.5% in 1993.

Here, the historical results again fail to support the Company's assumptions about the future. The management team increased SG&A expense from 20.6 percent of sales in 1983 to 22.0 percent of sales in 1987. In 1988, when they needed money to buy the Company, the forecast showed a dramatic reversal in the SG&A expense trend, which was estimated to drop to 19.5 percent of sales in 1993. One hopes the junk bond investors understood the ancient admonition "caveat emptor."

Working capital improvements are a common source of operating improvements in projections. This fact is demonstrated by another assumption listed in the Payless prospectus.

Forecast Assumption: Inventories and Accounts Payable

Payless forecasts that it will lower the level of inventories and improve inventory turnover as a result of the opening of the Sedalia distribution center and the implementation of its new inventory management system. Inventory and accounts payable leverage (trade accounts payable as a percentage of inventories) are forecast as follows:

	1989	1990	1991	1992	1993
Inventory turnover	4.2	4.5	4.6	4.7	4.8
Accounts payable leverage	35%	35%	35%	35%	35%

In this instance, the historical record was more supportive of management's numbers. Inventory turnover rose from 3.7× in 1985 to 4.2× in 1987, so a further increase in turnover wasn't out of line. In general, however, the overall forecast assumptions in the prospectus anticipated a turnaround in Payless's performance, despite a mediocre track record.

Actual Results 1989–1993

It is interesting to compare management's projections with what really happened. After all, who can predict a company's future better than its management? Exhibit 8–19 compares the projected data with the actual results for the five years ended November 30, 1993.

Actual sales consistently failed to meet management's targets because same-store sales projections weren't achieved in the real world. Payless obtained an increase in Pro sales, but the gain wasn't large enough to cover overall growth objectives. Actual net income exhibited shortfalls throughout the period as management's optimistic assumptions regarding gross margins, SG&A expense, and inventory turnover proved to be unreliable. A comparison of projected and actual data shown in Exhibit 8–20 illustrates the differences.

The inability of the Company to achieve its projections resulted in nervous moments for holders of the junk bonds. For months, the bonds traded below their original offering price, amid rumors of Payless having debt service problems. In 1993, the bondholders anxieties subsided when, after four years of losses, Payless completed a debt and equity refinancing in a favorable stock market. A short time later, the bonds were repaid in full. Shareholders in the leveraged buyout, in contrast, were more frustrated than bondholders. According to management's projects, earnings per share for

EXHIBIT 8–19. Payless Cashways, Inc.—Condensed Financial Data (in millions)

	Fiscal Year Ended November 30				
	1989	**1990**	**1991**	**1992**	**1993**
Projected-Sales	2,110	2,346	2,592	2,808	2,999
Actual-Sales	2,007	2,229	2,392	2,500	2,606
Projected-Net Income	(24)	(3)	18	45	70
Actual-Net Income	(32)	(21)	(13)	(16)	44

Note. Actual results were worse than the projections.

EXHIBIT 8–20. Payless Cashways, Inc.

	1993 Operating Results	
	Projected	Actual
Gross margin	30.4%	30.0%
SG&A expense	19.5%	21.9%
Inventory turnover	4.8×	4.4×

the LBO's shares were going to be $3.02 in 1993. In fact, EPS were only $0.16 in 1993, a negative difference of 95 percent. Earnings never recovered, and by late 1997, the company was bankrupt.

SUMMARY

Any evaluation of an established company's future prospects is based on prior events. Thus, a historical financial analysis precedes a projection of future results. Such analysis is conducted systematically using the financial statements as the raw materials and the four analytical devices—absolute amounts, percentage changes, common size statements, and financial ratios—as the tools. The would-be investor also prepares industry-specific statistics to measure the candidate's financial health. All this information is compared with data from similar businesses.

Experienced practitioners approach financial statements with a critical eye. Accounting firms are far from perfect and managements have an incentive to use liberal accounting methods, which may hide true economic returns. Furthermore, accounting profits are superseded by cash flow measures in certain situations.

Analysts sometimes fall in love with a stock and prepare projections while looking through rose-colored glasses. All forecasts benefit from a comparison with recent results.

QUESTIONS AND SHORT PROBLEMS

1. Why is financial statement analysis becoming a lost art?
2. Which assumption is the precursor to a financial statement analysis? Circle one answer:
   a. Statements are not fraudulent.
   b. Statements are prepared by a Big Six accounting firm.
   c. SEC has verified the audits.
   d. Accounting is similar among the competition.

3. During the late 1990s, Coca Cola stock generally traded at over 20 times its book value per share, yet investors continued buying the shares. Describe the intangible factors that contributed to the large difference between the stock price and historical accounting values.

4. Why do many software development firm shares trade at large premiums to book value per share when manufacturing companies with similar earnings trade at a more modest price to book multiples? Circle one answer:
   a. Software development requires few fixed assets in relation to potential earnings power.
   b. Most software firms have employed large R&D write-offs that reduce book value.
   c. Software firms use very high debt leverage, thus reducing book value per share and inflating the price to book ratio.
   d. All of the above.

5. Explain the respective purpose of each the four ratio categories used in financial statement analysis.

6. Alcott Co. 1999 accounts receivable to sales ratio increased from 0.12 to 0.20. Before concluding that this is a negative trend, what steps should the analyst implement?

Alcott Co. ($ millions)

	1998	1999
Sales	$100	$120
Accounts receivable	12	24

7. In 1987, Payless Cashways' annual sales grew by 16 percent. If same store sales were only 2.9 percent, what other factors contributed to the increase? (Exhibits 8–8, 8–14)

8. Payless' net income dropped in 1987 yet sales rose by 16 percent. Why?

9. Payless' net income declined by 2 percent in 1987, yet earnings per share increased 7 percent. How was that possible?

10. What caused earnings before interest and taxes for Payless to decline from 6.2 percent to 5.3 percent of sales?

11. How can a growing company, with *positive* net earnings, generate *negative* cash flow?

12. Why are financial results often considered over 3- to 5-year periods, as opposed to a one-year review?

13. In Exhibit 8–10, what factors contributed to Payless' negative cash flow in 1987?

14. Which of the following are true over the 1985 to 1987 period:
   a. Payless' pre-tax, pre-interest profit margins were declining.
   b. Payless was managing its inventory better.

   c. Payless' interest coverage ratio was at distressed company levels.
   d. Asset turnover was falling.
   e. Earnings per share were growing faster than net income.

15. Why do security analysts use the "same store" statistic for retailing companies? Indicate which of the following industries and related "same" statistics are appropriate for a security analysis:
   a. Restaurant, "same restaurant" sales.
   b. Cement, "same plant" sales.
   c. Hotel, "same room" sales.
   d. Airline, "same plane" sales.

16. Why do most "comparable company" financial analyses involve common size data? Why do practitioners strive to use normalized financial results in these studies? What is a "normalized" result (see Exhibits 8–5 and 8–6)?

17. Which *two* of the following *four* statistics were most supportive of Home Depot being the best do-it-yourself retailer in 1987?
   a. Inventory turnover.
   b. Current ratio.
   c. Earnings per share growth.
   d. Growth in same store sales.

18. Why do many Wall Street projections of corporate earnings turn out to be overly optimistic?

19. Over the last 10 years, a large U.S. cigarette company's sales have increased at an average ratio of 8 percent annually. Market share was constant, unit growth was 3 percent annually, and price inflation was 5 percent annually. The company informs you that U.S. sales for the next 5 years will climb at the rate of 17 percent annually. Provide three possible reasons that might be contained in the forecast assumptions.

20. The failure of one key assumption contributed to Payless' sales performance falling way short of its 1993 target. Which failed assumption was the most critical?

21. Using Altaire Corp.'s income statement for 1998 and 1999, answer the following questions:
   a. What was the 1998 EBIT to sales ratio?
   b. What was the firm's EBITDA in 1998?
   c. What was "normalized" EBITDA in 1999?
   d. Compute normalized net income and EPS for 1999, assuming a constant income tax rate.
   e. Complete a "common size" rendition of the 1998 and 1999 income statements.

Altaire Corp
Income Statement
(US$ millions, except per share data)

	1998	1999
Sales	$236.7	$240.2
Cost of sales	142.0	142.7
Depreciation	24.2	25.1
Non-recurring charge	—	8.0
Gross profit	70.5	64.4
General and administrative costs	46.3	47.2
Interest expense	12.0	9.5
Pre-tax income	12.1	7.7
Income taxes	4.3	2.7
Net income	$ 7.9	$ 5.0
Earnings per share	$ 2.03	$ 1.25
Shares outstanding	3.9	4.0

23. Three years' of summary balance sheets and annual sales results are presented for Gardenware Co. Complete these four exercises:
a. What trends do you notice?
b. What areas of potential concern are there for a potential investor?
c. Complete a common size balance sheet, an absolute amount changes table, and a percentage change table before answering (a) and (b).
d. Track the change in the current ratio, sales to inventory ratio, and sales to receivables ratio.

	1997	1998	1999
Assets			
Cash	$ 5.1	$ 6.2	$ 6.9
Accounts receivable	10.4	13.0	18.5
Inventory	12.6	14.0	15.1
Current assets	28.1	33.2	40.5
Fixed assets	32.4	35.6	38.5
	$ 60.5	$ 68.8	$ 79.0
Liabilities and Shareholders' Equity			
Accounts payable	$ 3.1	$ 3.9	$ 5.9
Other current liabilities	9.6	10.5	1.5
Current liabilities	12.7	14.4	17.4
Long-term debt	16.8	21.3	27.4
Shareholders' equity	31.0	33.1	34.2
	$ 60.5	$ 68.8	$ 79.0
Sales	$102.3	$104.8	$114.6

24. Why did the annual interest expense of Payless Cashways jump from $17 million in 1987 to $158 million in 1989?

Adopt-a-Company

A. Using the following four primary tools, provide a historical financial statement analysis for your company over the last three years. Be sure to "normalize" the company's results before beginning the exercise.
   1. Absolute amount changes.
   2. Percentage changes in growth.
   3. Common size percentage statement.
   4. Financial ratios.

B. Provide a brief written summary describing the reasons for:
   1. Changes in sales.
   2. Changes in net profitability and earnings per share.
   3. Changes in cash flow from operations.
   4. Changes in the company's debt to equity ratios from year 1 to year 3.

9

The Limitations of
Accounting Data

As shown in the previous chapter, intelligent financial analysis combines a thorough understanding of a company's business with a detailed review of its financial statements. Because the financials are constructed from accounting data, the practitioner appreciates the limitations of accounting as a means of describing a firm's financial condition.

A BEGINNER'S MISCONCEPTION

Many beginning students of security analysis regard financial statements as snapshots of absolute monetary values. After all, the statements are audited by a Big Six accounting firm, reviewed by a corporate board of directors, and passed through a quick SEC scrutiny. They thus carry the imprimatur of expertise and officialdom. To further support the notion of exactitude, the statements fit each other like a glove. The income statement carries over to the balance sheet, and both statements supply the raw information for the cash flow tables. All the accounts "balance" in a nice symmetry, and the package is then prefaced with an accountant's formal letter, followed by multiple footnotes explaining accounting policies and disclosure items.

THE NATURE OF FINANCIAL STATEMENTS

This appearance of numerical accuracy belies the fact that many accounting entries are not based on actual transactions, evidenced by certifiable records of money changing hands. Rather, a fair number of accounts rely heavily on the educated judgment of management and the corporate auditor. Ideally, these judgments provide financial statement users, such as security analysts, with a fair mathematical interpretation of the company's financial condition.

The fixed asset account is an excellent example of historical accounting's shortcomings. The economic life of specific asset classes varies widely among companies, and the depreciation charge attached to an asset represents simply a "best guess" on the accountant's part, particularly as the asset takes on unique attributes within its class. Likewise, the stated value of the asset (net of depreciation) on the balance sheet has curiosity value to the reader interested in original cost, but it typically has little economic meaning. Yet alternatives are lacking. Replacement cost is of minimal use if the firm has no plans to replace the asset in the near future. Liquidation value has little relevance if the company is a going concern, and "value in use" is difficult to separate from the totality of a company's operations. The practicality of traditional accounting wins out over the alternatives.

The accounting profession readily acknowledges the limitations of today's system, and it strives to update the methodology to respond to changing circumstances. Nevertheless, accountants caution analysts against taking financial statements literally, and the profession repeats the following precepts:

> Financial statements are prepared for the purpose of presenting a periodic report on progress by the management. They deal with the status of the investment in the business and the results achieved during the period under review.

> They reflect a combination of recorded facts, accounting conventions and personal judgments; and the judgments and conventions affect them materially. The soundness of the judgments necessarily depends on the competence and integrity of those who make them and on their adherence to generally accepted accounting principles and conditions.

As these statements imply, an appropriate financial investigation of a company extends past a review of the financial statements. It involves a meticulous study of the footnotes to the statements and an intelligent dialogue with the firm's financial executives.

Time and time again, investors are burned because a casual study of a firm's finances indicates a satisfactory condition, yet the actual situation is marginal. If a quick financial review reveals warning signals, the analyst is well advised to conduct a deep-probing analysis without cutting corners. This doesn't happen as often as it should. Many analysts lack extensive accounting training and are under pressure to focus singularly on future growth. As a result, Wall Street doesn't police accounting issues well. Corporations frequently get away with presenting a rosy scenario where none exists.

Many hi-tech firms, under pressure to raise equity money, pumped up their sales and earnings in recent years by using questionable accounting methods to inflate their market values. Some companies booked sales too early (i.e., when they still had an obligation for post-sale services or the customers had the right to a refund). Kendall Square Research Corp., a computer manufacturer, admitted that it counted as revenues numerous sales for customers who retained trade-in and refund privileges. Receivables growing faster than sales is one indicator of this overbooking.

BASIC ACCOUNTING ISSUES

While the current system of accounting works reasonably well, practitioners repeatedly confront six issues that complicate their work. The first three items are global problems that affect many analyses. The other three elements are company specific.

Global Issues

1. Accounting for service companies.
2. Growth in mergers and acquisitions.
3. Derivatives.

Company-Specific Issues

4. Flexibility in accounting methods.
5. Disclosure.
6. Potential for fraud.

GLOBAL ISSUES

Accounting for Service Companies

Much of the value added by companies today comes from services: business services, personal services, and financial services, where physical assets such as plants and inventories have little importance. Yet the accounting model used today was developed privately to fit (1) manufacturing companies, which produce a tangible product and sell it, and (2) merchandising companies, which buy tangible products and then resell them. With the sharp growth in service businesses, the traditional accounting measures assume less importance. How do you compute inventory turnover for a mutual fund company such as Fidelity? The primary assets of Genzyme Corp., a biotech company, are truly the intellectual abilities of its employees rather than the bricks and mortar of its office buildings. Is return on assets measurable for Kelly Services, a temporary help firm? These questions recur in the analysis of service firms and prompt analysts to rely on modified measurement techniques.

Growth in Mergers and Acquisitions

Since the early 1980s, merger and acquisition growth has exploded. In 90 percent of the transactions, the acquirer pays in excess of the seller's tangible book value (defined as net tangible assets minus liabilities). Since most buyers use purchase accounting, there is an upward revision of the seller's book value. Frequently, these revisions cannot account for all of the premium over book, and a large amount is registered as "goodwill."

The asset write-ups and goodwill additions of the typical deal result in big amortization charges against the buyer's income and thus complicate the analyst's job. A firm with multiple transactions under its belt has more accounting quirks than one whose business is internally grown. Practitioners deal with this problem by evaluating corporate results "above the line"; they look at "earnings before interest, taxes, depreciation, and amortization" (EBITDA) instead of "net earnings" as the primary measurement of performance. Other substitutes for net earnings are "free cash flow," earnings before interest and taxes and economic value added.

Exhibit 9–1 summarizes the write-ups when LEN Equipment buys DG Manufacturing to form Newco. Exhibit 9–2 illustrates the analyst's predicament. How does he compare the EPS of the newly merged Newco with its competitor, Telright Corp? The results are similar, but also different. Sales and EBITDA are the same for both firms but Telright's EPS are higher because amortization charges depress Newco's earnings.

Acquisition prices for companies are increasingly higher than net tangible assets. In 1986, net tangible assets represented 30 to 40 percent of

EXHIBIT 9–1. LEN Equipment Acquiring DG Manufacturing for $1 Billion
Newco—1997 Balance Sheet Data

	LEN Equipment	DG Manufacturing	Adjustments	Pro Forma Combined
Assets				
Current assets	$ 500	$225		$ 725
Fixed assets	500	225	+100[1]	825
Goodwill	—	—	+600[1]	600
Total assets	$1,000	$450	$700	$2,150
Liabilities and Stockholders' Equity				
Current liabilities	$ 300	$150	—	$ 450
Long-term debt	100	—	+600[2] −300[3]	700
Stockholder's equity	600	300	+400[3]	1,000
Total liabilities and stockholders' equity	$1,000	$450	$700	$2,150

Adjustments
[1] $1 billion purchase price exceeds $300 million DG equity by $700 million. The $700 million excess is allocated $100 million to fixed assets and $600 million to goodwill, amortized over 20 years,
[2] Issuance of $600 million of new debt for finance acquisition.
[3] Elimination of DG book equity and issuance of $400 million of new equity.

EXHIBIT 9–2. Similar Companies, Different Accounting (in millions except per share data)

COMPARATIVE BALANCE SHEET DATA

	Newco Combined	Telright Corp.
Assets		
Current assets	$ 725	$ 725
Fixed assets	825	825
Goodwill	600	
	$2,150	$1,550
Liabilities and Equity		
Current liabilities	$ 450	$ 450
Long-term debt	700	700
Stockholders' equity	1,000	400
	$2,150	$1,550

COMPARATIVE INCOME STATEMENT DATA

	Newco Combined	Telright Corp.
Revenues	$3,000	$3,000
EBITDA	250	250
Depreciation	100	100
Goodwill amortization	30	—
EBIT	120	150
Interest	50	50
Pretax income	70	100
Income taxes	40	40
Net income	$ 30	$ 60
EPS	$3.00	$6.00
Shares outstanding	10	10

Note. EBITDA = earnings before interest, taxes, depreciation, and amortization; EBIT = earnings before interest and taxes; EPS = earnings per share. Exhibit 9–2 shows that Newco and Telright financial results are similar with the exception of goodwill items.

takeover purchase prices. By 1999, this had fallen to just 20 to 25 percent. Two quotations illustrate the importance of intangibles to a business: From John Stuart, former Chairman of Quaker Oats, "If this business were split up, I'd be glad to take the brands, trademarks and goodwill and you could have all the bricks and mortar and I'd fare better than you." Per Gyllenhammer, CEO of Volvo, echoed a similar point, "Our most valuable asset is the Volvo trademark." By way of illustration, the shares of General Mills, the owner of such venerable brand names as Wheaties, Cheerios, and Betty Crocker, trade at 20× book value.

Of course, the value of brands, and goodwill, and other intangible assets can be overstated. The Schwinn brand used to represent excellence in bicycles; now it's a distant memory to consumers. Merrill Lynch bought

White Weld for its sterling reputation, client base, and banking experience, but the experienced personnel at White Weld left to join competitors after the deal, taking the clients with them. At times, the accounting convention of assigning a 20- to 40-year life to goodwill is out of line, particularly when most companies and product lines aren't even 40 years old. And increasingly, buyers incur large special charges immediately after consummating a deal, to curb the drag on income that results from goodwill amortization. For example, after buying Cheyenne Software for $1.2 billion in November 1996, Computer Associates International took a $0.6 billion charge in connection with the transaction. By writing off intangibles right away, the firm saved years of amortization expense. Such actions require the analyst to take extra care in reviewing the financials of active acquirers.

Accounting for Derivatives

A derivative financial instrument represents a contractual agreement between counterparties. It has a value that is "derived" from changes in the worth of some other underlying asset, such as the price of another security, interest rate, or currency exchange rate. Examples of derivatives include stock options, futures, and interest rate swaps. Once relegated to a small group of sophisticated financial institutions, the use of derivatives is spreading rapidly through corporate America. Commonly used as hedging devices that make income flows more predictable, derivatives have unforeseen side effects, and, if used for speculative purposes, can result in disaster. That's because a derivative's price tends to be more volatile than the price of the underlying security. Orange County, California, went bankrupt when rising interest rates caused its derivative portfolio to plummet in value.

The accounting profession and the Securities and Exchange Commission (SEC) are updating disclosure standards for the increasing variety of new and exotic derivatives, but for now, the information is off balance sheet and scattered throughout the footnotes. For corporations such as banks and insurance companies, which are the principal users of these instruments, the required disclosure is unintelligible to anyone but the most tenacious practitioner. Furthermore, derivative values are quite volatile, changing dramatically in days or weeks, yet the security analyst has to rely on quarterly reports that are released in three month intervals.

COMPANY-SPECIFIC ISSUES

Accounting for services, acquisitions, and derivatives is a generic problem encompassing many industries, and practitioners know to ask questions and make adjustments to conform the accounting to economic reality. This same diligence must be applied to specific firms because variations occur among similar companies, even within accounting conventions. A key source of these differences is management discretion. Generally accepted accounting principles permit economic transactions that receive accounting treatment to be recognized in different ways by different financial statement preparers. As a result, the analyst must examine not only the economic relevance of a given accounting method but also the manner in which the company and the auditors apply it in a given situation.

Flexibility in Accounting Methods

The accounting profession maintains a set of rules providing independent public accountants with instructions on how to translate economic activity into financial statements. These rules are called Generally Accepted Accounting Principles (GAAP). The Financial Accounting Standards Board (FASB), a nonprofit organization, has the primary responsibility for updating these rules and providing interpretations. Providing input to the FASB are the SEC, accounting groups such as the American Institute of Certified Public Accountants, and industry associations. Due to the lack of homogeneity among businesses and the changing of economic circumstances, the application of these rules is less than absolute and accountants make judgments to accurately represent a firm's condition. Therein lies the concept of management discretion.

Management discretion in the selection of an accounting policy is the enemy of the security analyst, who needs consistency of method over time and within industries. As shown by the Payless example, financial statement analysis concentrates on a series of consecutive statements. Particular attention is paid to observing changes from period to period. If management varies accounting methods over time, this interpretation of the data has less meaning. Likewise, an important part of the Payless financial and valuation analysis was the comparison of that company with similar enterprises. It follows that the accounting values used as a comparison should be based on similar methodologies. Substantial differences within an industry diminish the basis for a good comparison, as shown in Exhibit 9–3. Wisconsin Central's choice of 33 years for locomotive life is more liberal than that of the other companies.

This isn't to say that every business doesn't have its own idiosyncracies that deserve special accounting treatment, but the fundamental elements of a firm's accounts should conform to its competitors. Some managements use this flexibility to present results in a way that reflects neither economic reality nor industry convention, and it can be stated that management is not an innocent observer in the setting of policy. Management actively participates with the independent accounting firm in putting together corporate financial statements, and it exercises influence in the selection of accounting benchmarks. Should 100 percent of revenue be recognized immediately, or should 20 percent be withheld as future service and guaranty revenues?

EXHIBIT 9–3. Railroad Industry—Depreciable Lives of Locomotives and Railcars

Company	Years
Burlington Northern	21
Illinois Central	18–20
Norfolk Southern	23
Rail Tex	10–15
Wisconsin Central	33

Source. David Tice & Associates.

For a percentage-of-completion project, is the job 50 percent finished, or 60 percent? What is the estimated profit margin? Even experienced independent auditors need management's assistance in answering such questions intelligently.

Furthermore, the accounting profession has undergone an evolution, which, in the eyes of many practitioners, undercuts their objectivity. Peter Knudson, professor of accounting at Wharton, recalls the earlier times, "In the 1960s and 1970s accounting was like a gentlemen's club where boorish behavior resulted in expulsion. Standards were very high. Firms didn't advertise and they didn't directly solicit business." With the application of U.S. antitrust laws in the early 1980s, accounting firms began to advertise and grow other businesses, such as consulting, which sought fees from the same auditing clients. The resulting potential for a conflict of interest reminded the security analyst that independent auditors don't operate out of an ivory tower; they are susceptible to the same foibles as other businesspeople, such as bending the rules once in a while. At a 1996 American Institute of Certified Public Accountants (AICPA) conference, SEC Chairman Arthur Levitt said the accounting industry should view "auditing as the very soul of the public accounting profession—not as a loss leader retained as a foot in the door for higher-fee consulting services." SEC enforcement director William Lucas said, "The complex entanglement of services with clients poses a subtle but very real threat to independence." Thus, while the vast majority of financial statements are done properly, the practitioner cannot place blind faith in management's judgment and an auditor's report. He must look behind the numbers.

Disclosure and the Potential for Fraud

Given the flexibility inherent in Generally Accepted Accounting Principles, it is inevitable that corporate managements sometimes succumb to the temptation of providing misleading results to the public. The usual objective is to portray the business in a more favorable light than would otherwise be the case. In a minority of instances, the company may understate income statement and balance sheet values, either to save money on taxes or to keep earnings in reserve for later years. More often, management's tactics take the form of "liberal accounting," such as using unrealistically long asset lives for depreciation purposes or deliberately underestimating bad debt expenses (see Exhibit 9–4). At other times, financial statements mislead by way of omission. Management forgets an off-balance sheet support arrangement or dismisses a nettlesome lawsuit as "immaterial." In a severe situation, this manipulation leads to fraud, and managers purposely conceal items from auditors and forge accounting documentation.

Why are managers tempted to inflate corporate financial results? One reason is they can get away with it. Bill Berkley, Chairman of W.R. Berkley & Co. and a veteran of many public offerings, summarized it to me in a simple fashion, "Wall Street doesn't respect conservative accounting." Independent accountants, the supposed "keepers of the flame" of financial objectivity, are good, but less than perfect. Meanwhile, the institutional community and the SEC have a difficult time assigning sufficient resources to police the problem. Finally, it is an unusual set of financial statements that contains sufficient information for a comprehensive analysis. For verbal explanations and additional disclosures, the practitioner is forced to call the same managers who are motivated to exaggerate their performance.

Two recent books, *Financial Statement Analysis* by Martin Fridson (John Wiley & Sons: New York, NY, 1995) and *Financial Shenanigans* by Howard

EXHIBIT 9–4. Management Devices for Exaggerating Corporate Financial Performance

Accounting Method Selection	GAAP permits corporations, working with auditors, to have latitude in the way certain revenues and expenses are recorded. Management may deliberately select methods that don't reflect economic reality.
Disclosure	Footnote disclosure and management discussion may be vague, misleading, and suffering from omissions. The analyst is thus deterred from finding the truth.
Fraud	In extreme cases, management "cooks the books" by creating sales and earnings through fraudulent means such as forged receipts and double invoicing. Even skilled auditors have trouble detecting clever schemes, as suggested by Chris Nunn, risk management partner of Arthur Anderson. In response to an $80 million profit overstatement by Wickes, the English retailing chain, he said, "We were the victims of what is every auditor's nightmare—a skillfully executed, collusive fraud which deceived everybody."

Schilit (McGraw-Hill, Inc, New York, NY, 1993), cover well the incentives managers have to boost corporate financial results. A summary of these incentives appears as Exhibit 9–5.

The stage is thus set for the battle between corporate managers and security analysts. Managers try to convey the impression that their business is going well, and is getting better. Sure, risks are present in the business, but the management has crafted plans to deal with them, so prospective investors needn't worry. Taken at face value, such words are reassuring, but you can't accept them blindly, since management has incentives to

EXHIBIT 9–5. Management Rationales for Exaggerating Corporate Financial Performance

Rationale	Comments
Increase or Maintain Stock Market Valuation	A healthy stock price is helpful for several reasons: • *Obtaining Equity Finance.* Positive financial results (and continued expectations thereof) are critical to a company accessing the equity markets. • *Optimizing Equity Finance.* Access is important, but so is the pricing of a company's equity. Companies prefer receiving the most amount of money for the least ownership give-up. The appearance of good financial results provides a better valuation and a higher P/E ratio. • *Maximizing Management Compensation.* Most high-level corporate managers receive stock options as part of their compensation. Inflating the underlying stock price increases these option values.
Promote Access to the Debt Markets	Banks, institutional lenders, bond markets, trade creditors, commercial paper investors and rating agencies rely on financial statements to judge a company's creditworthiness. Managers may choose to exaggerate results to maintain the flow of finance and to keep pricing at reasonable levels. Consider of the cost a small change in perception. When Moody's dropped the debt rating of Lehman Brothers from A3 to Baa1 in 1995, analysts figured the change would cost the firm $25 million annually.
Preserve Job	Even when the financial markets aren't a big factor in corporate operations, management may have a temptation. A board of directors likes to see growth in sales and earnings. Keeping the directors happy with a steady stream of improving results may be necessary for a manager to keep his job.

place a positive spin on any situation. Even the veracity of financial statements is suspect, since auditors and accounting policies sometimes cannot portray properly the economic status of a business—either on a stand-alone basis or in fair comparison with similar companies. The analyst's role as a *financial detective* is thereby cemented alongside his multiple role as industry expert, business operations specialist, financial analyst, and valuation appraiser.

THE FUNDAMENTAL OBJECTIVE OF PUBLIC COMPANIES

In its quest to increase shareholder value, a public company management should be cognizant of the valuation methodologies outlined in this book. At a basic level, the executives should remember the following fundamentals of Wall Street:

- *Growth in Sales and Earnings Is Good.* Growth brings higher valuation ratios, such as a high P/E number.
- *Stability and Assurance of These Growth Objectives Are Good.* Stability brings higher valuation ratios.
- *Unpredictability and Volatility in Sales and Earnings Are Bad.* Unpredictability and volatility imply risk, which means a lower valuation ratio.

Management, therefore, should endeavor not only to achieve higher growth in sales and earnings, but to foster an image of stability. Preferably, annual sales and earnings grow in a consistent and seamless fashion from year to year, showing a trend line such as that shown in Exhibit 9–6.

General Electric is one of the all-time champions at displaying uninterrupted earnings growth. Its record is even more remarkable when you realize the company's main business lines are quite cyclical (see Exhibit 9–7). General Electric frequently offsets one-time gains from big asset sales with restructuring charges; this keeps earnings from rising so high that they can't be topped the following year (see Exhibit 9–8). GE also times sales of some equity stakes and even makes acquisitions to produce profit gains when needed. In 1991, a recession year that was problematic for most industrial companies, GE boosted earnings by $300 million through a simple financial calculation. It raised the assumed return on pension assets from 8.5 to 9.5 percent, thereby decreasing the required corporate contribution to the pension fund. According to Martin Sankey, CS First Boston analyst, "GE is certainly a relatively aggressive practitioner of earnings management," but Dennis Dammerman, GE's chief financial officer, declines to identify such actions as earnings management, "I've never looked at it that way."

Sustaining an image of constancy leads to accounting gimmickry at some companies, and the next section reviews a few methods by which management massages corporate financial results.

EXHIBIT 9–6. The Uninterrupted Sales and Earnings Growth of the "Ideal Company"

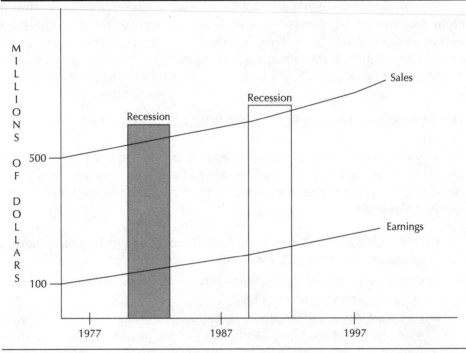

The Ideal Company has uninterrupted growth in sales and earnings. Recessions don't affect its results.

Case Study: Massage Corp. Exhibits 9–9 and 9–10 depict the summary income statement and balance sheet of Massage Corp., an imaginary manufacturer of packaging products. The key accounting items are discussed in a sequential fashion, beginning with sales, the top line of the income statement.

Income Statement

Sales

Typical means of exaggerating sales include the following:

- *Shipping Goods before a Sale Is Finalized.* Massage Corp. has ongoing service obligations on product lines and a liberal return policy, which means that not all revenues are recognized when the product is shipped to the customer.

   Revenue recognition has recently become a big issue in the software industry, where vendors are tempted to book revenues, despite continuing obligations to the customer. Oracle Corp. had a problem in 1994 when it failed to subtract revenue from returned equipment.

EXHIBIT 9–7. General Electric Company—Summary Track Record

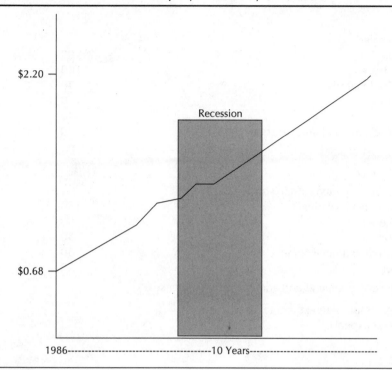

Note the smooth pattern of GE's Growth.
1986 EPS = $0.68. 1996 EPS = $2.20.

EXHIBIT 9–8. How GE Offsets Gains from Asset Sales

Year	Pretax Gain (millions)	Source of the Gain	Pretax Restructuring Charges (millions)
1993	$1,430	Sale of aerospace unit to Martin Marietta	$1,011
1987	858	Change in accounting for taxes and inventory	1,027
1986	50	Sale of foreign affiliate	311
1985	518	Sale of three coal properties and 37% cable stake	447
1984	617	Sale of Utal Int'l, small appliance unit, cable company	636
1983	117	Sale of radio/TV stations and Gearhart Industries stake	147

Source. General Electric Co., *Wall Street Journal.*

EXHIBIT 9–9. Massage Corp.—Summary Income Statement (in millions)

Sales		$1,000
Cost of sales		
Labor	300	
Raw materials	100	
Finished materials	40	
Utilities	40	
Rent	40	
Depreciation and amortization	80	
Total cost of sales		600
Gross income		400
Selling, General, and Administrative Expense		
Management salaries	150	
Marketing	50	
Insurance	30	
Research and development	50	
Other	20	
Total selling, general and administrative expense		300
Earnings before interest and taxes		100
Interest expense		30
Pretax income		70
Income tax		30
Net income		$ 40

EXHIBIT 9–10. Massage Corp.—Summary Balance Sheet (in millions)

Assets	
Cash	$ 50
Accounts receivable, net of reserves	80
Inventories	120
Other current assets	50
	300
Fixed assets, net of depreciation	250
Long-term equity investments	30
Other assets	20
Goodwill	150
	$750
Liabilities and Stockholders' Equity	
Short-term loans	$ 50
Accounts payable	100
Other current liabilities	50
Total current liabilities	200
Long-term debt	220
Postretirement benefits	30
Stockholders' equity	300
	$750

In 1997, Microsoft had over $700 million of deferred revenue, which the firm properly booked only when upgrades were delivered.

- *Selling Goods to Uncreditworthy Customers.* One way to boost revenues is selling to companies that can't find anyone else to sell to them for credit reasons. When sales are booked to these uncreditworthy customers, the aggressive firm downplays loss reserves. This is a short-term strategy for inflating revenues; but over the long term the inevitable write-off of receivables harms results. Schwartz Brothers, Inc., expanded its video distribution business dramatically in 1989 and 1990. With many of its new customers unable to pay, the firm went bankrupt in 1991 when it couldn't service the loans financing the bad receivables.

- *Selling Goods on Unrealistic Terms.* One way of obtaining new customers is to offer liberal repayment terms. If the industry norm is a 2 percent discount for 10-day payment, and full payment by 30 days (i.e., 2/10, net/30), an aggressive firm can generate additional sales by providing 3/30, net/60, for example. The cost of this tactic shows up in financing expense since the seller carries the receivables on its balance sheet.

- *Pushing Sales into a Quarter.* The desire for both favorable quarter-to-quarter sales comparisons and smooth upward sales trends prompts managers to manipulate the timing of sales. In some cases, the action is as benign as asking a salesperson to book a transaction on the first day of the following month instead of the 28th day of the current month. In other cases, the activity is more systematic. In 1994, Mattel boosted sales by forcing inventory on regular customers; in return, it promised free inventory in 1995. In 1993 and 1994, Bausch & Lomb stuffed its distributors with extra product, thereby increasing sales in those two years. Medaphis Corp. inflated 1996 sales by $16 million by reporting service revenues before the customer received a bill.

- *Understating Warranties and Returns.* When Maytag sells a washing machine, it recognizes a liability for the machine's repair guarantee. A $500 sale, might appear as $475 in the first year because of the warranty obligation.

$500 Sale
(25) Repair guarantee
$475 Net sale

Consider a company selling a new product with untested warranty experience. It may be tempted to underplay this obligation, pushing repair expenses into future years.

- *Abusing Percentage of Completion Accounting Method.* Some revenue generating activities require months and years to complete. Examples include sophisticated computer systems, large defense projects, and long-term construction jobs. Rather than book a huge sale when the contract is finished, the selling company accrues revenues and profits on a gradual basis, as the project meets certain completion goals. Since the company is likely to be far more knowledgeable about the project's "ins and outs" than its outside auditor, the temptation is for management to say the job is 60 percent complete and book 60 percent of the revenues, when, in fact, it is only 50 percent done.

- *Fraud.* The preceding tactics tend not to approach the level of criminal fraud. An example of such fraudulent action is creating phony sales invoices. When invoices for nonexistent sales enter the internal accounting system, managers achieve the illusion of growth. Well-designed schemes have avoided detection, even by outside auditors, for some time. Typically, the auditor is lax in spot-checking the veracity of sales documents. Coated Sales, Inc., a high-flying stock in the late 1980s, fooled its auditors and bank lenders with a phony invoice scheme over several accounting periods. Top executives later received jail sentences. At other times, firms seemingly permit improper billing practices. In 1997, Smith Kline Beecham paid $325 million to the federal government to resolve allegations that it over-billed Medicare and Medicaid for unnecessary tests. In 1996, Horizon/CMS Healthcare settled similar claims. In 1995, Structural Dynamics Research Corp. and Sunrise Medical both admitted that earlier profits were overstated due to fraudulent sales reporting practices by subsidiaries.

COST OF SALES

Despite the long history of inflation, a few U.S. firms still record the cost of sales using the first-in, first-out method (FIFO), rather than last-in, first-out (LIFO). LIFO is more reflective of current costs in an inflationary environment. Steelmaker J&L Specialty Steel finally adopted LIFO in 1994, cutting that year's net income by $6.5 million.

Labor. A popular tactic for recording a misleading labor expense lies in the calculation of future benefits. Fringes such as pension, medical care, and vacations add up to one-third of labor costs. The determination of the "current cost" of future items such as pensions and medical plans is inherently uncertain, and shading actuarial assumptions one way or another makes a big difference. Outside actuaries assist the auditors in many instances, but the corporation can influence numerous actuarial variables, such as the variables affecting future medical and retirement costs:

- Number of eligible employees in 20 years.
- Cost of future medical care.
- Number of employees requiring medical care.
- Annual financial discount rate for future benefits.

- Eligibility assumptions (service time, future layoffs, etc.).
- Future employee salaries.
- Employer versus employee contributions.
- Assumed future rate of return on pension assets.

Wilbros Group, for example, assumed annual pay increases of 6 percent and annual pension returns of 8.5 percent in 1996. Weyerhaeser had more liberal estimates, 4.5 percent and 11.5 percent, respectively. If Weyerhaeser had used 8.5 percent instead of 11.5 percent for its pensions, annual earnings would have declined by 6 percent.

Raw Materials/Finished Materials.   Management has little ability to manipulate raw materials. One exception is the accounting method selection, such as LIFO versus FIFO versus lower of cost or market.

Utilities.   It is difficult to massage utility expenses.

Rent.   Rent is a large item for companies that lease rather than own. It becomes an accounting issue when the lease is really a noncancelable financing and should therefore be capitalized as debt. For many firms, access to debt financing is dependent on low leverage, so management struggles to classify lease costs as rent (an operating lease) versus debt service (a capitalized lease.)

Depreciation.   Although independent auditors have benchmarks that match assets with depreciable lives, there are ranges within the reference points and numerous exceptions. Thus, depreciable lives vary among similar assets of similar companies, because judgment and discretion are involved. The short-term earnings benefit of using a long depreciable life is obvious for a $10 million asset. A five-year life reduces annual income by $2 million; a ten-year life by only $1 million:

$10 Million Asset

Depreciable life	5 years	10 years
Annual income reduction	$2 million	$1 million

For a new asset with an untested economic life, it is never a cut- and dry-issue. When Blockbuster Entertainment went public, analysts complained about the three-year life attached to its primary asset, movie videos. Wall Streeters argued that (1) few people wanted to rent a video after it had been in the store for 12 months; (2) most depreciation, therefore, should occur over the first 12 months; and (3) the company's earnings, therefore, were overstated with the three-year video life.

Amortization of Goodwill.   The substantial increase in merger-and-acquisition activity means that corporate income statements are increasingly affected by goodwill amortization. Acquirers write off any excess purchase price that cannot be attributed to the seller's tangible assets (like plant and equipment) as goodwill. The life of goodwill incurred in an acquisition is a subjective determination, set jointly by management and the independent auditors. Similar to the depreciation account, a long goodwill life represents a smaller impact on earnings. The annual difference between a 10-year life and a 40-year life (the longest permitted by the SEC) on a $100 million goodwill account is $7.5 million annually.

$100 Million Goodwill Account

	10 years	40 years
Estimated life	10 years	40 years
Annual charge to income	$10 million	$2.5 million

The inconsistency of the longer life is that most companies aren't 40 years old, and neither are most products. Also, in many acquisitions, the buyer fires the seller's executives, diminishing the duration of the *intangible* value.

Newell Company, a consumer products manufacturer, relies on acquisitions to grow. In 1996, it was amortizing $900 million of goodwill over a 40-year period. Reducing this economic life to 20 years would have cut Newell's 1996 net income by 9 percent.

Amortization of Other Intangible Assets.   Other intangible assets are registered on corporate balance sheets, and not all are derived from acquisitions. In studying Gibson Greetings' financial statements, I learned that a $50 million intangible asset represented shelf-space rights. The company paid drugstore chains this amount to reserve shelf space for its greeting cards for a 10-year period. Other common intangibles include covenants not to compete, leasehold rights, contract rights, patents, and software.

Thanks to an obscure accounting rule, hi-tech acquirers are assigning excess-over-book values to the seller's intangible research and development costs, which are then written off in one large chunk, rather than being drawn out over multiple years like normal goodwill. This suppresses the long-term cost of the technology that supplies the buyer with future revenues. In 1995, IBM wrote off $1.8 billion of the $3.2 billion it paid to acquire software developer Lotus Development Corp., relieving itself of $1.8 billion of write-offs over the acquired software's five-year economic life. Abraham Briloff, a well-known accounting expert, estimated that this action boosted IBM's annual earnings by 10 percent over the period. What happens when the accounting benefits end? In an August, 1997 *Forbes* article on Disney's liberal accounting, one executive remarked, "We call it the cliff. Either we come through with real earnings or we fall off the cliff."

SELLING, GENERAL, AND ADMINISTRATIVE COSTS

Management Salaries.   Like other labor costs, management salaries include a heavy component of fringe benefits, the current cost of which is based on actuarial estimates. In bringing management's interests more in line with those of shareholders, more firms offer top managers attractive stock option packages, the cost of which doesn't appear on the income statement. When Michael Ovitz left Walt Disney Company with $38 million worth of stock options, none of this amount was expensed. Similarly, in 1998, Microsoft compensated its employees with $1.1 billion of stock options, in addition to salary and other fringes. If this amount had been paid in cash, earnings would have been 17 percent less.

Marketing. In addition to normal media advertising, companies use dozens of schemes to promote their products. Rebates, allowances, credits, shelf-space payments, and long-term commissions are a few marketing practices that complicate accounting. One English retailer, Wickes plc., overstated profits by $80 million through the improper booking of supplier rebates related to Wickes (1) achieving certain sales levels, (2) providing shelf space, and (3) instituting marketing programs for the suppliers. Wickes booked these items as current year profit rather than spreading them over the term of the supply agreements.

A common corporate practice in the United States is capitalizing a portion of the monies used to attract new customers. By capitalizing such costs and amortizing them over the expected customer life, companies avoid big up-front expenses. The big question is: Do the customers keep coming back? One growing mail-order company, Seattle Filmworks, capitalizes the costs of its direct mailings to prospective customers, expensing them over three years rather than using the conservative approach of expensing such costs in the year they're incurred. This liberal accounting method produced 50 percent higher net earnings in 1996.

America Online, the popular Internet company, spread its marketing costs over two years. A poor history of retaining subscribers led the firm to change this policy in late 1996, resulting in a $385 million write-off of marketing costs on the balance sheet, and management's belated acknowledgment that earlier earnings were overstated. Similarly, in 1996, Toys 'Я' Us took a $400 million special charge to reverse capitalized marketing costs.

Insurance. You need to ensure that the company under study carries adequate insurance for its operations. Management may try to pinch pennies (and thus increase earnings) by not buying enough coverage.

Research and Development. A lot of companies capitalize a portion of their research and development costs and amortize them over a period of years. This policy attempts to match costs against future revenues, much like the depreciating value of a paper factory is allocated to each ton of paper produced. The problem with placing R&D on the balance sheet is the uncertainty attached to whether the R&D will actually produce earnings. Many innovations fail and others are minimally profitable. A disclosure item in the auditor's report for a hi-tech firm is vague:

The establishment of technological feasibility and the ongoing assessment of recoverability of development costs require considerable judgment by management with respect to certain external factors, including, but not limited to, anticipated future revenues, estimated economic life and changes in software and hardware technologies.

With this kind of elusive disclosure, the analyst evaluates R&D accounting carefully, particularly when hi-tech stocks play a large role in the stock market today.

INTEREST

Companies have a variety of means to disguise debt financings. For example, interest costs can be hidden in the rent expense category.

INCOME TAXES

A company with a heavy fixed asset base typically pays less in cash income tax than the income tax accrual indicates. Federal income tax depreciation schedules have shorter lives than GAAP, meaning that true taxable income is less than GAAP pretax income. Financial statement footnotes provide details on cash tax payments.

THE BALANCE SHEET

ASSETS

Cash.   Massage Corp. can do little to inflate this account short of fraud. I have seen a few firms commingle the operating cash account with dedicated cash accounts (i.e., those set aside for lenders, landlords, and other special parties) in the consolidation.

Accounts Receivable, Net of Reserves.   The receivables from sales are not reflected at 100 percent of face value. A reserve is established for the possibility of nonpayment, returns, warranties, and other items. Of particular note is the company that has a large receivable from an uncreditworthy customer. This problem pops up in certain "emerging market" deals, where state-owned enterprises are the issuer's largest customers. These governments don't pay their bills on time.

The proper level of reserves is a major issue for any finance company, whose principal assets are receivables from others. Advanta, the eighth largest credit card issuer, had its problems in 1997. Earlier it set a low level of bad debt reserves on the credit extended to its cardholders. When many couldn't repay their card balances, Advanta reduced earnings by adding to its loss reserves.

In 1996, Sears Roebuck was accused of the opposite situation: *having overly generous credit card reserves.* With a $1 billion reserve (twice as large in percentage of receivables versus similar firms), Sears drew down on the balance sheet reserve when times got tough, rather than accruing additional bad debt losses on the income statement.

Bad debt reserves are especially important for banks, insurance companies, and savings and loans. The latter's voluminous bad debts cost the U.S. government billions in the 1980s.

As noted earlier, the counterfeiting of receivables has been used to jigger financial statements. The analyst relies on the independent auditors to police this fraud, although a studied examination of receivables' performance can present clues to such shenanigans.

Inventories.   Fashion changes, product innovations, and technological advances can quickly reduce the value of a firm's inventory. In 1987, I worked with a stationery company that failed to write off its inventory of unsold 1986 calendars. Ann Taylor Stores, the upscale apparel retailer, was accused of accumulating large amounts of unsold inventory in 1994, but refusing to reduce earnings by writing down such values. Leslie Fay Companies, the apparel manufacturer, failed to report inventory problems in 1994. Acclaim Entertainment took big losses on its playstation inventory in 1995 as technology changed. Not being experts in all products, many accountants have trouble identifying diminished value, so the analyst has to ask questions if inventories seem high by historical standards.

One colorful fraud involved Crazy Eddie Corporation, which moved the same inventory to different warehouses, enabling the auditors to count the same items twice.

Fixed Assets, Net of Depreciation.   If Massage Corp. deliberately understates depreciation, the economic value of the fixed assets may be less than the accounting value. In certain cases, the asset is worth more than the balance sheet value, particularly as an alternative use. Such is frequently the case in real estate, which tends to increase in value with inflation. In one of my merger transactions, the seller, Young Drug Products, operated a distribution center in a tony office park. After the deal, the location was rightly converted into a high-rent office building.

Rather than depreciate fixed assets in an orderly fashion, managers are tempted to take the occasional "big bath" write-off, so future earnings are enhanced while past earnings are history. In other instances, a company husbands a hidden value, waiting to offset down earnings with a profitable asset sale.

Natural Resource Reserves.   Historical accounting for the ownership of natural resources, such as timber and mineral reserves, is practically meaningless from the analyst's standpoint. The practitioner is only interested in the statistical compilations of these reserves and the estimated cost of extraction, so he can attach estimated market values to them. A useful piece of accounting data is the tax basis of the reserves, but this information is unavailable to the public.

Long-Term Equity Investments.   You should try to "mark to market" long-term equity investments, since management cannot be relied on to perform this task. Most companies wait too long to write down impaired investments, while profitable equity sales are deferred until normal operations are having problems.

Overstating the value of a securities portfolio—particularly hard-to-value private securities—is a common practice among unscrupulous executives. In 1996, Christopher Bagdasarian, an investment manager once heralded as the next Warren Buffett, was caught overstating the value of his firm's security portfolio to obtain financing.

Goodwill.   The economic value and life of goodwill is a subjective decision. Acquired goodwill is an accounting item, but the value of internally generated goodwill is decided in the stock market on a day-to-day basis. Most companies trade at a multiple of net tangible accounting value. Trademarks, reputations, patents, customers, distribution systems, employees, and production processes are just a few items lending goodwill to a company's business.

Other Intangible Assets.   Under GAAP, as noted earlier, companies can capitalize the value of customer acquisition expenses, mailing lists, research and development costs, leasehold interests, contractual rights, software, patents, and shelf space, among other items. Even with the help of professional appraisers, companies and auditors have problems in establishing fair value for these assets.

LIABILITIES AND STOCKHOLDERS' EQUITY

Short-Term Loans.   This is a difficult item for managers to massage.

Accounts Payable.   Short of outright fraud, accounts payable balances are difficult to manipulate.

Long-Term Debt.   To reduce perceived financial risk and to enhance access to debt financing sources, corporations like to understate their true leverage positions. Direct debt financing often has the lowest cost, but it appears prominently on the balance sheet. Accordingly, companies seek alternative sources of debtlike financings such as long-term operating leases, supplier credits, and off-balance sheet transactions. While the analyst can get a grip on operating lease exposure by investigating the footnotes, off-balance sheet deals are harder to figure out.

Lenders to securitization and project financings typically turn to a specific asset base when things go bad, but in many deals lenders have subsequent recourse to the lead sponsor. Rather than outright guarantees, the support arrangements involve nomenclature that mean the same thing (e.g., a project may have a working capital maintenance agreement, "first loss" coverage protection, or take-or-pay contract with the sponsor). Due to legal and accounting nuances, such supports don't qualify as outright debt, but in judging the sponsor's economic value the analyst considers their potential impact on corporate performance. Debt rating agencies, for example, usually capitalize leases and consolidate off-balance sheet financings (along with the related assets) in calculating a firm's total debt picture.

Postretirement Liabilities: Pensions. The analyst wants to verify that: (1) the actuarial calculations for pension funding are reasonable; and (2) the pension plan is fully funded. Given the difficulties in estimating pension liabilities, the objective here is to ensure that the company's calculations have a safety margin. The corporate investor relations officer provides information in this regard, as do the footnotes to the financial statements.

Postretirement Benefits Other Than Pensions. Since 1993, companies have treated retiree medical and other non-pension benefits as a form of deferred compensation. The cost of these benefits accrues over the period that employees render the services necessary to earn them, instead of expensing on the pay-as-you-go plan. Like pensions, postretirement benefit liability and expense calculations are highly sensitive to the underlying actuarial assumptions.

Undisclosed Liabilities. In addition to project financing arrangements, a firm may have undisclosed liabilities that seriously affect its value. Auditors may have a hard time catching these items if management is not forthcoming. Potential damages from lawsuits are difficult to quantify, for example. Environmental liabilities can be open ended and present real problems in the chemical industry. Until recently, an airline didn't report its liability for frequent flyer miles.

Deferred Taxes. The deferred income tax reported on the balance sheet does not have the attributes of a liability. It lacks legal obligation, relative certainty of amount, and estimation of payment date. Moreover, unlike a pension liability, the amount shown is not a present value computed using a discount rate. For 99 percent of firms using accelerated depreciation on the tax return, this tax payment is deferred indefinitely.

STATEMENT OF CASH FLOWS

The statement of cash flows is a collection of (1) income statement data, and (2) selected changes in balance sheet items, as set forth in Exhibit 9–11. Liberal accounting methods in the first two statements thus flow through to the statement of cash flows.

EXHIBIT 9–11. Massage Corp.—Statement of Cash Flows (in millions)

Cash flows from operating activities	
Net income	$ 40
Adjustments to reconcile net income to net cash provided by operating activities:	
Depreciation	25
Deferred taxes	5
Changes in operating assets and liabilities	
Accounts receivable	(10)
Inventories, net	(15)
Other current assets	(5)
Accounts payable	15
Other current liabilities	5
Net cash provided by operating activities (1)	60
Cash flows from investing activities	(40)
Capital expenditures	(5)
Acquisitions, net of liabilities	(45)
Net cash provided by investing activities (2)	
Cash flows from financing activities	
Proceeds from loans	35
Payments on loans	(20)
Proceeds from equity sales	5
Dividends paid	(15)
Net cash provided by financing activities (3)	5
Net increase in cash (1) + (2) + (3)	$ 20

Note. Massage dedicates most of its operating cash flow ($60 million) to capital expenditures ($40 million).

Because of the leeway in accounting rules, net income can be reported in different ways, but cash in the bank is hard to fake. As a result, analysts consult the statement of cash flows to verify that cash follows reported earnings. Many is the junior analyst who has had this question: "My target company's accounts show profits, but it has problems paying bills and cash is getting smaller and smaller. Are capital investments increasing for the company, or is cash being absorbed by unsold inventories and unpaid receivables?"

FOOTNOTES TO THE FINANCIAL STATEMENTS

The footnotes describe accounting policies and provide additional information. They are indispensable to a financial analysis. Most practitioners prefer more disclosure, and corporate investor relations officers are usually agreeable to answering questions, particularly if the questioner works for a large institution or brokerage firm.

"BIG BATH" WRITE-OFFS, RESTRUCTURING CHARGES, AND EXTRAORDINARY WRITE-OFFS

Over the past 15 years, companies have become enamored with taking one-time charges to earnings in lieu of properly matching periodic costs to the related revenues. A typical tactic is to use a liberal accounting method for several years, thus boosting perceived earnings performance. Perhaps depreciation lives are understated. The R&D expenses are capitalized, rather than expensed. Eventually, economic reality sets in; the fixed assets and R&D aren't producing sufficient earnings.

Management can admit its financial errors and restate past earnings, or with the auditor's consent, they can post a large nonrecurring charge that marks down asset and R&D values in one fell swoop. This popular tactic has several benefits: (1) It negates the need to show restated earnings, which would give a true picture of past earnings power; (2) by exaggerating

EXHIBIT 9-12. Two Companies Amortizing the Same Asset (in millions)

The Scenario:
- On January 1, 1997, Conservative Corp. and Liberal Corp. each place a $60 million asset on their respective balance sheets.
- Conservative Corp. chooses a three-year economic life and Liberal Corp. selects a six-year life.
- Both companies have 1997 earnings before interest, taxes, and amortization (*on this asset only*) of $100 million.
- Liberal Corp. incurs a special charge in 1999, after deciding the asset's value has been impaired. The data follow:

Accounting 1997–2002

	1997	1998	1999	2000	2001	2002
Conservative Corp.						
EBITA	$100	$110	$120	$130	$140	$150
Amortization	(20)	(20)	(20)	—	—	—
EBIT	$ 80	$ 90	$100	$130	$140	$150
Liberal Corp.						
EBITA	$100	$110	$120	$130	$140	$150
Amortization	(10)	(10)	(10)	—	—	—
EBIT before nonrecurring charge	90	100	110	130	140	150
Nonrecurring charge[1]	—	—	(30)	—	—	—
EBIT	$ 90	$100	$ 80	$130	$140	$150

[1] 1999 write-down of asset from remaining $30 million value to zero.

The Result:

Liberal Corp.'s EBIT *exceeds* Conservative Corp.'s EBIT for the first two years. After 1999, Liberal Corp.'s EBIT matches Conservative Corp.

Liberal Corp's short-term earnings record (1997–1998) appears better, helping its stock price over this time.

the one-time write-off, future depreciation and amortization expenses are reduced, thus providing an artificial bonus to future earnings; and (3) several one-time charges can be lumped together in a big bath restructuring loss, complicating investors' ability to ferret out the impacts of each charge. The big bath announcement gets the bad news out in one large chunk. Earnings are not penalized year by year in a Chinese water-torture style, and the overall negative impact on the company's share price is lessened.

The acceptance of the nonrecurring charge is reaching absurd levels. Over the past 10 years, AT&T took four "one-time" restructuring charges totaling $14. 2 billion, which exceeded the company's $10.3 billion in reported earnings during that time. AMR Corp. (American Airlines) recorded large nonrecurring charges in each of the five years from 1992 to 1996, exceeding in total $1.9 billion. The company's net income ranged from negative $1 billion to positive $1 billion over this time. How does the analyst determine the normal earnings power of a company like AMR that takes repeated write-offs? Exhibit 9–12 shows how Liberal Corp. achieves higher earnings than Conservative Corp. by using the special charge tactic.

SUMMARY

In closing, accounting rules permit a company to represent its financial condition in a number of ways. The pressure for management to tinker with earnings is intense. Rising earnings mean a higher stock price, while missed growth targets can send the stock price into a free fall. Firms are thus tempted to base a financial statement presentation on overoptimistic assumptions and sporadic one-time charges. In determining earnings power, practitioners check the veracity of a company's accounting policies, substitute their own assumptions if need be, and recalculate the reported financial data. If the situation doesn't inspire confidence, a proper investigation might reveal misrepresentations, concealed losses, and window dressings.

In today's market, a fundamentally adverse relationship remains between security issuers and analysts. Professional investors are resigned to the fact that companies take liberties with accounting policy. Alert to the need to question accounting policies and the assumptions behind them, every practitioner hopes for more progress in the accounting profession's movement toward uniform reporting standards.

QUESTIONS AND SHORT PROBLEMS

1. Which of the following accounting entries is based on the educated judgments of management and the independent auditor? Circle all that apply:
   a. Depreciation.
   b. Amortization.

   c. Reserve for bad debts.

   d. Interest expense.

   e. Short-term loans.

2. Why do financial statements rely on the judgment, integrity, and competence of those whom make them?

3. Why doesn't Wall Street usually perform extensive financial analysis of historical financial statements?

4. How does buyer goodwill arise in a corporate acquisition completed for cash consideration?

   a. Buyer pays a premium to the market price of the target's shares.

   b. Buyer pays more than the historical book value of the seller's equity.

   c. Buyer writes down to realizable value the seller's assets and liabilities.

   d. Buyer completes a reorganization at the acquisition's closing.

5. What is a key business reason for the common shares of General Mills trading at 20 times historical book value in 1998?

6. Match the assets and depreciable lives:

   a. Video rental tape of recent movie   (i)   5 years

   b. New automobile   (ii) 18 months

   c. Railroad car   (iii) 23 years

   d. New office building   (iv) 30 years

7. Atlas Co. is acquiring 100 percent of the equity of Cyron Corp. for $300 million in cash. Atlas is financing the transaction with $300 million of new 9 percent debt and is allocating all of the excess of purchase price over equity book value to fixed assets. Complete the balance sheet adjustments and pro forma combined:

Balance Sheet Data
(in millions)

	Atlas	Cyron	Adjustments	Pro Forma Combined
Assets				
Current assets	$192	$ 88	—	—
Fixed assets	302	172	—	—
Goodwill	53	—	—	—
	$547	$260	—	—
Liabilities and Stockholders' Equity				
Current liabilities	$112	$ 50	—	—
9% long-term debt	35	—	—	—
Stockholders' equity	400	210	—	—
	$547	$260	—	—

8. Using the pro forma combined balance sheet prepared in Question 7, and the following income statements, complete the pro forma income

statement. Assume depreciation on fixed assets represents a 10-year average life. On a pro forma basis, Atlas Co. expects to realize cost-saving synergies of $8 million annually, by laying off 75 of Cyron's middle managers (assume *no* extra charges for termination expense).

Income Statement Data
(in millions except per share)

	Atlas	Cyron	Adjustments	Pro Forma Combined
Sales	$1,100	$ 548	—	—
Depreciation	30	17	—	—
Amortization	1	—	—	—
EBIT	58	31	—	—
Interest expense	3	—	—	—
Pre-tax income	55	31	—	—
Income taxes (40%)	22	12	—	—
Net income	$ 33	$ 19	—	—
Earnings per share	$ 3.00	$1.20		

9. Atlas' chief financial officer is trying to convince the company's independent auditors that the average life of fixed assets should be increased from 10 years to 12 years. If the auditors agree to the change, what would be the revised pro forma earnings per share as reflected in Question 8?

10. Most biotech companies have few fixed assets in relation to the stock market value of the companies. Does this mean the stocks should be worth less?

11. The application of many accounting principles is not a hard and fast exercise with each securities issuer. Why not? Aren't the principles available from the Financial Accounting Standards Board?

12. Why don't independent auditors operate in a manner that's totally detached from the company being audited? Circle all that apply:
   a. Independent auditors are essentially paid employees of the company.
   b. The auditors often need management's help in applying generally accepted accounting principles in a meaningful way.
   c. Management direction in accounting principles is allied with the auditor's role.
   d. Many audit-firms run lucrative consulting businesses that advise their audit clients, presenting possible conflicts of interest.

13. Provide three accounting tactics that might be construed as liberal accounting—but not fraudulent accounting.

14. A privately-owned, high-tech growth company is marginally profitable and is considering an initial public offering of common stock.

Why might it be tempted to exaggerate its financial results by using liberal, aggressive accounting? Circle all that apply:

a. Obtain access to public equity markets.

b. Preserve investment-grade debt rating.

c. Negotiate better IPO terms with the independent auditors.

d. Receive a higher stock price.

e. All of the above.

15. Many large, publicly traded companies engage in "earnings management." What is earnings management and how do these companies benefit from it?

16. Which of the following tactics is *not* directed at exaggerating a corporation's accounting sales?

a. Overstating warranties and returns.

b. Pushing sales orders into an earlier quarter.

c. Selling goods on unrealistic terms.

d. Selling to uncreditworthy customers.

17. To fund fully all of its employees pensions, Wheelbow Corp. needs a pension fund worth $75 million at the end of 10 years. For the first year, the company's actuary is suggesting an annual contribution to the fund of $5.1 million and an assumed 10-year compound rate of return on assets of 7 percent. Believing the actuary's rate of return assumption is too conservative, Wheelbow's chief financial officer is suggesting 8.5 percent. If the higher figure is selected, how much expense savings (and higher pre-tax income) will the company realize per year?

18. Some security analysts claimed that Blockbuster's net earnings were overstated at its initial public offering. Why?

19. Marie Kohl, a security analyst, notes that Hi-Tech Corp. is assigning a 10-year life to its computing equipment. It Marie believes the true economic life of the equipment is only 4 years, she should:

a. Call the company and ask it to correct its financial statements.

b. Increase the company's depreciation expense for such equipment by 2.5 times in her normalized analysis.

c. Notify the relevant stock exchange, which will inform the auditors.

d. Include in her report a statement of generally accepted accounting principles.

20. Why might the auditors of a retailer of ladies' fashion apparel have the occasional problem in evaluating inventory accurately?

21. Match the following inventory items with the difficulty in assigning accurate value:

a. 18-carat gold bars   (i)   Most difficult

b. Used automobiles   (ii)   Very difficult

c. Prerecorded compact discs   (iii)   Moderate difficulty

d. Residential real estate   (iv)   Easy

22. Why do publicly traded companies like using project financings and asset securitizations?

23. Many publicly traded companies take large restructuring charges, even though such charges create significant losses in a fiscal year. What long-term benefits can companies sometimes derive from a large one-time charge?

24. Consult Exhibit 9–12. Assume Conservative Corp. and Liberal Corp. are both going public in 1998.
    a. All things being equal, which company would likely receive a higher stock market valuation? Why?
    b. How does your answer defy economic logic?

Adopt-a-Company

Critically examine the accounting methods of your company by reading the footnotes to the financial statements; calling the company's investor relations officer to fill in missing information; and comparing the company's accounting practices with those of similar firms. Conclude whether your company's accounting is relatively liberal or conservative.

10

Financial Analysis and Stock Characterization

What are the financial clues enabling practitioners to classify a company as pioneer, growth, mature, or declining? Chapter 10 provides the tools for making these investigations.

In Chapter 8, we reviewed the financial results of Payless Cashways, an established firm functioning in a mature industry. In Chapter 9, we learned to look at reported financial data with a critical eye. Continuing with Section 5 of the research report (see Exhibit 10–1), we consider financial markers that place a company in the corporate life cycle. Historical financial analysis thus complements industry and company analysis in characterizing a business as pioneer, growth, mature, or declining. The financial analysis of cyclical firms is also discussed in Chapter 10, as well as how changes in shares outstanding and leverage alter earnings per share results.

EXHIBIT 10–1. Model Research Report

1. Introduction
2. Macroeconomic Review
3. Relevant Stock Market Prospects
4. Review of the Company and Its Business
5. Financial Analysis✓
6. Financial Projections
7. Application of Valuation Methodologies
8. Recommendation

THE TRAINING ENVIRONMENT

Financial analysis textbooks study the mature, established business. This is appropriate for the graduate school environment, where the student is getting accustomed to manipulating financial data and ratios. Examining a business with minor variances in income statement and balance sheet items from year to year is a good place to start.

As the student transforms into the practitioner, he is subject to a rude awakening. The public company landscape is littered with firms that fall outside the teaching model. Many firms exhibit sharp changes in year-to-year operating performance—for positive and negative reasons. Others complicate the analyst's job by engaging in numerous acquisitions, so one doesn't know where the real business ends and the new acquisition begins. The basic work is covered under Section 5 of the research report (see Exhibit 10–1).

THE MATURE ESTABLISHED COMPANY

As the Payless case illustrated, the prototypical mature business exhibits steady, if unspectacular, gains in sales and earnings. The standard financial ratios show only small year-to-year variances, and the impact of acquisitions and divestitures is easy to distinguish. With a few adjustments from the footnotes, the analyst can evaluate the progress of the base businesses separate from acquisitions. An example appears in Exhibit 10–2 for Belden, Inc., an established manufacturer of wire and cable products.

EXHIBIT 10–2. Mature, Established Company—Belden, Inc.
(in millions, except ratios)

	1995	1996	1997(E)
Sales			
Base businesses	$506	$624	$714
New acquisitions	103	43	90
Total sales	609	667	804
EBIT	80	94	110
Net income	46	55	65
Ratios			
Net margin	9.1%	8.8%	9.1%
Asset turnover	1.8×	1.9×	1.9×
Current ratio	2.1×	2.3×	2.3×
Sales growth	38.4%	9.5%	20.5%

Source: Securities and Exchange Commission reports and Belden, Inc.
Note. Belden complements its base business with acquisitions that spur income growth. EBIT = earnings before interest and taxes.

In classifying a business as mature, the practitioner likes to see a moderate uptrend in base business revenues and a stability in profit margins. From this predictable pattern, he forms an opinion on annual earnings power, absent acquisitions.

THE GROWTH COMPANY

A growth company shows consistent above-average growth in sales and earnings. The definition of "above average" shifts with the times, but a 12 to 15 percent annual rate (or higher) usually qualifies as a growth trajectory. Profit margins are stable or increasing, yet the business is likely to consume cash, since investment in new facilities, accounts receivable, inventories, and acquisitions outstrips internal cash generation. Regular issues of debt and equity are required to fuel the expansion. Because management is still learning the business and competitors are jockeying for position, the growth company may hit a bump in the earnings road from time to time. Overly generous sales promotions, excess inventories, and supply bottlenecks are three common problem areas.

PeopleSoft fit well the description of a growth company in 1996. Without the use of acquisitions, sales and earnings were rising at a rapid pace, and the company required common stock issues in 1993, 1995, and 1996. PeopleSoft used the funds to finance a big jump in accounts receivables and a $130 million increase in capital expenditures. Exhibit 10–3 shows selected income statement data and financial ratios.

EXHIBIT 10–3. PeopleSoft, Inc., a Classic Growth Company—Selected Financial Data (in millions, except for ratios and percentages)

	Year Ended December 31		
Income Statement Data	**1994**	**1995**	**1996**
Revenues	$113	$232	$450
% Growth	93%	105%	94%
Net income	$ 13	$ 27	$ 36
% Growth	73%	101%	31%
Ratios			
Net margin	11.5%	11.6%	8.0%
Asset turnover	0.8×	0.9×	0.9×
Current ratio	1.9×	1.6×	1.4×
Cash Flow Data			
Increase in receivables	$15	$50	$64
Capital expenditures	18	55	57

Three Types of Growth Companies

Not all growth companies expand from the same set of underlying factors. There are three types of growth companies. They are described as follows (and as set forth in Exhibit 10–4):

1. *Classic Growth Company.* This company offers a new product that no one (or company) knew they needed before the product's invention. These products are frequently the result of technological innovation (e.g., cellular phones and VCRs). PeopleSoft is a classic growth company, offering a human resource software system specifically designed for new client/server computing architecture. The classic growth company often forms part of a new industry offering innovative products.

In many instances of new product offerings, the practitioner has no "comparable companies" with which to compare the subject firm. The industry is too new to have more than one or two similar stocks. For example, in 1996 there were no true comparables for Starbucks, the coffee bar company. To avoid conducting analysis of Starbucks in a vacuum, analysts consulted the results of fast-growing companies in related consumer fields, such as restaurants and low-price novelty retailers.

2. *Market Share Growth Company.* This company participates in a mature industry, with GNP-like unit sales growth. Due to superior product differentiation or a better mousetrap, the company grabs market share away from its competitors. The mathematics appear as shown in Exhibit 10–5.

American Greetings is a good example of a company increasing its share in a mature market. Its sales grew 39 percent over the past five years, as its share in greeting cards rose from 33 to 35 percent. Its two principal competitors, Hallmark with 41 percent and Gibson Greetings with 8 percent, experienced declines in share.

EXHIBIT 10–4. Three Kinds of Growth Companies

Classic Growth Company	Offers a new product for which there was no established demand. The product is typically the result of new innovation and technology.
Market Share Growth Company	Participating in a mature industry, this company grows quickly because it boosts market share through better product quality, image, or service.
Consolidator	Operating in a fragmented and mature industry, the consolidator grows by acquiring numerous other firms. Paying the right price and realizing synergies are critical factors for success.

EXHIBIT 10–5. Market Share Growth Company (in millions, except for percentages)

	1997	1998	1999
Market revenues	$1,000	$1,060	$1,124
% Growth in the market	6%	6%	6%
Company revenue	$ 200	$ 233	$ 270
% Market share	20%	22%	24%
% Increase in company sales	15%	17%	16%
Result: Company's growth exceeded market growth by:	9%	11%	10%

3. *Consolidator.* A consolidator operates in a mature industry that is highly fragmented. Rather than achieving share through internal product and marketing developments, the consolidator buys numerous "mom and pop" firms operating in its industry. Each acquisition of a competitor means more market share. In addition, operating synergies may result from the combination. The technique is discussed fully in my previous book, *M&A: A Practical Guide to Doing the Deal* (New York: John Wiley & Sons, 1997).

The consolidator's business has two drivers: (1) acquiring companies at a reasonable price, and (2) achieving cost savings and/or revenue gains in the acquisitions. Due to the number and frequency of acquisitions consummated by the consolidator, the accounting is complex and the security analysis is difficult. Reviewing the results, the practitioner confirms several important aspects of the consolidator's status:

- *Base Businesses Are Stable.* The acquired businesses prosper after going under the consolidation umbrella. A big risk in acquisitions is poor integration, causing a corresponding loss in customers.

- *Purchase Prices Are Reasonable.* In its zeal to expand, the consolidator is tempted to pay high purchase prices, particularly when other consolidators are at work. The analyst's research should show that acquisitions provide a fair return on investment.

- *Estimates of Synergies Must Be Realistic.* To attract financing, consolidators sometimes exaggerate the cost savings and revenue enhancements that are realized from a transaction.

There are dozens of publicly traded consolidators, in various industries. An active consolidator is U.S. Office Supply, which acquired dozens of office stationers in 1995 and 1996, on its way to building a $3 billion business. Two other examples are Carmike Cinema and United Waste Systems. Annual sales, net income, and acquisitions for the three firms appear in Exhibit 10–6. Note how multiple acquisitions promote rapid growth.

EXHIBIT 10-6. Selected Data for Three Consolidators (in millions, except for acquisitions and earnings per share)

	1994	1995	1996	
U.S. Office Supply—65 Acquisitions				
Sales	$268	$356	$702	Sales almost
Net income	5	6	9	tripled in
Earnings per share	—	—	0.37	two years
Carmike Cinema—13 Acquisitions				
Sales	$232	$254	$296	Sales up
Net income	17	13	31[1]	28% in
Earnings per share	2.00	1.16	2.74	two years
United Waste Systems—110 Acquisitions				
Sales	$146	$228	$336	Sales more
Net income	19	27	35	than doubled
Earnings per share	0.65	0.77	0.87	in two years

[1] Before $45 million special charge.

THE CYCLICAL COMPANY

Both mature businesses and growth companies exhibit stable trends that lend confidence to estimates of current earnings power. Without a strong argument to the contrary, practitioners continue these trends into their earnings projections. After all, will people stop drinking Coca-Cola or eating at McDonald's? Cyclical companies pose another problem. Since their own earnings exaggerate the movement in the business cycle, boom times are followed by bust times, and this pattern is repeated with every cycle. Exhibit 10–7 shows earlier data from Exhibit 6–3.

Given the ups and downs of a cyclical business, there is no point in using the current year's earnings as a base, since that performance level is only temporary. If the cycle is peaking, the analyst knows that earnings declines are just around the corner. Similarly, particularly low earnings may signal a bottom, and one is justified in anticipating a recovery. Accordingly, the historical financial analysis should focus on the firm's earnings over the last full business cycle. Of particular interest to the analyst are the firm's average performance, operating leverage, and debt service capability. These items are examined for each year in the last cycle.

Average Performance and the Cyclical Company

Determining the average annual earnings power for the cyclical company complements the standard analytical strategies. The average is computed over the entire cycle, which probably includes one or two bad years and

EXHIBIT 10–7. Business Cycle Earnings Comparison—GNP versus Earnings per Share

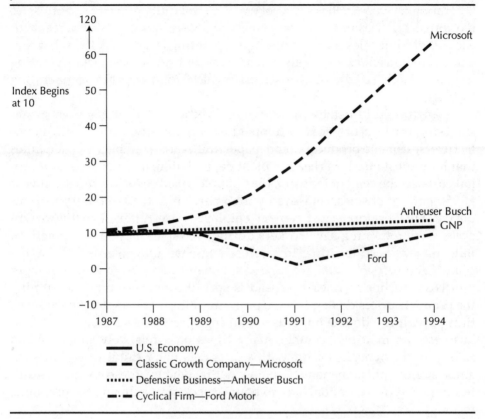

three or four good years. Analysts perform similar calculations for EBIT, EBITDA, and other performance measures. The averages are then used in various valuation estimates. The data for Bearings, Inc., a cyclical distributor of industrial bearings, appears in Exhibit 10–8. Cyclical company managements often encourage the practice of averaging by maintaining constant dividend growth over the cycle.

EXHIBIT 10–8. Bearings, Inc.—Averaging Cyclical Performance

	Economy's Performance									
	Expansion		Recession			Expansion				
	1988	1989	1990	1991	1992	1993	1994	1995	1996	Average
EPS	1.26	1.63	1.13	0.41	−0.16	0.82	1.12	1.46	1.90	1.06
EBIT (in millions)	25	33	25	17	5	21	28	37	49	27
Cash dividends/share	0.33	0.37	0.43	0.43	0.43	0.43	0.43	0.47	0.54	0.43

Note. Normalized data. Shares outstanding were stable. Observe the peak in 1989 and the bottom in 1992.

Recession began in 1990 and continued through 1992. EPS = earnings per share; EBIT = earnings before interest and taxes.

Operating Leverage and Cyclical Companies

Operating leverage is the degree of earnings volatility associated with sales movements. For example, a company whose earnings climb 30 percent for each 10 percent sales increase has high operating leverage. A firm that registers a 10 percent earning gains on a 10 percent sales boost lacks operating leverage. High fixed-cost firms usually have high degrees of operating leverage.

Many cyclical businesses have high fixed costs, resulting from a substantial infrastructure needed to operate economically. Automobile manufacturers, cement producers, and paper mills are examples of companies that have substantial overhead in plant depreciation, maintenance, and capital costs. In the cement industry, for example, fixed costs in a recession year are 50 percent of sales, compared with 5 percent in the temporary help industry. Furthermore, most cement employees are retained in the down-cycle, since retraining new workers during the rapid upcycle is impractical. But, this overhead is a drag in a recession, when unit sales are down, because fixed costs per unit are high. As demand picks up in a recovery, per unit costs decline as fixed overhead is spread over more units. Assuming the products prices don't go down, profit margins increase along with sales, thus providing a double impetus to earnings growth. As a result, a cyclical business can multiply earnings many times on a relatively small gain in sales (but the opposite occurs with a sales decline). Exhibit 10–9 shows examples of the phenomenon. Note how net income for these companies suffered during the recession, only to bounce back strong during the economic recovery.

As the practitioner examines cyclical company historical performance, he refers regularly to his industry study, which provides a link between the

EXHIBIT 10–9. Volatility of Cyclical Company Performance[1]

	1988	1989	1990	1991	1992	1993	1994	1995	1996
	Peak ⇨		Recession			⇨ Recovery ⇨			
WEYERHAEUSER—paper producer									
Sales (billions)	9.3	10.2	9.1	8.8	9.3	9.5	10.4	11.8	11.1
Net income (millions)	566	601	394	83	372	543	589	985	463
TRINOVA—industrial products									
Sales (billions)	1.7	1.7	2.0	1.7	1.7	1.6	1.8	1.9	2.0
Net income (millions)	81	72	41	(29)	14	44	66	95	103
AMERICAN AIRLINES—air transport									
Sales (billions)	8.8	10.5	11.7	12.9	14.4	15.8	16.1	16.9	17.8
Net income (millions)	477	455	(40)	(240)	(475)	(9)	228	196	1105

[1] "Normalized net income." These companies, like many others, incurred regular restructuring changes, special items, and extraordinary gains. Such items are eliminated in normalized net income.

firm's revenues and key macroeconomic factors, such as growth of gross national product, housing starts, and capital goods demand. Having established drivers for corporate sales, he looks for those aspects of operating leverage that influence earnings. If the company has a limited product line, the financial analysis can synthesize changes in historical profit margins into a few relationships. For example, Asarco, Inc., is a reasonably pure copper mining play. Just a \$.01/lb change in the price of copper causes an annual change in EPS of \$0.15. Aracruz Celulose, S.A. exclusively manufactures eucalyptus paper pulp. From 1992 to 1996, production costs per ton of pulp inched up with U.S. inflation. As a result, I calculated that a \$10 variation in price/ton affected Aracruz's bottom line by \$0.05 per share. Naturally, the results of such calculations factor in other elements affecting a company's health, such as industry shipments, market share movements, and cost control.

For cyclical businesses, quantifying operating leverage is difficult. Many participate in multiple lines of business and it is hard to separate cost of goods sold and other expense items by segment. Also, few firms disclose enough details on shipments, volume, and prices to facilitate the determination. Gaining insights typically involves telephone calls to management. Exhibit 10–10 shows how William Wigdon, CS First Boston analyst, singled out operating leverage for Williamette Industries, a multiline forest products company. By predicting paper price trends, he forecasts earnings per share changes.

Cyclical Companies and Financial Leverage

Lenders must be repaid, whether or not the borrower is enduring a recession. The debt service issue takes center stage for cyclical firms that rely on debt to finance their large fixed asset bases. Most are obligated to pursue

EXHIBIT 10–10. Operating Leverage and the Multiline Cyclical Company— Williamette Industries, Inc.

EPS Leverage per $40 per Unit Price Change Product	Leverage per $40 Price Change in per Ton Product Price
Linerboard	$0.74
Uncoated free sheet	0.46
Old corrugated containers	0.48
Lumber	0.20
Panel products	0.94

Assumes 40% tax rate.
Annual sales are $2 billion for Williamette Industries.
Source. 1996 research report of CS First Boston.

sizable capital investment programs because growth requires continued capacity expansions. In this way, they combine financial leverage with high operating leverage, and the combination adds to default risk. Accordingly, the review assesses cash flows carefully. Did cash flow cover debt service and capital expenditures over the cycle? Did the company borrow to pay dividends? Were cash reserves sufficient? Exhibits 10–11 and 10–12 show conservative and aggressive debt service approaches. The aggressive company should plan for a cash reserve to cope with the bottom of the cycle.

Another evaluative method is reviewing debt service coverage. Low coverage suggests that management risked creditor problems. On a forward-looking basis, the practitioner must be confident that the business can fulfill debt obligations during a cyclical downturn. Otherwise, it won't participate in the upturn. General Motors survived the 1991 recession by dipping into its large cash reserves (see Exhibit 10–13). Exhibit 10–14 shows why auto companies need to prepare for the cycle.

Other Cycles

As noted in Chapter 6, besides the general business cycle, other cyclical phenomena affect performance. Brokerage firms, for example, show cyclicality

EXHIBIT 10–11. Cyclical Firms and Debt Service Coverage—Conservative Firm

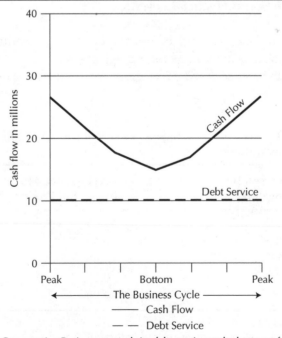

The Conservative Business exceeds its debt service at the bottom of the cycle.

EXHIBIT 10–12. Cyclical Firms and Debt Service Coverage—Aggressive Firm

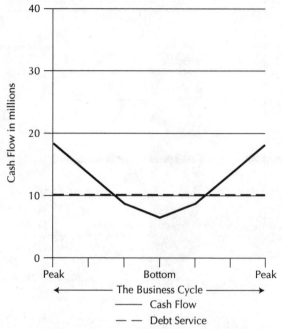

The Aggressive Business pays debt service out of cash reserves at the bottom of the cycle.
It should plan for a cash reserve to cope with the bottom of the cycle.

based on the ebb and flow of stock prices and trading volumes. Product re-placement cycles in the computer industry lead to volatile swings in semi-conductor demand. Other cycles arise from predictable variations in supply, which produce price cycles in commodities that are independent of the business cycle. Exhibits 10–15 and 10–16 show a recent aluminum price cycle and illustrate Alcoa's earnings record. Observe how Alcoa's earnings fell a lot more than aluminum prices.

Supply imbalances occur in commodity industries that rely on gigantic production facilities to stay effective. Examples include iron ore mining

EXHIBIT 10–13. General Motors Corporation—Interest Coverage

	Economy's Performance							
	Expansion		Recession			Recovery		
	1988	1989	1990	1991	1992	1993	1994	1995
EBIT (billions)	$6.2	$5.5	$0.9	$(2.8)	$(0.9)	$4.2	$8.0	$10.0
EBIT/Interest (×)	11.7×	10.7×	1.0×	(2.0)×	(0.6)×	2.9×	11.2×	17.5×

Note. Excluding captive finance operations and special charges. GM survived the 1990–1992 recession by dipping into cash reserves.

EXHIBIT 10–14. Factory Sales of New Motor Vehicles

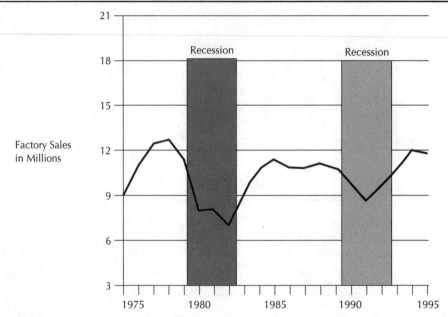

The impact of recessions on auto sales is quickly apparent in Exhibit 10–14.

($500 million to $1 billion per mine), petrochemical ($1 billion plus for a large plant), and paper production ($500 million plus for a paper mill). Participants all tend to construct new facilities at the same time (i.e., in the middle to end of the cycle when times are good and lenders are flush). The facilities then come on line at similar times, and a new supply floods the market, depressing prices until demand catches up. The paper industry is a perfect example of the pattern of capacity expansion and retrenchment, and price changes in pulp prices indicate the extent of the problem: $600 per ton in 1990, dropping to $350 per ton in 1993 before jumping to $800 per ton in 1995, and dropping again to $600 per ton in 1997.

EXHIBIT 10–15. Average U.S. Market Price per Pound for Aluminum Ingot

	1989	1990	1991	1992	1993	1994	1995
Aluminum Price/LB	88¢	74¢	59¢	58¢	53¢	71¢	86¢
Index	100	84	67	66	60	81	98
Alcoa EPS	$5.34	$1.70	$0.36	$0.12	$0.02	$2.10	$4.43
Index	100	32	7	2	—	39	83

Note. 1992 data excludes effect of accounting change. Alcoa's EPS were more volatile than aluminum prices.

EXHIBIT 10-16. Alcoa Earnings per Share versus Ingot Price

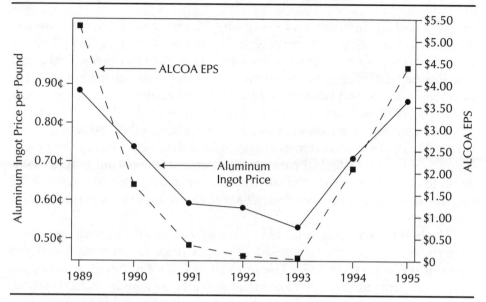

THE DECLINING COMPANY

It's important to distinguish between a cyclical company in the downcycle and a company in a permanent state of decline. Sometimes, purely cyclical factors are hard to differentiate from coincident changes in fundamentals such as shifts in customer preferences or changes in product technology. The industry study provides guidance in this area, but the firm may be operating in a submarket that functions separately.

Falling unit volumes and lower profit margins are stark evidence of a declining business. "Current earnings power" is going to be a continuation of this downward spiral, all things being equal. Few people want to invest in a modern-day buggy whip manufacturer. Cash flow and balance sheet analysis assist in determining a company's sustainability.

A recent buggy whip example was Smith Corona Corp., a major typewriter manufacturer. Faced with obsolescence by the personal computer/word processor, the company (and its investment banker, Lehman Brothers) argued in the firm's 1989 initial offering (at $21 per share) that typewriter demand would continue, nonetheless, in the Third World, where people couldn't afford personal computers. Smith Corona's revenues kept declining, however, as developing economies leapfrogged to word-processing technology. After two appearances in bankruptcy court, the company's stock now trades over the counter at 3 cents per share.

THE TURNAROUND

In every mature industry and every growth business, there's a company whose star has fallen. Once a profitable enterprise with rising sales, the turnaround is now a laggard. Its sales growth is flat to negative, and profit margins lag far behind the competition. Reasons behind the collapse are many and varied, and while historical financial analysis synthesizes some of the problems in statistical form, it offers little in the way of predictive ability. Typically, management has a plan to revitalize the business (i.e., the turnaround), but the implementation requires time and money. The practitioner focuses on historical cash flow patterns and existing leverage concerns to determine if the company has the time and resources needed for management to pull off the plan. Chapter 23 reviews valuing turnaround candidates.

The best known turnaround in recent years was IBM. A high cost structure and a one-time charge caused IBM's earnings to fall from $10.51 per share in 1991 to zero in 1993. The stock price fell off a precipice, dropping like a stone from $150 to $50 in 24 months. With new management installed, the computer giant recovered and the stock price returned to $150 in 1997.

Analysts ignored one key item when avoiding IBM stock in those dark days—the company's vast base of installed machines. These machines generated cash flow month in and month out, regardless of IBM's failures in developing new products in a timely fashion. IBM had the ability to stay afloat for years.

THE PIONEER

Historical financial analysis is almost useless for the pioneer company. With few sales and no earnings, the company is a poor candidate for the standard tools of absolute amount, percentage change, common size, and ratio analysis. Valuations of these stocks, in fact, are tied 100 percent to projections that have little connection with the firm's past. With little history to go on, practitioners use fanciful projections to justify prices. They are willing to absorb losses in the hope of a big payoff, as demonstrated by Internet investors. While waiting for the earnings to arrive, practitioners emphasize one historical statistic—the company's "burn rate."

In establishing itself, the pioneer company runs negative cash flows. Operating expenses, R&D, and capital investment far exceed the cash derived from sales and working capital changes. Using the naive assumption that outside financings are unavailable, the analyst calculates "monthly negative cash flow." This is called the burn rate because the company burns through that much cash in a typical month. This amount is then divided into cash on hand, and the analyst has a rough idea of how long the firm can last without outside assistance. If the firm has $24 million in cash and a $1 million burn rate, it implies a two-year window. During this time, the

EXHIBIT 10–17. Calculation of Cel-Sci's Burn Rate

Year Ended September 30, 1996	($ millions)
Annual cash operating expenses	$6.4
Capital expenditures per year	—
	6.4
Divided by months per year	÷ 12.0
Burn rate	$0.5 per month
Cash on hand at 9/30/96	$10.0
Divided by burn rate	÷ 0.5
Number of months to external finance	20 months

enterprise can avoid selling equity securities, which dilute existing share-holders' claims on future earnings. It also gives an indication of management's flexibility in concentrating on R&D, instead of selling stock.

Exhibit 10–17 shows the calculation of Cel-Sci's burn rate and indicates that the company has financing-free funding for 20 months. Cel-Sci is a biotech company with few sales and no earnings, but it has a promising technology with enthusiastic supporters.

FINANCIAL GAMES

For much of this book, financial analysis has been discussed in terms of total corporate performance. Higher sales and net income were naively assumed to translate into higher earnings and dividends per share. In numerous instances, this logical progression does not occur. Instead, companies issue more common shares to finance the innovative products, market share expansions, and acquisitions that provide growth. If earnings from the new initiatives aren't sufficient to cover the added shares, shareholders suffer a diminution of their investment's earning power.

Since we are discussing the purchase of common shares in this book, performance statistics on a per share basis take precedence. For example, hypothetical Big Sky Corp. prefers to grow sales rather than earnings per share. As shown in Exhibit 10–18, net income increased 20 percent annually from 1995 to 1997. To the casual observer, Big Sky qualifies as a growth company. The experienced practitioner, however, continues his inspection to *earnings per share,* which dropped 8% annually over the same period. Net income growth failed to travel to the bottom line—earnings per share. To achieve the net income gains, Big Sky issued too many new shares.

Utilicorp United is a good example of the Big Sky phenomenon. From 1990 through 1996, sales and net income increased 30 percent and 10 percent,

EXHIBIT 10–18. Higher Earnings, but Lower EPS—Big Sky Corp.—Selected Income Statement Data (in millions, except per share data)

	1995	1996	1997	Compound Annual Growth Rate (%)
Sales	$100.0	$120.0	$144.0	20
Net income	20.0	24.0	28.8	20
Average shares outstanding	10.0	13.0	16.9	30
Earnings per share	2.00	1.85	1.70	(8)

A higher number of shares meant EPS went down, even as net income went up.

respectively, on a compound annual basis, but EPS failed to keep up, rising only 1 percent annually. Over this time period Utilicorp grew the number of its shares outstanding by 62 percent. See Exhibit 10–19.

A historical analysis reveals the faulty financial mechanics of Utilicorp in achieving growth. The follow-up question is whether similar share issuances are needed to support the firm's future performance.

With some companies, the analyst may notice that top-line growth is moderate or nonexistent, yet earnings per share keep rising. The culprit in this case is either (1) a share repurchase program, or (2) a larger financial leverage.

The Share Repurchase Program

When net income is flat, a company can often *increase* EPS by *decreasing* the number of shares outstanding. With board authorization, the firm buys its own shares and then places them into a treasury account, so they aren't

EXHIBIT 10–19. Utilicorp United Inc.—Top-Line Growth without Corresponding EPS Gains

	1990	1991	1992	1993	1994	1995	1996	Compound Annual Growth Rate
Revenues (billions)	0.9	1.1	1.3	1.6	2.4	2.8	4.3	30%
Net income (millions)	59	74	53	84	91	78	104	10%
Earnings per share	2.03	2.15	1.31	1.85	2.06	1.71	2.19	1%
Shares outstanding (millions)	29	34	40	45	44	46	47	8%

Even though net income rose 10% annually, EPS failed to keep up. Utilicorp issued too many shares.

counted as "outstanding shares." The EPS numerator is therefore divided by a smaller denominator:

$$EPS = \frac{\text{Net Earnings}}{\text{Number of Shares Outstanding}}$$

The effectiveness of a share buyback is dependent on several variables, such as the opportunity cost of cash, the cost of debt, the share price, the tax rate, and the P/E ratio.

International Dairy Queen, Inc. practiced this technique. As shown in Exhibit 10–20, the company's EBIT growth was moderate over the past five years, but EPS rose over 35 percent. The reason for this difference was Dairy Queen's repurchase program, which reduced shares outstanding from 26.0 million in 1992 to 22.6 million in 1996.

Increasing Financial Leverage

When faced with mediocre earnings prospects, some companies prop up EPS growth by increasing debt levels. Rather than financing a portion of additional investment by issuing new shares, these firms opt to use debt for external cash needs. Shareholder dilution is thus avoided because the number of shares remains constant, but this objective is accomplished at the expense of making the firm's earnings stream more volatile and, therefore, more risky.

Consider the plight of Industrial Distribution Company. In December 1999, it had to decide how to raise $100 million to fund the completion of a new warehouse facility, along with the associated inventory. At a board

EXHIBIT 10–20. International Dairy Queen Inc. —EPS Effects of Share Repurchase Program (in millions, except for per share data)

	1992	1993	1994	1995	1996	Compound Annual Growth Rate
Net revenues	$228	$242	$269	$298	$308	8%
Earnings before interest and taxes	48	48	50	53	55	3
Net income	29	30	31	33	34	4
Earnings per share	1.12	1.19	1.30	1.43	1.52	8
Average shares outstanding	26.0	25.1	24.3	23.2	22.6	(3)

Dairy Queen 8% EPS growth rate was double the 4% net income growth rate. Share repurchases decreased shares outstanding 3% and boosted EPS results.

meeting, the chief financial officer pushed an all-debt option, and trotted out his projections showing how EPS increase faster with leverage.

"Projected EPS growth is now below-average," he said, "We can't afford equity." In contrast, the chief operating officer argued for the conservative all-equity option, "We're sensitive to the business cycle," he argued, "and EBIT doesn't go up in a staircase fashion. Debt stands at $100 million already." An assistant controller prepared the numbers and presented the board with three alternatives, as set forth in Exhibit 10–21's hypothetical case.

Which financing alternative should the board select?

The financing debate boiled down to the company's appetite for risk and its perception of future operating results. In the "Sunny Day" forecast, the all-debt option was the clear winner, EPS increased 11 percent on a compound annual basis versus 8 percent under the all-equity alternative. The "Rainy Day" forecast assumed a cyclical downturn in the middle of the period, threatening the firm's ability to pay cash dividends and service debts. Rainy Day EPS were higher under the equity scenario. Exhibit 10–22 provides the details.

With a shift in financing strategy, Industrial Distribution Company can change its projected EPS performance. Other companies perform similar sleights of hand to remedy poor prospects. Some conservatively leveraged firms incur huge debts to complete large acquisitions. Others incur sizable debts to fund massive share repurchases, thus increasing leverage and cutting outstanding shares simultaneously. A proper financial analysis uncovers such EPS-building strategies in short order.

EXHIBIT 10–21. Industrial Distribution Co. Three Financing Alternatives (in millions)

	Alternatives		
Capital Structure	1 Do Nothing	2 Issue Long-Term Debt	3 Sell Equity
Short-term debt	$100	$ —	$ —
Long-term debt	100	200	100
Equity	200	200	300
Total capitalization	$400	$400	$400
Average shares outstanding	20	20	26
Projected 2000 EBIT	$50 million		
Income tax rate	40%		
Stock price	$17.00		
Estimated 2000 EPS	$ 1.00		

Note. EBIT = earnings before interest and taxes; EPS = earnings per share.

EXHIBIT 10–22. Industrial Distribution Co.—Financing a New Warehouse (in millions, except per share data)

	2000	2001	2002	2003	2004
Sunny Day forecast:					
Sales	$1,000	$1,100	$1,150	$,250	$1,350
Earnings before					
interest and taxes	50	54	58	63	68
Earnings per Share:					
Debt financing	$1.02	$1.14	$1.26	$1.41	$1.56
Equity financing	1.00	1.09	1.18	1.29	1.38

All-debt EPS are higher in the Sunny Day forecast.

	2000	2001	2002	2003	2004
Rainy Day forecast:					
Sales	$900	$800	$700	$800	$900
Earnings before					
interest and taxes	40	35	30	35	40
Earnings per Share:					
Debt financing	$0.75	$0.60	$0.45	$0.60	$0.75
Equity financing	0.76	0.65	0.53	0.65	0.76

All-equity EPS are higher in the Rainy Day forecast.

Extra Shares Outstanding?

Another thing to look for is the ownership dilution attributable to hybrid securities. Fifteen years ago, analysts needed to consider only convertible bonds and employee stock options, but recent advances in financial technology have created equity-oriented hybrids that are difficult to figure out. Also, companies grant more stock options than ever before, and this means a greater potential for future share issuances. Only a studied review of the footnotes to the financial statements and the proxy statement can provide the answers.

SUMMARY

Security analysis would be a lot easier if all companies exhibited steady upward trends in sales, net income, and earnings per share. Because the real world doesn't operate that way, the practitioner is confronted with a bewildering variety of performance patterns.

A deliberate financial study simplifies the analyst's conundrum. It enables him to weave his way through the confusion and to identify forms of operating behavior that fall within the six business classifications used by the stock market:

1. Mature company.
2. Growth company:
    Classic growth.
    Market share growth.
    Consolidator.
3. Cyclical company:
    Business cycle is dominant.
    Other cycles.
4. Declining company.
5. Turnaround.
6. Pioneer.

As the classification process unfolds and earnings drivers are clarified, a secondary objective is ensuring that top-line performance is in sync with bottom-line EPS. Abrupt increases in leverage and sizable issuances of equity upset the traditional relationship between EBIT, net income, and EPS. Companies divorce the top and bottom lines in the following ways:

- Going overboard in issuing new shares to finance growth.
- Repurchasing shares to increase EPS results.
- Boosting leverage to accelerate EPS growth.

Now that the analyst has a good comprehension of the factors underlying his subject company's historical performance, he can proceed to the development of a financial forecast. In today's market, forming a view on the future is more important than describing the past.

QUESTIONS AND SHORT PROBLEMS

1. The 1999 annual report of Stocall, Inc., indicated a 19 percent compound annual growth in sales.

Stocall, Inc.
Year Ended December 31

US$ (millions)	1997	1998	1999
Sales	$460	$550	$660

On January 1, 1998, Stocall acquired a business growing at 10 percent annually and recording $30 million in sales in 1997. On January 1, 1999, it acquired another business growing at 12 percent annually and recording $42 million in sales the previous year. What was the internal growth rate of Stocall's base business over the 1997–1999 period?

2. Define a growth company. Do most growth companies generate excess cash from operations? Explain your answer.

3. Exhibit 10–3 shows that Peoplesoft had net income of $36 million in 1996. The year's increase in receivables and capital expenditures totaled $121 million, more than 3 times net income. How did Peoplesoft finance these two items?

4. Outline the principal differences between a classic growth company, a market share growth company, and a consolidation growth company.

5. Which of the following industries might be ripe for a consolidation? Circle all that apply:
   a. Car washes.
   b. Automobile manufacturers.
   c. Cable TV providers.
   d. Dry cleaners.
   e. Pulp and paper manufacturers.

6. Many cyclical companies have high operating leverage. With a 10 percent sales increase, operating earnings can jump by 20 percent or more. How does operating leverage work to their advantage in an economic recovery?

7. Alcott Corp. is a cyclical producer of commercial aircraft parts. Assume (a) all of its debt is represented by long-term notes with fixed interest rates; and (b) the company's 1999 results reflect the peak of its industry cycle. What is a risk for Alcott if the cycle turns negative in 2000?

Alcott Corp.
(in millions)

Income Statement	1998	1999
Sales	$751	$832
EBIT	66	80
Interest expense	53	61
Pre-tax income	13	19
Net income	7	12

Balance Sheet		
Cash	$ 38	
Other current assets	212	
Fixed assets	301	
Total assets	551	
Debt	460	
Equity	91	

8. Which of the following is not a cyclical industry?
   a. Paper manufacturing.
   b. Aluminum processing.
   c. Home building.
   d. Cigarette manufacturing.

9. Which of the following popular products turned into virtual dinosaurs? Circle all that apply:
   a. Mainframe computers.
   b. Manual typewriters.
   c. 8-track tapes.
   d. Contact lenses.
   e. CB radios.

10. Curetech, Inc. is a young biotech company with a monthly negative cash flow of $1.3 million. Annual capital expenditures are $2.4 million. Given the balance sheet below and your estimate of Curetech's "burn rate," how much longer can the company survive without external finance?

Curetech, Inc. Balance Sheet
(in millions)

Cash on hand	$18.3
Other current assets	5.2
Fixed assets	3.9
Total assets	27.4
Current liabilities	3.6
Total debt	1.7
Stockholder's equity	22.1

11. Is the burn rate statistic used in the same manner as the P/E ratio?

12. Business media commentators would call Big Sky Corp. (Exhibit 10–18) a growth company because sales and net income were increasing at a 20 percent compound annual rate. Why should the investor look skeptically at that characterization of Big Sky Corp.?

13. Up through 1998, Tellide's sales, EBIT, net income and earnings per share grew at 10 percent per year. In 1999, management believes sales and EBIT will only increase 8 percent. To avoid a hostile takeover, management needs to show 10 percent growth in earnings per share. As a result, the company is considering a share repurchase. It is now January 1, 1999; approximately how many shares must Tellide repurchase to achieve 10 percent EPS growth in 1999?

   Assume:
   (a) Tellide can borrow up to $100 million at 6 percent annually.
   (b) It can acquire an unlimited amount of its shares on January 1, 1999 at $45 per share.
   (c) Tellide will not pay a cash dividend.

Tellide Corp.
(in millions except per share)

Income Statement	1998 (Actual)	1999 (Estimated)
Sales	$ 300	$ 324
EBIT	50	54
Interest	—	?
Pre-tax income	50	?
Income taxes @ 40%	20	?
Net income	30	?
Earnings per share	$3.00	$3.30

Balance Sheet

Assets	$ 200	$ 220
Debt	—	?
Equity	200	?

Market Data at January 1, 1999

Shares outstanding	10 million
Market price per share	$45.00
Dividend per share	None
P/E ratio	15.0 times

Adopt-a-Company

Determine whether your company's EPS results correspond to its EBIT and EBITDA performance.

11

Financial Projection Pointers

Before jumping into the business of making financial projections,
you should know popular approaches and common pitfalls. Moderat-
ing optimistic assumptions with reality checks is an important part
of projection work.

Constructing accurate financial projections is a difficult task. As the top-down approach in Chapter 5 illustrated, so many variables affect a firm's performance—and they originate in so many sectors of the economy, the industry, and the company itself that the forecasting process appears well nigh impossible. The academic literature is full of studies showing the inaccuracy of earnings estimates. Even one-year forecasts have a mean error of 25 percent according to a 10-year study by Trinity Investment Management, but what choice do we have? Everyone knows the Graham and Dodd approach of picking dirt-cheap stocks on the basis of low P/E and price/book ratios, so these opportunities are almost nonexistent. Relative value analysis identifies inefficiencies, but the investor risks plunging into an already overvalued sector.

Notwithstanding the fundamental problem of forecasts, the basis for stock prices today is almost 100 percent forward looking, and there are solid rationales for this approach. That's why Part 6 of the research report (see Exhibit 11–1) is critical.

Practitioners aren't seers, so it is fortunate that no one seeks perfection in security analysis. As noted earlier, the analyst who is right 60 to 70 percent of the time is considered a Wall Street superstar. And being right doesn't mean predicting earnings per share down to the penny year after year. Just detecting when the consensus forecast falls out of the bounds of

EXHIBIT 11–1. Model Research Report

1. Introduction
2. Macroeconomic Review
3. Relevant Stock Market Prospects
4. Review of the Company and its Business
5. Financial Analysis
6. Financial Projections✓
7. Application of Valuation Methodologies
8. Recommendation

common sense is a great service to investors, who use this information as a signal to buy and sell.

In this chapter, we cover projection methodology at the company-specific level and review principles that can make you a better forecaster. The "nuts and bolts" of projections, such as assigning growth percentages to revenues and applying inventory to sales ratios, are covered in Chapter 8 (Payless Cashways case), Chapter 12 (Mars case), and Chapter 22 (USSB case and Cel-Sci case).

THE CASCADE OF PROJECTIONS

As Chapter 5 illustrated, the top-down approach isolates the important macroeconomic, capital market, and industry variables that affect a company's performance. These relationships tie into each other in a sequential fashion, leading to the cascade of projections summarized in Exhibit 5–5 and reproduced here as Exhibit 11–2.

THE TYPICAL FINANCIAL PROJECTION

The typical financial projection relies heavily on what happened in the past. The Payless Cashways forecast was a classic illustration. Key statistics such as same store sales, gross margins, and selling, general, and administrative (SG&A) expenses were anticipated to improve modestly over historical results, and neither a recession, a new competitor, nor a major market change was predicted. The vast majority of financial projections follow this pattern of the future reflecting the immediate past. Indeed, it is difficult for investors to argue against the rearview-mirror approach. Financial analysts, economists, and other investment experts are notoriously poor at gauging when a reasonably stable company, such as Payless, is going to face either a serious downturn or a rejuvenating upturn. As a result, most projections involving established businesses extend recent historical performance into

EXHIBIT 11–2. Cascade of Forecasts, Homebuilding Company

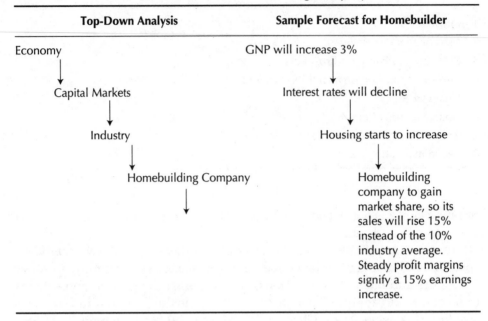

Top-Down Analysis	Sample Forecast for Homebuilder
Economy	GNP will increase 3%
Capital Markets	Interest rates will decline
Industry	Housing starts to increase
Homebuilding Company	Homebuilding company to gain market share, so its sales will rise 15% instead of the 10% industry average. Steady profit margins signify a 15% earnings increase.

the future, usually through a loosely derived mathematical model such as a regression, moving average, trend line, or exponential smoothing.

An exception to this convention should be the cyclical business, yet most practitioners are loathe to predict downturns. Accordingly, most published forecasts of cyclical firms move upward in lockstep, like the projections of stable companies. United Airlines provides one example in Exhibit 11–3. Note how this projection shows no business cycle.

ALTERNATE MEANS OF FORECASTING

To prevent a total reliance on historical data for established concerns—and to construct projections from the ground up for new firms—analysts consider alternatives to trending past history. These alternate approaches

EXHIBIT 11–3. United Airlines Inc.—Cyclical Company Forecast without the Cycle (revenue in billions, EBIT in millions)

	1994	1995	1996	1997	1998	1999	2000
Revenues	14.7	15.8	17.0	17.8	18.8	19.7	20.6
EBIT	249	377	502	532	472	536	632

Source. United Airlines 1993 Proxy Statement
Note. EBIT = earnings before interest and taxes.

are appropriate for businesses which have little track record or which participate in a volatile industry. Examples of the former are start-up ventures. Examples of the latter are innovative firms dependent on rapidly changing technology. Fashion-oriented businesses also require specialized techniques. Clothing, toy, and entertainment businesses fall into the fashion category.

The critical component of a financial forecast is the revenue projection. Most expense and balance sheet items flow directly from sales. Your first assignment is thus determining which technique is best for estimating sales. The initial reaction of the average analyst is to look at past sales as the anchor for predicting future revenues. While this technique is valid for many businesses, it must be tempered with a considered review of prospective changes in the company's product offerings, product prices, competitive environments, and required technologies. Even when firms operate in the same industry, they contain unique elements that make each projection a situational exercise. Many of these elements contain a strong historical bias while others require an independent interpretation.

A common approach to sales forecasting is placing the company in the corporate life cycle chart. Alternatively, the candidate falls into an industry designation. Both the corporate life cycle positions and industry categories carry sales growth patterns that are now well known to the reader (see Exhibit 11–4).

EXHIBIT 11–4. Defining the Candidate for Sales Forecasting

Corporate Life Cycle	Expected Sales Performance
Pioneer	Unpredictable and volatile sales movements.
Growth	Steady growth in sales as product acceptance widens.
Mature	Moderate increases in sales as the market for the company's product matures.
Decline	Decrease in sales as customers are attracted to newer, innovative products.

Industry Characterization	Expected Sales Performance
Growth	Steady growth in sales as product acceptance widens.
Cyclical	Established business in sector where sales are dependent on the economic cycle (e.g., autos, home construction).
Defensive	Sales movements that are resistant to changes in the economic cycle (e.g., bread, beer, and cigarette companies).

When the analyst establishes the fit between the company, its industry, and its corporate life cycle position, he is in a position to select the appropriate projection technique. Sales projection techniques fall into three categories: (1) time series, (2) causal, and (3) qualitative.

Time Series Forecast Techniques

The basic assumption underlying time series analysis is that the future will be like the past. Analysts prepare sales forecasts, therefore, by examining historical results, which are then brought forward through the use of moving averages, exponential smoothing, or trendlines. Using this technique, a company with a five-year growth rate of 10 percent has an estimated future growth rate of 10 percent. This rearview-mirror approach is difficult to counter effectively unless someone has a fresh reason for promoting a dramatic change.

The time series method has proven itself well in basic industries such as food, electricity, and medical care. As a result, it is popular in projections of stable and defensive concerns. Accurate projections can be difficult at the company-specific level, although it is easier when the business controls a significant market share. Dominant firms, like Budweiser in the beer business, are really a proxy for the entire industry.

The weakness of the time series technique is its inability to predict turning points in a company's performance. Turning points are often the result of hard-to-predict new competition or product innovation. How could a time-series analysis have forecasted the total demise of record player sales in the 1980s after 30 years of LPs dominating the recorded music sector? Or, the near complete collapse of U.S. television manufacturing in favor of Japanese, Korean, and Taiwanese TVs? How about the explosive growth in four-wheel drive vehicles, after these products had been consigned to the recreation and contractor markets?

The times-series technique also encounters a problem with business cycles. These phenomena do not appear on a preset schedule, and they vary considerably in their duration and magnitude. As a result, other predictive measures are required.

Causal Techniques

The causal methods forecast a company's sales by establishing relationships between sales and variables that are independent of the corporation. At times, these relationships involve broad economic variables such as gross national product or housing starts. To illustrate, cement demand is tied closely to gross national product (GNP) growth, so a cement industry projection relies heavily on GNP estimates. In other instances, demographic factors may influence a firm's future sales. For example, the "greying" of

America inevitably leads to predictions that nursing homes are a "growth industry." With other companies, industry-related factors drive sales. In the 1980s, for example, videotape sales and rentals related directly to VCR purchases.

Company-specific factors may be causal. In lodging, a hotel chain's future sales are influenced by its new hotel construction program. A computer chip company's revenues are impacted by a new production plant.

Quantifying these causal relationships means regression formulas and econometric calculations. Complementing these results are customer surveys and feasibility studies connecting future sales to variables that are not observable from the past. For example, hotel room rentals went up sharply in Florida after the construction of Walt Disney World. A tourist survey would have quantified that future link to lodging increases.

Causal forecasting is used frequently for companies in the stable and decline phases of the corporate life cycle. It is also applied to established firms operating in cyclical or defensive industries. A company in the later stages of its growth phase is a causal candidate since its operating record is long enough to relate to external variables.

Qualitative Techniques

Qualitative projection techniques are applied to pioneer or growth companies offering new products and services. With little history to act as a guide, the sales forecaster is left with expert opinions, market research studies, and historical analogies as his analytical tools. Sometimes, the result is nothing more than educated guesswork. The market reaction of truly new products is hard to gauge. Even experienced professionals have difficulty answering questions such as, What will be the level of acceptance? What price will the consumer pay? For example, direct satellite TV services and computer notebooks confounded Wall Street prognosticators.

Any would-be analyst is well advised to use qualitative techniques in developing projections, even if the business in question has a consistent sales record. The added work is part of an effective research report. Important qualitative methods for predicting sales are described in Exhibit 11-5.

Confronted with a historically derived projection from an established firm such as Payless Cashways, a careful analyst would have considered alternate means of forecasting. In 1988, the do-it-yourself (DIY) retailing industry was in the process of consolidation, as the larger, national chains gathered market share from smaller participants. The handful of national players, which included Payless, resembled a growth industry in this regard. Payless's own sales performance exceeded the growth in total DIY revenues, despite the firm's mediocre earnings indicating the stable phase of the life cycle. Causal forces affecting DIY sales, such as housing starts, would have been interesting to project alongside Payless's revenues. Also, qualitative factors could have modified the projection. Home Depot was in

EXHIBIT 11–5. Qualitative Forecasting Methods

Experts	The practitioner consults with an industry expert(s) to develop assumptions on sales projections.
Market Research	Consumer studies are made to estimate future demand and pricing for a potential or existing product line.
Historical Analogy	The analyst makes a connection between the company's potential sales and those of firms that offered a related concept in the past. For example, CD player manufacturers examined the prior introduction of the TV and VCR into the American household.
Futurists	A long view, say 5–10 years into the future, may require an unconventional interpretation. The force, intensity, and speed of contemporary business brings unpredictable change. Every industry has its visionaries who try to look beyond the obvious near-term developments.

the midst of expanding a "superstore" concept that had achieved consumer acceptance, and industry experts agreed Payless needed to fight back. A reasonable analyst would have expected the superstore's emergence to be a negative for Payless. An equally important qualitative factor—with a positive spin—would have been the anticipated rebound of the "oil patch" stores, since the region couldn't remain depressed forever.

PREPARING PROJECTIONS

Accompanying the preparation of top-line sales projections are conclusions from the historical financial review. Will the gross margin change in the future? Will SG&A expense stay constant as sales rise? Will inventory turnover jump in the coming years? Applying the answers provides you with a framework for making a projection. In the case of Payless, an objective practitioner would have prepared a forecast that was less sanguine than the junk bond prospectus. Exhibit 11–6 shows the prospectus forecast alongside hypothetical data developed by a sensible analyst.

Because the U.S. economy was in a seven-year upcycle, 1988's rational investor would have suggested a mild recession in 1990 and 1991, reducing DIY activity because of lower home sales. Profit margins would increase but fail to reach the levels presumed in the prospectus. Of course, both sets of forecasts in Exhibit 11–6 assume a leveraged corporate structure. Without a heavy debt load, Payless would have grown faster than indicated; cash flow previously targeted to debt service payments would have been devoted to expansion.

EXHIBIT 11–6. Payless Cashways—Condensed Forecast Financial Data (in millions)

	1989	1990	1991	1992	1993
Prospectus		**Optimistic Forecast**			
Sales	$2110	$2346	$2592	$2808	$2999
EBIT	127	161	196	237	276
Sales growth	10%	11%	11%	8%	7%
EBIT margin	6%	7%	8%	8%	9%
Rational Investor		**Realistic Forecast**			
Sales	$2030	$2120	$2210	$2340	$2530
EBIT	100	120	130	160	180
Sales growth	6%	5%	4%	6%	8%
EBIT margin	5%	6%	6%	7%	7%

Note. The junk bond prospectus contained optimistic projections that didn't fit the company's prior results. A rational investor uses realistic data. EBIT = earnings before interest and taxes.

With Payless, or any projection, the practitioner should follow these seven steps:

Seven Steps in Making Projections

1. Complete historical financial analysis.
2. Match company classification with appropriate sales forecast a technique.

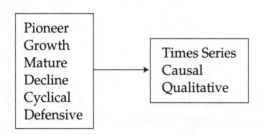

3. Select reasonable assumptions for other top-down variables.

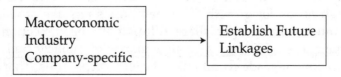

4. Prepare income statement down to the EBIT line.

5. Estimate external cash needs, if any, and structure future finances, such as additional debt and common stock.

6. Complete all forecasts down to earnings per share.

7. Perform reality check.

Steps 1, 2, and 3. Focus on Top-Down Study and Historical Financial Analysis

The first three steps draw from the analyst's top-down study and historical financial analysis. Experience dictates a focus on the critical assumptions and linkages. For the average publicly traded stock, you summarize these items in one or two typed pages. The normal forecast period is 5 to 10 years.

Step 4. Project the EBIT Line First

As noted in the previous chapter, the corporate financing decision influences per share earnings. If the company is going to issue more shares, EPS can fall behind income growth. Before predicting pretax income, net income, and EPS, the analyst balances future debt use against new equity finance. That's why EBIT is a good stopping point. You have to know future interest expense before projecting net income.

The capital structure assumptions are intertwined with the company's forecasted needs for property and equipment, inventory, receivables, and other operating requirements. These items usually change in tandem with sales.

Step 5. Structure Future Finances

The firm's operating performance, stock market value, and creditworthiness play an important role in the formulation of the forward capital structure. A company with a strong track record and conservative balance sheet like Campbell Soup can raise debt financing easier than a high-flying technology business like Biogen. The analyst can logically assume that the latter firm is more likely to use equity.

A common mistake among junior analysts is naively assuming that debt is available to fill in any gaps between future cash flows from operations and cash needs for growth. This beginner's mistake of using debt avoids unwanted earnings per share dilution in the projection, but it doesn't fit the real world. Only a small minority of publicly traded firms qualify as investment-grade credits (i.e., the elite corporations that have an easy time accessing debt markets). Most publicly traded firms are junk bond credits, and their debt financing options are limited. Presumed leverage parameters have to be realistic, even if that means your company issues more shares.

Step 6. Complete the Earnings per Share Forecast

With your financing scheme in place, you estimate interest expense and outstanding shares over the projected period. You then calculate pretax income, net income, and earnings per share for the income statement. Finally, you fill in the balance sheet and the statement of cash flows.

Step 7. Reality Check

With the final projection in hand, it's time for you to step back, perhaps for a few days, and consider whether your numbers are sensible. From my experience, many a practitioner gets swept up in running endless scenarios on his personal computer, when he should be taking a second look at the fundamental assumptions driving his forecast. Sometimes, another set of "eyes" helps spot obvious inconsistencies, and I recommend that analysts show abbreviated data to a disinterested third party, such as a colleague or an industry observer.

On the sell side, I've noticed that the reality check leans heavily on the subject company's management. Even after doing painstaking research and financial modeling, the brokerage firm analyst feels insecure. Anxious to have the benefit of the company's in-house projections and its knowledge of competing analyst opinions, he lays out his numbers in front of the firm's executives, who then have the opportunity to dissuade him of any P/E-deflating assumptions. While managers are an important source of information, their opinions are obviously biased and should be reviewed with caution. Yet, the sell-side analyst feels pressure to conform to the consensus.

THREE SCENARIOS

During the refinement of Steps 1 to 6, the practitioner runs numerous scenarios, testing the earnings and cash flow effects of different assumptions. These scenarios produce multiple forecasts, but they are variants of three versions: (1) the Upside Case (optimistic), (2) the Base Case (best guess), and (3) the Downside Case (pessimistic). For the established business in a mature industry, the initial EBIT spread is usually ±10 percent off the Base Case, and future EBIT moves off this level. Exhibit 11–7 provides scenarios from a recent research report on Boeing Corp.

The Upside Case of the average research report assumes no recessions, smooth product introductions, and moderate competition. Included in the

EXHIBIT 11–7. Boeing Corp.—Three Forecast Scenarios (EBIT in billions)

	Forecast							Compound Annual Growth Rate
	1997	1998	1999	2000	2001	2002	2003	
Upside Case								
EBIT	$2.6	$3.1	$4.3	$4.7	$4.5	$5.2	$6.2	16%
EPS	5.71	7.24	10.19	11.75	11.87	13.84	16.26	19%
Base Case								
EBIT	$2.2	$2.4	$3.5	$3.9	$4.3	$4.7	$5.2	15%
EPS	4.85	5.43	8.01	8.97	10.40	11.79	13.36	18%
Downside Case								
EBIT	$2.2	$2.4	$3.5	$3.9	$3.5	$3.1	$2.8	4%
EPS	4.85	5.30	7.71	8.42	8.03	7.50	7.05	6%

Note. The financial projection exercise calls for three scenarios. EBIT = earnings before interest and taxes; EPS = earnings per share.

Downside Case are the effects of recessions, price wars, and turning points. Gunslinging portfolio managers dismiss Downside Cases as too pessimistic, but thoughtful investors need to examine the financial cushion of a business if things go bad. They also need to consider a stock's potential bottom if events don't turn out as planned.

CYCLICAL COMPANY FORECAST

Because of the inevitability of a recession, it should be mandatory that practitioners include a one- or two-year down period in any Base Case of a cyclical business. Nevertheless, most analysts ignore this advice, as evidenced by the Boeing Corp. Base Case, which showed earnings climbing in lockstep fashion for seven years. That particular research report illustrated the firm's deep cycles over the past 20 years—three periods of strong growth, followed by three periods of steep declines—but the author maintained that things were different this time. Entertaining the notion that Boeing can escape the aircraft order cycle is speculative indeed.

A more practical approach is provided by Jim Rudolph, a veteran steel analyst at Fahnestock & Co., "You know there's going to be a downturn for these capital-intensive companies, so your forecast has to show the effects of the waves (of economic prosperity) coming in and out." Thus, while the overall sales trend over the future cycles moves upward, it is interrupted periodically with a couple of down years. If one assumes a repetitive seven-year cycle for aircraft orders, then Boeing's revenue tops out in 2000, to be followed by a couple of years of declines. Logic suggests that investors study carefully the Downside Case in Exhibit 11–7.

The same rationale is appropriate for the larger universe of cyclical enterprises, which includes capital goods and consumer durables companies.

EXHIBIT 11–8. Long-Term Cyclical Company Forecast

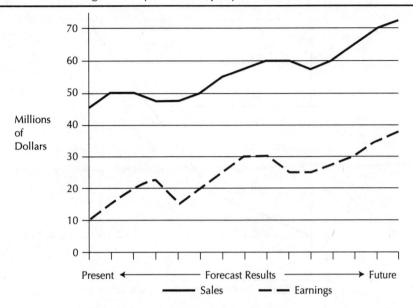

A realistic analyst expects the cyclical company's future results to be uneven.

Assuming the underlying business shows promise, the relevant sales and earnings forecast should look like Exhibit 11–8.

HOCKEY STICK PHENOMENON

The hockey stick phenomenon occurs as follows: (1) a professional evaluates a steadily growing business and makes a financial projection; (2) to justify an investment recommendation, he kick starts the company's earnings the year after an investment starts; and (3) others use his forecast to sign off on the recommended stock, which otherwise appears overpriced or risky. Graphically, the optimistic projection resembles a hockey stick (see Exhibit 11–9). Note how results suddenly get better in this projection.

Hockey sticks are prevalent in the latter stages of a bull market, since investors make increasingly optimistic assumptions to rationalize the high prices they're paying for stocks. Hockey sticks are also endemic to the merger and acquisition business. Consider the comments of Travis Engen, Chairman of ITT Industries, in justifying the $800 million acquisition of Goulds Pumps, "The pump business isn't very sexy, but the growth prospects are tremendous." In their quest to build larger empires, CEOs and merchant bankers often inflate numbers to promote a deal. Common sense is left behind.

This is exactly what happened in the $2.7 billion acquisition of Riverwood International, a paper and packaging company, by Clayton, Dubilier

EXHIBIT 11–9. Typical Hockey Stick Projection

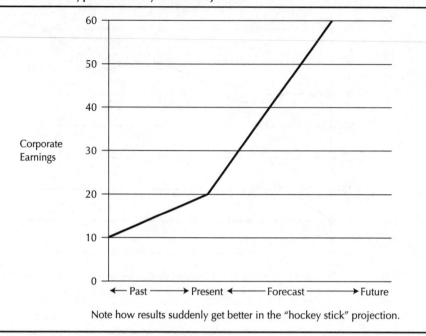

Corporate Earnings

←—— Past ——→ Present ←——— Forecast ———→ Future

Note how results suddenly get better in the "hockey stick" projection.

EXHIBIT 11–10. Hockey Stick Projection—Riverwood International Buyout

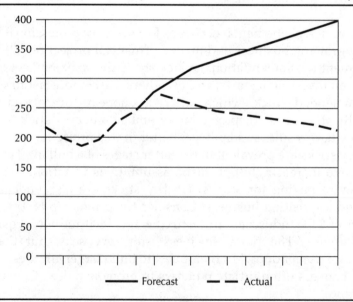

——— Forecast   — — Actual

Source. Company reports, *Wall Street Journal* (April 3, 1997).

& Rice, a leveraged buyout firm, in March 1996. In outbidding two industry players, International Paper and Georgia Pacific, the firm assumed a significant jump in earnings, which never happened. Instead, a downturn in income caused concerns among the buyout's lending group and it showed how even experienced investors can succumb to overoptimistic thinking, Exhibit 11–10 summarizes the situation.

SUMMARY

The critical variable for projections is sales, and practitioners emphasize three techniques to forecast this item—times series, causal, and qualitative. Once a sales forecast methodology is selected, the analyst follows a seven-step process to round out the remainder of his projection. Common missteps during this task include naively filling in easy debt financings and using overoptimistic assumptions. Positive thinking is an occupational hazard in the investment business, and all practitioners are advised to prepare multiple scenarios and seek independent counsel from time to time.

QUESTIONS AND SHORT PROBLEMS

1. Most corporate earnings projections made by analysis are inaccurate. Consequently, what's the point of completing a financial forecast as part of the evaluation of a company's shares?

2. Why do most earnings projections rely heavily on what happened in the company's past? Provide two hypothetical situations in which an analyst may want to place a reduced emphasis on a company's immediate past results.

3. Using the definitions from Exhibit 11–4, assign each of the following 10 companies an appropriate sales forecasting technique:

Company	Technique
Amazon.com	
United Water Company	
Baltimore Gas & Electric	
Merck	
Ryland Homes	
McDonald's	
Boston Celtics	
Kellogg	
Ciena	
Microsoft	

4. Assume you are a Lucent Technologies manager reviewing a sales plan for a new, miniature "picture phone" (i.e., a phone with a small video screen for everyday use in businesses and homes). The price of the phone is about 2 times the price of a normal phone. Which one of the four qualitative methods in Exhibit 11–5 should receive the most emphasis in the sales plan?

5. The Gap is planning to make yellow the new fashion color for the next season. Which of the four qualitative sales forecasting methods should it emphasize before proceeding?

6. Why must security analysts evaluate with a skeptical eye the financial forecasts provided by corporate issuers? Consider the Payless Company case as one example.

7. Xtride, Inc. has a solid track record and moderate leverage, but certain aspects of its business have a cyclical component. The company is considering the acquisition of a new $100 million factory (at book value) that will add $15 million of EBIT to Xtride's results over the next three years. *Without* the new factory, Xtride is forecasting the following results:

Xtride, Inc.
(US$ millions, except per share)

	Current Year Actual Results	Forecast 1	Forecast 2	Forecast 3
EBIT	$ 30	$ 33	$ 37	$ 41
Interest	8	8	10	10
Pre-tax income	22	25	27	31
Taxes (40%)	9	10	11	12
Net income	$ 13	$ 15	$ 16	$ 19
Earnings per share	$1.30	$1.50	$1.60	$1.90

Xtride can (a) borrow $100 million at 9 percent by selling a bond issue, (b) sell 6.25 million shares at $16 per share, or (c) do a combination offering of $50 million of 7 percent bonds and 2.5 million shares at $20.00 per share. Which financing option (a, b, or c) provides the highest EPS in the third year?

Option c enables the company to sell stock at a higher price than option b and to sell bonds at a lower yield than option a. Provide a likely explanation for the disparities.

8. Describe the "hockey stock" phenomenon. Why does the phenomenon tend to get repeated during bull markets for U.S. equity securities?

9. Place the following financial projection steps in the proper order:
    a. Match company classification with appropriate sales forecasting technique.

    b. Complete historical financial analysis.

    c. Complete projected income statement of the EBIT line.

    d. Select top-down variables.

    e. Structure future financing plan.

10. What's the purpose of a reality check in a corporate financial projection? Circle one answer:

    a. Verify industry "top down" variables.

    b. Gauge overall "common sense" attributes of the projection.

    c. Coordinate the analyst's financial model with the issuer's management.

    d. Ensure the "cascade of projections" flows from sales.

Adopt-a-Company

A. Which projection technique is most suitable for your company?

B. If previous security analysts reports on your company are available, compare the analysts' earlier earnings forecast to actual results.

C. Has your company used any "financial games" to enhance its earnings per share over the last five years?

PART III

Valuation and the Investment Decision

At the conclusion of the research report, the analyst answers two questions: (1) Is this security fairly valued? and (2) based on the previous answer, should I recommend buying or selling the stock? Part III provides the modern valuation framework.

12

Modern Approaches
to Valuation

Chapter 12 reviews the manner in which valuation techniques are applied in the 1990s, and covers one technique, intrinsic value, in specific. The equally important relative value method is stressed in Chapter 13.

The following three valuation approaches instill a discipline in the stock market and form the basis for Section 7 of the research report (see Exhibit 12–1):

1. *Intrinsic Value.* A stock's price equals the net present value of its dividends.
2. *Relative Value.* A stock's value is determined by comparing similar stock values.
3. *Acquisition Value.* Calculate a company's share price by determining its worth to a third party acquirer.

EXHIBIT 12–1. Model Research Report

---

1. Introduction
2. Macroeconomic Review
3. Relevant Stock Market Prospects
4. Review of the Company and Its Business
5. Financial Analysis
6. Financial Projections
7. Application of Valuation Methodologies✓
8. Recommendation

EXHIBIT 12–2. Valuation Approaches

---

1. *Intrinsic Value.* A business equals the net present value of its dividends. Intrinsic value is sometimes called "fundamental value" or the "discounted cash flow" technique.

2. *Relative Value.* A firm's value is determined by comparing it to similar companies' values.

3. *Acquisition Value.* Calculate a company's share price by determining its worth to a third party acquirer.

4. *Technical.* Future share prices can be divined from prior trading patterns.

There are four broad approaches to common stock valuation (see Exhibit 12–2), but only these three lend themselves to the quasi-scientific method outlined in this book. They forecast stock prices on the basis of economic, capital market, industry and company information.

STARTING WITH INTRINSIC VALUE

A stock's intrinsic value is the present value of its stream of future cash dividends. This value is calculated with different formulas, depending on the situation at hand. The simplest formula is used for firms that have a stable capital structure and growth rate:

Discounted Cash Dividend Valuation Approach
Constant Growth Model

$$P = \frac{D_1}{k - g}$$

where P = Intrinsic value (i.e., correct price)
   D_1 = Next year's cash dividend
   k = Annual rate of return required by shareholders
   g = Expected annual growth rate of dividends

To calculate the intrinsic value, the practitioner plugs in the variables D_1, k, and g. He derives D_1 and g from his financial projections. We discuss k later in the chapter.

For companies that are not expected to have anything approaching a constant growth rate, such as a cyclical business, a start-up venture, or a firm with a history of special dividends and spin-offs, the formula is modified. The practice is to predict dividends for a 5- or 10-year period, after which time the company is assumed to pay out dividends in a constant fashion. A 10-year time horizon is shown here:

Discounted Cash Dividend Valuation Approach
Two-Step Growth Model

Step 1: Variable Growth
Rates (Years 1 to 10)

Step 2: Constant Growth
Rate (Year 11)

$$P = \frac{D_0(1+g_1)}{(1+k)^1} + \frac{D_1(1+g_2)}{(1+k)^2} + \ldots + \frac{D_9(1+g_{10})}{(1+k)^{10}} + \frac{\dfrac{D_{10}(1+g_{11})}{k-g}}{(1+k)^{10}}$$

where P = Intrinsic value

D = Current year's dividend

k = Annual rate of return required by shareholder (which is the sum of the risk-free rate plus a premium for "risk")

g = Yearly growth rate

g_{11} = Constant growth rate after year 10

In the two-step model, g_1 is the growth rate of the dividend in year one, g_2 in year two, and so on until year 11 when the model becomes steady state. Alternative dividend models value stocks that don't pay dividends, consider situations involving short-term holding periods, and allow for periods of varying discount rates. The research department of Morgan Stanley & Co. uses multiple discount rates for speculative growth stocks (see Exhibit 12–3).

EXHIBIT 12–3. Multistage Discounted Cash Flow Analysis—Speculative Growth Stocks

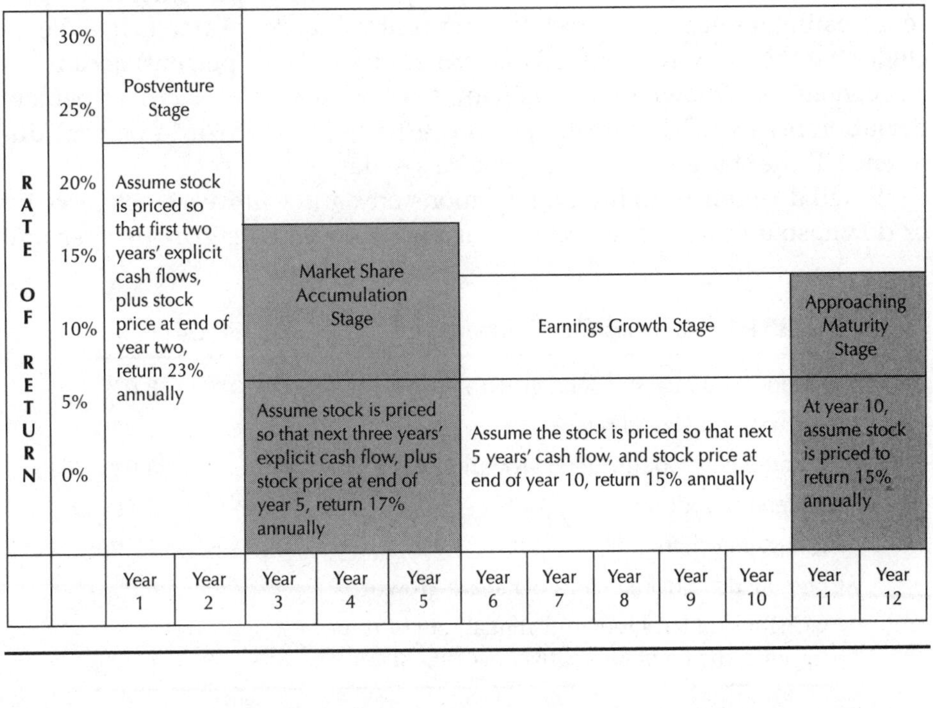

The inability of businesspeople to predict accurately the future growth rates of a company's dividend, and the lack of a market consensus on the appropriate discount rate for almost any stock, combine to generate an enormous amount of trading activity based on differing views regarding these two fundamental aspects of a stock's worth. Even if there appears to be an underlying consensus on future dividends and on what an equity holder's expected return should be, minuscule differences in the D_1, g, and k estimates provide a broad band of trading values.

An analysis of the fictitious Atlas Gas Company (AGC) is shown in Exhibit 12–4.

The AGC stockholder's 11.0 percent rate of return objective is reasonable. Alternative investments with less risk provide expected returns that are below 11 percent, so the AGC stockholder is getting "paid" for the extra risk. Exhibit 12–5 shows alternative investments. AGC stock (and any corporate stock) is a riskier investment than a U.S. government bond or a high-quality corporate bond. For this reason, AGC offers its shareholders the potential for a superior return.

Using the prior information, the analyst applies the dividend discount formula to derive a $50 share value:

$$AGC\ Price = \frac{D_1}{k - g}$$

$$AGC\ Price = \frac{\$1.50}{.11 - 08}$$

$$AGC\ Price = \$50.00$$

An investor who disagrees just slightly with the 11 percent k and 8 percent g estimates has a substantially different value. For example, if you conclude that the growth rate is 7.5 percent annually (vs. 8 percent) because of an economic slowdown in the company's service area, this small 0.5 percent deviation prices AGC shares at $43 (i.e., $1.50/.11 − .075), a 14 percent difference. If the shares trade at $50, you're a seller.

Small differences in investor opinions on k and g move a stock price up or down, so a public company pays attention to how its growth rates and

EXHIBIT 12–4. Atlas Gas Company (AGC) Common Stock

Compound annual dividend growth	8.0%
Next year's dividend rate	$1.50
Expected constant dividend growth rate ("g")	8.0%
Dividend payout ratio	50.0%
Earnings per share	$3.00
Compound annual earnings per share growth	8.0%
AGC stockholder's required annual rate of return ("k"), given a choice of alternative investments	11.0%

EXHIBIT 12–5. Sample Alternative Investments, March 1997 Annual Expected Rates of Return

U.S. government bonds	7.0%
"AA" rated bonds	7.5
"BB" rated bonds	8.0
AGC stock	11.0

required returns are perceived by outsiders. Even a minor decline in the consensus view of a firm's growth rate is damaging. A small increase in k, the investor's desired rate of return (i.e., the discount rate) produces a similar result (increase k from 11% to 11.5% and stock price drops to $43 again). Thus, in addition to implementing strategies which actually achieve higher dividends, companies foster an image of predictable growth. This image of constancy is quite valuable, because complacent investors view the firm's shares in a less risky light. They award a lower discount rate to its cash flows, resulting in a bigger present value.

This portrait of stability is in obvious contrast to the volatile environment that is endemic to a market economy. Nevertheless, in an effort to defy economic gravity, public companies avoid cutting dividends, notwithstanding earnings declines, and seek to "smooth out" or "manage" the natural variability in annual income by timing revenue recognition, incurring special charges, or taking one-time gains. This feigned stability provides confidence to investors, who then consider the stock as having a lower risk profile than reality might indicate.

Once you determine a stock's intrinsic value, your job is monitoring the situation for developments that change D, k, or g significantly. Separating short-term factors from truly fundamental issues is the real challenge here. Large acquisitions, for example, demand immediate attention. Their size, immediate balance sheet impact, frequent diversification aspects, and earnings growth implications influence dramatically the value equations.

A large acquisition deal causes a security analyst to revise the buyer's dividend prospects. After completing "what if" projections, he looks to the quality of the dividend stream being forecast. Did the buyer finance the deal entirely with debt? If so, the combined company's leverage may indicate that future dividends are subject to greater volatility, thereby mandating a higher required rate of return than before the deal. Likewise, a diversification acquisition might lead to a lower k by reducing the buyer's risk. For example, if a volatile hi-tech firm purchases a stable food business, investors will consider the combined earnings stream as less risky than the hi-tech company on a stand-alone basis, assuming no change in leverage ratios. This sentiment of "less risk" results in a lower k for the surviving company. If an electric utility purchases a biotech firm, the opposite happens since the latter has a greater risk profile.

The use of k and g as individual company statistics independent of the broader market is a key tenet of the intrinsic value crowd, but the sheer difficulty of forecasting corporate dividends and determining the appropriate discount rate spawns many arguments. Discussions among intrinsic value investors typically involve comments such as "How can you assign an 11 percent growth rate to the stock's dividends when the historical growth rate is 14 percent?" "Other firms in the industry are growing at 12 percent; why is your projected growth rate only 8 percent?" "Your 18 percent discount rate is too high; if we drop it to 16 percent, we can justify buying the stock." "How can our estimates of g equals 12 percent and k equals 17 percent be correct; they indicate a $14 stock price when the market price is $24. Our numbers must be wrong!"

RELATIVE VALUE APPROACH

Although k and g are popular subjects in business schools, the inability of investors and analysts to agree on exact estimates for individual stocks, and the huge price differences created by only small differences in these statistics, reduce their relevance in the real world. While believing that the intrinsic value concept is intuitively correct, a large portion of the investment community abandons it as unworkable from a practical point of view. In its stead, analysts rely on the "relative value" concept, which uses comparisons as the basis for establishing value. The theory is simple enough. If they participate in the same industry, companies with comparable track records and balance sheets should have comparable valuation yardsticks. Since k and g statistics are indeterminate, the relative value school adopts substitute measures, the most popular being the P/E ratio.

Relative value adherents can be spotted when they are saying something like "Merck's stock is undervalued at a 19 P/E ratio, yet it is growing faster than Eli Lilly, which has a 22 P/E ratio" or "Union Carbide is overvalued. Its 20 P/E ratio is 33 percent higher than the industry's 15 P/E ratio, but its projected growth is only 14 percent higher than the industry's."

Relative value investors employ many financial statistics. Ratios such as the Enterprise Value to Earnings before Interest and Taxes, Share Price to Book Value, and Share Price to Sales per Share are popular. Many industry-specific ratios exist. For example, retail analysts use Share Price to Number of Stores per Share Ratio as one barometer of relative value. Cable TV analysts use the Share Price to Number of Connected Homes per Share Ratio; cement analysts, Tons of Production Capacity per Share Ratio, and so on. The P/E ratio, however, remains the most popular relative valuation statistic.

The P/E Ratio

Wall Street synthesizes the k and g variables of the dividend discount model into one statistic, the price/earnings ratio. Business publications constantly print statements such as "Philip Morris is trading at a 16 P/E ratio, 10 percent over the market average," "Dow Chemical looks cheap at a 15 P/E ratio," or "Bell Atlantic is overpriced at a 22 P/E ratio." Individual P/E ratios are often expressed in relative terms. When a firm's P/E ratio exceeds the P/E ratio of the stock market as a whole, that company is considered to have earnings growth potential exceeding the prospects of the average listed company. Conversely, a relatively low P/E indicates a profile that is below average. Analyst extend these comparisons to a firm's peers.

In the case of either a "high growth" company or a "low growth" company, the P/E ratio is a function of two perceptions: (1) What is the company's future growth rate? and (2) How much should this stock return relative to other investments? Consider the interrelationships involved in the following two formulas:

Dividend Discount Model

$$P = \frac{D_1}{k - g}$$

Price/Earnings Multiple

$$\text{P/E Multiple} = \frac{P_A}{EPS}$$

where

P = Intrinsic value (i.e., appropriate stock price)
P_A = Actual market price
D_1 = Expected dividend rate
k = Investors' required rate of return
g = Expected growth rate in dividends
EPS = Current earnings per share
P/E multiple = Price/earnings ratio

For every publicly traded stock, its actual price, dividend rate, and earnings per share are known facts, which cannot be disputed. These statistics are available in various business newspapers. The variables that are open to interpretation and educated guesswork are k and g; these same publications provide only estimates of these statistics. It's up to the analyst to decide if

EXHIBIT 12–6. Atlas Gas Company—P/E Calculation Using Intrinsic Value Variables

$$P/E = \frac{\left[\dfrac{D}{k - g}\right]}{EPS}$$

$$= \frac{\left[\dfrac{\$1.50}{11.0\% - 8.0\%}\right]}{\$3.00}$$

$$= \frac{\$50.00}{\$3.00}$$

$$= 16.7\times$$

EXHIBIT 12–7. Atlas Gas Company—Adjusted P/E Calculation for New Contract

$$P/E = \frac{\left[\dfrac{\$1.50}{11.0\% - 10.0\%}\right]}{\$3.00}$$

$$P/E = \frac{\$150.00}{\$3.00}$$

$$P/E = 50.0\times$$

his intrinsic value calculation matches the current market price. Changes in the perception of a stock's risk or growth characteristics alter the P/E ratio. Exhibit 12–6 shows the substitution of "$D_1/k - g$" for "P_A" in the P/E Multiple calculation.

Assume that AGC announces a major new contract, unanticipated by investors. If the Street decides the deal increases the growth rate, the P/E ratio goes up considerably. Suppose AGC's growth rate increases to 10 percent from 8 percent. The stock price then reaches $150 and the P/E ratio climbs to 50 times (Exhibit 12–7). If the P/E had stayed at 16.7 times after the contract's implementation, investors would have considered AGC a Buy.

However, assume AGC incurs substantial debt to build capacity for the new contract. The perception is now one of increased earnings volatility. Investors thus demand a higher rate of return, reducing the 50.0 times multiple to a number more down to earth. Exhibit 12–8 shows the impact of a 13 percent return instead of the earlier 11 percent return. In this case, the new contract doesn't improve the P/E ratio.

The P/E ratio is a statistic that incorporates the *growth* and *risk* aspects of a stock. The P/E ratio climbs when investors boost a stock's indicated growth rate. Likewise, the P/E ratio increases or decreases with changes in the perception of a stock's risk characteristics. This having been said, Wall Streeters focus on growth rates far more than perceived risks, which is why investors have to be doubly careful with speculative growth investments.

EXHIBIT 12–8. Atlas Gas Company—Adjusted P/E Calculation for New Contract and New Debt

$$P/E = \frac{\left[\dfrac{\$1.50}{13.0\% - 10.0\%}\right]}{\$3.00}$$

$$P/E = \frac{\$50.00}{\$3.00}$$

$$P/E = 16.7\times$$

THE PRICE OF RISK

A stock's required rate of return is based on a relative analysis of the returns being offered by competing investments, taking into account the respective risks involved. Investments perceived as risky because of checkered track records or questionable prospects provide investors with a high expected rate of return. Exhibit 12–9 illustrates a risk/return matrix for competing investments and Exhibit 12–10 shows the matrix in graphic form.

The notion that the risks of competing investments can be (1) measured and then (2) priced comes from the Capital Asset Pricing Model (CAPM), a theoretical concept refined in the 1960s. The principal measure of risk under CAPM is beta (ß), which is a statistic that measures the historical volatility of a given investment's rate of return with the historical return of the U.S. stock market. The beta (ß) of an individual stock is calculated empirically, and lists of corporate betas are available from data services.

The logic of the CAPM is simple. Unpredictability and volatility in investment returns are bad. Stability and assurance of returns are good. The required return of any stock should equal the rate of return on a relatively riskless investment, such as a U.S. government bond, plus a premium for the added risk incurred by the investor for holding a non-government-guaranteed investment. The premium is obtained in a two-step process. First, the government bond rate is subtracted from the expected return of the stock market. Second, the result of this subtraction, which is defined as the "market premium" for risk, is multiplied by the stock's beta to determine the applicable risk premium. If government bonds yield 7 percent and people believe the stock market has an *expected rate of return* (i.e., dividends plus capital gains) of 14 percent, the estimated "market premium" is 7 percent (14% minus 7%). If the *relevant beta of the stock* is 1.50, this means that the risk premium for the investment is 1.50× the 7 percent market premium, or 1.50× 7 percent = 10.5 percent. The calculation appears in Exhibit 12–11.

EXHIBIT 12–9. Risk and Return, August 1997

Investment	Annual Expected Return (%)
U.S. government bonds	7.0
"A" rated corporate bonds	8.0
Utility stock mutual fund	13.5
Industrial stock mutual fund	14.0
Biotech company common stock	20.0–22.0
Leveraged buyout equity	30.0–35.0

EXHIBIT 12–10. Risk and Return Graph for August 1997

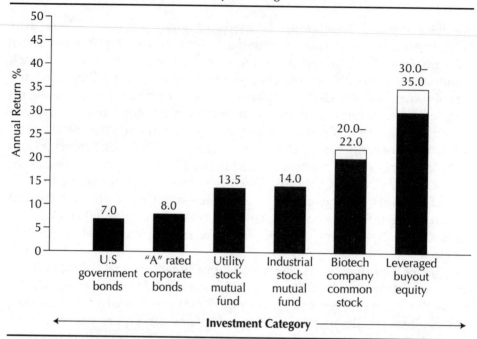

Once the individual stock risk premium has been calculated, k is computed by adding the government bond yield to the previous calculation:

1. k = Government Bond Yield + Individual Stock Risk Premium
2. $k = 7\% + 10.5\%$
3. $k = 17.5\%$

Based on the preceding information, a rational investor purchases the stock when he believes he can achieve a 17.5 percent return. Projected cash returns from the stock are discounted at 17.5 percent and the resultant present value is then compared with the stock price. If the present value is higher than the market price, the stock is a Buy.

Suppose a seasoned analyst forecasts cash flows from Thor Corp. shares, which have a 1.5 beta and trade at $60 per share (Exhibit 12–12). Are

EXHIBIT 12–11. Sample Calculation of Risk Premium for an Individual Stock

1. Market Premium × Beta = Individual Stock Risk Premium ("ISRP")
2. [Expected Return on Stock Market – Yield on Government Bond] × Beta = Individual Stock Risk Premium (ISRP)
3. $(14\% - 7\%)1.5 = $ ISRP
4. $10.5\% = $ ISRP

EXHIBIT 12–12. Thor Corp. Share Projection, Investment Cash Flows at $60 Price

	1998	1999	2000	2001
Purchase cost	$(60.00)	—	—	—
Cash dividends	—	$4.00	$4.40	$ 4.84
Sale of shares	—	—	—	72.00
	$(60.00)	$4.00	$4.40	$76.84

Thor Corp. shares a Buy? The answer is no. The $54 present value of the cash flows is below the $60 market price (see Exhibit 12–13).

BETA

The beta statistic premium is, by itself, a mathematical calculation involving a comparison of a stock's historical returns to the market's. The beta of a security whose return just matches the return of the broad market has a value of 1.0. If the stock market is forecast to provide investors with capital gains and cash dividends equivalent to a 10 percent return, the 1.0 beta stock has an expected return of 10 percent. Should the market forecast drop to negative 5 percent, the prognosticators will say the stock's forecast mirrors the –5 present market movement. A stock with a beta of 1.5, on the other hand, moves one and one-half times the movement of the market. So if the market is projected to return 10 percent in the next year, the 1.5 beta stock has an estimated 15 percent return. Likewise, a –5 percent market return leads to a –7.5 percent return estimate. Because volatility in investment returns is bad, investors require higher returns for a 1.5 beta stock, compared with the assumed return for a 1.0 beta stock.

A stock's beta is only a measure of its *past* sensitivity to market moves. For any stock, beta's applicability as a predictor of future price sympathy with the market is limited. All stock prices have a tendency to go up and

EXHIBIT 12–13. Present Value of a Thor Share

Year	Cash Flow ($)		Discount Factor		Present Value ($)
1999	4.00	÷	1.175	=	$ 3.40
2000	4.40	÷	1.36 $(1.175)^2$	=	3.19
2001	(4.84 + 72.00)	÷	1.58 $(1.175)^3$	=	47.37
	Present value of cash flows				$53.96

Investment Conclusion: Sell. The estimated $54 present value is less than the $60 market price.

down with the market, but individual share prices are heavily influenced by factors peculiar to that one company: a management change, a new product, and so on. An investor's portfolio can largely eliminate firm-specific risks by combining 20 or more stocks into a portfolio. The diversification achieved thereby tends to bring the portfolio's expected returns more into line with what its weighted average beta would predict, as aberrant individual returns cancel each other out.

Designed and nurtured by the academic community in the 1950s and 1960s, beta and the CAPM achieved wide acceptance with portfolio managers by the 1970s. Indeed, the CAPM makes common sense: Corporate investments should yield more than U.S. government bonds, and risky firms should offer investors higher prospective returns than conservative businesses. Today, the CAPM offers distinct advantages for practitioners, who need a logical risk framework in which to compare and contrast securities. The CAPM allows them to grade the risk of competing investments and discount the relevant cash flows accordingly. More importantly, the CAPM is widely accepted in the institutional investment community, so a knowledge of this theory is a prerequisite for obtaining an analyst position.

Besides enjoying the benefits of a wide acceptance, the CAPM has another advantage: Its elements are easy to find. The government bond rate is available from daily newspapers. The expected return on the stock market is arguable, but over long periods it has yielded 6 to 8 percentage points more per annum than government bonds. To develop a shorthand corporate discount rate, the analyst can use the Expected Market Return as (1) the 10-year government bond rate plus (2) 7 percent, the average additional return provided by the market. Betas are found in business publications, such as Value Line and Standard & Poor's, to complete the calculation. While this shorthand method is not totally accurate from an academic point of view, the result is acceptable for most security valuation proposes. Exhibit 12–14 shows sample k calculations.

EXHIBIT 12–14. Sample k Calculations March 1997

$$\frac{\text{Corporate Dividend}}{\text{Discount Rate}} = k = \frac{\text{Government}}{\text{Bond Rate}} + \text{Beta}\left[\begin{array}{cc}\text{Expected} & \text{Government} \\ \text{Market Return} & \text{Bond Rate}\end{array}\right]$$

Black & Decker (1.15 Beta)
   $k = 7\% + 1.15\ (14\% - 7\%)$
   $k = 15.1\%$

Allied Signal (1.35 Beta)
   $k = 7\% + 1.35\ (14\% - 7\%)$
   $k = 16.5\%$

Where:
10-year government bond rate = 7% (from the *Wall Street Journal* or similar publication).
Expected market return = 14% (market premium of 7% plus the 7% bond rate).
Betas were obtained from Value Line.

EXHIBIT 12–15. Betas of Publicly Traded Drugstore Companies—Summary Information March 1997

| Company | Beta | Sales | Latest Fiscal Year (In Millions) | | |
			Net Income	Debt/Total Capital	P/E Ratio
Arbor Drugs	0.7	$ 826	$ 27	0.1	20.1
Genovese	0.8	660	9	0.4	17.5
Long's Drug	0.8	2,765	60	0.0	14.3
Revco	1.0	5,088	83	0.4	21.1
Rite Aid	0.9	5,920	180	0.8	16.7
Walgreen	1.1	11,780	370	0.0	23.1
Average	0.9				

Actual 1996 data or estimated using 9-month results. P/E using latest 12 months' earnings per share.
The 0.9 beta can be used as a proxy for a nonlisted drugstore company.

These two k calculations involve prominent publicly traded companies, but sometimes professionals study privately held concerns or new offerings that don't have betas. For these investments, the beta of a similar publicly traded company is a good proxy. If a close match cannot be found, the average beta of a group of similar public companies provides a substitute. To illustrate, a large privately owned drugstore chain with a consistent record and good balance sheet should have a 0.9 beta estimate, given the average of similar firms found in Exhibit 12–15.

DIFFICULT DISCOUNT RATES

For unusual stocks that defy a logical k calculation, I recommend placing the investment in one of the following risk categories and then applying the relevant discount rate. Exhibit 12–16 assumes a 10-year U.S. Treasury bond yield of 6 to 8 percent. Note how the riskier investments require a higher assumed return.

Case Study: Discounted Cash Flow—Mars Company.   Suppose Mars Company, the large candy company, decides to go public and you need to value the new shares. Its earnings record and leverage are similar to Hershey Foods, Tootsie Roll, and Wrigley. First, assign a k to the new stock using a 0.9 beta, the average of its three competitors. Second, project Mars Company's income statement, balance sheet, and statement of cash flows on the basis of a top-down analysis and develop a five-year projection of per share earnings and cash dividends. Third, assign a terminal value to your investment. Fourth, discount the five years of dividends and the terminal value to the present, and then compare the resultant net present value (NPV) to the proposed offering price.

EXHIBIT 12–16. Risk Categories

Risk Category	Minimum Discount Rate for Projected Cash Flows (%)
Stable, mature business (Kellogg)	13–15
Cyclical firm (Asarco)	15–17
Seasoned growth company (Coke)	16–18
Speculative growth company with short track record (PeopleSoft)	20–22
Untested enterprise, with few sales and no earnings (Cel-Sci)	25–35
Second-stage venture capital investment	25–35
First-stage venture capital transaction	35–50
Leveraged buyout (i.e., mature business with a 4:1 debt-to-equity ratio and a 1.3× interest coverage)	30–35

Note how the riskier investments require a higher assumed return.

Step 1: Setting a Discount Rate

$$k_{Mars} = \text{Government Bond Yield} + \text{Beta} \left[\begin{array}{cc} \text{Expected} & \text{Government} \\ \text{Market Return} & \text{Bond Rate} \end{array} \right]$$

$$k_{Mars} = 7\% \times 0.9(14\% - 7\%)$$

$$k_{Mars} = 13.3\%$$

Step 2: Projecting Cash Flows for Mars Company

	Actual	Projected				
Per Share	1997	1998	1999	2000	2001	2002
Earnings ($)	3.00	3.45	3.90	4.40	5.00	5.60
Dividends ($)	1.00	1.15	1.30	1.45	1.67	1.87

Step 3: Terminal Value

Either the constant growth model or P/E statistic can determine a terminal value in 2002. Using both is a good check:

Constant Growth Model

$$P_{Year\,5} = \frac{D_6}{k - g}$$

$$P_{Year\,5} = \frac{\$2.08}{.133 - .11}$$

$$P_{Year\,5} = \$90.44$$

P/E-Based Value

A reasonable P/E for a quality candy stock is 14× to 20× earnings. Using the midpoint of 17×, the terminal value for Mars equals $95.20 (i.e., 17× $5.60 EPS in the year 2002)

Step 4: Calculate NPV and Compare with the Proposed Offering Price

	Present Value of Cash Flows @ 13.3%					Net Present Value
	1998	1999	2000	2001	2002	
Constant Growth Model						
Cash dividends	1.02	1.01	1.00	1.02	1.02	
2002 terminal value ($90.44)	—	—	—	—	49.09	
	1.02	1.01	1.00	1.02	50.11	$54.16
P/E Based Value						
Cash dividends	1.02	1.01	1.00	1.02	1.02	
2002 terminal value ($95.20)	—	—	—	—	50.99	
	1.02	1.01	1.00	1.02	52.01	$56.06

- The per share NPV equals *$54.16* or *$56.06*. This difference is attributable to the terminal values, since dividends are the same under both models.
- Your margin of safety is ±15 percent, setting a possible buying range of $46 to $65.
- An offering price of $46 or lower is a clear Buy. Any price over $65 is a theoretical short sale.
- The procedure is identical for seasoned equity securities.

SUMMARY

Of all the valuation methods used in the stock market, the discounted cash flow method is the most valid from a theoretical point of view. It also makes common sense. However, the large number of assumptions and calculations involved in devising a stock's intrinsic value limit this method's practical use on Wall Street.

Professionals prefer short, concise value indicators, such as the P/E ratio, which summarize the relevant DCF statistics into one number. The subject firm's value ratios are then compared with those of similar businesses, just as the historical financial analysis used comparable company ratios to study a firm's financial condition.

Chapter 13 covers popular relative valuation techniques.

QUESTIONS AND SHORT PROBLEMS

1. Describe the four valuation approaches that dominate the stock market.

2. Outline the principal weaknesses of the discounted cash dividend valuation approach.

3. Sally Smit, a security analyst at Brimfield Investment Partners, is studying Holfield Corp. stock in January 2000. In her financial projection models, "free cash flow" for Holfield is paid out entirely as cash dividends to shareholders. She has projected Holfield's cash dividends per share under current management as shown below. She has projected a 12 percent growth rate in dividends thereafter and assumed a 16 percent discount rate.

Holfield Corp.
Year Ending December 31

	Projected Earnings per Share	Cash Dividends per Share
2000	$2.00	$1.20
2001	2.50	1.50
2002	2.80	2.00

   a. Calculate the present value of a Holfield common share.
   b. One of Sally's colleagues suggests she derive a more "scientific" discount rate. She decides to use the formula in Exhibit 12–14 and the following information:

   10-year U.S. government bond yield = 6%
   Holfield common stock beta = 1.5
   Expected return on stock market = 13%

   What is the present value per share using the revised discount rate?
   c. The Holfield stock is trading in the market at $30 per share. Using the margin-of-safety concept, state whether it is a "buy," under the conditions of (a) or (b).

4. Zet.com is considered a growth company, but Russell Siegel, a Merrill Lynch security analyst, isn't sure that it has enough cash-on-hand and credit lines to fund its near-term growth.

Zet.com
Results for Immediate Preceding Year

	US$ millions	% of Sales
Income Statement		
Sales	$ 100	100
Depreciation and amortization	10	10
Gross profit	50	50
Selling, general and administrative expense	20	20
EBIT	30	30
Interest	—	—
Pre-tax income	30	30
Income taxes (40%)	12	12
Net income	$ 18	18
Earnings per share	$1.80	
Shares outstanding	10 million	
Balance Sheet		
Assets:		
Cash		$ 20
Other current assets		40
Total current assets		60
Fixed assets	80	
Less accumulated depreciation	(20)	
Net fixed assets		60
Total assets		$120
Liabilities and stockholders' equity:		
Short-term debt		$ —
Other current liabilities		20
Total current liabilities		20
Long-term debt		—
Stockholder's equity		100
		$120

Mr. Siegel's assumptions for his Zet.com financial projection are as follows:

- Sales grow 35 percent in year 1, 20 percent in year 2, and 15 percent in year 3.

- Selling, general and administrative expenses remain at 20 percent of sales.

- Existing fixed assets of $80 million depreciate at $10 million per year. New fixed assets depreciate over an eight year life (initial year depreciation is one-half of full year). Capital expenditures for new fixed assets are $40 million in year 1, $40 million in year 2, and $32 million in year 3.

- The Company can borrow up to $50 million at 8 percent annual interest. Due to Zet.com's risky high-tech business, $50 million is the maximum debt available for the next three years. Zet.com prefers new debt over new equity.

- New shares can be sold at 16 times the previous years' earnings per share, if the Company needs extra cash for growth.

- Other current assets and other current liabilities grow at the same rate as sales.

- The Company pays neither cash dividends nor stock dividends.

- The minimum cash balance is zero.

(a) Prepare three-year forecasts of Zet.com's income statement, balance sheet, and sources and uses of funds statement. Use the assumptions.

(b) How much new debt and equity financing are required by Zet.com over the three years?

(c) What are Zet.com's earnings per share by the end of year 3?

(d) Assume a 16 times P/E multiple at the end of year 3, sale of the stock at the end of year 3, and a 20 percent cost of equity capital. What's a share of Zet.com worth today?

5. Using the methodology of Exhibit 12–14, calculate the equity discount rates for Merck, Procter & Gamble, Amazon.com, and Bowater.

6. Estar Bank, a privately owned regional commercial bank, has total assets of $6 billion. Its financial results over the last five years are within industry standards. Management wants to estimate the bank's cost of equity capital. Using the Exhibit 12–15 example, select five regional banks and determine a good proxy for Estar's cost of equity.

Adopt-a-Company

A. Prepare summary forecasts of your company's income statement, balance sheet, and sources and uses of funds statement. To simplify the number of assumptions, combine smaller income statement and balance sheet accounts into fewer, but larger, accounts. For example, combine accounts payable and accrued expenses into one line item.

B. Justify the reasonableness of your forecasts.

C. Estimate your company's cost of equity capital.

13

The Relative Value Approach

The relative value approach is favored by Wall Street today. Chapter 13 takes a close look at this popular valuation technique and offers a disciplined methodology for implementing it.

The reliance of the fundamental school on uncertain projections and arguable discount rates reduces its relevance in the real world. Indeed, Morgan Stanley analyst, Madhav Dhar, suggests there's no such thing as the "intrinsic value" of a stock, "You have to figure out where you are relative to everybody else," he says. "It's an investment decision overlaid by game theory." With many institutions sharing this view, practitioners increasingly turn to relative values to price companies. Instead of a fair price based on discounted cash flows, practitioners use "relative value" analysis where the positive and negative aspects of a stock are evaluated against those characteristics of similar stocks falling in the same industry category. Value parameters are then compared and contrasted, resulting in statements such as "Kroger is undervalued relative to Safeway because Kroger's growth rate is higher, yet its P/E ratio is lower." Other popular comparators include the Price/Book, Price/Sales, (Price + Debt)/EBITDA, and (Price + Debt)/EBIT ratios.

Professional analysts refer to equity values in these standard terms. In fact, intrinsic value is rarely discussed. With the exception of speculative stocks, which have no earnings (E) or earnings before interest and taxes (EBIT), you rarely see intrinsic values in research reports. Inevitably, a stock price is characterized as "20× earnings," "8× EBIT," or "3× book value." When the analyst is asked how he justifies this valuation, the response is invariably something like "comparable companies are trading at 20× earnings, 8× EBIT or 3× book value." If the subject company's multiples are higher than the comparables, the investor asks the obvious question, "Why is this firm's price higher than its peers?" The answer is typically a recitation of

EXHIBIT 13–1. Model Research Report

---

1. Introduction
2. Macroeconomic Review
3. Relevant Stock Market Prospects
4. Review of the Company and Its Business
5. Financial Analysis
6. Financial Projections
7. Application of Valuation Methodologies✓
8. Recommendation

---

the firm's positive attributes, such as a better growth outlook, a better track record, or a better balance sheet. Set forth in Section 7 of the Research Report (Exhibit 13–1), these value-defining characteristics are important elements of the relative value process.

PROBLEMS WITH RELATIVE VALUE

The main problem with the comparable company approach is that it doesn't tell you whether the industry as a whole is cheap or expensive at any specific time. Some analysts look back to historical norms to identify clear aberrations, but staying with this idea requires a contrarian view. In 1997 and 1998, for example, the P/Es of most industries climbed significantly above past averages, but most investors continued to buy equities. A second problem with relative analysis is the lack of true comparables. Even within the same industry, companies have different characteristics that limit the relevance of such studies. Accordingly, I recommend discounted cash flow (DCF) as a reality check for every comparable valuation. If the two calculations are significantly different, the analyst should refrain from making a recommendation until the matter is resolved. Exhibit 13–2 lists the problems associated with both approaches.

EXHIBIT 13–2. Problems with Valuation Approaches

Intrinsic Value (Discounted Cash Flow)
- Theoretically appropriate, but practitioners are reluctant to utilize discounted cash flow.
- Difficult to reach consensus on k and g variables.

Relative Value
- There is no yardstick to indicate whether the entire group of comparables is properly valued, on a commonsense basis.
- Many firms lack true comparables, diminishing the technique's relevance.

EXHIBIT 13–3. Key Valuation Data of Publicly Traded Stocks—February 1997

	Compound 5-Year Annual Growth in EPS	Valuation Multiples		
		P/E	Price/Book	Enterprise Value/EBIT[1]
Retail Drug Stores				
Walgreen	13.6%	23.1×	4.4×	15.0×
Arbor Drugs	12.8	20.1	3.3	13.4
Longs Drug	2.2	14.3	1.5	8.7
Rite Aid	8.5	16.7	2.5	10.5
Grocery Chains				
Safeway	26.1%	23.2×	7.5×	12.5×
Albertson's	15.0	18.0	3.8	11.1
American Stores	11.9	17.1	2.3	10.4
Weis Markets	1.5	16.5	1.6	10.5

[1] Enterprise value equals (1) market value of equity, plus (2) outstanding debt, minus (3) cash on hand. *Note:* The chart shows how firms with high growth rates have higher value multiples.

Because the future is uncertain, the historical track record is the easiest way to differentiate companies in the same industry. Usually, the market places higher multiples on those firms with growth-oriented performance records. In Exhibit 13–3, I selected four stocks from two industry groups that offered reasonably pure comparables. Highly leveraged companies, inconsistent earners, and takeover candidates were excluded from the comparison. Note the connection between high growth and high P/E multiples.

Sometimes, a poor performer has an inexplicably high earnings multiple compared with successful enterprises. As shown in Exhibit 13–4, Delchamps' EPS declined dramatically from 1991 to 1996 yet it had a 33× P/E multiple. Despite its poor record, this supermarket operator's P/E exceeded those of four chains with good growth histories. This situation reflected investors'

EXHIBIT 13–4. Comparing a Poor Performer to Strong Companies—March 1997

	5-Year Annual EPS Growth (1991–1996)	P/E	Price/ Book	Comments
Delchamps	(24.1)%	33.0×	1.3×	Poor performance with a high P/E.
Grocery chain average (from Exhibit 13–3)	13.8	18.7	3.8	Strong track records, but lower P/Es.

belief in (1) the company's recovery potential, and (2) its underlying asset value to a third party (i.e., a potential takeover price).

The P/E and Enterprise Value/EBIT are good measures for companies with steady performance. Inconsistency adds complexity to the analysis. Exhibit 13–5 summarizes the records of the next two companies, both operating in the casual dining industry. The two firms have similar revenues, growth rates, and leverage ratios, but only Luby's shows a *consistent* increase in sales and earnings. NPC International exhibited erratic performance on a normalized basis and had frequent nonrecurring charges. The P/E ratio is most relevant in establishing Luby's value in relation to other *consistent* casual dining chains. When the comparison is between Luby and NPC, the P/E has less significance.

A constant earnings stream implies less risk, so the earnings are awarded a higher multiplier. A spotty record carries the connotation of reduced predictability and more risk, which means a lower multiplier. (This is one reason the P/E ratio of the cyclical firm carries a discount to a steady business.) In this example, NPC's inconsistency stands in stark contrast to Luby's steadiness. All things being equal, Luby's receives the higher P/E ratio. But, the relationship between P/E ratios and earnings volatility is not linear. Other "relative value" comparisons play a role. Professionals look at price/sales, price/book value, price/number of restaurants, and similar multiples in determining whether a casual dining chain is fairly valued.

A few calculations appear in Exhibit 13–6. The additional ratios show that Luby's book value, sales, EBIT, and restaurants had higher values than NPCs. The market penalized NPC.

One complication with the P/E multiple is the different degrees of leverage found among companies in the same industry. How does an analyst

EXHIBIT 13–5. Casual Dining Company Track Records (in millions, except for per share data and ratios) January 1997

	1991	1992	1993	1994	1995	1996 (E)	5-Year Compound Growth Rate	P/E Ratio
Luby's Cafeterias								
EPS	1.18	1.19	1.31	1.45	1.55	1.66	7.1%	13.8×
Yr-to-Yr. EPS Change	Up	Up	Up	Up	Up	Up		
NPC International								
EPS	0.50	0.36	0.45	0.44	0.66	0.75	8.4%	10.7×
Yr-to-Yr. EPS Change	Down	Down	Up	Down	Up	Up		

Note. NPC's erratic record penalized its P/E ratio, despite a higher growth rate.

EXHIBIT 13–6. Alternative Valuation Ratios—Casual Dining Companies—January 1997

| | Share Price Divided By | | Enterprise Value Divided By | | |
	EPS	Book Value	Sales	EBIT	Number of Restaurants[1]
Luby's	13.8	2.4	1.3	8.9	$2,700,000
NPC	10.7	1.9	1.0	7.9	760,000

[1] Luby's restaurants are larger, justifying a higher value per restaurant.

compare a risky, highly leveraged business to a safer, debt-free company? On the one hand, a highly leveraged firm deserves a lower P/E multiple because of the higher risk. On the other hand, the potential for EPS growth is enhanced through leverage, providing a justification for a higher P/E. The components of the

$$\frac{\text{Price}}{\text{Earnings}} = \frac{\left[\dfrac{D_1}{k-g}\right]}{\text{EPS}}$$

formula can be tinkered with, so almost any P/E can be rationalized by a crafty analyst, but the real argument plays out in the stock market on a daily basis. Many times, high leverage penalizes the P/E. In February 1997, Kroger had a better growth record than conservative Albertson's, but Kroger's debt hurt its P/E ratio. (See Exhibit 13–7.)

RELATIVE EBIT RATIOS

To reduce the leverage effect on comparative valuations, practitioners review two statistics: "earnings before interest and taxes" (EBIT) and "earnings

EXHIBIT 13–7. High Leverage Can Lower the P/E Ratio, Even When Growth Is Superior

Operating Results	1996 Sales	5-Year Compound Annual Growth Rate in EPS	P/E Ratio
Kroger	$25 billion	19%	17×
Albertson's	$14 billion	15%	18×

Leverage	Debt/Total Capitalization	Interest Coverage	P/E Ratio
Kroger	100%	3×	17×
Albertson's	23%	12×	18×

Note. Total capitalization equals debt outstanding plus shareholders' equity. Kroger's equity was a negative $1.2 billion, making the ratio 100%.

before interest, taxes, depreciation, and amortization" (EBITDA). Correspondingly, corporate value is defined as the sum of "market equity value plus outstanding debt minus cash on hand" (i.e., "enterprise value"). This grosses up corporate values for the addition of interest expense to the denominator. Thus, Kroger's market equity value was $6 billion, while its enterprise value was $9.5 billion. Enterprise value is the numerator for the commonly used EBIT ratio:

$$\text{EBIT Ratio} = \frac{\text{Market Value of Company's Equity} + \text{Net Outstanding Debt}}{\text{Earnings before Interest and Taxes}}$$

Is the same as

$$\text{EBIT Ratio} = \frac{\text{Enterprise Value}}{\text{Earnings before Interest and Taxes}}$$

Analysts increasingly use EBIT and EBITDA ratios instead of P/Es, but I don't subscribe to this practice. Passive shareholders only own a small percentage of a company's shares so their focus should remain on dividends and earnings per share. In my opinion, EBIT and EBITDA calculations are more relevant in the mergers and acquisitions field, where a buyer can change the leverage of its acquisition after the deal is completed.

The following EBIT ratios show that investors valued Kroger's EBIT less than Albertson's, despite Kroger's higher growth rate.

	Enterprise Value/EBIT	EPS Growth Rate	Debt Total Capitalization
Kroger	10.5×	19%	100%
Albertson's	11.1×	15	23

In diversified company valuations, the EBIT ratio is helpful because the firm is broken down into its component parts. In determining a corporate division's worth, the analyst faces a business that does not report a true net income, since its capital structure is artificial or nonexistent. The division may report an operating earnings figure, which is equivalent to the EBIT of a publicly traded firm. He thus has an indicator from which to begin a valuation. This topic is discussed further in Chapter 16.

WHAT'S THE RIGHT P/E RATIO?

In the relative value approach, there isn't a gold standard that says how many P/E multiples you knock off if your subject company lacks certain financial characteristics. Life would be easier if a 2 percent substandard growth rate mechanically reduced a firm's P/E multiple by 3× (i.e., from 17× to 14×), but it doesn't work that way. Too many extraneous variables enter the process, particularly those hard-to-define future expectations. Nevertheless, as one means of quantifying the relative performance of similar businesses, I recommend historical rankings as part of the process.

Unlike the DCF method, relative value relies mostly on historical results. To set the stage for a quantitative comparison, I rank companies according to a few ratios germane to the industry. If the firm with the best ranking has the lowest valuation multiple, I search for concrete reasons that explain the discrepancy. Finding none, I conclude the stock is cheap on a relative basis.

Case Study: Consumer Food Companies.   Ann Solan, a security analyst at Montclair Securities, decides to look at the relative values of six consumer food stocks. Her goal is to determine whether one of the share prices is out of balance with the group. The following list shows the shares and their respective P/Es:

Company	P/E	Rank
CPC International	19.8	4
Campbell Soup	24.1	2
Flowers Industries	27.0	1
H.J. Heinz	18.5	6
Kellogg Company	22.0	3
Sara Lee	18.6	5

For performance measurements, she selects several ratios from each of the four categories:

Four Ratio Categories	Solan's Selection for Consumer Food Comparison
Profitability	EBIT margin, net profit margin, return on total capital, return on equity
Activity	Asset turnover, capital turnover
Credit	Debt to equity ratio, interest coverage ratio
Growth	Sales per share, cash flow per share, earnings per share, dividends per share

Referring to her database, which has the normalized results for the six firms, she looks at trends in the ratios and runs a series of averages for the group. Changing trends merit special attention and she highlights them in boxes. A small section of her calculations appears as Exhibit 13–8.

After reviewing many ratios, Ms. Solan grades each company. Rapidly improving (or declining) results are given extra weight, and she develops the rankings in Exhibit 13–9.

A quick glance at the chart shows three companies monopolizing the top two spots in each category: Kellogg, Campbell Soup, and Flowers Industries. Indeed, these three firms have the highest P/E multiples. However, her

EXHIBIT 13–8. Consumer Food Companies—Selective Rankings by Ratio

	Year	Group Average	CPC	Campbell Soup	Flowers	Heinz	Kellogg	Sara Lee
Profitability Ratio				Positive Trend				
Return on								
Equity	1986	22%	23%	15%	16%	24%	37%	18%
	1996	27	26	29	17	24	46	20
	Rank		3	2	6	4	1	5
Activity Ratio							Positive Trend	Negative Trend
Asset	1986	2.8×	2.6×	2.3×	2.5×	2.3×	2.9×	4.3×
Turnover	1996	2.8	2.6	2.3	2.7	2.0	4.0	3.0
	Rank		4	5	3	6	1	2
Credit Ratio								
Debt to Equity	1986	0.5×	0.8×	0.2×	0.7×	0.4×	0.3×	0.4×
	1996	0.5	0.7	0.3	0.7	0.7	0.2	0.4
	Rank		4	2	4	4	1	3
Compound Annual Growth							Negative Trend	
Earnings per	Latest							
Share	10 yrs.	11%	13%	14%	8%	9%	8%	13%
	Latest							
	5 yrs.	10	9	15	13	10	4	11
	Rank		5	1	2	4	6	3

Note. Each company's performance is ranked vs. its competitors and recorded next to the group average.

EXHIBIT 13–9. Cumulative Rankings by Ratio Analysis

Profitability	Activity	Credit	Growth
1. Kellogg	1. Kellogg	1. Kellogg	1. Campbell Soup
2. Campbell Soup	2. Flowers	2. Campbell Soup	2. Flowers
3. CPC	3. Sara Lee	3. Sara Lee	3. Sara Lee
4. Heinz	4. CPC	4. Flowers	4. Heinz
5. Sara Lee	5. Campbell Soup	5. CPC	5. CPC
6. Flowers	6. Heinz	6. Heinz	6. Kellogg

Note that Kellogg, Campbell Soup, and Flowers control the top two rankings.

EXHIBIT 13–10. Weighted Ranking by Historical Financial Performance

Company (Score)	Ranking	P/E	Comments
Campbell Soup (2.2)	1	24.1	—
Kellogg (3.0)	2	22.0	—
Flowers (3.2)	3	27.0	P/E seems relatively high
Sara Lee (3.4)	4	18.6	—
CPC (4.4)	5	19.8	P/E seems relatively high
Heinz (4.8)	6	18.5	—

evaluative system emphasizes growth and she assigns a 40 percent weighting to a firm's ranking in that important category. The other categories receive 20 percent weightings. To illustrate, she calculates Kellogg's overall score as follows:

Kellogg's Overall Rank = The sum of:
   (i) profitability rank × 20%
   (ii) activity rank × 20%
   (iii) credit rank × 20%, and
   (iv) growth rank × 40%.
= 1(0.2) + 1(0.2) + 1(0.2)
   + 6(0.4)
= 3.0

A table of weighted rankings is prepared, and shown alongside P/E multiples (see Exhibit 13–10). The data indicate that Flowers and CPC are expensive relative to their comparables. Their P/E multiples are higher than their weighted rankings suggest.

In the case of Flowers Industries, the company was in the process of absorbing a large acquisition, which cut profit margins—supposedly on a temporary basis—so the 27 P/E was calculated on lower-than-normal EPS. CPC's out-of-line multiple wasn't easily explained. After reviewing her top-down analysis and intrinsic values, Ms. Solan issued a sell recommendation on CPC.

HOW HIGH IS UP?

In mid-1999, tapewatchers commented on the high P/Es ascribed to established businesses, such as Coca-Cola (45 P/E) and General Electric (37 P/E). Before plunging forward, a smart investor is well advised to consider the mathematics involved in buying a high P/E stock. If you buy a 50 P/E stock today and plan on selling it at a 20 P/E (which is still above average) in five years (when the issuer's business is likely maturing), the earnings per share

EXHIBIT 13–11. Growth Expectations and High P/E Stocks

Buy-in P/E	Exit P/E after 5 Years	Required EPS Growth Over 5 Years to Realize Market Return[1] (%)
100	20	860
50	20	380
40	20	280
30	15	290

[1] To realize 14% market return; assumes no cash dividends.

of the company must *quintuple* for you to realize a market-type return. Exhibit 13–11 outlines the EPS growth required by high P/E stocks to achieve market returns.

SUMMARY

The valuation of common stocks is an inexact science. Modern methods provide a range of prices rather than a precise number.

Today's security analysts operate within two frameworks (1) intrinsic value; and (2) relative value. Intrinsic value is the academically pure approach which stipulates that a business is worth the discounted value of its future dividends. While theoretically correct, dividend discounting carries little weight among practitioners, who decided long ago not to argue interminably among themselves about the merits of one projection against another. Nor do they care to debate the merits of one discount rate against another. Instead, most practitioner debates center on relative values. If the auto parts group is trading at 16× annual net earnings, then this 16× multiple is the starting point for an auto parts stock. If research shows that the subject company is a better performer than its peers, it deserves a higher multiple. If its record is worse and it has fewer prospects, it merits a lower multiple. Nonearnings-based factors, such as "hidden" asset values or off-balance sheet liabilities, are then added or deducted from the benchmark estimate.

QUESTIONS AND SHORT PROBLEMS

1. Compare and contrast the merits and defects of (a) the discounted cash dividend approach and (b) the relative value approach.

2. Name three problems involved with the relative value approach.

3. If you were a relative value adherent, which of the following statements would you consider true? Assume the companies operate in the same retailing industry, have similar capital structures, and reasonable prospects:

a. Alme Stores has a higher earnings per share than Dott Shops, and Alme is therefore a better investment.

b. Phillips Retailing has higher compound annual growth in net income than Capital Stores Corp., and all things being equal, Phillips deserves a better P/E multiple.

c. Trendy Stores, Inc. has a more erratic earnings per share record than Simpson Shops, even though their 10-year, annual compound growth rates in EPS are the same. Nevertheless, Trendy Stores deserves a lower P/E ratio than Simpson.

d. Candy Shops and T-Stores both have a troubled history of marginal performance. The EV/Number of stores ratios for the companies are $2.0 million and $1.4 million, respectively. T-Stores represents the better investment value.

e. Treller Retailing has a 16 percent annual growth rate in earnings per share and a 19 times P/E ratio. Boston Stores Corp. has a 14 percent growth rate and a 15 times P/E ratio. An investor should buy Treller shares and sell Boston stock.

4. Why is a discounted cash dividend valuation a good "back-up" check for relative valuation?

5. On May 1, 1999, Delfone stock traded at $42 per share, or 21 times earnings per share for the most recent 12-month period. On May 10, the Company announced a risky expansion into the former Soviet Union, and the share price declined by $4, even though analysts' EPS and dividend estimates didn't change. Explain, theoretically, how Delfon's higher perceived risk meant (a) a higher cost of capital; (b) a lower P/E ratio; and (c) a lower share price.

6. Assume you are a relative value adherent. Rank the following comparable companies in descending order of likely P/E ratios:

	Debt/ Equity	Compound Annual Growth	
		in EPS	in EBITDA
Cettron Corp.	60%	14.2%	13.1%
Intolt, Inc.	53	14.9	13.0
Ctec Company	41	13.2	11.8
Wellstone, Inc.	43	13.0	12.2

7. Upon performing a relative value analysis, you determine the fair value of a Cendron Company share is $16. As a check, you prepare a discounted cash flow analysis that shows a $24 value. The stock is trading at $20. What do you do now?

a. Buy the stock because it exceeds the margin of safety.

b. Sell the stock because it exceeds the margin of safety.

c. Simultaneously buy puts and calls out of the money.

d. Double check the assumptions in your DCF model.

e. Both (a) and (c).

8. Using the summary financial results for Penn Cable Co., a cable TV company, with a current share price of $28, that serves 1.9 million subscribers, calculate the following valuation ratios:
   a. Enterprise value/EBITDA.
   b. Enterprise value/EBIT.
   c. Enterprise value/Number of subscribers.
   d. Price/Earnings per share.
   e. Price/Book value per share.

Penn Cable Co. Latest Annual Results
(in US$ million)

Income Statement	
Revenues	$1,200
Depreciation and amortization	210
Other operating expenses	855
Operating profit	135
Interest expense	90
Pre-tax income	45
Income taxes	15
Net income	$ 30
Earnings per share	$1.00
Shares outstanding	30 million
Balance Sheet	
Assets:	
Cash	$ 40
Other current assets	85
Total current assets	125
Fixed assets, net	1,135
Goodwill	340
Total assets	$1,600
Liabilities and Stockholders' Equity:	
Short-term debt	$ —
Other current liabilities	40
Total current liabilities	40
Long-term debt	1,420
Stockholders' equity	140
	$1,600

9. Should individual investors de-emphasize the use of EBITDA and EBIT ratios relative to the use of the P/E ratio?

10. A security analyst is recommending Super Hi-Tech Corp. at $90 per share. Current earnings are now $2.00 per share, and the company is in its growth phase. After six years, the analyst believes growth will

moderate and the stock will trade at 20 times earnings. What must be Super Hi-Tech's EPS in six years for an investor to earn an 18 percent internal rate of return? Assume Hi-Tech pays no cash or stock dividends over the period.

11. Set forth below are selected statistics for Kraft Foods:

Selected Statistics for Kraft Foods for 1989 and 1994
(in US$ millions except per share)

	1989	1994
Income Statement		
Sales	5,341	7,267
Net income	305	436
Earnings per share	2.58	3.63
Dividends per share	1.51	2.09
Balance Sheet		
Current assets	342	530
Total assets	2,111	3,030
Current liabilities	204	310
Debt	600	800
Equity	1,400	1,920
Market Data		
Stock price per share at 12/31/94	46.00	65.00

Valuation data in 1994 for similar food companies were:

Comparable Public Companies	P/E	Enterprise Value/ EBIT	Growth Rate	Debt/ Equity
Campbell Soup	20 times	11 times	10%	32%
Kellogg	22 times	12 times	11	5
Heinz	17 times	9 times	7	33
Borden	36 times	7 times	2	88

Using comparable company analysis, was Kraft stock trading at a "fair price" relative to other stocks? Justify your answer?

Adopt-a-Company

A. Select three publicly traded companies that represent the best "comparables" for your adopted company.

B. Utilizing top-down reviews and historical financial analysis, rank your company and the three comparables in terms of operating performance.

C. Determine whether your company is fairly valued on a relative basis.

14

Valuing Marginal Performers

How can you apply relative value multiples when the subject company has either no earnings or a rocky track record? This chapter explains how professionals evaluate less-than-ideal corporate performance.

The previous chapter focused on the usefulness of applying earnings-based valuation ratios to the appraisal process. Price/earnings per share (P/Es) and earnings before interest and taxes (EBIT) ratios are helpful indicators for solid, growing companies, but many firms lack a steady trend of improving sales and earnings. For these businesses, earnings-based multiples are less than an ideal means of discerning relative value.

CATEGORIES OF APPRAISALS

To meet the requirement of Section 7 of the research report (Exhibit 14–1), professionals use alternative methods for these problem candidates, which generally fall into three categories:

1. *Corporate Value Based on Operating Track Record.* A Category 1 company has a good historical trend, but it suffered a one-year "earnings hiccup" over the past five years.

2. *Corporate Value Based More on Potential than Past Performance.* Companies falling into Category 2 are erratic performers, cyclical businesses, or money losers. The future earnings potential of these businesses is more speculative than that of Category 1 companies.

3. *Corporate Value Based on Assets That Don't Provide Income Now, but Have the Potential to Generate Income in the Future.* Category 3 firms frequently have substantial underutilized real estate values

EXHIBIT 14–1. Model Research Report

1. Introduction
2. Macroeconomic Review
3. Relevant Stock Market Prospects
4. Review of the Company and Its Business
5. Financial Analysis
6. Financial Projections
7. Application of Valuation Methodologies✓
8. Recommendation

or dormant natural resource assets, such as oil reserves, metallic ore reserves, or extensive timberlands. To generate income, the real estate must be sold or developed, while the natural resource assets must be extracted, harvested, and then sold. An equity investor calculates the future costs of real estate development, oil drilling, ore mining, or timber-cutting, and compares these costs with estimated revenues.

Underperforming government-mandated monopolies fall into Category 3. Examples include television stations, cellular bandwidths, and cable TV franchises. The key assets of these businesses are not tangible assets like timberlands, but they are nonetheless quite valuable if placed into the hands of a management that can improve the franchise.

Harvesting underutilized assets can be both capital and management intensive. For example, a company with substantial iron ore reserves faces considerable expense to exploit the reserves. Mining equipment, rail spurs, utility connections, and start-up costs represent huge investments. Constructing this infrastructure on time and within budget is uncertain, as are the risks that the ore reserves, after some development work, are not what they appeared to be at the time of the analyst's research. The behavior of future iron prices is another uncertainty.

The next section provides some businesses with erratic records, along with the relative valuation methods applied to them.

Corporate Value Based on Track Record

Companies with Extraordinary Gains or Losses on the Income Statement. By definition, an extraordinary event is something that happens on rare occasions. Practitioners consider these items to be "one-time" occurrences that won't happen again. When using earnings multiples, they eliminate extraordinary gains or loses from the calculation of a firm's net income and EBIT, providing normalized data (i.e., as if the extraordinary event had never occurred). Needless to say, the valuation multiples of similar companies have to be adjusted in the same fashion to facilitate a comparison.

Companies with Discontinued Operations in the Income Statement.   Large corporations regularly sell off divisions that do not fit in with their long-term goals. Following the divestitures, the sales and profits (or losses) of these discarded businesses are included in a separate part of the corporate income statement for accounting purposes, such as the "discontinued operations" section. For valuation purposes, practitioners eliminate a discontinued operation from historical results, thereby producing pro forma data for a meaningful comparative analysis.

Corporate Value Based More on Earning Potential than Past Performance

Companies with Uneven Earnings Records.   Companies that do not exhibit smooth upward earnings trends are nevertheless valuable commodities, primarily because investors believe management (or a new management) can reform the inconsistent earnings pattern. You can compute a simplistic "estimated value," for an inconsistant firm by multiplying *(x)* a one-year earnings statistic (such as EPS or EBIT) by *(y)* the comparable company multiple. However, this basic calculation has less meaning for an erratic performer than the same multiplication performed for a consistent moneymaker. Several averaging methods moderate the problematic effects of uneven track records. A common remedy is to "smooth" out the firm's spotty performance by averaging three to five years of results. Instead of using the last year's earnings (or next year's estimated earnings), you calculate an average of the last three years' results. This average is multiplied by the one-year EPS ratios applicable for similar businesses, thereby creating a meaningful estimate.

Cyclical Firms.   As discussed, many profitable firms have earnings streams that are highly sensitive to the business cycle of the economy. Boom times for these firms are followed by bust times and their historical results show a repeated pattern of peaks and troughs. Other kinds of cyclical firms experience earnings patterns that do not correlate well to the general economy, but trend against other economic variables. Brokerage firms, for example, show cyclicality based on stock and bond prices, while agricultural firms exhibit earnings tied to the crop price cycle. Security analysts are hard pressed to place precise relative values on these enterprises. In practice, one-year and average earnings multiples are complemented by other methods, including the following multiples:

- *Value as a multiple of earnings power over the cycle.* Average the company's EPS over an entire cycle, which can last from five to eight years. Assume reasonable secular growth in the next cycle and multiply estimated EPS over the next cycle by an appropriate P/E.

- *Value as a multiple of the most recent peak year results.* Consider the P/E for similar firms in the subject company's industry. Apply this multiple to the subject's peak year EPS to determine a reasonable valuation.
- *Value as a multiple of the most recent bottom year results.* Repeat the preceding exercise for bottom-of-the-cycle earnings.

Money-Losing Companies. The first reaction of many investors is to shy away from money-losing firms. The operating, managerial, and financial problems of the money-losers create analytical headaches over and above those accompanying normal equity investments. Furthermore, the risk of overpayment is magnified, since money-losers are hard to value, and their earnings are notoriously difficult to predict. These considerations increase the chances of the stockholder not collecting what was anticipated on his investment.

Nevertheless, dozens of money-losing companies trade at substantial equity values, notwithstanding the aforementioned complications, and the stockholders of these underperformers represent a cross section of investors. How does an analyst look for valuation guideposts in these circumstances? Discounted cash flow analysis is helpful for the analyst's own work, but few institutions place much stock in it. Earnings-based multiples are of minimal use since there are no earnings to multiply. The primary attraction of the underperformer is its potential to make money. How do investors measure this potential in the real world, where *all* projections are suspect?—they consider valuation benchmarks besides those derived from historical earnings. Many such tools are based on accounting statistics, while others rely on operating data. Popular accounting-based ratios for valuing a money-losing company are shown in Exhibit 14–2.

NON-EARNINGS BASED MULTIPLES

Cash Flow Multiples

The idea of valuing a company as a multiple of cash flow, rather than earnings, became popular in the 1980s. Corporate acquirers, particular leveraged buyout (LBO) firms, relied heavily on cash flow to evaluate a target's ability to repay acquisition debts. The practice spread to security analysts, who used it to gauge the likely takeover pricing of companies, as well as the economic value of businesses reporting losses. Most of Wall Street defines cash flow as EBITDA (earnings before interest, depreciation, and amortization). Depreciation and amortization are noncash accounting charges reflecting assumed drops in the value of corporate assets.

EXHIBIT 14–2. Value Multiples for Companies with Negative Earnings per Share

- *Cash Flow Multiples.* Suppose the company has negative EPS, yet it has positive cash flow because of sizable depreciation and amortization expenses. The latest year's cash flow per share is then multiplied by a benchmark such as 5 or 6 to set a rough estimate of equity value (after debt is subtracted).

- *Book Value Multiples.* The money-losing firm doesn't generate profits, but its shareholders' equity account is positive, indicating that the accounting value of assets exceeds liabilities. The price/book value ratio of profitable manufacturing companies is usually 2× to 4×. Similar ratios for money losers are 1.0× or less.

- *Sales Multiple.* A company with a high sales volume may have the potential to make money. Perhaps unneeded expenses can be cut, or prices raised. Recognizing this possibility, Wall Street says something like, "Well, the equity value is only 1× sales," as if this is a bargain for a money-losing business. To make sense out of this comment, investors examine price-to-sales ratios of comparable publicly traded firms. A discount is then applied to establish a reasonable value.

Accounting theory implies that D&A cash should be plowed back into the business if net earnings are to be maintained, but the theory isn't always right. In the 1970s and 1980s, for example, real estate prices rose far above depreciated values. Also, many LBOs registered large amortization costs, but nevertheless had big value gains in the 1980s and 1990s.

Price to cash flow is used to appraise many industries, including the cable TV, cellular phone, oil, hotel, real estate, and gambling industries. If there's a substantial up-front capital investment, equity value sometimes holds up without the reinvestment of depreciation and amortization. This worked well for cable TV stocks such as Comcast Corp., whose stock went up 200 percent over the past 10 years, despite never recording an annual net profit, but the party may be over. New technology from direct broadcast satellites and phone companies threatens the cable industry's prospects. Likewise, real estate investment trusts (REITs) can skimp on refurbishments and tenant improvements when the office building market is tight, but these capital items mushroom when tenants have many options. Cash flow valuation is covered extensively in Chapter 18.

Book Value Multiples

This calculation is computed as current share price divided by book value per share. Book value is based on historical accounting data, and it has shortcomings as a measurement device. Besides excluding the extra value of the business as a going concern (along with related intangible assets), book value fails to write up increases in tangible assets, such as real estate. The price/book ratio is most meaningful for a troubled business, where liquidation is an option and book value helps define downside risk. Financial companies are quoted in price/book terms since their principal assets, corporate bonds and loans, have little intangible value.

Price to Sales Multiples

Measuring the relationship of price to sales is useful when the money-losing company (1) has turnaround potential, (2) is introducing a new product, or (3) is developing a market franchise. The idea is that sales translate into earnings down the road. You see this ratio most frequently with speculative, hi-tech companies. Their sales are accelerating rapidly, but they lack sufficient economies of scale to realize a profit until achieving wider product acceptance.

Shorthand Relative Value Ratios

Money-losing firms do not lend themselves to valuation multiples based on accounting data, which work better for profitable firms with upward earnings trends. Nevertheless, comparable-company P/E, Enterprise Value/EBIT, Enterprise Value/Cash Flow, Price/Book, and Enterprise Value/Sales are factored into most distressed company research reports. The general lack of similar money-losing firms (or M&A transactions) limits the usefulness of this data, but practitioners try to make "lemonade out of lemons" by applying a money-loser discount from profitable firm ratios. Projected cash flow analysis is also of questionable use with the problem firm because of the uncertainty attached to the underperformer's prospects. Uncomfortable relying on either (1) value multiples based on historical result, or (2) cash flows derived from doubtful projections, practitioners use numerous shorthand value ratios. These ratios depend on something other than historical and forecast financial data. Typically, they can be calculated quickly, using available asset or production statistics related to the firm's business. Shorthand indicators complement accounting-based ratios because they provide another value for the earnings potential of a problem company.

Most shorthand value ratios are based on industry operating criteria. For example, the value of a money-losing retailing firm is often expressed in terms of its enterprise value divided by the number of stores. The money-loser's enterprise value per store statistic is then compared with other retailing firms.

Shorthand calculations are in everyday use and unscientific as these calculations are, they make up part of the valuation landscape. Most appropriate for erratic, cyclical, or money-losing firms, they are also calculated for businesses with long and successful track records, to ensure the completeness of an appraisal and to showcase possible discrepancies in the accounting-derived techniques. Common shorthand valuation ratios, segmented by industry, appear in Exhibit 14–3.

EXHIBIT 14–3. Shorthand Valuation Ratios Used in Security Analysis

Restaurants

$$\frac{\text{Enterprise Value}}{\text{Number of Restaurants}} = \text{Value per Restaurants in Operatio}$$

Telephone Services

Hard Line: $\dfrac{\text{Enterprise Value}}{\text{Number of Restaurants}} = \text{Value per Phone Line}$

Cellular: $\dfrac{\text{Enterprise Value}}{\text{Number of Persons in Coverage Area}} = \text{Value per Potential Customer}$

Cable Television

$$\frac{\text{Enterprise Value}}{\text{Number of Subscribers}} = \text{Value per Subscriber}$$

Cement, Steel, Petrochemical

$$\frac{\text{Enterprise Value}}{\text{Tons of Annual Production Capacity}} = \text{Value per Ton of Capacity}$$

Hotels

$$\frac{\text{Enterprise Value}}{\text{Number of Rooms}} = \text{Value per Room}$$

Average Nightly Room Rate × Number of Rooms × 1,000 = Enterprise Value

Airlines

$$\frac{\text{Enterprise Value}}{\text{Annual Passenger Miles}} = \text{Value per Passenger Mile}$$

$$\frac{\text{Enterprise Value}}{\text{Number of Annual Seats Filled}} = \text{Value per Seat Filled}$$

Movie Theater

$$\frac{\text{Enterprise Value}}{\text{Number of Movie Screens}} = \text{Value per Movie Screen}$$

Oil, Gas, Timber, and Mining

Equity Value = The Following Sum:

-   + Net working capital
-   + Fixed assets
-   − Accounting liabilities
-   + Value of natural resource reserves based on recent prices paid solely for such reserves (e.g., 1997 price for oil-in-the-ground reserves were $5 per barrel, compared to above-the-ground price of $18 per barrel)

Small Company Discount

Small company stocks usually trade at a discount to the valuation multiples of large capitalization issues. Two factors support the continuation of this practice. The first is technical. Small company shares, by definition, have a limited float so the big institutions can't participate. Demand for the stock is thus diminished. Second, small companies have higher operating risks. Compared with the big firms; they exhibit greater earnings fluctuations, rely on fewer customers, and have little or no management depth. Small business discounts can be as high as 30 percent off large company multiples.

SUMMARY

The investor of the 1990s emphasizes the relative value approach, which compares stock prices with earnings-based valuation ratios, such as price/earnings and price/cash flow. These ratios are particularly appropriate for firms with upward earnings trends, but they are less helpful in evaluating companies with erratic performance records. Should the subject company have an uneven track record or earnings problems, practitioners turn to averaging, peak-year, and shorthand value indicators. These stress the future potential of the company to make money, as opposed to its actual profit history. Many of the indicators are industry-specific, and include ratios based on sales, production capacity, or mineral reserves.

QUESTIONS AND SHORT PROBLEMS

1. Payless Cashways had a one-time special charge of $24 million in fiscal 1987. How did the analysis in Chapter 8 "normalize" this charge in evaluating the company? (See Exhibit 8–6.)

2. In comparing Payless Cashways to similar firms, why did the analysis in Chapter 8 use a net income figure of $41 million for Payless Cashways in fiscal 1987, instead of the reported $28 million?

3. In the year ended December 31, 1999, Dunrite Corp. incurred a special charge of $12 million related to the settlement of litigation and recorded a one-time $25 million profit from the sale of a subsidiary. Reported net income was $50 million. What was Dunrite Corp.'s normalized net income in 1999?

Dunrite Corp.
Year Ended December 31, 1999
(in millions of dollars)

Sales	$670
Cost of sales	440
Gross profit	330
Selling, general and administrative expenses	274
Special charge from litigation	12
Operating profit	44
Interest expense	8
Pre-tax income before disc. ops.	36
Income from disc. op.	22
Pre-tax gain from sale of disc. ops.	25
Pre-tax income	83
Income taxes	33
Net income	$ 50

4. Lsoftware, Inc., has an erratic record of earnings per share performance, as indicated for the years ending December 31:

1994	1995	1996	1997	1998
$1.44	$1.82	$1.75	$3.15	$2.46

Comparable companies have an average P/E ratio of 18 times in early 1999. Using this statistic, what is the suggested stock price of Lsoftware using: (a) current year EPS, (b) three-year average EPS, and c) five-year average EPS?

5. Why is income averaging an appropriate tool for a cyclical stock?

6. Exhibit 10–15 shows the earnings per share of Alcoa over an aluminum price cycle. What is the company's average annual EPS over the cycle? How is this statistic relevant to a "relative value" evaluation of Alcoa stock?

7. Explain why Wall Street analysts began to use Enterprise Value/ EBITDA multiples as a basis for relative value comparisons.

8. Depreciation and amortization are expenses, according to generally accepted accounting principles, yet many analysts believe such expenses are not totally legitimate. Why?

9. Radio broadcasting firms are trading at an average EV/EBITDA multiple of 10 times. A privately held radio broadcaster, Royce Radio, is considering an initial public offering. Assuming Royce Radio's financial attributes and prospects are close to the average, what is a reasonable estimate of its per share common stock price, using the relative value method?

Royce Radio
(in millions except per share)

Income Statement	
Revenues	$ 221
EBITDA	32
Depreciation and amortization	26
EBIT	6
Interest	18
Pre-tax income	(12)
Income taxes	—
Net income	$ (12)
Earnings per share	$(0.63)
Shares outstanding (MM)	19.0
Balance Sheet	
Assets	$ 159
Total debt	212
Stockholders' equity	(53)

10. Analysts sometimes use the EV/sales multiple as a "relative value" measurement for a company with a net loss. What is the logic behind calculating this statistic, and then comparing it to the EV/sales multiples of profitable firms participating in the same industry as the money losing company?

11. In 1999, many Internet companies had equity valuations based on multiples of sales rather than earnings. Why were investors willing to rely on the price/sales multiples as an accurate indicator of relative values?

12. What are the principal shortcomings of using the price/book value ratio?

13. Describe "short-hand relative value" ratios.

14. Which of the following is not a "shorthand relative value" ratio:
    a. EV/Number of rooms.
    b. EV/EBITDA.
    c. EV/Ton of capacity.
    d. EV/Customers.
    e. EV/Movie screens.

15. Which of the following factors contribute to small company stocks often trading at valuation multiples lower than big company stocks? Circle all that apply.
    a. Small companies have less management depth than big companies.
    b. Large institutional investors place less emphasis on small company stocks.

   c. Compared with large firms, small companies typically have higher
      earnings fluctuations.
   d. All of the above.

Adopt-a-Company

Your company should have a consistent earnings record; and, therefore, it
should not require significant adjustments or averaging as described in this
chapter.

15

The Mergers and Acquisitions Market, Leveraged Buyouts, and Takeovers

As a means of complementing discounted cash flow (DCF) and relative valuation methods, practitioners examine takeover-based pricing. Chapter 15 shows how to integrate mergers and acquisitions (M&A) values into your analysis.

Given the qualitative judgments involved in the relative value and DCF techniques, I recommend several alternative approaches as good reality checks. Our research report encompasses multiple value applications in Section 7 (see Exhibit 15–1). In this chapter, leveraged buyout (LBO) and takeover values are discussed. Chapter 16 examines breakup analysis.

- *LBO Valuation.* A company's minimal worth in the takeover market is its value to a financial buyer who can't realize operating synergies.

EXHIBIT 15–1. Model Research Report

1. Introduction
2. Macroeconomic Review
3. Relevant Stock Market Prospects
4. Review of the Company and Its Business
5. Financial Analysis
6. Financial Projections
7. Application of Valuation Methodologies✓
8. Recommendation

The analyst applies a 25 percent discount to the LBO value to reach a reasonable market price.

- *Takeover Pricing.* Optimum takeover prices are achieved when one operating business buys another. Companies trading at substantial discounts to industry acquisition multiples can be good investment opportunities.

- *Breakup Analysis.* A diversified business is examined as the sum of its parts. If the component values substantially exceed the stock price, the shares are a buy.

THE MERGERS AND ACQUISITIONS MARKET

There has been a tremendous amount of merger and acquisition activity in the 1990s. In fact, the years 1995 through 1999 have set new records in terms of transaction value, indicating that corporate America has fully accepted the idea that growth is accomplished either by *building from within,* or by *buying businesses.* This notion has also been embraced by the capital markets, and active acquirers receive plenty of interest from banks, institutional lenders, and equity investors. Since operating corporations are active buyers of equities—usually for the purpose of gaining 100 percent control over the investment—analysts must be cognizant of what price level stirs takeover interest in a company.

While the maximum price of what one operating business can logically pay to acquire another is beyond the scope of this book (the reader can refer to my earlier work, *M&A: A Practical Guide to Doing the Deal,* New York: John Wiley & Sons, 1997), a minimum takeout price is established for many companies by applying the leveraged buyout method. I refer to the "minimum" price because an LBO firm tends to pay a lower valuation multiple than an operating business. The LBO firm can't realize the same operating synergies that come from combining two similar companies, so its pricing formula tends to reflect a lower number.

A typical corporate acquirer justifies a takeover by assuming that its skills and resources, once applied to the seller's business, will ratchet up the seller's sales and earnings performance. When Microsoft bought tiny Vermeer Technology, the inclusion of Vermeer's front-page software into Microsoft's marketing and distributing system propelled sales from thousands of copies annually to hundreds of thousands. Bank of Boston's acquisition of Bay Banks didn't meaningfully increase Bay Banks' revenue base, but the cost savings resulting from eliminating duplicative headquarters, marketing, and branch functions increased the company's operating earnings significantly. In many deals in which I participated as an investment banker, synergies boosted the acquisition's bottom line by 10 to 20 percent. As a result, it follows that an operating company can afford to pay more than an LBO firm in most instances.

EXHIBIT 15–2. Target Co.'s Effective Price/Earnings Multiple (US$ millions)

	Historical Results of Target Co.	Adjustments[1] for a Synergy Merger with Similar Co.	Pro Forma Results of Target Co.
Sales	$100.0	$ —	$100.0
Operating expenses	88.0	(2.0)	86.0
Earnings before interest and taxes	12.0		14.0
Interest	2.0	—	2.0
Pretax income	10.0	2.0	12.0
Income taxes	4.0	0.8	4.8
Net income	$ 6.0	$1.2	$ 7.2
Asking price	$120		$120
	Financial Partners		*Similar Co.*
Effective P/E ratio at asking price[2]	20.0×		$16.7×

[1] Adjusted to reflect pro forma decrease of $2.0 million in staff compensation. Assumes no purchase accounting adjustments.

[2] Synergies mean Similar Co. is only paying 16.7× earnings, while Financial Partners pays 20× earnings.

Exhibit 15–2 illustrates the effective P/E multiples paid by Financial Partners, an LBO firm, and Similar Co., an operating business, should one of them purchase Target Co. for $120 million. Without synergies, Financial Partners pays 20× net income. Similar Co., on the other hand, is in the same business as Target Co., so it consolidates many of Target's executive and staff functions into Similar Co.'s overhead. The total savings equal $1.2 million after taxes. The resultant 20 percent gain in Target's net income, adjusted for the acquisition, means that Similar Co. pays less per dollar of earnings than Financial Partners. Similar Co. thus has a bidding advantage in the auction, enabling it to pay more.

UNDERSTANDING LEVERAGED BUYOUTS

There are four basic principles behind the leveraged buyout (see Exhibit 15–3). The first one is simple: "OPM," or "Other People's Money." The leveraged buyout firm attempts to acquire companies while investing as little as possible of its own money. The bulk of the purchase price is borrowed from banks or other knowledgeable lenders engaged in the field of highly leveraged transactions. The LBO firm does not guarantee the related debt financing, which is secured solely by the assets and future cash flows of the target company. Nor does the LBO firm promise the lenders much in the way of operating expertise, since it is typically staffed with financial professionals who know little about how to run a large manufacturing or

EXHIBIT 15–3. Four LBO Principles

1. *Other People's Money.* Use as much leverage as possible in deals, thus enhancing prospective equity returns.
2. *Buying Right.* Search for businesses which can be acquired at relatively low value multiples.
3. *Out-of-Fashion Industries.* Focus efforts on out-of-fashion industries where valuation multiples are low.
4. *Improve Operating Performance.* Shift management's orientation to acting as owners instead of employees.

service business. The LBO firm is basically a transaction promoter, which is a full-time job in and of itself. Finding an acquisition candidate, pricing the deal, performing due diligence, finding financing, and negotiating legal documents is a lengthy and complex process requiring combinations of contacts and skills that are not easily duplicated.

Since the LBO business emerged from obscurity in the early 1980s, it has become institutionalized. Today, about 150 investment firms specialize in arranging leveraged buyouts. Another 50 to 100 investment banks, venture capital firms, and general investment funds, dabble in the field, closing one or two deals per year. Collectively, these buyers work with many of the Fortune 500 companies and in some cases are significant corporate shareholders, having bought some of these large companies in the frenetic late 1980s, when the LBO market hit its peak. The success of LBO investments has attracted blue-chip state, corporate, and employee pension plans to the field, and they are now the primary funding sources behind the vast equity pools commanded by the buyout firms. The top five firms control $12 billion in equity, which could, if leveraged at 4:1, acquire corporate assets worth $60 billion.

By using large amounts of leverage, the LBO firm enhances its investment returns because lenders share little or none of the increase in value of the corporate assets. It can only lose its initial investment, perhaps 20 percent of the deal's purchase price, while enjoying practically 100 percent of the upside. (See Exhibit 15–4.) Since corporate earnings tend to have upward tendencies because of inflation and economic growth, the LBO tactic of using lots of borrowed money to buy corporate assets is sensible, particularly if the related acquisition prices are reasonably in line with historical standards.

"Buying right" is the second linchpin of the LBO artist because a premium price can spell failure quickly. Overpaying for a business is costly for two key reasons: (1) Like any other corporate acquirer, an LBO firm faces smaller returns with each extra dollar it pays for a deal; (2) an LBO firm operates with a small margin for error, even when it buys a deal "right." When it overpays, the acquisition is loaded up with even more debt than would normally be the case. If the deal's operating earnings come in even slightly lower than forecast, its ability to pay debt service is in jeopardy with the higher debt load.

EXHIBIT 15–4. Leveraged Buyout Capitalization

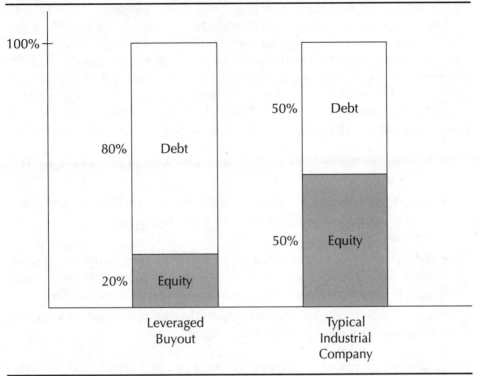

Third, to avoid paying top dollar, LBO firms turn to acquisitions in out-of-fashion industries that corporate America is avoiding. The auctions for businesses in these unpopular industries draw little interest from synergy players and asking prices are low compared to the popular industries. Furthermore, a robust company may need ongoing capital injections that complicate the LBO financing. After buying the business, the LBO firm seeks to improve the operation and hopes for the fashion cycle to turn.

The fourth leg of the LBO table is enhancing the operating performance of the firm. After acquisition, LBO firms seek above-average efficiencies from their management teams. Top managers are provided with a meaningful equity participation and they are expected to run the business like owners instead of employees. Many respond by cutting expenses that otherwise would be tolerated under the public ownership model. The result for the LBO firm is a more profitable acquisition that can exceed its projections.

LBO MECHANICS

The mechanics of implementing an LBO are well known and center around finding a business that can support the debt needed to finance about 80 percent of its purchase price. While this degree of leverage is typical in real estate, autos, and airplanes—to name a few asset categories—it is uncommon in operating companies that manufacture a product or provide a service. Why? Because operating company values fluctuate widely from year to year. Even the values of big-name corporations exhibit wide ranges. In 1998, the price of Coca-Cola stock traded between $53 and $88, a 40 percent difference in just 12 months. Computer Associates shares moved within a $26 to $62 range, a 42 percent difference. To justify taking the risk of a significant value drop, LBO lenders look for borrowers with a few key characteristics:

- *Low-Tech.* LBO lenders prefer businesses relying on technology that is not subject to rapid change.
- *Solid Track Record.* LBO lenders prefer low-tech businesses with a history of consistent profitability and a pro forma ability to cover LBO debt service.
- *Hard Assets.* As an insurance policy against potential operating problems, LBO lenders prefer borrowers with lots of tangible assets, such as real estate, plant and equipment, inventory, and receivables.
- *Low Indebtedness.* To support acquisition debt, the target company needs to have low leverage in the first place.

In reviewing potential buyout candidates, LBO firms balance these lender preferences against likely purchase prices. Basic calculations are performed to determine a would-be acquisition's attractiveness to the lending community.

Case Study: Roto-Rooter, Inc. In late 1996, Roto-Rooter, Inc., a provider of sewer, drain, and pipe cleaning services, was bought out by an affiliated company, Chemed Corp. Roto-Rooter had a consistent record of profitability and participated in a low-tech business. Six months prior to Chemed's tender offer, Roto-Rooter's share price was in the low 30s, and the company had ample LBO debt-servicing capabilities. Exhibit 15–5 provides selected financial information.

How Much Can the LBO Firm Pay?

Roto-Rooter is a good LBO candidate, but how much can an LBO firm pay? The $20.4 million EBIT number is the first place to start. Using a 1.4 EBIT/Interest ratio as a "rule of thumb" for lenders, Roto Rooter can support $14.6 million per year of interest payments (i.e., $20.4 ÷ 1.4 = $14.6). Figuring a 9.50 percent interest rate on LBO debt (2.50% over the 10-year U.S. Treasury bond), Roto-Rooter can shoulder about $153 million of debt (i.e., $14.6 ÷ 0.095 = $153). Applying a debt-equity ratio of 80/20 to the transaction means the LBO firm can give Roto-Rooter a total price of $190

EXHIBIT 15–5. Roto-Rooter, Inc.—Selected Financial Information (in millions except per share data)

	Year Ended December 31		
	1994	**1995**	**1996**[1]
Income Statement Data			
Net revenue	$171.9	$179.8	$199.2
EBIT[2]	16.5	17.5	20.4
Net earnings	8.8	9.7	11.6
Earnings per share	$1.73	$1.90	$2.27
Balance Sheet Data	*At December 31, 1996*		
Current assets	$ 59.6		
Total assets	159.1		
Current liabilities	61.7		
Long-term debt	8.5		
Shareholder's equity	84.1		
Share Data			
Price range, June 1995–June 1996	$28 to $36		
Shares outstanding	5.3 million		

[1] 1996 data was actual through June 30. Estimated thereafter.
[2] EBIT excludes interest income (except from statutory deposits and non-recurring items).

million, including $37 million of new equity and the assumption of net outstanding debts (see Exhibit 15–6).

Roto-Rooter's long-term debt in early 1996 totaled $8.5 million. Since this debt must be either assumed or repaid by the LBO borrower, it is subtracted from the enterprise value while cash is added back. The final amount is the equity acquisition value, which is divided by the number of shares outstanding to provide an LBO per share value (see Exhibit 15–7).

This $36.89 per share value is a guide to LBO affordability. Given that it is higher than the market trading range of $28 to $36, it holds open the possibility of Roto-Rooter selling out to an LBO firm. The number, however, is a rough estimate. Further due diligence might uncover hidden assets or liabilities that could increase or decrease the value.

EXHIBIT 15–6. Roto-Rooter LBO Enterprise Value

	Millions	**%**
LBO debt	$153	80
Equity	37	20
LBO enterprise value	$190	100

EXHIBIT 15–7. Roto-Rooter LBO per Share Value (in millions except per share)

Enterprise value	$190.0
Less: Existing debt	(8.5)
Add: Cash-on-hand	14.0
Adjusted enterprise value	195.5
Divided by outstanding shares and options	÷ 5.3
LBO per share value	$36.89

Projections prepared by the Company and made available to the public indicated that Roto-Rooter was in a position both to support an LBO-type debt load and to provide lenders with an appropriate safety margin. Exhibit 15–8 provides summary projected data for a $190 million deal.

The projections reflect the usual seller's optimism with respect to future results, and the Company's EBIT is forecast to increase at a compound annual rate of 13 percent. Even if management's projections are trimmed, however, Roto Rooter still covers its debt service easily on a pro forma basis. Accordingly, the LBO price of $36.89 is the likely bottom for a takeover bid. In fact, Chemed paid $41 per share, reflecting, in part, its ability to realize operating synergies.

LBO Valuation in the Security Analysis

For manufacturing and service firms that fit the lenders' LBO criteria, the practitioner computes an LBO equity value following the three steps of the Roto-Rooter example:

1. Verify the low-tech nature and solid track record of the company.
2. Determine the affordability quotient of an LBO buyer by using guideposts of 80/20 leverage and 1.4× interest coverage.

EXHIBIT 15–8. Roto-Rooter—Hypothetical $190 Million LBO—Summary Financial Projections (in millions)

	Estimated	Projected[2]			
	1996	1997	1998	1999	2000
Income Statement Data					
Net revenue	$199.2	$221.4	$247.8	$277.7	$311.6
EBIT	20.4	23.1	26.4	28.5	32.8
Assumed LBO interest	14.6	14.6	14.6	14.6	14.6
EBIT/Interest ratio[1]	1.4×	1.6×	1.8×	2.0×	2.2×

[1] Minimum acceptable ratio is 1.4×.
[2] Projections are from Roto-Rooter's SEC filings in connection with Chemed's offer.

3. Develop projections with a top-down analysis and make sure that future LBO debt service is covered.

When the stock is trading at less than 75 percent of the LBO price, the company is considered relatively cheap as a takeover candidate. The stock may be an attractive buy, particularly if the shares are widely held and the corporate charter has few takeover protections.

Occasionally, the discounted cash flow and relative value techniques produce inconsistent results. The LBO value-method is an excellent reality check for manufacturing and service firms.

ALTERNATIVE TAKEOVER VALUES

LBOs represent less than 20 percent of merger activity, but their pricing parameters are easier to surmise than the other 80 percent. Operating-to-operating company mergers have so many situational variables that estimating one given firm's value to another—and the likely timing of a deal—is almost impossible. Nevertheless, a healthy business trading at less than 75 percent of the multiples of comparable acquisition transactions (or as Warren Buffett would say, "private market values") is fundamentally cheap. For example, in 1996 five retail drug takeovers occurred at 22× to 26× earnings. A retail drugstore chain trading at 16× to 18× earnings appeared attractive, and most institutions considered such a stock a good investment.

Researching M&A comparables is difficult because the number of deals in an industry is much smaller than the universe of participants. Moreover, the statistical information that the analyst compiles at any given time is dated, since generating a representative sample of industry transactions requires going back a year or more. As a result, practitioners maintain a running inventory of transaction statistics, which are amended as new deals crop up. Investors just beginning to track an industry can buy M&A

EXHIBIT 15–9. Selected 1996 HMO Takeovers

Seller/Buyer	Purchase Price (millions)	Purchase Price as a Multiple of		
		Net Earnings	Sales	Book Value
Caremark/Med Partners	$2,300	29.1	1.0	4.8
FHP/Pacificare	2,100	24.4	0.5	1.8
Healthwise/United Healthcare	290	42.6	1.8	14.5
Ramsey HMO/United Healthcare	420	35.3	1.5	8.2
Takecare/United Healthcare	820	32.6	1.3	5.4
U.S. Healthcare/Aetna	8,900	21.2	2.1	9.3
Wellpoint/Blue Shield	4,500	21.0	1.8	3.6

data from a number of services, such as Mergers & Acquisition magazine, Corporate Growth Outlook publications, and Compustat. An abbreviated compilation of 1996 HMO deals appears as Exhibit 15–9. In this exhibit, note how the bigger deals have lower value multiples.

In 1996, large HMOs sold for P/Es averaging in the low 20s. A large HMO stock trading in the mid-teens would have appeared relatively cheap, assuming its track record and prospects were satisfactory. Small HMOs were purchased at higher multiples, and small-cap HMO stocks reflected this differential.

SUMMARY

Including M&A values in a security analysis is a good idea. Companies trading substantially below their private market values are often takeover candidates, besides being good fundamental opportunities. Nevertheless, a transaction review is only a supplement to the DCF and relative value process.

Industries go in and out of fashion in the M&A business. Ten years ago, investment bankers couldn't give away real estate investment trust securities (REITs). Nowadays, active acquirers are buying REITs at 12 to 15 times cash flow. Recognizing the vagaries of the market, the analyst uses top-down research to verify whether the prospects of an industry justify M&A pricing.

QUESTIONS AND SHORT PROBLEMS

1. Why can an operating company often afford to pay more than a leveraged buyout firm in bidding for the acquisition of another operating company? Select one answer.
   a. The operating company can realize higher rates of return from the acquisition by realizing synergies, such as reduced overhead.
   b. The LBO firm's cost of capital is much higher than the operating company.
   c. LBO firms typically underbid all acquisitions in order to maximize profit.
   d. Operating companies can usually offer high P/E multiple stock as acquisition currency, rather than cash.

2. List the four principles that underlie the leverage buyout phenomenon.

3. How can leveraged-buyout equity investors sometimes achieve above-average investment returns?
   a. Large amounts of leverage allow them to retain much of the upside performance of the investment, while lenders incur most of the downside risk.
   b. Corporate earnings always increase, enhancing the prospects of leverage.

c. LBO firms tend to pay lower prices for acquisitions, thus realizing eventual higher returns.

d. LBO firms buy into popular industry trends, and thus follow momentum investors to higher profits.

4. List the four key characteristics of a prime leveraged buyout candidate.

5. Why are lenders generally reluctant to provide "loan-to-value" ratios of 80 percent for acquirers of operating businesses?

6. Why is a high-tech firm an unlikely LBO candidate? Select the best answer.

a. Its earnings are likely to grow faster than a low-tech firm, thereby reducing its ability to incur debt.

b. The future earnings stream of the high-tech firm is generally considered more uncertain than that of a low-tech firm, and lenders are reluctant to provide high leverage.

c. The high P/E multiples given to all high-tech firms make them too expensive for LBO sponsors.

d. The management teams of high-tech firms are not used to operating businesses with heavy debt loads.

7. Tilbourne Foods' majority owners are considering sponsoring an LBO of the company with the assistance of an investment firm. Here are the financial data for this manufacturer and marketer of consumer packaged foods:

Tilbourne Foods, Inc.
(in millions except per share data)

Income Statement	Year Ended December 31		
	1997	1998	1999
Net revenue	$ 256	$ 278	$ 299
EBIT	25	27	30
Net earnings	13	15	18
Earnings per share	$1.63	$1.88	$2.25

Balance Sheet	At December 31, 1999
Cash on hand	$ 12
Other assets	228
Total assets	240
Total debt	22
Shareholders' equity	138

Answer the following questions:

a. Using a 1.4 EBIT/interest expense ratio as a lender guideline, how much interest expense can Tilbourne reasonably expect to support in an LBO?

b. If the 10-year U.S. Treasury rate is 6 percent, and LBO lenders, on average, demand 2.5 percent over Treasuries, how much debt can Tilbourne carry in an LBO?

c. Given your answer in (b), what is the minimum amount of equity necessary in a hypothetical LBO?

d. What is your estimate of Tilbourne's per share value in a leveraged buyout? Assume 8.0 million shares outstanding and no stock options.

8. Tilbourne Foods' stock is trading at $28 per share. Should it be considered a "buy" on the basis of your answer to Question 7(d)?

9. Over the last two years, four companies comparable to Tilbourne Foods have been acquired. The acquisition value multiples are:

Seller/Buyer	Purchase Price (MM)	P/E Ratio	EV/EBIT
Twill Foods/Campbell Soup	$340	17 times	11 times
Chase Products/Flower Ind.	216	22	13
Constant Foods/Quaker Oats	425	18	11
Total Food/P&G	648	16	10

At a public market price of $28 per share, is Tilbourne Foods' stock a "buy," given the relative values of recent acquisitions?

Adopt-a-Company

A. Using the technique in Chapter 15, calculate the LBO value of your company on a per share basis.

B. Identify acquisitions of similar companies over the last two years. Using tender offer documents, proxy statements, and similar materials, calculate the acquisitions' P/E, EV/EBIT, and Price/Book multiples.

C. By utilizing the data in (2), determine whether your company is a "buy," according to the private market "75 percent rule of thumb."

16

Breakup Analysis

A multiline business poses an extra challenge for the practitioner. Breaking it down into its component parts and valuing each separately is discussed in this chapter.

One of the problems with security analysis is the diversity of public corporations. Many are engaged in disparate product lines, which means the evaluation of one stock turns into the study of a series of businesses. The painstaking methodology of performing a top-down analysis and making projections is thus repeated for each and every business. As a result, the proper analysis of a conglomerate can involve two or three times the effort of evaluating a one-line company. This chapter examines the process of valuing a multiline company, and it represents a continuation of the research report's Section 7 (see Exhibit 16–1).

EXHIBIT 16–1. Model Research Report

1. Introduction
2. Macroeconomic Review
3. Relevant Stock Market Prospects
4. Review of the Company and Its Business
5. Financial Analysis
6. Financial Projections
7. Application of Valuation Methodologies✓
8. Recommendation

BACKGROUND

Because the businesses of a truly diversified enterprise have little to do with one another, a practitioner does not appraise the company as one large going concern. He views it as a collection of separate units, each of which can be peeled off to realize value.

Breakup analysis is applied best either to conglomerates with divisions engaged in unrelated businesses or to companies with complementary businesses that don't fit together. The term "breakup" became popular in the mid-1980s when takeover artists performed such analyses, bought diversified companies at prices below their collective divisional values, and then sold off the companies division by division, thereby unlocking value not recognized by the market. The larger operation was thus "broken up" into its component parts. My last book, *M&A: A Practical Guide to Doing the Deal* (New York: John Wiley & Sons, 1997), covered this technique.

Actual breakup transactions are rare these days. Responding to an upsurge in this activity, the government closed loopholes in the tax law that promoted them. Now, the revised tax burden makes most prospective breakups uneconomic. In its place, diversified companies realize the value of noncore businesses by spinning them off to shareholders. The parent declares the business's shares as a noncash dividend, after gaining an IRS ruling guaranteeing that such distribution is tax-free. Prominent spinoffs have included several well-known conglomerates, including Dun & Bradstreet, General Instrument, and Pepsico.

Dun & Bradstreet, the giant information services company, spun off A. C. Nielsen, the TV information business, and Cognizant, a new firm formed from two fast-growing D&B units: IMS International, which supplies market information to drug companies, and Gartner Group, which sells research and analysis on computer hardware. General Instrument proposed to split into three new companies: The largest contained its telephone and cable equipment business ($1.7 billion in sales), and the other two held the coaxial wire business ($600 million in sales) and the electrical components operation ($360 million in sales), respectively. PepsiCo, which had been criticized for damaging its P/E multiple by holding onto its low-growth restaurant business (Taco Bell, Pizza Hut, and Kentucky Fried Chicken), finally decided to spin off the $11 billion in sales represented by these operations, thus slimming the parent down to two consumer product lines, soft drinks (Pepsi) and snacks (Frito-Lay).

Case Study: Sample Breakup Analysis for Teleflex, Inc.   Teleflex, Inc., provides an example of how to approach breakup analysis. In February 1997, Teleflex comprised three core businesses—auto parts, medical devices, and aerospace products—which had no operating synergy. Despite its varied operations, Teleflex's formula worked. Earnings had risen in each of the previous 10 years, and occasional downturns in one business line were offset by growth in others. The company's balance sheet was strong and return on equity was favorable. Summary operating and market data at February 1997 are shown in Exhibit 16–2.

Business Segment Valuation

The first step in my breakup analysis was valuing each of Teleflex's business segments as a stand-alone company. Summary operating performance of the divisions appears in Exhibit 16–3. When an analyst seeks to determine the worth of a corporate division or a holding company subsidiary, he faces a business that does not report a true net income since its capitalization structure is artificial or nonexistent. The business unit, however, will report an operating earnings figure, which is equivalent to the EBIT of a publicly traded firm. He thus has an indicator from which to begin a valuation.

Large corporations like Teleflex use a holding company to segment their various businesses for legal and financial purposes. Each business line is encapsuled in a subsidiary, a separate legal corporation that receives its permanent capital in the form of equity (and sometimes debt) from the mother

EXHIBIT 16–2. Teleflex, Inc.—Summary of Financial and Market Data (in millions except per share and ratios)

Income Statement	Year Ended December 31, 1996	1991–1996 Compound Annual Growth Rate %
Revenues	$931	14
EBIT	100	11
Net income	57	14
Earnings per share	3.16	12

Balance Sheet	At December 31, 1996
Cash	$ 68
Net working capital, including cash	270
Fixed assets	292
Total debt	266
Stockholders' equity	409

Market Data	At February 28, 1997
Share price	$45
P/E multiple	14.2×
Price/book value	2.0×
Enterprise value/EBIT	10.0×
Dividend yield	1.5%

Note. Company data indicate strong growth rate, solid balance sheet, and moderate valuation multiples.

EXHIBIT 16–3. Teleflex, Inc.—Business Segment Information for the Year Ended December 31, 1996

Business Segment	In Millions		5-Year Compound Growth Rate	
	Revenues	Operating Income	Revenues (%)	Operating Income (%)
Auto parts	$422	$ 58	20	24
Medical devices	308	35	19	12
Aerospace products	201	21	2	(1)
	$931	$114		
Corporate expense		(13)		
Interest expense		(18)		
Interest income		4		
Pretax income		$ 87		

Note. The auto parts and medical devices divisions showed strong growth results.

company. The subsidiaries own inventory, receivables, and plant and equipment, whereas the mother company's primary assets are the common shares of these subsidiaries. Its primary liabilities are the debt it issues to finance its subsidiaries' operating activities (i.e., the subsidiaries actually make the product or provide a service that is sold to an outside party). The mother company accesses large sums of financing at a cheaper cost than its subsidiaries can obtain on a stand-alone basis; and furthermore, it can afford to be staffed with the finance, legal, tax, and accounting experts required to administer specialized services to the operating businesses. Exhibit 16–4 presents a diagram showing a common organizational structure for a holding company.

The relevant subsidiary (or division as the case may be) does not have an independent capital structure. Its few long-term debts are owed to the mother company, which also owns its common equity. The concept of "subsidiary net income" does not exist on a stand-alone basis, since income tax obligations are consolidated at the parent company level.

Because the Teleflex divisions were consistently profitable over the past five years, earnings-based multiples and DCF were appropriate valuation tools, but first I needed to construct individual income statements for each division "as if" it were independent. I allocated each division a portion of corporate overhead and then applied a 35 percent corporate income tax rate. With the divisional depreciation from the financial statements, I had pro forma EBITDA, EBIT, and net income numbers to use for DCF forecasts and relative values. Exhibit 16–5 summarizes this procedure.

The remainder of the divisional valuation process follows the intrinsic value and relative value techniques described earlier. Due to the lack of full balance sheet and footnote data, the divisional analysis relies heavily on relative value multiples, as opposed to classical cash flow forecasts. The following summary provides highlights of the work:

EXHIBIT 16–4. Financial and Management Structure of a Holding Company with Three Subsidiaries

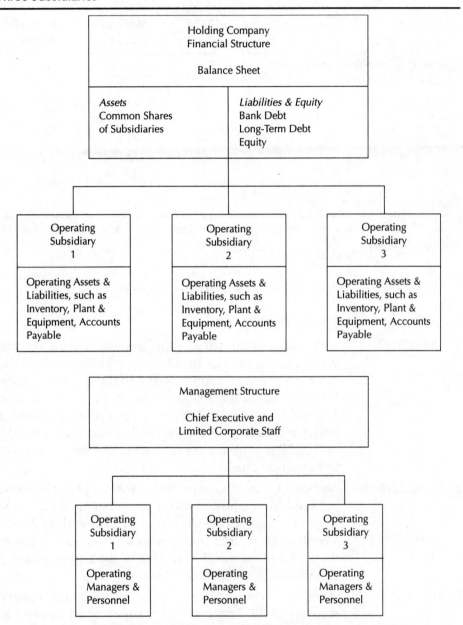

EXHIBIT 16–5. Teleflex, Inc.—Pro Forma Divisional Net Income Year Ended December 31, 1996 (in millions)

	Auto Parts	Medical Devices	Aerospace Products
Operating income from annual report	$58	$35	$21
Allocated overhead	(7)	(4)	(2)
EBIT	51	31	19
Interest	—	—	—
Pretax income	51	31	19
Proforma taxes (35%)	18	11	7
Net income	$33	$20	$12
Depreciation from annual report	$12	$16	$10

Note. Allocating corporate overhead and income taxes provides an estimate of stand-alone profitability.

Summary Valuation of Teleflex Divisions

Value (in millions)	Teleflex Division
$ 460 to $495	*Auto Parts.* Auto parts suppliers with solid records were trading at 11× to 12× net earnings, which reflected a market discount owing to the sector's cyclicability. Because of its superior growth record and favorable prospects. Teleflex's operation deserved a better multiple, perhaps 14× to 15× earnings. EBITDA and EBIT multipliers conformed to the $460 million to $495 million range.
$ 340 to $360	*Medical Devices.* In early 1997, medical product stocks suffered from a lack of investor interest, and valuation multiples had dropped from earlier premium levels. The division's niche business and strong sales growth merited a premium (17× to 18×) to the slower-growing diversified stocks (14× to 15×).
$ 215 to $225	*Aerospace Products.* The division experienced a sharp recovery in 1995 and 1996. Anticipating an uptrend in the aircraft spending cycle, investors bid up most aerospace stocks to high P/Es. Consider the February 1997 quote of Laurence Chapman, chief financial officer of Rohr, Inc., a large aircraft component manufacturer, "There's a tremendous demand out there for new aircraft." Trading independently, the division justified an 18 to 19 P/E.
$1,015 to $1,080	*Total Value of Divisions*

Netting Out Nonoperating Assets and Liabilities

The Teleflex analysis evaluates the worth of divisional assets (and liabilities) that actually create sales and earnings. Each division is a separate value unit. From this $1,015 million to $1,080 million total must be added (or subtracted) the net value of extraneous assets and liabilities that are not involved in operations.

In my experience, nonoperating items tend to be centered in the holding company and have a financial orientation. Sometimes, operating businesses hold onto valuable assets, such as a real estate parcel, which have little operating importance. This is referred to as a "hidden value." In one transaction, the Limited acquired a large retailer, Lane Bryant, that owned a small property on Fifth Avenue in New York. Lane Bryant operated a successful store at this location, but the Limited quickly realized that the site was far more valuable as prime office space. The two-story store was demolished and a 37-story office tower replaced it.

In the case of Teleflex, the two largest nonoperating items were excess cash ($68 million) and outstanding debt ($266 million). Long-term investments ($17 million), unfunded pension liabilities ($9 million), and unexercised option values ($10 million) were also represented. The net breakup value before capital gains taxes was $45.28 to $48.61 per share, slightly above the $45 market price (see Exhibit 16–6).

EXHIBIT 16–6. Teleflex Breakup Value as of February 1997

	Value Range (in millions)
Auto parts	$ 460–495
Medical devices	340–360
Aerospace products	215–225
Other	$1,015–1,080
Add:	
Corporate cash	+68
Other investments	+17
Subtract:	
Corporate debts	−266
Pension liabilities	−9
Value of management options	−10
Net breakup value before taxes	$815–$875
Net Breakup Value per Teleflex Share:	$45.28–$48.61

Note. The breakup value is only slightly higher than the $45 market price.

Unlocking Breakup Values

Unlocking breakup values can be accomplished in four ways: (1) a corporate takeover; (2) a cash sale of certain divisions; (3) a dividend of divisional shares to corporate equity holders; or (4) a spin-off of shares to corporate equity holders. Being taken over isn't the first option of most managements, but more companies are considering the other three choices. From both a corporate and stockholder viewpoint, a spin-off is usually most beneficial, particularly if it is ruled tax-free by the IRS. In contrast, selling a division at a profit means capital gains taxes. Shareholders sometimes pay income taxes on the value of division shares received as dividends.

With Teleflex, the breakup value per share was practically the same as the $45 market price. As a result, there was no compelling need to buy the stock on the basis of a presumed discount to breakup value. Many professionals like to acquire shares of companies trading at 70 to 80 percent of breakup value, thus minimizing downside exposure. More aggressive investors, such as Michael Price and Mario Gabelli, actively build positions in such businesses and pressure management to unlock the values, thus providing an impetus to a higher stock price. Frequently, such investors include acquisition premiums into their calculations, believing external force can lead to outright action.

SUMMARY

The value of a diversified business is reached by calculating the sum of its individual parts. Because of the lack of information available on divisional operations, breakup analysis is more dependent on relative valuation techniques than a conventional one-line business evaluation. Although it's not perfect, breakup analysis is a good reality check for other techniques. Tracing hidden values and discounts-to-breakup value is a common avocation of the practitioner community.

QUESTIONS AND SHORT PROBLEMS

1. A break-up valuation analysis is best performed for which kind of company?
   a. A company that is consistently losing money and is a takeover candidate.
   b. A company with substantial unrealized real estate values that are not reflected in historical accounting reports.
   c. A company with core businesses that complement each other well.
   d. A diversified conglomerate with several unrelated product lines.

2. Why did the Telefex analysis calculate pro forma EBIT and net income results for each division?

3. In most break-up evaluations, the divisional valuation process relies heavily on the relative value technique, as opposed to the discounted cash flow method. Why?
   a. Discounted cash flow has too many uncertainties regarding projections and discount rates.
   b. SEC reports do not provide full disclosure regarding divisional financial results, thus making cash flow forecasts problematic.
   c. Relative value is a more accurate method of assessing divisional pricing in the private market.
   d. Analysts cannot properly estimate the amount of corporate overhead allocable to the divisions.

4. The remaining questions incorporate the following financial data:

Regent Co. Financial and Market Data
(in millions, except per share and ratios)

Income Statement	Year Ended December 31, 1999	1994–1999 Compound Annual Growth Rate %
Revenues	$1,390	7%
EBIT	152	9
Net income	86	10
Earnings per share	$ 4.00	9

Balance Sheet	At December 31, 1999
Cash	$102
Net working capital, incl. cash	378
Fixed assets	441
Total debt	390
Stockholders' equity	612

Market Data	
Share price	$60
P/E multiple	15.0 times
Price/book value	2.1 times
Enterprise value/EBIT	10.4
Dividend yield	1.5%
Shares outstanding (MM)	21.5

Note: Regent data indicate strong growth rate, solid balance sheet, and moderate valuation multiples.

Regent Co. Business Segment Information
(for the Year Ended December 31, 1999)

	In Millions		5-Year Growth Rate	
	Revenues	Operating Income	Revenues %	Operating Income
Electronics	$ 623	$ 87	6%	9%
Business forms	460	53	12	10
Metal distribution	307	33	(2)	(2)
	$1,390	$173		
Corporate expenses		(21)		
Corporate EBIT		$152		
Interest expense		(24)		
Interest income		4		
Pretax income		$132		

Note: The electronics and business forms divisions showed strong growth results.

a. Allocate corporate overhead to the divisions on the basis of the divisions' respective contributions to corporate sales. Complete the next table:

Regent Co. Pro Forma Divisional Net Income
Year Ended December 31, 1999 (in millions)

	Electronics Manufacturing	Business Forms	Metal Distribution
Operating income	$87	$53	$33
Allocated overhead	—	—	—
EBIT	—	—	—
Interest	—	—	—
Pretax income	—	—	—
Pro forma taxes (35%)	—	—	—
Net income	$—	$—	$—
Depreciation by division	$18	$23	$15

Note: Allocating corporate overhead and income taxes by division provides an estimate of stand-alone profitability by division.

b. The average growth rates and trading multiples for selected industry groups comparable to Regent's divisions are shown. Using the material provided, calculate the net "break-up value" per Regent Co. share, assuming no income or capital gains taxes on the breakup.

Industry Group	Average Growth Rates	P/E	EV/EBIT
Electronics Mfg.	10%	20 times	12 times
Business Forms	8	16	10
Metal Distribution	(1)	9	6

c. Based on your answer to (b), is Regent Co. stock a good value on a break-up basis?

Adopt-a-Company

If your company was selected by using the requisite criteria, it is not a break-up candidate because it only has one line of business.

17

Recommended
Investment Decision

Chapter 17 presents a case study in which the four approaches to valuation are applied to a real-life company. It demonstrates a decision making process that is rational and systematic. The investment recommendation concludes the chapter.

In Chapters 12 to 16, we covered four approaches to equity valuation:

1. *Intrinsic Value.* A business is worth the net present value of its dividends.
2. *Relative Value.* Determine a company's value by comparing it to similar companies' values.
3. *Acquisition Value.* Calculate a company's share price by determining its worth to a third party acquirer, such as another operating business, a leveraged buyout firm, or a liquidator. Then apply a 25 percent discount for a passive minority investment.
4. *Breakup Analysis.* One values a multi-line company by segmenting its components and valuing each separately. The whole is thus the sum of its parts.

In this chapter, I apply each valuation technique to Ruddick Corp., a successful company with two divisions, Harris Teeter and American & Efird:

- *Harris Teeter* operates a 140-store grocery chain in the southern United States with a leading position in the North Carolina market.

Sales and operating income for the 12 months ended March 30, 1997, were $1.9 billion and $48 million, respectively.

- *American & Efird* (A&E) produces industrial sewing thread for use by apparel, automotive, home furnishings, and footwear manufacturers. A&E is the largest producer in the U.S. industrial thread market with a 35 percent share, and is increasing its international presence. A cyclical business, A&E's sales and operating income totaled $351 million and $45 million, respectively, for the 12 months ending March 30, 1997.

EXHIBIT 17–1. Ruddick Corporation—Summary Financial and Market Data (in millions except per share data and percentages)

Income Statement	Year Ended September 30			12 Months Ended March 30, 1997	10-Year Compound Annual Growth Rate
	1994	1995	1996		
Net Sales					
Harris Teeter	$1,579	$1,712	$1,833	$1,877	10%
American & Efird	277	298	309	351	11
Total net sales	1,856	2,010	2,142	2,228	
Operating Profit					
Harris Teeter	37	42	48	48	18
American & Efird	27	35	35	45	12
Total operating profit	64	77	83	93	
EBIT	60	70	74	85	12
Net income	32	39	43	48	12
Earnings per share	0.67	0.84	0.92	1.03	10

Balance Sheet	At March 30, 1997
Cash	$ 14
Fixed assets	439
Total assets	853
Total debt	218
Stockholders' equity	363

Market Data	At May 15, 1997
Ruddick share price	$15
P/E multiple	14.6×
Price/book	1.9
Enterprise value/EBIT	10.7
Dividend yield	2.1%

Ruddick's two divisions have nothing in common, so the company is a good break-up candidate. Furthermore, Ruddick's profitable history, low-tech orientation, and conservative balance sheet make it a potential leveraged buyout. In sum, the firm is a good case study for using the valuation tools set forth in the earlier chapters. Financial and market data as of May 1997 appear in Exhibit 17–1.

SUMMARY TOP-DOWN ANALYSIS

A proper top-down study can easily fill 20 to 30 pages in a typed format. For the sake of illustration, I only present a few remarks regarding (1) the study's conclusions, and (2) the assumptions for the financial projections.

CONCLUSIONS OF THE TOP-DOWN STUDY

Macroeconomy

The U.S. economy is expected to advance within historical performance parameters. Reflecting the likelihood of a recession after continuous growth through the 90s, a mild economic downturn is predicted for 1999. Accordingly, the 1999 operating income of Harris Teeter and A&E will only increase 4 percent and 2 percent, respectively, before rebounding in 2000.

Capital Markets

Forecasting the stock and bond markets is a hazardous exercise. This case assumes a moderate upward trend in share prices, responding to the growth in corporate earnings and a slight decline in P/E ratios. P/E and EBIT multiples for the supermarket and thread industries fluctuate within previous limits.

Industry

Supermarkets. The grocery store industry is "mature" within the corporate life cycle framework. From the business cycle viewpoint, it is a defensive industry. The low-tech nature of supermarkets indicates few rapid changes, and the basic need for food ensures continued demand for the industry's products. The primary threat to the industry's growth is the warehouse club phenomenon. In the Southeast, where Harris Teeter operates, warehouse clubs have entered the market without seriously damaging the supermarket industry. Grocery store sales in the region are rising faster than in other areas and the trend should continue. Expected sales growth thus exceeds nominal GNP growth (3% real growth + 4% inflation = 7% nominal growth) by 2 percent annually. Profit margins are assumed to remain stable.

Thread Industry.   With a 35 percent share of the industrial thread market, A&E is a proxy for the industry. Within the corporate life cycle, the industrial thread industry is mature; in the business cycle model, it is cyclical. The low-tech aspect of industrial threads and the diversified nature of the industry's customer base suggest few important developments over the medium-to-long term. Sales growth corresponds to nominal GNP growth. Profit margins are stable.

The Company

Harris Teeter.   The leader in its core North Carolina market and expanding gradually into adjacent areas. Besides name recognition, a key Harris Teeter differentiation is its upscale image relative to the competition. Cultivating this image requires an emphasis on perishable areas, such as produce, deli, seafood, bakery, and meat. Capital expenditures will be substantial in this division, reflecting ongoing renovation, improvement, and expansion programs.

American and Efird.   A leader in a niche market. Divisional management demonstrates a strong ability to maintain growth and profit margins. To boost sales in excess of GNP growth, the division acquired a competitor in 1996 for $50 million. Corporate management has a long history in producing quality results for Ruddick shareholders. A large insider ownership preserves management's ability to take the long view.

Historical Financial Analysis

Ruddick is an ideal candidate for a historical financial analysis—sales have increased in each of the past 10 years and net income has grown in 9 out of the last 10 years. "Same store" sales increases have exceeded inflation. Over the past decade, profit margins of both Harris Teeter and A&E have proved to be a model of consistency, varying only slightly on a year-to-year basis.

Furthermore, management didn't play financial games to enhance earnings per share performance. Leverage declined over the period and the number of shares outstanding rose 24 percent. The share increase explains why the compound annual growth rate for net income was 12 percent, versus only 10 percent for earnings per share. Most of the growth has been derived from internal sources, rather than acquisitions.

By today's standards, the company's accounting was straightforward. Unlike many publicly traded firms, Ruddick incurred no significant charges" over the last 10 years. The only twist was the firm's $2 million annual expense on "key man" whole life policies, which provided some $3 million in annual investment income. (Six top executives were insured for large multi-million dollar policies.) The balance sheet was reasonably "clean" with no hint of hidden liabilities. Other assets consisted primarily of undeveloped real estate (for new stores) and whole life surrender values.

Financial Projections

From Chapter 11, there are three projection techniques:

Time Series Techniques.   This method suggests that the future will be like the past. It is well suited for basic industries such as food, brewing, and electricity.

Causal Techniques.   The causal techniques forecast results by establishing relationships between corporate sales and certain external variables, such as housing starts or interest rates. Supermarket sales, for example, are dependent on population growth, among other factors.

Qualitative Techniques.   Qualitative projection techniques are applied to pioneer companies, which have little history to act as a guide for the future. The forecaster is left with expert opinions, market research, and historical analogies as predictive tools. Hi-tech companies frequently use qualitative projection techniques.

The Ruddick Corporation forecast assumptions rely heavily on the time series methodology. Causal techniques assisted me in developing the Harris Teeter store opening program and in predicting a thread acquisition in 2001.

Key Forecast Assumptions

Harris Teeter.   Given the Southeast's healthy economy and the division's superior ability to capture new store sites, nominal sales growth should exceed the presumed 7 percent nominal GNP growth rate by three percentage points over the long term. Hannaford Bros. and Food Lion will continue to encroach on the division's market, fostering a competition that prevents any rise in profit margins. Working capital and capital expenditure needs track sales gains.

American & Efird.   Despite a promising entry into the international arena, the division's underlying growth rate corresponds to nominal GNP growth. However, A&E boosts its market-leading share by two percentage points with an earnings-per-share accretive acquisition in 2001. Profit margins stay constant with the exception of the recession year.

EXHIBIT 17–2. Ruddick Corp.—Condensed Forecast Financial Data (in millions except per share)

	For the Fiscal Year Ended September 30						
	Actual	Estimated	Forecast				
Income Statement	1996	1997	1998	1999	2000	2001	2002
Net Sales			-Recession-				
Harris Teeter	$1,833	$1,930	$2,100	$2,200	$2,420	$2,710	$2,980
American & Efird	309	370	395	400	445	490	560
	2,142	2,300	2,495	2,600	2,865	3,200	3,540
Operating Profit							
Harris Teeter	48	50	55	57	65	70	77
American & Efird	35	47	50	51	58	62	66
	83	97	105	108	123	132	143
EBIT	74	89	97	100	114	123	133
Net income	43	51	56	58	68	78	87
Earnings per share	0.92	1.09	1.20	1.23	1.44	1.60	1.73
Cash dividends	0.28	0.32	0.36	0.36	0.44	0.48	0.52
Balance Sheet							
Cash	$ 21	$ 16	$ 15	$ 12	$ 26	$ 19	$ 18
Fixed assets	411	455	492	523	572	681	745
Total assets	802	866	942	990	1,110	1,252	1,365
Total debt	171	210	232	235	165	200	240
Stockholders' equity	347	382	421	462	580	635	695

Corporate Finances. Corporate overhead, expressed as a percentage of sales, declines over the projected period. The company's Employee Stock Ownership Plan provides an income tax shield. Capital expenses require moderate increases in debt levels until 2000, when the firm sells three million shares to raise $75 million. The dividend payout remains 30 percent of net income.

Summary financial forecasts appear in Exhibit 17–2.

DISCOUNTED CASH FLOW VALUATION

The critical components of a DCF valuation are (1) cash dividend forecast; (2) discount rate; and (3) terminal value. The dividend projections are available from Exhibit 17–2. The discount rate calculation uses Ruddick's 0.7 beta (from Value Line Investment Services), the 10-year U.S. Treasury bond yield (from the *Wall Street Journal*), and a 13.5 percent estimate for the market return. The computation follows:

$$\begin{matrix} \text{Ruddick Dividend} \\ \text{Discount Rate} \end{matrix} = k = \begin{matrix} \text{Government} \\ \text{Bond Rate} \end{matrix} + \text{Beta}\begin{bmatrix} \text{Expected} & - & \text{Government} \\ \text{Market Return} & & \text{Bond Rate} \end{bmatrix}$$

$$= 6.5\% \qquad +0.7 \qquad [13.5\% - 6.5\%]$$

$$= 6.5\% \qquad +0.7 \qquad [7\%]$$

$$= 11.4\%$$

The third variable—the terminal value—is problematic. Projections become less accurate as the time period lengthens, and our dividend discount model requires a stock price prediction in 2002, five years after the initial purchase date. In Ruddick's case, most practitioners would figure a terminal value by applying an average historical P/E multiple to the company's 2002 earnings per share. Others might consider a modified breakup approach, achieved through determining the 2002 values of Harris Teeter and A&E. A small minority would utilize the "constant growth" dividend discount model (DDM). Exhibit 17–3 illustrates the P/E multiple and DDM methods (breakup valuations are covered later in this chapter). Note that the terminal values are $21.63 and $20.00, respectively.

With terminal values in hand, the rest of the DCF exercise consists of filling in the variables of the two-step dividend discount model, reviewed in Chapter 12. In the first computation, I insert the $21.63 estimate of the terminal value:

$$\begin{matrix} \text{Ruddick 1997} \\ \text{Share Value} \end{matrix} = \frac{D_1}{1+k} + \frac{D_2}{(1+k)^2} + \frac{D_3}{(1+k)^3} + \frac{D_4}{(1+k)^4} + \frac{D_5 + \text{Terminal Value}}{(1+k)^5}$$

$$\begin{matrix} \text{Ruddick 1997} \\ \text{Share Value} \end{matrix} = \frac{\$0.36}{1.114} + \frac{\$0.36}{(1.114)^2} + \frac{\$0.44}{(1.114)^3} + \frac{\$0.48}{(1.114)^4} + \frac{\$0.52 + \$21.63}{(1.114)^5}$$

$$= \underline{\underline{\$14.15}}$$

EXHIBIT 17–3. Terminal Value Computation—Ruddick Corp. Valuation

P/E Approach	Constant Growth Dividend Discount Model
2002 EPS = $1.73	2003 Dividend = $0.58
Estimated 2002 P/E Multiple = 12.5×	Constant Growth Rate = 8.5%
Terminal Value 2002 = P/E × EPS = 12.5 × $1.73 = $21.63	Discount Rate = 11.4% Terminal Value 2002 $= \dfrac{D_{2003}}{k-g}$ $= \dfrac{\$0.58}{11.4\% - 8.5\%}$ $= \underline{\underline{\$20.00}}$

Note. I recommend using both forms of terminal value calculation. In complete appraisals, practitioners complement the P/E approach with EBIT and EBITDA multiples.

EXHIBIT 17–4. Ruddick's Share Price

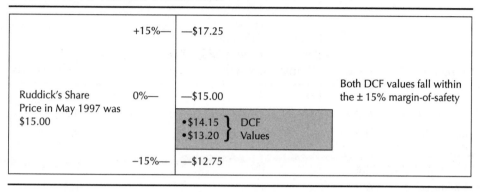

If I use the $20.00 terminal value provided by the constant growth DDM in Exhibit 17–3, the equation produces a $13.20 Ruddick share value.

As set forth in Exhibit 17–4, Ruddick's share price in May 1997 was $15.00 per share, which was slightly higher than the $14.15 and $13.20 per share values determined under the discounted cash flow method. However, neither of the two values inspired an investment decision independently because both fell within the 15 percent margin of safety. In my experience, this no-action event occurs in 80 to 90 percent of valuations. Sensible people perform similar analysis in the financial markets, resulting in reasonable valuations for most shares.

RELATIVE VALUE/BREAKUP VALUATION APPROACH

Because of the differing nature of Ruddick's two divisions, the relative valuation approach necessarily adopts the breakup technique. Thus, each division is valued separately by looking at "comparable company" multiples. To these values, we add nonoperating corporate assets, and subtract nonoperating corporate liabilities. The net result is then divided by the number of shares outstanding, as outlined in Chapter 16.

Harris Teeter Valuation

To start the Harris Teeter valuation, I prepared Exhibit 17–5, which shows valuation multiples for publicly traded supermarket chains. The average P/E and EBIT ratios for the group were 18× and 12×, respectively. Based on a comparative study of the chains' prospects and operating records, I decided that Harris Teeter merited a better-than-average multiple. Since the

EXHIBIT 17–5. Regional Supermarket Comparisons

Company	Beta	Annual Sales (Billions)	5-Year Compound Annual EPS Growth	P/E Ratio	EV/EBIT	Debt/Equity
Harris Teeter	—	$1.9	—	—	—	—
Giant Food	0.7	3.9	3%	21×	12×	0.2
Hannaford Bros.	0.9	3.0	11	19	12	0.5
Marsh Supermarkets	0.8	1.5	(6)	13	11	1.1
Quality Food	0.9	0.8	10	22	15	1.4
Weis Markets	0.6	1.8	1	17	9	0.0
Average	0.8			18×	12×	

Company	Region of Operations
Harris Teeter	North Carolina, Southern U.S.
Giant Food	Mid-Atlantic
Hannaford Bros.	New England and Southeast
Marsh Supermarkets	Ohio, Indiana
Quality Food	Seattle and Pacific Northwest
Weis Markets	Mid-Atlantic

Note. We use these comparisons to value the Harris-Teeter supermarket division of Ruddick Corp. The division's 10% long-term growth record and promising prospects suggest a premium multiple.

division had no net earnings, I used EBIT comparisons. A 13 EV/EBIT multiple for Harris Teeter provided a $624 million value:

$$\text{Harris Teeter Value} = \left[\begin{array}{c} \text{Divisional operating} \\ \text{income} \end{array} - \begin{array}{c} \text{Allocated corporate} \\ \text{overhead} \end{array} \right] \times \frac{\text{EV}}{\text{EBIT}} \text{Multiple}$$

$$= [\$50 \text{ million} - \$2 \text{ million}] \times 13$$

$$= \$624 \text{ million}$$

American & Efird Valuation

The American & Efird division had no direct comparables, but textile manufacturing companies were similar in many respects. Average textile P/E and EV/EBIT multiples were in the 11× to 12× and 7× to 8× ranges, respectively, at the time of this writing. With its consistent growth rate and stable performance through the cycles, A&E deserved a superior multiple, and I applied the division's results against an 8.5× EV/EBIT multiple:

$$A\&E\ Value = \left[\begin{array}{c}\text{Divisional operating} \\ \text{income}\end{array} - \begin{array}{c}\text{Allocated corporate} \\ \text{overhead}\end{array}\right] \times \frac{EV}{EBIT}\text{Multiple}$$

$$= [\$47\ \text{million} - \$2\ \text{million}] \times 8.5$$

$$= \underline{\underline{\$383\ \text{million}}}$$

CORPORATE ASSETS AND LIABILITIES

Ruddick's two divisions had an aggregate value of $1.0 billion (i.e., $624 million plus $383 million). To this amount, I added two nonoperating corporate assets—cash and the surrender value of whole life insurance policies—and then subtracted outstanding corporate debt, accrued interest, unfunded pension liability, and management options. The net breakup value was $781 million, as illustrated by Exhibit 17–6. The estimated per share value was $16.65, 11 percent higher than the $15 market price. My estimate thus fell within the 15 percent margin of safety, indicating no investment action.

EXHIBIT 17–6. Ruddick Corp.—Breakup and Relative Value Approaches—May 1997 (in millions except per share)

	Valuation
Relative Values	
Harris Teeter	$ 624
American & Efird	383
Subtotal	1,007
Add:	
Corporate cash	14
Whole life policies	25
Subtract:	
Corporate debt	(218)
Accrued interest	(21)
Unfunded pension liability	(21)
Management options	(5)
Net breakup/relative value	$ 781
On a per share basis	$16.65

Note. The $16.65 net breakup value (using the relative value technique) was 11% higher than the $15 per share market price.

ACQUISITION VALUE

I have now shown how to price the shares with the DCF, relative value, and breakup methods. Acquisition pricing is the next process. To determine Ruddick's value in the M&A market, I considered two methods: (1) comparable company acquisition multiples; and (2) the company's leveraged buyout value.

Since Harris Teeter and American & Efird are so different, I calculated the value of each division separately, using comparable acquisition multiples. Exhibit 17–7 shows acquisition prices for supermarket chains.

Given the heavy amortization charges of several of the grocery acquisitions, EBITDA was the most appropriate multiplier. The average acquisition multiple was 8.5×, but I assigned 9.0× to Harris Teeter since its historical results and future prospects indicated superior performance. On this basis, the division's "private market" value was $765 million. This number was 23 percent higher than the $624 million "comparable company" appraisal because of the control premium factored into takeover values.

$$
\begin{aligned}
\begin{array}{c} \text{Harris Teeter} \\ \text{Private Market} \\ \text{Value} \end{array} &= \left[\begin{array}{c} \text{Division} \\ \text{operating} \\ \text{income} \end{array} + \begin{array}{c} \text{Division} \\ \text{depreciation} \end{array} - \begin{array}{c} \text{Allocated} \\ \text{corporate} \\ \text{overhead} \end{array} \right] \times \frac{\text{EV}}{\text{EBITDA}} \text{Multiple} \\
&= \left[\$50 \text{ million} + \$37 \text{ million} - \$2 \text{ million} \right] \times 9.0 \\
&= \$765 \text{ million}
\end{aligned}
$$

Performing a similar exercise for A&E provided a divisional private value of $428 million.

EXHIBIT 17–7. Comparable Acquisition Transactions—Supermarket Chains

Target/Acquirer	Date	$MM Purchase Price	Purchase Price as a Multiple of			
			Net Earnings	Book Value	EBIT	EBITDA
Riser Foods/Giant Eagle	06/97	$ 340	17.7×	3.2×	10.9×	8.1
Smith Food/Fred Meyer	05/97	710	n.m.[1]	n.m.[1]	14.2	8.5
Vons/Safeway	12/96	2,400	23.3	4.0	16.3	11.2
Kash 'N' Karry/Food Lion	12/96	121	n.m.[1]	2.3	10.7	6.0
Stop & Shop/Ahold N.V.	08/96	1,750	21.9	5.1	11.4	8.3
Fresh Fields/Whole Foods	08/96	120	n.m.[1]	2.4	n.m.[1]	8.6
Average			22.6	3.4	12.7	8.5

[1] Ratios were not meaningful because net earnings, book value, or EBIT were marginal or negative.

Note. We use these statistics to estimate the private market value of the Harris Teeter division of Ruddick Corp.

EXHIBIT 17–8. Ruddick Corp.—Private Market Value Approach May 1997 (in millions except per share)

	Valuation
Private Market Values × 75%:	
Harris Teeter ($765 × 75%)	$574
American & Efird ($428 × 75%)	321
Subtotal	895
Add:	
Corporate cash	14
Whole life policies	25
Subtract:	
Corporate debt	(218)
Accrued interest	(21)
Unfunded pension liability	(21)
Management options	(5)
Net value of private market approach	$669
On a per share basis	$14.26

Note. The $14.26 per share value, derived from the private market value approach, was 5% lower than the $15 per share market price.

Ruddick's stock should trade at a minimum of 75 percent of private market value, so the price should have been at least $14.26 per share, as indicated in Exhibit 17–8. This estimate was 5 percent below the actual $15 market price, indicating no investment action.

LEVERAGED BUYOUT METHOD

To estimate Ruddick's per share value to a leveraged buyout firm, we follow the steps outlined in Chapter 15.

1. Approximate the company's interest carrying ability. LBO lenders like to see a 1.4 EBIT/interest coverage ratio on a pro forma basis. Depending on market conditions and the specific transaction's attributes, this coverage ratio can drop as low as 1.2×. Ruddick can carry $61 million of annual interest.

$$\text{LBO Interest Carrying Ability} = \frac{\text{EBIT}}{1.4}$$
$$= \frac{\$85 \text{ million}}{1.4}$$
$$= \$61 \text{ million}$$

2. Gauge LBO debt capacity. The debt of a typical LBO is equally divided between banks and junk bond investors. As senior lenders, the banks charge about 1 percent over the U.S. Treasury bond with a comparable maturity. As subordinated lenders, junk bondholders incur more risk. They charge the U.S. Treasury bond rate plus 2.5 percent and they sometimes require a small equity participation in the deal. The average yield spread is thus 1.75 percent (i.e., 1% plus 2.5% divided by 2). This division of debt represents a slight modification to the Chapter 15 formula.

In May 1997, the 10-year Treasury bond yielded 6.5 percent. Assuming a yield spread of 1.75 percent, the LBO interest cost was 8.25 percent (i.e., 6.5% + 1.75%). Dividing this number into the $61 million "interest carrying ability" meant a debt capacity of $740 million:

$$
\begin{aligned}
\text{LBO Interest Carrying Ability} &= \frac{\text{LBO Debt Capacity}}{\text{Interest Rate}} \\
&= \frac{\$61 \text{ million}}{.0825} \\
&= \$740 \text{ million}
\end{aligned}
$$

3. Calculate the LBO enterprise value. Banks refuse funds to LBOs unless the sponsor puts up 20 percent of the purchase price in equity. Applying a debt-equity ratio of 80/20 to the hypothetical transaction gave Ruddick a $925 million enterprise value, as shown in Exhibit 17–9.

4. Derive an LBO per share value. In a real leveraged buyout, Ruddick's long-term debt would either be assumed or repaid by the sponsor. Corporate cash would be applied toward the purchase price. The net amount is Ruddick's LBO equity value, which is divided by the number of shares to compute a per share LBO price. According to this methodology, Ruddick's value to an LBO firm is $14.89 per share (see Exhibit 17–10).

5. Compare LBO value to the market price. Warren Buffett and other value investors consider a stock "cheap" when it is trading at less than 75 percent of its LBO value. Since Ruddick's stock was trading at $15 per share at the time of this writing, it was not cheap relative to the $11.17 LBO pricing marker (i.e., 75% × the $14.89 LBO value per share = $11.17). Thus, on the basis of LBO values, no investment action was recommended.

EXHIBIT 17–9. Ruddick Corporation LBO Enterprise Value

	Millions	%
LBO debt	$740	80
Equity	185	20
Enterprise value	$925	100%

EXHIBIT 17–10. Ruddick Corporation—LBO Value per Share (in millions except per share)

Enterprise value	$925
Subtract:	
Existing debt	(218)
Accrued interest on debt	(21)
Add:	
Excess cash	14
Adjusted enterprise value	700
Divided by outstanding Ruddick shares	÷ 47
LBO value per share	$14.89

In buoyant stock markets, LBO sponsors are hamstrung by the lofty prices accorded to most acquisition candidates. To pursue transactions, they (1) ask lenders to soften the interest coverage limitation, perhaps from 1.4× to 1.2×; (2) suggest that the lenders compute the ratio on forward-year EBIT rather than prior year EBIT; (3) commit themselves to a higher equity investment, such as 25 to 30 percent of the purchase price (instead of 20%); and (4) immediately assume a 3 to 5 percent rise in EBIT from postacquisition cost savings. By using all four modifications, I increased Ruddick's theoretical LBO value per share from $14.89 to $21.54 (a 45% increase). Applying the 75 percent fraction to the modified $21.54 LBO value suggested a public trading price of $16.16, which was only 8 percent higher than the actual $15 market price. Again, no investment action was recommended by the LBO valuation technique.

The modified $21.54 LBO value was equivalent to 20.9× Ruddick's trailing 12-months' earnings per share. Although this multiple appeared high for a debt-financed transaction, it was consistent with numerous LBO's announced in 1997.

INVESTMENT RECOMMENDATION AND CONCLUSION

In this chapter, we appraised Ruddick Corporation shares by using four basic approaches, the results of which appear in Exhibit 17–11.

The company's actual share price was close to the valuations determined by the practitioner approaches. With the valuations falling into the 15 percent margin of safety, this analysis recommended neither a buy nor a sell. Ruddick's expected investment return was in line with its future prospects and the returns of competing securities.

EXHIBIT 17–11. Results of Four Valuation Approaches

Approach	Per Share Value Estimate	Recommended Investment Action
1. *Intrinsic Value* A business is worth the net present value of its dividends.	$13.20 and $14.15	The intrinsic values fall within the 15% margin of safety. No action.
2. *Relative Value* Determine a company's value by comparing it to similar companies' values.	$16.65	Because of the differing nature of the company's two divisions, we used relative values while "breaking up" the company. The breakup value was within the margin of safety. No action.
3. *Acquisition Value* A public company's share price should exceed 75% of private market values.	$14.26 (Comp. cos.) $11.17 (LBO) $16.16 (Modified LBO)	Given the $15 market price, the comparable companies and modified LBO values were within the margin of safety. Since the $15 market price exceeded the $11.17 LBO value, it suggested that the stock was not cheap on the basis of a potential LBO. No action.
4. *Breakup Analysis* A diversified company's value equals the sum of its parts.	$16.65	The relative value approach integrated the breakup analysis. No action.

SUMMARY

Using this book's approach, "no recommended action" is the conclusion of 90 percent of security analyses. This result is a reflection of the market's effectiveness in processing information and the tendency of practitioners to follow similar evaluative methods. In this particular instance, my conclusion didn't mean Ruddick was a poor stock selection. Rather, it suggested that a shareholder couldn't reasonably expect to receive a superior return on an absolute or relative basis. For those investors who wanted to seek superior performance, the Ruddick analysis told them to look elsewhere.

QUESTIONS AND SHORT PROBLEMS

1. Why is Ruddick Corporation a good LBO candidate?
2. Why is Ruddick Corporation a good candidate for break-up analysis?

3. Circle the correct attributes of the supermarket industry:
   a. Mature.
   b. Cyclical.
   c. Pioneer.
   d. Defensive.
   e. Decline.

4. Circle the correct attributes of the thread industry:
   a. Mature.
   b. Cyclical.
   c. Pioneer.
   d. Defensive.
   e. Decline.

5. Select the appropriate methodology for forecasting Ruddick's operating results:
   a. Time series.
   b. Causal.
   c. Qualitative.

   Explain your decision.

6. The discounted cash flow valuation technique can utilize two different terminal values: (a) constant growth DDM or (b) P/E approach. Explain the difference.

7. Using the following information on Teldon Corp., calculate Teldon's per share value at January 1, 2000 using the (a) constant growth DDM and (b) P/E approach.

1999 earnings per share	$1.00
Forecast dividend payout ratio	40%
Forecast earnings per share growth rate through 2005	11%
Post 2005 growth rate	8%
Capital cost of equity (Ke)	16%
P/E ratio 1999	20 times
Expected P/E ratio 2005	15 times

8. In Exhibit 17–5, the average EV/EBIT multiple for regional supermarkets was 12 times; however, the Harris Teeter valuation used a 13 times multiple. Why was there a discrepancy?

9. Harris Teeter's acquisition value was estimated at $765 million, but the "comparable company" appraisal yielded a value of only $624 million. Explain the discrepancy.

10. Which of the following actions enable LBO sponsors to pay higher prices than this book's formula will predict? Circle all that apply.

   a. LBO sponsors invest more equity in the deal.

   b. Lenders provide a lower leverage ratio.

   c. Interest coverage ratio applied to forward-year EBIT.

   d. Assume instant operating cost savings after the deal closes.

Adopt-a-Company

Using the appropriate appraisal techniques, determine if your company's stock is a "buy" or a "sell."

The rest of the book involves security analysis and special situations. Accordingly, Adopt-a-Company assignments will not appear in subsequent chapters.

PART IV

Special Cases

The model company for the "typical security analysis" is an industrial manufacturer or a service business with a history of improving sales and earnings. Most publicly traded firms don't fit this model, and Part IV reviews popular special cases including international stocks.

18

Cash Flow Stocks

According to some investors, cash flow is "king" on Wall Street. In this chapter, we'll examine companies that generate lots of cash, but no earnings.

Most listed securities can be evaluated reasonably well using the methods examined in Chapters 12 to 17. However, many stocks require complementary forms of analysis, often tailored to a particular industry. Chapters 18 to 21 provide the basic tools for evaluating such situations, including the following:

- Cash flow stocks.
- Natural resource stocks.
- Financial industry stocks.
- Quasi-monopoly stocks.
- Real estate stocks.

This chapter discusses several stock categories valued by practitioners on the basis of cash flow, rather than on reported earnings.

CASH FLOW STOCKS

Cash flow stocks fall into three classifications:

1. Capital-intensive quasi-monopolies such as cable TV, radio, and cellular phones.
2. Firms with heavy depreciation charges, such as hotel or real estate companies.

3. Companies with large goodwill accounts, such as public leveraged buyouts.

Such firms typically have little or no earnings, so the relative value types can't use the popular P/E ratio, because there's no "E." In fact, for many of these companies, the income statement shows major losses as interest, depreciation, and amortization expense wipe out reported earnings. Items from the 1996 income statement of Cablevision Systems, a leading cable TV provider, are instructive (see Exhibit 18–1). Even though Cablevision incurred a large net loss, its EBITDA (earnings before interest, taxes, depreciation, and amortization; i.e., cash flow from operations) was $452 million, a huge number that helped practitioners place a $2 billion value on the firm's equity.

Cash flow adherents believe net earnings are not the best measure of a company's ability to grow in its business or pay dividends over the long term; they prefer to add back noncash costs (depreciation and amortization), interest, and taxes to earnings to form EBITDA, a statistic that shows the firm's ability to generate cash from operations, once it is theoretically stripped of obligations to reinvest in the business, service debt, and pay income taxes. Given the tenuous nature of these assumptions, the accounting profession refuses to recognize EBITDA as a performance measurement. Nevertheless, many firms reporting net losses include the number in their press releases, the Securities and Exchange Commission permits its use in prospectuses, and Wall Street follows EBITDA regularly.

Before accepting EBITDA as a useful comparator, the analyst should recognize that its use flies in the face of accounting theory. Depreciation and amortization are noncash accounting charges reflecting assumed drops in the value of corporate assets. For example, the accounting value of a car decreases each year, reflecting not only the normal wear and tear of usage, but also the decline in resale value as new technologies and fads gradually make the car less attractive than an up-to-date model. The same can be said for most tangible corporate assets such as office equipment, computers, machinery, and physical plant. To stay whole, the corporation must reinvest the cash generated by depreciation.

EXHIBIT 18–1. Cablevision Systems Inc. 1996 Income Statement Data (in millions)

Net loss	$(332)
Interest expense	265
Depreciation & amortization	399
Other non-cash losses	120
Income tax benefit	—
EBITDA	$ 452

QUASI-MONOPOLIES

That interpretation of depreciation is okay for most practitioners, except when the target company is building an infrastructure to run a quasi-monopoly, such as a cable TV system. Once the local franchise is fully wired, the theory goes, the big money has been spent, and the cable operator can kick back and watch the cash from his captive subscribers roll in. As the business matures, capital expenditures drop to a minimal amount and depreciation charges fall off, allowing net earnings to accelerate rapidly. The theory is shown in Exhibit 18–2.

According to EBITDA believers, the accounting lives of cable TV assets are all wrong. After physical completion, the system provides earnings indefinitely, without the necessity of major reinvestment in new equipment. Thus, cable TV infrastructure is like real estate, which traditionally has risen in value, defying the accounting convention that says buildings have a limited economic life, usually assumed to be 20 to 40 years.

The "cable TV equals real estate" analogy took hold in the early 1980s, but after 15 years it remains unproven. Just as cable operators thought they were coming out of the woods on system buildups, technological improvements in satellite broadcasting and channel compression brought unexpected sources of competition, prompting a new wave of cable capital investment in the 1990s. On top of the billions spent on wiring America's homes, the cable firms are now faced with tens of billions dedicated to upgrading their technology, so

EXHIBIT 18–2. Hypothetical Cable TV Company: Net Income Rises as Depreciation Falls

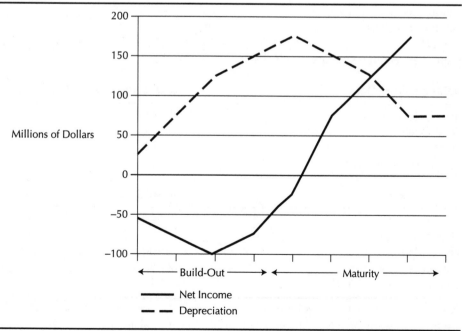

they can offer the additional channels, increased services, and better reception promised by satellite TV operators, phone companies, and Internet providers. The "pot of gold" of positive earnings is elusive, and time will tell if cable valuations hold up.

The real estate analogy is applied to other quasi-monopoly franchises such as broadcast TV, radio, paging services, and cellular phones. For example, Sinclair Broadcast Group (see Exhibit 18–3) had a $900 million market value in April 1997, despite minimal profitability and a goodwill-laden balance sheet. PageNet, the leading paging service, had a $1.2 billion valuation although net income had been consistently negative (see Exhibit 18–4).

Broadcast TV and radio cash flows have shown a steady uptrend over the years, vindicating those who compared the related license values with real estate, but the ongoing value of the intangible assets of cellular phone operators is open to question. License costs are being amortized over 10 to 40 years on the basis of quasi-monopoly status, yet it is apparent that advances in personal communications service (PCS) technology allow paging firms to offer an identical mobile telephone service. New competition means price cutting and marketing costs as paging companies and cellular

EXHIBIT 18–3. Summary Financial Data—Sinclair Broadcast Group, Inc.—Large Equity Valuation with Minimal Net Earnings (in millions except per share data and ratios)

Income Statement Data	1994	1995	1996
Total revenues	$129	$206	$378
Net income	(3)	—	1
Earnings per share	(.09)	—	.03
EBITDA	75	125	216
Capital expenditures before acquisitions	2	2	13

Balance Sheet Data	At December 31, 1996
Intangible assets	$1,344
Total assets	1,707
Total debt	1,288
Stockholders' equity	237

Market Data	At April 30, 1997
Price per share	$24
Shares outstanding	37.4
Equity value	$900
Enterprise value	$2,188
Enterprise value/EBITDA	10.1×

Note. Sinclair Broadcast Group operates numerous TV and radio stations across the United States. Intangible assets represent over 75% of total assets.

EXHIBIT 18–4. Paging Network, Inc.[1]—Summary Financial Data—Large Equity Valuation with Minimal Net Earnings

Income Statement Data (in millions)	1994	1995	1996
Total revenues	$490	$646	$823
Net income	(18)	(44)	(82)
Earnings per share	(0.18)	(0.43)	(0.80)
EBITDA	140	201	257
Capital expenditures	213	312	403

Balance Sheet Data (in millions)	At December 31, 1996
Intangible assets	$ 490
Total assets	1,462
Total debt	1,459
Stockholders' equity	(160)

Market Data	At May 15, 1997
Price per share	$12
Shares outstanding	102 million
Equity value[2]	$1.2 billion
Enterprise value	$2.7 billion
Enterprise value/EBITDA	10.4×
Enterprise value/subscribers	$300

[1] PageNet is the largest paging service in the United States, with over a million subscribers.
[2] Note how Wall Street assigns PageNet a $1.2 billion equity valuation, despite the company's lack of earnings.

providers fight for the same customer. A 1990s' change can upset 1980s' accounting.

Putting competitive concerns on the back burner, sell-side analysts continue to forecast higher net income and lower capital investment for cellular companies. A research report by a Wall Street analyst illustrates the conventional wisdom for Vanguard Cellular Systems, Inc., which just completed the infrastructure build-out for its five markets. As shown in Exhibit 18–5, Vanguard's five-year trend of losses and increasing capital expenses reversed in 1996, after which time the report predicts rapid income growth and declining capital needs.

The broadcast TV, cable TV, radio, and cellular phone industries represent quasi-monopolies that have shown steady increases in equity values, despite many participants exhibiting a history of net losses. In supporting these industries, practitioners explain away the losses by valuing the businesses on the basis of current cash flow and the presumption of eventual accounting profitability. A central tenet to this methodology is the belief that the relevant industry has few technological or competitive threats, once the infrastructure investment has been made.

EXHIBIT 18–5. Vanguard Cellular Systems, Inc.—Financial Model for a Cellular Company (in millions except per share data)

	Actual						Forecast			
	1991	1992	1993	1994	1995	1996	1997	1998	1999	2000
Revenues	56	73	99	146	217	250	347	409	459	487
Net income	(33)	(27)	(15)	(14)	(7)	6	21	62	95	120
EPS	(0.96)	(0.72)	(0.40)	(0.36)	(0.17)	0.14	0.50	1.50	2.30	2.89
EBITDA	4	14	25	36	68	50	138	176	206	231
Capital Investment	17	18	21	63	130	100	110	85	70	70
		Infrastructure build-out					Leveraging of prior investment			

Note how this cellular company's net income was supposed to skyrocket once its infrastructure was in place.

REAL ESTATE

Because Wall Street respects earnings more than assets, the common wisdom is that real estate is never given its true value by the stock market. As a result, real estate finance is better left to the private investor rather than the public market. Like many investment adages, the Street's aversion to real estate is suspended periodically, and this recurrent interest usually coincides with an upturn in real estate prices. Such was the case from 1994 to 1997 when recovering real estate markets sparked a huge growth in offerings by real estate investment trusts (REITs), the primary vehicles through which the stock market participates in real estate. REITs own portfolios of apartments, office buildings, or other real estate.

Like cable TV firms, REITs argue that cash flow is the best relative measure of performance. REIT net income, they say, is artificially depressed by noncash charges for depreciation and amortization, which represent a significant portion of the expenses incurred to operate a real estate property. Such charges must be taken over 5 to 40 years to reflect that buildings and other assets may decline in value over time and need to be replaced or refurbished. Because real estate has traditionally been resold at prices far in excess of accounting-depreciated worth, the argument goes that GAAP is simply inaccurate. Institutional investors accept this logic and REIT analysts use funds from operations (FFO) as a proxy for earnings per share (EPS). FFO equals the sum of EPS plus depreciation per share (see Exhibit 18–6 for a typical REIT income statement and Exhibit 18–7 for a balance sheet).

Practitioner forecasts of FFO encompass many industry-specific factors, such as lease renewal rates, tenant history, and site location, but they also cover operating-type investment concerns such as general economic trends, local market economies, competition, and management expertise. Besides the inclusion of these variables, implicit in the use of FFO is the assumption

EXHIBIT 18–6. Typical REIT Income Statement Merry Land & Investment Company, Inc., Year Ended December 31, 1996 (in millions except per share and percentages)

	Amount	Percentage
Income		
Rental income	$177	94%
Other income	11	6
	188	100
Expenses		
Rental expenses	50	27
Real estate taxes and insurance	20	10
Interest expense	23	12
Depreciation and amortization(1)	35	19
Operating income	60	32
Gains (losses) on sales of property	4	2
Net income(2)	$ 64	34%
Funds from operations (1 + 2)	$ 99	
Per share data:		
Earnings per share	$1.23	
FFO per share	$2.13	
FAD per share[1]	$1.90	
Dividends per share	$1.48	

[1] Qualified REITs must pay 95% of taxable income in cash dividends to avoid federal income taxes. Funds available for distribution (FAD) equals FFO less recurrent capital expenditures.

that real estate is a natural hedge against inflation because (1) leasing rates should go up with the consumer price index; and (2) land, which comprises 20 to 30 percent of the cost of a real estate venture (and isn't depreciated in GAAP), should also climb in price.

Financial Analysis of REITs

Because the real estate industry is cyclical, the experienced analyst balances a REITs growth potential against its ability to withstand the inevitable downturn. To be classified as a "pass through" for income tax purposes, a REIT must pay at least 95 percent of its net income to stockholders. With substantial cash flow paid out as dividends, the REITs property acquisitions and rental revenue growth are heavily reliant on its ability to regularly raise new funds, either through the debt or equity markets. Cyclical downturns restrict the supply of financing.

Key ratios used by stockholders and lenders in the financial analysis of REITs are as shown in Exhibit 18–8.

EXHIBIT 18–7. Typical REIT Balance Sheet—Merry Land & Investment Company, Inc. (in millions)

	December 31, 1996	
Assets		
Land	$ 249	21%
Buildings	995	82
Accumulated depreciation	(103)	(8)
Net real estate	1,141	95
Other assets	67	5
Total assets	$1,208	100%
Liabilities and Stockholders' Equity		
Mortgages and other debts	$ 388	32%
Other liabilities	21	2
Stockholders' equity	799	66
Total liabilities and stockholders' equity	$1,208	100%

Note. Most of the REIT's assets are tied up in income-producing rental properties.

EXHIBIT 18–8. Key Financial Ratios for REITs

REIT Ratio	Comments	Merry Land's Results
Dividends paid/FFO (Substituting FAD for FFO is common.)	FFO ratios exceeding 80% are worrisome because little cash flow is available for investment to promote growth. FAD ratios breaking 90% are causes for concern.	Merry Land's payout ratio was 70% in 1996.
Debt service coverage: EBITDA/(interest plus principal payments)	2.0× is the bare minimum for investment grade, the debt rating that heightens financial flexibility.	Assuming a 10-year debt amortization schedule, Merry Land's coverage is 2.0×. It's bonds are investment grade (BBB+).
FFO/total debt	Under 15% impacts the credit rating negatively.	Merry Land's 26% is substantially over the benchmark.
EBITDA/(total debt plus equity): This statistic is considered to be similar to the return on equity result used for an industrial company.	Established REITs have 11% to 13%. Newer REITs, with less asset appreciation, show lower percentages ranging from 8% to 10%.	Merry Land's ratio is 10.3%. This relatively low number reflects its recent acquisition program.

EXHIBIT 18–8. *(Continued)*

REIT Ratio	Comments	Merry Land's Results
EBITDA/real estate cost (before accumulated depreciation)	This ratio is like a cash return on invested assets measurement. It's an indicator of acquisition prices.	Merry Land's 9.8% result is slightly below average.
"Same store" rent change	This ratio separates the percentage increases of established properties from the rent increases attributable to new properties. It shows the health of the REIT's base business.	In 1996, Merry Land's same store rental income rose 2.1%, slightly below the 3.2% national average.
Total debt/total capitalization	50% to 60% is the highest ratio found among the investment grade REIT's.	Merry Land's ratio is a conservative 33%.
Real estate/shares outstanding	An indicator of the "hard asset value" behind each share.	Merry Land has $26 of real estate per share, before subtracting debt of $8 per share.
Compound annual growth rates: The growth rates of rent revenues, assets, FFO, and dividends are important performance barometers.	Over the long term, shareholders hope for dividend growth of 5% annually, accompanied by moderate asset value increases. Cyclicality makes the growth uneven.	Over the 1986 to 1996 period, compound annual dividend growth was 6.3%. The dividend was cut from 80 cents in 1989 to 30 cents in the 1990 recession, only to increase later.
Occupancy	A high occupancy rate suggests that the REIT has room to increase rents.	Merry Land's occupancy rate was an acceptable 94% in 1996.
(Net assets before depreciation minus debt)/shares outstanding = NAV (net asset value).	Another indicator of hard asset value per share.	Merry Land's result is $19 per share based on historical cost accounting. Many analysts consider their subjective measures of the firm's real estate values rather than use the book values. Such calculations are referred to as "market-based" NAVs.

EXHIBIT 18–9. Key Valuation Measures for REITs

REIT Valuation Measure	Merry Land's Results
Dividend yield (annual cash dividends/ market price per share)	At April 21, 1997's price of $21, the shares yielded 7.0%.
Price/FFO (used as the proxy for the P/E ratio)	Merry Land's 9.9× FFO multiple was slightly lower than the average REIT.
Share price/real estate per share	At 84%, the ratio was conservative. Many REIT's trade at ratios in excess of 100%.
Enterprise Value/EBITDA	Merry Land's ratio was 11.3×.
Share price/NAV	At 115%, the ratio was conservative, reflecting moderate growth prospects for Merry Land. "Net asset value is my major indicator for protection on the downside," says Patrice Derrington, fund manager for Victory Real Estate Investments. Russell Platt, who manages real estate funds for Morgan Stanley, prefers REITs that trade at less than 110% of NAV.

REIT Valuation Considerations

Equity holders buy REITs for capital gains and income. The 95 percent payout requirement means that REITs have higher dividend yields than most stocks, and the inflationary hedge of real estate, along with the REIT's use of leverage, provides the potential for a modest annual increase in share values. To see that REIT's fulfill this dual objective, investors look for fundamentally good business prospects, as well as favorable relative values. The statistics listed in Exhibit 18–9 are good measuring tools.

Comparative valuation data for prominent REITs at this writing are shown in Exhibit 18–10.

EXHIBIT 18–10. Comparative Valuation Data Real Estate Investment Trusts— April 1997

Apartment REITs	P/E	P/FFO	P/NAV	Dividend Yield
Merry Land & Investment	17×	10×	115%	7.0%
Camden Property	29	11	125	7.0
Columbus Realty	23	12	133	7.1
Equity Residential	25	9	164	5.6
Mid-America Apartment	21	10	122	7.9
Walden Residential	26	11	122	8.1

Note. Merry Land's valuation multiples are slightly lower than the competition's.

COMPANIES WITH LARGE GOODWILL ACCOUNTS

As described in Chapter 9, when one company buys another for a price in excess of accounting book value, a portion of the excess is often assigned to a goodwill account. The value of the intangible asset is then amortized over a 5- to 40-year period. The average listed company doesn't have enough acquisition activity for goodwill to become a major accounting issue, but there remain several hundred firms whose acquisition-related goodwill amortizations significantly depress net income. For these stocks, the practitioner uses EBITDA as a performance substitute for net income, and the relevant valuation ratio becomes Enterprise Value/EBITDA instead of P/E. Most companies receiving this treatment are leveraged buyouts, highly leveraged acquirers, or platform consolidators. An explanation appears in Exhibit 18–11.

PLATFORM CONSOLIDATOR AND LBO

The Coinmach Laundry Corporation, a leading supplier of coin-operated laundry equipment services for apartment buildings, is an example of the EBITDA phenomenon. In January 1995, management and a venture capital firm started the company through the leveraged acquisition of an established

EXHIBIT 18–11. Why Some Companies Have Large Goodwill Accounts

Leveraged Buyouts	Comments
Leveraged Buyouts LBOs start life with substantial goodwill.	During favorable stock markets, many private LBOs became public companies, as their owners seek to raise equity funds to repay debt and reduce financial risk. Goodwill usually represents over 50% of book assets.
Highly Leveraged Acquirers Some managements prefer to operate with high leverage. Large acquisitions are financed with debt. Purchase accounting is required, and goodwill is created.	For leveraged acquirers, the use of EBITDA softens the EPS "hit" of large acquisitions. Some firms incur major write-offs on closing a deal to avoid amortization charges (see Chapter 9 regarding the IBM/Lotus deal).
Platform Consolidators A platform consolidator builds a large firm by making multiple acquisitions in a fragmented industry. The "platform" is the initial business from which the consolidation process begins.	The intense acquisition efforts of the consolidator create substantial goodwill. Practitioners believe these aggressive concerns create value through the combination process, implying that the GAAP goodwill practice is invalid. EBITDA thus becomes the substitute for net income.

business. Growth was accomplished through acquisitions, and the firm's installed machine base rose in 18 months from 54,000 machines to 245,000 machines. By June 1996, debt had ballooned to $203 million (against negative $1 million of stockholder's equity) and in July the company successfully completed a $58 million initial public offering. Summary financial data appears in Exhibit 18–12.

In its IPO prospectus, Coinmach studiously avoided an emphasis on earnings per share. EBITDA was prominently mentioned as the industry's measure of corporate operating performance, and, on this basis, the company performed well. Annual EBITDA tripled over a short period of time, although such growth was accompanied by a substantial increase in acquisition-related borrowings. Since interest and principal payments have priority over stockholders' dividends, research reports properly examined debt service coverages when showing DCF projections and relative (EBITDA) value models.

EXHIBIT 18–12. Example of a Leveraged Consolidator—Coinmach Laundry Corporation—Summary Financial Data at the Initial Public Offering (in millions except per share data and ratios)

Income Statement Data	Twelve Months Ended March 29, 1996	
Revenues	$178.8	Contrast the $49 million EBITDA against the $8.6 million net loss.
Depreciation and amortization	36.6	
EBITDA	49.0	
EBIT	12.4	
Net loss	(8.6)	

Balance Sheet Data	At March 29, 1996		
Property and equipment, net	$ 82.7	33%	Even with negative shareholders' equity, Coinmach borrowed over $200 million.
Intangible assets	133.7	54	
Total assets	249.1	100	
Total debt	202.8	81	
Other liabilities	47.6	19	
Stockholder's equity	(1.3)	—	

Market Data[1]	At July 17, 1996
Per share price	$14.00
Earnings per share	$(0.57)
P/E Ratio	Not applicable
EBITDA per share	$5.38
Market value of company's shares	$146.3 million
Enterprise value/EBITDA	6.3×

[1] Pro forma for 4.1 million share IPO and consolidation of a small acquisition.

EXHIBIT 18–13. Enterprise Value/EBITDA Ratios—Platform Consolidators

	Enterprise Value ÷ EBITDA
Coinmach	6.3×
American Medical Response	9.4
G-Tech Holdings	10.4
Protection One	12.2
Premier Ranks	11.5
Outdoor Systems	16.6

A historical financial analysis showed the steady noncyclical nature of Coinmach's business, and one analyst, Dillon Read's Thomas O'Halloran, summarized the consensus view on the firm's high leverage, "We are not troubled by the (financial) risk. The company's cash flow is very predictable, and interest coverage on a cash flow basis is more than two times. The company is generating ample cash flow to reduce the debt going forward. If it chooses instead to redeploy these funds toward additional acquisitions, it will generate even higher levels of cash flow."

Indeed, all three research reports I read on Coinmach highlighted EBITDA measures, such as the annual EBITDA growth rate, EBITDA/sales margin, adjusted EBITDA (i.e., EBITDA minus recurring capital expenditures), and EBITDA/interest. "Comparable company" values were considered from an EBITDA viewpoint, as Coinmach was evaluated against other consolidators with heavy goodwill charges. Exhibit 18–13 provides comparable multiples indicating that Coinmach was a relative bargain. Its 6.3 ratio was far lower than the other firms.

EARNINGS BEFORE INTEREST, TAXES, DEPRECIATION, AND AMORTIZATION VERSUS EARNINGS PER SHARE

Comparing consolidators to nonacquisitive firms would be easier if purchase accounting didn't interfere. For example, by (1) adding back Coinmach's $23 million of intangible amortization expense to pretax income and (2) applying a 40 percent tax rate to the new total, I increased the company's earnings per share from *negative 57 cents* to *positive 92 cents* (see Exhibit 18–14). Dividing the adjusted EPS into the $14 IPO price produced a 15.2× P/E ratio (i.e., $14 ÷ $0.92 = 15.2×).

At the time of this writing, service firms with normal leverage and stable growth records were trading at 18 to 20 P/Es, so Coinmach's adjusted 15.2 P/E looks a little cheap. However, the higher risk of Coinmach's leverage justified a P/E discount to the "normal" companies. A 20 to 30 percent discount, for example, supported the pricing of Coinmach's stock.

Of course, purchase accounting has some basis in fact. The earnings power of many an acquisition hasn't increased as expected, and some

EXHIBIT 18–14. Coinmach Laundry Corporation—Adding Back
Amortization to Pretax Income

GAAP Pretax income	$(7.0)
Add Back: Intangible amortization expense	23.0
Adjusted pretax income	16.0
Assumed income taxes @ 40%	(6.4)
Adjusted net income	$ 9.6
Adjusted EPS	$0.92
Adjusted P/E on $14 IPO price	15.2×

Note. Adding back amortization charges increases net income.

intangible assets have a determinate economic life (e.g., below-market leases, patents, and service contracts). Furthermore, common sense tells us that a change in ownership (which can mean a replacement of management) may lead to operating dislocations and customer poachings that diminish an acquisition's value. Even a stable business loses about half of its customer base every five years. Notwithstanding these issues, the past 15 years of increasing merger activity have contradicted GAAP. In the majority of transactions, there has been little or no impairment of goodwill values. In fact, many deals contributed to increases in the acquirer's worth far and above the acquisition purchase price.

From a financial viewpoint, practitioners gain confidence that intangibles will hold their value when they see the buyer reinvesting cash in the acquired business. For capital-intensive industries such as mining and heavy manufacturing, this relationship is apparent, but service businesses also require substantial reinvestment to remain healthy. They too must develop new products, enhance existing services, and retain customer allegiance. The service industry's commitment is less to bricks and mortar, and more to marketing, personnel, and technology.

SUMMARY

The equities of quasi-monopolies, REITs, and active acquirers are often valued on the basis of cash flow rather than net earnings. The reason for this practice is that such firms have high depreciation and amortization charges, which depress reported earnings. Relative value adherents thus resort to cash-oriented performance measures such as EBITDA and FFO to contrast and compare firms. The accounting profession doesn't officially accept such statistics, but they represent a useful valuation tool on Wall Street.

Along with his review of historical cash flow, the analyst prepares financial projections that show the subject company "growing out" of its accounting-loss predicament over time. He then uses the conventional P/E ratio to assign a terminal value multiple.

QUESTIONS AND SHORT PROBLEMS

1. Define a cash flow stock.

2. How does Wall Street's use of the EV/EBITDA multiple contradict accounting theory?

3. In May 1997, Paging Network had an equity market valuation of $1.2 billion. Nevertheless, the company had incurred an $82 million loss in the year ending December 31, 1996, and its balance sheet showed $2.7 billion in debt. Provide reasons for why Wall Street placed a high value on Paging Network.

4. Which of the following statements is *not* true:
   a. EV/EBITDA multiples are reasonable tools for evaluating capital-intensive quasi-monopolies.
   b. EV/EBITDA is frequently used in the cable TV industry.
   c. EV/EBITDA is similar to a cash flow multiple.
   d. EV/EBITDA is not used in the hotel industry.

5. Explain how analysts forecasted the revenues and earnings of Vanguard Cellular to increase in 1997–2000, even as the projected capital investment declined.

6. What comprises the "funds from operations" statistic for a real estate investment trust (REIT)?
   a. Earnings per share plus depreciation.
   b. EBITDA.
   c. EBITDA, less capital expenditures.
   d. EBITDA, less capital expenditures and debt principal repayments.

7. When a practitioner forecasts the REIT "funds from operations" statistic, he incorporates assumptions regarding:
   a. Tenant history.
   b. Local market economics.
   c. Lease renewal rates.
   d. REIT management expertise.
   e. All of the above.

8. Suburban Real Estate's stock price is $70 per share. Using the data provided, calculate the following statistics:
   a. Dividend yield.
   b. Share price/FFO per share.
   c. P/E ratio.
   d. EV/EBITDA.
   e. FAD per share.
   f. FFO/total debt.
   g. Real estate/shares outstanding.

   Compare Suburban's 1996 results to the results of Merry Land in Exhibits 18–6 and 18–7. On a relative basis, which stock was the better value?

Suburban Real Estate Investment Co.
Income Statement Data
Year ended December 31, 1996
(in millions except per share and percentages)

	Amount	Percentage
Income		
Rental income	$ 126	90%
Other income	14	10
	140	100
Expenses		
Rental expenses	42	30
Real estate taxes and insurance	14	10
Interest expense	14	10
Depreciation and amortization	28	20
Operating income	42	30
Gains (losses) on sales of property	8	6
Net income	$ 50	36%
Capital expenditures	$ 32	
Earnings per share	$3.20	
Dividends per share	$3.35	

Balance Sheet
(in millions)

	December 31, 1996
Assets	
Land	$185
Buildings	750
Accumulated depreciation	(120)
Net real estate	815
Other assets	35
Total assets	$850
Liabilities and Stockholders' Equity	
Mortgages and other debts	$275
Other liabilities	15
Stockholders' equity	560
Total liabilities and stockholders' equity	$850

10. How does a company typically produce a significant amount of goodwill on its balance sheet?

11. What is a platform consolidator?

12. Platform consolidators encourage investors to consider EBITDA as a performance measurement related to earnings power, as opposed to net income. Why?

19

Natural Resource Stocks

*Natural resources stocks require a truly unique valuation approach.
Replenishing the resource is a critical necessity to corporate survival.*

Manufacturing and service companies compete on a variety of considerations. Price, quality, reputation, service, brand name, technology, and other differentiating characteristics of their respective product lines enable them to compete and succeed in many ways. Natural resource companies, in contrast, participate in commodity markets where the basic product—oil, timber, or iron ore, for example—is essentially the same. Furthermore, the success of these firms is dependent on the regular replacement of resource reserves. These industry characteristics call for a special form of analysis, which we review in this chapter.

GENERAL METHODOLOGY

In evaluating a natural resource stock, you focus on four analytical factors:

1. *The appraisal of the company's resource reserves* is the major component of equity value. Depending on the industry, the reserve value to stock price has a range. In the oil and gas exploration and production business, a band of 50 to 80 percent is not uncommon. Oil reserves are the equivalent of long-term inventories, waiting to produce revenues. (See Exhibit 19–1.)

2. *The value of other physical assets* is a contributing factor. The extraction, processing, and distribution of a natural resource requires substantial capital investment in the form of machinery and equipment. Furthermore, like any other business, the natural resource company has cash on hand, accounts receivable, and other tangible assets. In addition, most companies carry substantial acreage that has yet to be explored and exploited.

EXHIBIT 19–1. Pumping Oil from Underground Reserves

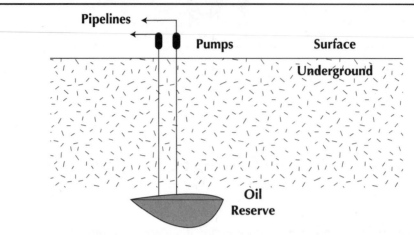

3. *Net tangible assets* are derived in this way: From the sum of reserve values and physical assets is subtracted the accounting value of liabilities, providing a *net tangible asset* calculation, or net asset value (NAV) in Street jargon.

4. *Management's ability to replenish the company's reserves* on an economical basis is that part of the share value not traceable to NAV. Like an industrial firm, a natural resource company's prospects are reliant on management generating new revenue streams. The industrial firm extends a brand name into a complementary product line or introduces a new service to produce more sales. The natural resource management, on the other hand, continually searches for new reserves that can be exploited and sold. At the time of this writing, most natural resource stocks were trading above NAV, indicating confidence in the managers' respective abilities to find new reserves.

This four-factor approach is quite unlike the discounted cash flow (DCF) and relative value methods used earlier in this book, and the reasoning behind it stems from the importance of reserves to the natural resource company. Unlike the brand name of the consumer products firm, the reputation of the business service provider, or the intellectual capital of the software developer, the principal assets of the natural resource firm—its reserves—have a finite life that is easy to calculate.

Suppose an oil exploration and production (E&P) company has 100 million barrels of oil reserves (i.e., "oil in the ground") and a production rate of 10 million barrels yearly. Assuming the reserve base can be depleted evenly, the company, absent any reserve replenishment, has a 10-year life (100 million bbls. ÷ 10 million bbls./year = 10 years). Assigning an exact economic life to industrial assets is far more complicated (as discussed in Chapters 7 and 9), and this difference accounts for much of the change in valuation

EXHIBIT 19–2. Natural Resource Stocks—Evaluation Methodology

+	Market value of natural resource reserves
+	Value of other physical assets, including working capital
−	Accounting value of liabilities
+	Intangible value of management's ability to replenish the reserve base
Net amount	Appropriate equity value

This is the four-step approach to valuing a natural resource company.

technique. P/E and EBITDA ratios play a diminished role with the natural resource company, because the price/NAV ratio takes more importance.

Furthermore, since natural resource reserves relate to widely traded commodities, their actual cash value out-of-the-ground is easy to determine. One need only pick up the *Wall Street Journal* or any commodity newsletter to see the market price of oil, timber, or iron ore. That present price can then be extrapolated into the future, and multiplied by annual production volumes, to form a sales projection. As illustrated earlier, projecting revenues for an industrial firm is a great deal more problematic.

In-the-ground values are obtainable for the visible commodities such as oil and gold. Transactions in mineral reserves take place frequently and the prices are publicized in specialized periodicals. Each reserve transaction has unique elements. Thus, the $5 per barrel of oil-in-the-ground statistic used in several 1997 E&P transactions was a value guide, rather than a precise appraisal, of an E&P company's reserve base. Exhibit 19–2 shows the evaluation methodology for natural resource stocks.

In the research report, the practitioner compares the probable future revenues from reserves against the cost of extracting them (or cutting them down in the case of lumber). An equally important part of the security analysis is gauging the firm's ability to replace reserves. This skill is critically important to sustaining and growing the enterprise, and a company's record in economically finding and/or purchasing new reserves is a significant performance measure. Some companies are better at doing this than others, and investors assign such shares the highest intangible values.

THE FINANCIAL REPORTING OF NATURAL RESOURCE COMPANIES

As shown in Exhibits 19–3 and 19–4, the income statement and balance sheet of a natural resource firm have historical data that is similar to the industrial company presentation. However, the accounting information set forth in the financial statements has less interpretative value for the natural resource firm, and practitioners use special accounting-based measurements to track reserves and units of production.

Over the years, the accounting profession and the SEC have tried to make financial reporting relevant to the valuation process of a natural

EXHIBIT 19–3. Pogo Producing Company—Summary Income Statement Data (in millions except per share data)

	Year Ended December 31		
	1994	**1995**	**1996**
Revenues			
Oil and gas production revenues	$ 174	$ 158	$ 204
Other revenues	1	4	1
Operating Expenses			
Depreciation, depletion and			
amortization	63	68	62
Production	30	35	38
General and administrative	16	16	18
Exploration cost of dry holes	5	6	17
Dry hole and impairment	7	6	9
Operating Income	52	23	61
Interest expense	9	9	9
Income before Income Taxes	43	14	52
Income tax provision	16	5	18
Net Income	$ 27	$ 9	$ 34
Earnings per Share	$0.82	$0.28	$0.96

Note. Pogo Producing Company explores for, develops, and produces crude oil and natural gas; 75% of the Company's reserves are located in the United States. Using the successful efforts method of accounting, Pogo expenses immediately the cost of dry holes.

resource company, but the end result is still quite confusing to the inexperienced analyst. The financial information and operating data needed for a research report are scattered throughout the SEC filings, forcing you to hunker down and comb through the public documents to pick out the required statistics. Leading performance criteria for the oil and gas industry are set forth in Exhibit 19–5. Note how net income, EPS, and EBITDA don't appear on the list.

Because historical accounting doesn't do justice to mineral reserve values, a natural resource firm must have its reserves evaluated by an independent engineering firm each year. A summary of the engineer's reserve calculations is included with the financial statements. For oil and gas companies, the issuer prepares an abbreviated calculation of the present value of such reserves, using year-end oil and gas prices and a statutory 10 percent discount rate. The engineer's report thus complements the recording and measurement functions of the independent accountant and actuarial consultant.

EXHIBIT 19–4. Pogo Producing Company—Summary Balance Sheet Data at December 31, 1996 (in millions)

Assets		
Cash	$ 3	
Accounts receivables	30	
Other current assets	42	
Total current assets	$ 75	
Oil and gas reserves, on the basis of successful efforts accounting:		80% of Pogo's assets are represented by its oil and gas reserves.
Proved properties	$1,079	
Unproved and properties under development	112	
Other property and equipment	9	
Less: accumulated depreciation, depletion and amortization	(815)	
	385	
Other assets	19	
	$ 479	
Liabilities and Shareholders' Equity		
Accounts payable	$ 7	
Other payables	4	
Accrued expenses	57	Pogo's ability to incur leverage is highly dependent on its reserve position. Debt to total capital ratio is 70%.
Total current liabilities	68	
Long-term debt	247	
Deferred income taxes	46	
Other liabilities	11	
Shareholders' equity	107	
	$ 479	

Because of the prominence of the oil and gas industry, I use it to illustrate the evaluation process. To simplify the exercise, we'll cover Pogo Producing Company, a medium-size, independent oil and gas exploration and production company, rather than a large integrated oil company like Exxon. The big firms supplement their exploration and development businesses with substantial downstream operations in chemicals, oil refining, and gasoline retailing, and analyzing such conglomerates is quite complicated.

Case Study: Pogo Producing Company.   Although Pogo's historical financial statements don't tell the whole story, they provide the best starting point. Summary data appear as Exhibits 19–3, 19–4, 19–6, 19–7.

As shown in Exhibit 19–3, Pogo reported an accounting profit in each of the preceding three years. Revenues increased sharply in 1996 due to increasing oil and gas prices. The debt-to-total-capitalization ratio was 70

EXHIBIT 19–5. Oil and Gas Industry—Financial Performance Criteria

Reserves Measurement	Comments
Reserve production ratio	Dividing total in-the-ground proved reserves by annual production provides a ratio that indicates expected reserve life, before any new additions. Specific data is provided in the body of the Form 10-K. There is no guarantee that all indicated reserves can be extracted economically.
Estimated quantities of proved reserves	The footnotes to the financial statements have a tabular summary of reserves which engineers have determined are economically viable for exploitation. Proved "developed" reserves can be recovered through existing wells. Proved "undeveloped" reserves need to be drilled, so there remains uncertainty about extraction costs.
Reserves per share	This is a shorthand measure of hard assets per share.
Standardized measure of discounted future net cash flows to proved reserves	Using current energy prices and extraction costs, the company provides a DCF value of proved reserves. To foster standardization, the SEC mandates a 10% discount rate (although it doesn't reflect true risk in most cases) and prices are not escalated.
Underdeveloped acreage and cost per acre	E&P companies typically acquire mineral rights in promising regions in anticipation of future exploration. Unless there is information available to the contrary, practitioners value these assets at historical cost.

Operating Data	
Average prices received in the sale of oil and gas	Either the footnotes or SEC 10-K form provide a tabular summary of average prices per barrel of oil and mcf of natural gas. Some E&P companies hedge prices by entering into long-term contracts.
Lifting costs per barrel	In their financial statements, E&P companies separate the cash operating costs needed to extract (i.e., "lift") the resource, from (1) general and administrative expenses; and (2) noncash depletion, depreciation, and amortization charges. Cash operating costs are then divided by annual barrels of production. Low lifting costs are favorable for the corporation. Note that 6 mcf of gas equal one-barrel-of-oil-equivalent (BOE).

EXHIBIT 19–5. *(Continued)*

Reserves Measurement	Comments
General and administrative costs	G&A costs are expressed both as (1) a percentage of revenues and (2) cost per BOE production. Low G&A costs indicate efficiencies.
Cash flows and DDA (depreciation, depletion, and amortization)	DDA represents the runoff of the substantial exploration and development expenses that E&P companies capitalize with respect to reserves. DDA is usually the major expense of an E&P business, and it is generated on a unit-of-production basis. DDA is a noncash charge and represents a significant portion of E&P operating cash flow. In most firms, the bulk of this cash flow is reinvested in the search for more reserves.

Reserve Replacement	
Reserve replacement ratio	Using footnote data, the analyst divides new reserves by annual production. Obviously, a ratio of 1.0 or higher is necessary to sustain the corporation. High ratios imply favorable search abilities.
Finding costs per BOE	In the footnotes or 10-K form, the firm should summarize the capitalized costs incurred in exploration, development, and reserve acquisition activities. New reserve additions are then divided into the newly capitalized costs. To remain profitable, the company's finding costs per BOE, taken with lifting and G&A costs per BOE, have to be less than the BOE selling price. Low finding costs indicate a capable management. In 1995, for example, average U.S. replacement costs were $4.30/BOE. Typical sale prices were $16.50/barrel of oil and $10.00/natural gas BOE (or $1.67/mcf).

EXHIBIT 19–6. Pogo Producing Company—Summary Cash Flow Data (in millions)

	Year Ended December 31, 1996
Cash Flows from Operating Activities	
Net income	$ 33
Adjustments to reconcile net income to net cash provided by operating activities:	
Depreciation, depletion, and amortization	62
Deferred income taxes	7
Dry holes and impairment of capitalized reserves	9
Other	(3)
Changes in operating assets and liabilities, net	(15)
Cash flows from operations	$ 93
Cash Flows from Investing Activities	
Exploration and development expenditures on successful wells	$172
Proceeds from asset sales	—
Purchases of proved reserves	—
Net cash used by investing activities	$172
Cash Flows from Financing Activities	
Borrowings, net	$ 78
Issuance of common stock	3
Cash dividends	(4)
Net cash provided by financing activities	77
Net decrease in cash	$ (2)

As oil and gas are extracted from the ground, their accounting values on the balance sheet are "depleted." Depletion is a noncash charge. Note Pogo's sizable commitment to exploration and development.

percent, which was higher than most E&P companies. Note how reserves represented 80 percent of accounting assets. (See Exhibit 19–4.)

CERTAIN ACCOUNTING ASPECTS

The typical E&P company spends huge amounts exploring for oil and preparing reserves for lifting. Many times, a well is drilled on it's acreage and no oil is found (i.e., a "dry hole"). Participants use one of two accounting methods to capitalize and expense exploration and development costs:

1. *Full Cost Accounting.* All drilling costs, including those of dry holes, are capitalized on the balance sheet. The resultant capitalized costs are then amortized on the unit of production method.

EXHIBIT 19–7. Pogo Producing Company—Key Performance Measures

	1994	1995	1996	Trend
Reserves				
Reserve production ratio				
(reserves/production)	5.4 years	7.9 years	9.6 years	Favorable
Reserves per share (BOE)	2.2	3.0	3.3	Favorable
Reserve DCF per share				
(SEC basis)	$ 8.79	$11.42	$20.79	Favorable
Before-tax DCF per share	$11.58	$16.12	$28.91	Favorable
Operating Data				
Sale price				
Oil (barrel)	$16.88	$17.80	$22.12	Favorable
Natural gas (Mcf)	1.88	1.63	2.40	Favorable
Lifting costs/BOE production	2.16	2.82	3.18	Unfavorable
Gen. & ad. cost/BOE				
production	$ 1.17	$ 1.31	$ 1.58	Unfavorable
Gen. & ad. cost/revenues	9.2%	10.4%	8.8%	Favorable
DDA/BOE	4.62	5.47	5.42	Mixed
Cash flow per share	3.20	2.67	3.25	Mixed
Reserve Replacement				
Reserve replacement ratio	154%	304%	187%	Favorable
Finding costs/new BOE				
reserves	$ 5.46	$ 2.74	$ 9.02	Mixed

Note. Six Mcf of gas approximates one BOE.

2. *Successful Efforts Accounting.* The firm capitalizes successful well expenses like an office building. Dry hole costs, however, are immediately charged against earnings. The successful efforts method is more conservative. (The analyst should remember to add back dry hole costs to capital investments to determine finding costs.) Pogo uses the successful efforts method.

Under both methods, the E&P company should write down the capitalized amounts if events indicate that such values cannot be recovered in the future. For example, in 1995 Burlington Resources recognized a noncash charge of $490 million, as falling natural gas prices impaired reserve values. In 1996, gas prices subsequently increased 20 to 30 percent, but the firm did not make an upward revision.

Most E&P companies that I have examined pay little or no federal income taxes. Resource depletion allowances for federal income tax purposes are much faster than book depletion rates, so income taxes are deferred until the firm's production eventually falls off. In practice, obligations can be postponed indefinitely.

Statistics for Pogo Producing Company

As an illustration of the key criteria used to evaluate E&P corporate performance, Pogo's statistics for the three years ended December 31, 1996 (as shown in Exhibit 19–7), enable the reader to reach the following conclusions:

- *Reserves.* Under any measurement, the Company's reserve position improved. Reserve life rose to 9.6 years and BOE per share were up 50 percent to 3.3. Aided by energy price gains, the net present value of reserves per share rose to $20.79, without a commensurate increase in debt or shares outstanding.

- *Operating Results.* The sharp increase in oil and gas price boosted the Company's operating results, as the sale price per barrel jumped from $16.88 to $22.12 in just two years. The trend in lifting costs was unfavorable, but Pogo's $3.18/BOE production cost was still $1 to $2 lower than many similar firms. The Company's general and administrative (G&A) costs as a percentage of revenues (8.8% in 1996) were higher than competing firms, because the firm's relatively small size didn't permit it to spread overhead easily.

- *Reserve Replacement.* Pogo's reserve replacement performance was above average. This fact and the oil and gas price increase supported a doubling of the stock value over the period. Note that the $9.02 finding cost/BOE in 1996 was out of line with earlier results. 1996 was adversely affected by an unusual nine million BOE downward revision in Thai reserves. Assuming a "normal" year, the finding cost would have been $7.30/BOE. This figure is relatively high for the industry, but not excessive. E&P analysts prefer to average finding costs over a three-year period to moderate the effect of such aberrations.

Reserve Value per Share on Liquidation Basis

A thorough research report on an E&P company contains a breakup calculation. The analyst estimates the present value of the firm's reserves (usually by the DCF method), adds other assets to this amount, and subtracts accounting liabilities. To begin this process, he first assumes a future production curve for existing reserves (see Exhibit 19–8), and then applies the appropriate selling prices and lifting costs to annual barrels of production. Sample calculations for Pogo are provided in Exhibit 19–9.

Once the production curve and financial model are in the analyst's personal computer, he is free to manipulate the assumptions to see the effect of higher discount rates, lower prices, and other changes.

Breakup Value Estimate

With the liquidation data from Exhibit 19–9, the Company's SEC filings, and available independent asset appraisals, the analyst is ready to estimate Pogo's breakup value. Exhibit 19–10 reviews the mechanics of this calculation.

EXHIBIT 19–8. Typical Production Curve of an Oil Reserve

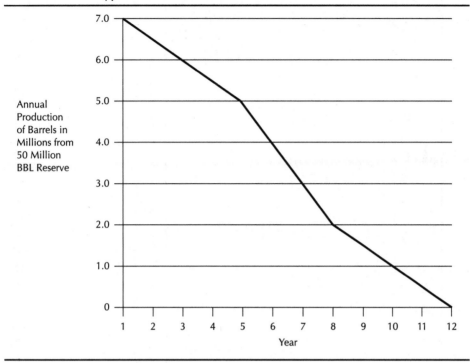

Annual Production of Barrels in Millions from 50 Million BBL Reserve

Year

REACHING A CONCLUSION

The breakup value provided an appropriate takeover price for Pogo, absent the intangible benefits of a management team that knows how to replenish a depleting reserve base. Such intangible qualities had considerable value in Pogo's case. For example, in April 1997, Pogo's share price was $36, yet the breakup value I calculated in Exhibit 19–10 was only $23 per share. The $13 difference was attributable to the intangible assets of management. Exhibit 19–11 shows summary market data for Pogo's stock.

To justify the market's 57 percent premium over the $23.30 breakup value, analysts had faith in Pogo's ability to increase shareholder value. Over the previous three years, the Company had increased reserves per share by 50 percent without a corresponding rise in debt, so the premium appeared warranted.

Confidence in a firm's exploration ability generally leads to premium P/E and price/cash flow ratios, relative to similar companies. Management's experience in generating new reserves at low finding costs is of paramount concern, but analysts also examine the E&P company's leverage, its efforts to control lifting and administrative costs, and the qualitative aspects of the existing reserves. How much is oil versus gas? Where are the reserves located? And so on.

In assessing *relative* values, the practitioner compares the E&P industry's unique operating statistics across specific companies. As shown in

EXHIBIT 19–9. Reserves' Present Value on a Per Share Basis—"Liquidation Stock Price"—Pogo Producing Company

Year	Oil Reserves (Mmbbls)	Oil Production (Mmbls)	Oil Pricing $/Bbl.	Natural Gas Reserves (Bcf)	Natural Gas Production (Bcf)	Natural Gas Pricing $/Mcf	Revenues Oil ($MM)	Revenues Gas ($MM)	Total Revenues ($MM)	Expenses Oper./Dev. Cost ($MM)	Total Costs ($MM)	Undisc. Pre-Tax Net CF ($MM)	NPV Pre-Tax CF@10% ($MM)
1997	50	7	$20	360	36	$2.15	$140	$77	$217	$42	$52	$ 165	$150
1998	43	6	19	324	32	2.10	114	67	181	38	48	133	110
1999	37	6	19	292	29	2.15	114	62	176	38	43	133	100
2000	33	5	19	263	28	2.20	95	62	157	40	40	117	80
2001	28	5	20	235	26	2.30	100	60	160	35	35	125	78
2002	13	5	21	209	26	2.39	105	62	167	37	37	130	73
2003	18	4	22	183	25	2.49	88	62	150	34	34	116	59
2004	14	4	23	158	25	2.59	92	65	157	35	35	122	57
2005	10	3	23	133	24	2.69	69	65	134	31	31	103	44
2006	7	3	24	109	24	2.80	72	67	139	32	32	107	41
2007	4	2	25	85	23	2.91	50	67	117	28	28	89	31
2008	2	2	26	62	20	3.03	52	61	113	27	27	86	28
2009	—	—	—	42	16	3.15	—	50	50	14	14	36	10
2010	—	—	—	26	10	3.27	—	33	33	9	9	26	7
2011	—	—	—	16	6	3.41	—	20	20	6	6	14	4
2012	—	—	—	10	3	3.54	—	11	11	3	3	8	2
Sub-Total	—	50	—	—	353	—	—	—	—	—	—	1,510	874
Remainder	—	—	—	7	7	3.68	—	26	26	7	7	19	4
Total Future	—	—	—	0	360	—	—	—	—	—	—	$1,529	$878

Pricing Parameters: In this model oil and gas prices escalate gradually. Note that SEC standardized calculation does not escalate price or cost.

Cost Parameters: Operating, Developing and Abandonment costs: $3.25 per BOE escalating at 4% annually. Additional $25 million in years 1–3 for extra developmental drilling, field preparation and closing costs.

Net present value/share	$ 26.37
Net debt/share	(7.39)
LIQUIDATION STOCK PRICE	$ 18.98

Net present value (MM)	$878
Net debt (MM)	$246
Shares outstanding (MM)	33.3

EXHIBIT 19–10. Breakup Value Pogo—Producing Company at December 31, 1996

	SEC Case		Author's Case		Simplistic $5/Bbl Value In-the-Ground[2] Case	
	Amount	Per Share	Amount	Per Share	Amount	Per Share
Proved oil and gas reserves	$ 954	$28.65	$ 878	$26.37	$550	$16.52
Undeveloped acreage	111		111		111	
Property & equipment, net	7		7		7	
Other assets	19		19		19	
Net working capital	7		7		7	
Gross asset value	1,098	32.97	1,022	30.68	694	20.83
Long-term debt	(246)	(7.38)	(246)	(7.38)	(246)	(7.38)
Net asset value[1]	$ 852	$25.59	$ 776	$23.30	$448	$13.45

[1] Depending on the assumptions, the breakup value has a wide range.

[2] The $5 per barrel in-the-ground estimate ignores the rapid production curve of the company's reserves. A short reserve life increases the net present value of reserves and supports the author's case.

Chapter 13 for industrial companies, a good exercise is ranking E&P firms by historical performance. Those firms receiving the best grades have a reasonable basis for deserving a premium valuation. Exhibit 19–12 shows a hypothetical ranking for four firms. Depending on the defining characteristics, Pogo has between 20 and 30 comparables that can be used in a ranking scheme.

In conjunction with relative value analysis, the practitioner prepares corporate financial projections that elaborate on the breakup value calculations. Rather than showing a static production curve, the company is assumed to continue (or improve on) its record of finding reserves in excess of

EXHIBIT 19–11. Pogo Producing Company—Summary Market Data at April 1997

Share price	$36.00
P/E multiple	37.5×
P/Cash flow per share	11.1×
Price/book	11.2×
Price/break-up value	157%
Reserves/share (BOE)	3.3 bbls.
Dividend yield	0.3%

Note how accounting-based value multiples appear out of line. P/E and price to book are largely irrelevant for the natural resource company.

EXHIBIT 19–12. Ranking Exploration and Production Companies

	Oil and Gas E&P Company			
	A	**B**	**C**	**D**
Existing reserve situation	Good	Excellent	Average	Average
Operating performance	Excellent	Good	Good	Average
Reserve finding ability	Poor	Average	Good	Average

Note. The company with the best grades may deserve a premium valuation.

annual production. By making the requisite assumptions with regard to selling prices, operating expenses, and finding costs, the analyst constructs a five- to ten-year financial forecast. At the end of the period, a terminal value is assigned to the firm, based on a P/E or cash flow multiple, rather than a net asset value. Doug Cannon, a portfolio manager at Jenswold King & Associates, a Texas-based money manager, suggests, "5× to 6× cash flow as a reasonable multiple, because its a good historical indicator of E&P values."

MINING COMPANIES

Mining company analysts employ several of the techniques used in oil and gas appraisals, but the performance parameters are very different. For example, the lifting cost (per sales dollar) of a mining operation tends to be much higher than its E&P counterpart. Tons of ore must be extracted and processed to obtain a few hundred pounds of the lesser grade metals (such as copper and zinc) or just a couple of ounces of the precious metals (such as gold and platinum). This costs a lot of money. Operating expenses for a mining company can exceed 60 percent of sales, whereas a typical ratio for an E&P firm might be 30 percent. However, the mining company has fewer finding and amortization costs (as a percentage of the sales dollar), and its shipping costs are lower due to the higher value-to-weight ratio enjoyed by metals (e.g., $18 per barrel oil equals six cents per pound, whereas silver has a value of $90 per pound).

Like the oil and gas appraisals, mining company valuations are heavily dependent on reserve calculations. Reserve life and replacement experience are important. In addition to examining ore quantities per share, the analyst reviews the grade (or purity) of the reserves. High-grade ore implies less processing (i.e., less operating expense) per pound (or ounce) of salable product. To assist investors, mining companies disclose reserves, grades, and operating costs per ton in their SEC filings.

In the United States, mining company reserve disclosures are verified by independent mining engineering firms. The importance of third-party checking was highlighted by the 1997 scandal affecting Bre-X Minerals, a small Canadian gold mining company. From an obscure penny stock operation with a market value of less than $10 million, Bre-X ran claims of a fantastic Indonesian gold strike into a capitalization of $6 billion. Only independent testing by Freeport McMoRan, a possible merger partner, uncovered fraudulent reserve calculations by the company, which suddenly collapsed into bankruptcy, costing investors huge losses.

As the *Washington Post* noted on July 17, 1997:

> Bre-X's public statements and official filings frequently noted that estimates of the size of the find had been prepared by a respected engineering firm, Montreal-based SNC Lavalin. Not as publicized was the fact that the engineering company had been hired only to make its calculations based on samples of earth extracted and processed by Bre-X.

Few sophisticated players thought to ask Bre-X for a legitimate double-check of its reserve claims, and the list of those hoodwinked by the firm

EXHIBIT 19–13. Echo Bay Mines, Ltd.—Round Mountain Gold Mine

Selected Operating Data	Year Ended December 31, 1996
Gold produced (ounces)	410,974
Mining cost/ton of ore and waste	69¢ per ton
Production cost/ounce of gold:	
Direct mining expense	$228 per ounce
Deferred stripping and other costs	(7)
Cash operating costs	221
Royalties paid	32
Production taxes	4
Total cash cost	257
Depreciation and amortization	69
Reclamation	5
Total production cost[1]	$331 per ounce

[1] Sale price per ounce was $384 in 1996, against the $331 production cost.

Ore Reserves[2]	Tonnage (millions of tons)	Average Grade of Gold (ounces per ton)	Gold Content (millions of ounces)
At December 31, 1996			
Round Mountain Pit	326.1	0.022	7.3
Offloads and leach stockpiles	147.8	0.011	1.6
Mill stockpiles	2.5	0.040	0.1
Total proven and probable	476.5	0.019	9.0

[2] Reviewed by independent engineering firm.

comprise a veritable "who's who" of finance: Fidelity, the giant fund company; J.P. Morgan, the global banking concern; Nesbitt Burns, Canada's most prestigious investment bank; the Toronto stock exchange, Canada's largest securities market; the National Association of Securities Dealers (NASD), which listed the shares in the United States; and the SEC, which processed the company's U.S. regulatory filings. Nesbitt Burns provided a typically lame excuse for failing to uncover the problem, "Our analysts rely on publicly available information that is released by reputable companies, but in this case there is fraud. Our experts are not experts in uncovering fraud." As stressed in this book, an effective security analysis extends past information spoon-fed to the public by the issuer.

As an example of reserve estimate disclosure, Exhibit 19–13 provides information regarding the Round Mountain gold operation of Echo Bay Mines, Ltd. The values of mining stocks reflect the market price of the related commodity. Thus, if gold prices jump 10 percent, the share price of Echo Bay Mines will frequently rise in sympathy. At other times, investors ignore gold's volatility in favor of the benign view that price fluctuations will average out in the future.

SUMMARY

Natural resource companies participate in commodity markets where the basic product—oil, gas, or metallic ore—is essentially the same. With no brand name, service component, or technology to differentiate one firm's products from another, the research focuses on two factors: (1) the net tangible value of the company's reserves, using the DCF method and the recent transactions approach; and (2) the presumed ability of the existing management team to find new reserves in an economical fashion. The average natural resource stock trades at a price in excess of net tangible value. The larger this excess, the more confidence investors have in the company's ability to replace current production with new reserves.

The share values of these firms move in sympathy with underlying changes in the market price of the relevant natural resource. Thus, if oil prices jump 10 percent, shares of oil companies are bound to rise, unless a strong consensus emerges on the price increase being temporary.

QUESTIONS AND SHORT PROBLEMS

1. The evaluation of natural resource stocks is fundamentally different than the evaluation of most manufacturing and service company stocks. Why?

2. a. Tinder Oil Company has oil reserves of 40 million barrels when oil-in-the-ground has a market value of $6 per barrel.

b. The company's stock price is $30 per share and 10 million shares are outstanding.

c. The balance sheet summary is as follows:

Tinder Oil Company
Balance Sheet
(in millions)

Current assets	$ 15
Fixed assets, net	25
Oil and gas reserves, net	160
Total assets	200
Current liabilities	10
Long-term debt	70
Other liabilities	20
Shareholders' equity	100

d. How much "intangible value" are investors assigning to management's ability to replenish the reserve base in the future? Estimate this intangible value on a per share basis. Show the calculations.

3. How does the "depletion" expense of an oil and gas E&P company resemble the "depreciation" expense of a manufacturing firm?

4. The next several questions relate to Pogo Producing Company:
   a. What factors contributed to the increase in Pogo's revenues over the 1994 to 1996 period?
   b. What are lifting costs? What was Pogo's lifting cost trend?
   c. The reserve production ratio increased. Why was this favorable?
   d. Describe the behavior of the finding costs/new reserve ratio?
   e. Pogo's break-up value per share was less than its market value? Why?

5. Bangier Oil stock analysis incorporates the following data:
   a. The company's reserves are 100 million barrels.
   b. The reserves will be extracted at the rate of 10 million barrels per year.
   c. The price of oil is $12 per barrel and the forecast indicates a 2 percent annual price increase.
   d. Total operating costs for Bangier Oil are $46 million per year, and they should increase at 2.5 percent annually.
   e. The discount rate is 15 percent.
   f. No income taxes will be payable.
   g. Shares outstanding are 20 million. Net debt per share is $3.

   What is the liquidation stock price of Bangier Oil? If oil prices increase from $12 to $14 per barrel tomorrow, what happens to the liquidation stock price?

6. Why are operating expenses (as a percentage of sales) for a mining company typically much higher than those of an oil and gas exploration and production firm?

7. Why do mining company investors like companies with high-grade ore bodies?

8. In 1996, what percentage of Echo Bay Mine's production cost related to direct mining expense? What gold price was "breakeven" for Echo Bay on a "cash" basis?

9. Is it appropriate for an analyst to use ore reserves as a proxy for liquidation value for a mining company?

10. How did Bre-X hoodwink many of its equity investors? Why didn't the brokerage research analysts discover the situation earlier?

20

Financial Industry Stocks

Like natural resource companies, financial stocks require a special analysis, replete with individualized ratios and performance measurements. Chapter 20 covers the basics of valuing these investments.

Evaluating a financial business like a savings and loan, bank, or insurance company requires analytical tools that have not been employed previously in this book. The reasons for the modification in our approach stem from the singular nature of financial assets. Unlike a manufacturing or a service business, a financial company's tangible assets are almost entirely pieces of paper, most of which are contractual in nature such as loans or bonds. The liability side of these businesses also contributes to a specialized approach, since financial firms are highly leveraged and deal in many activities that have uncertain future obligations, such as insurance underwritings and derivative securities. Finally, the regulatory environment influences this sector more than the average industrial business.

The pieces of paper controlled by financial institutions often represent the savings and peace of mind of the average citizen. Reckless behavior by just one company can undermine confidence in the financial system and contribute to depositor runs, policy withdrawals, or other panics. To reduce the likelihood of this problem, government has created a complex regulatory structure that sets the industry's ground rules. Outside of big-picture structural and pricing concerns, the enforcement of these regulations is best characterized as benign. Accordingly, the research analyst addresses government influence on an infrequent basis, such as when the regulations are being altered to help one financial sector at the possible expense of another.

This chapter examines the analytical process involved in three financial sectors:

1. *Savings and Loans.* S&Ls represent one of the last pure "spread" businesses, whereby cash income is principally derived from borrowing money at a low rate and lending it out at a higher rate.

2. *Finance Companies.* These firms are fundamentally spread businesses, but many realize more income from packaging loans than from spread activities.

3. *Commercial Banks.* The spread business is augmented by a large volume of fee-based activities.

Chapter 21 reviews a fourth sector, the insurance industry:

4. *Insurance Companies.* By using the law of large numbers, these firms absorb the risk of catastrophic events that are too costly for a single business or individual to incur.

Brokerage firms and mutual fund companies are part of the financial industry, but the limited number of significant publicly held players diminishes the need for attention here.

GENERAL INFORMATION ABOUT THE FINANCIAL INDUSTRY

With the exception of mutual funds and brokerage firms, the financial sector can be characterized as both mature and cyclical. Furthermore, the products and services offered within each subsector are fairly homogeneous, giving the industry a commodity orientation that limits profitability. These factors combine to keep the P/E ratios of financial stocks below their operating company counterparts.

Innovation provides one way that a company can differentiate itself from another without cutting price, but few financial inventions can be patented and most are copied shortly after their introduction. Also, the fact remains that product lines are quite similar within sectors. For example:

1. *Bank and Other Lenders.* Except for interest costs and related fees, the money borrowed from one bank is identical to that from another.

2. *Insurance Firms.* Except for price and the insurer's long-term ability to pay a claim presented to it, insurance policies are similar.

3. *Brokerage Firms.* From the individual's point of view, there is little difference between the services provided by most brokerage firms. Institutional and corporate services are only differentiated in a meaningful way by the top 10 investment banks.

4. *Mutual Funds.* Despite their claims to the contrary, the vast majority of mutual funds cannot beat stock or bond market indices on a regular basis. Their money management abilities are distressingly similar.

EXHIBIT 20–1. The Financial Industry

Subsector	Principal Products/ Services	Nonprice Competitive Elements
Banks, S&Ls	Loans, transaction processing and custodial services, charge cards.	Government deposit guarantees, reputation, service efficiency, convenience, personal relationships.
Insurers	Insurance against unanticipated events, various tax-deferred investment products, third-party claims processing services.	Creditworthiness, reputation, specialized expertise, service efficiency, personal relationships.
Brokerage Firms	Order execution and custodial services. Financial advisory services for individuals and corporations. Asset management.	Reputation. Personal relationships. Distribution and trading ability for corporate accounts.
Mutual Funds	Management of individual and corporate pension and savings accounts, in exchange for a fee.	Reputation. Claims of above-average performance potential. Marketing abilities. Convenience.

Note. Competition in the financial industry is heavily dependent on nonprice factors.

As a result, success in these sectors rests on intangibles—such as marketing clout, reputation, and personal contacts—which de-commoditize the product, as well as on the operating controls and cost efficiencies that keep a firm's pricing in line with the competition. Exhibit 20–1 provides further information.

THE NATURE OF FINANCIAL ASSETS

The intangible elements of a financial business frequently represent the engine of growth, and the practitioner assesses these qualities carefully in his analysis. At the same time, he must evaluate the company's asset portfolio in the here and now, not only to appraise the accuracy of accounting estimates, but also to measure management's ability to run the business.

Above all, the analyst remembers that financial assets are contractual in nature. Contracts, in the United States and elsewhere, are rarely 100 percent enforceable according to their terms. Thus, when a corporation stops repaying a $10 million loan or bond, the foreclosure process doesn't immediately begin. Rather, this nonpayment is the start of a negotiation. Similarly, a property and casualty insurer is circumspect in honoring a large claim. The firm defers payment until it investigates the situation, and it may contest the size and validity of the claim, depending on its interpretation of the policy. The analyst acknowledges firstly that financial assets are not governed by an absolutist legal framework.

Furthermore, the economic values of financial assets—whether they are bonds or stocks—are subject to systematic change. Bond prices are directly influenced by movements in interest rates, which impact common stock values also. Depending on the industry, the historical accounting presentation may not accurately reflect such changes in economic value.

The valuation of certain financial assets is judgmental. The economics of the asset may be clear, but near the margin the value depends on the manner in which the appraiser interprets (1) the wording of the related contract, (2) the likely enforceability of the contract in a court of law, and (3) the ability of each party to live up to its obligations. Independent auditors are not expert in understanding the nuances of complex legal contracts; and thus, the notion of management flexibility in defining operating results is alive and well in the financial sector. The securities analyst must be alert to the possibility of inflated asset valuations, as well as the likelihood of deflated bad loan estimates or faulty insurance underwritings.

The daisy chain of paper shuffling, the complicated nature of legal contracts, the inherent uncertainty attached to financial asset values, and the speed with which large sums of money change hands make the financial industry a fertile area for promoters and charlatans. While most publicly traded firms uphold reasonable standards of operation, the experienced analyst is on guard for the disreputable management that seeks to take advantage of weak links in the reporting system.

TWO SETS OF SKILLS

As this chapter and Chapter 21 indicate, much of a financial institution's success relies on managerial judgment, since few loans or investments made by the institution are 100 percent guaranteed. The bank executive must select those borrowers which are creditworthy out of the many presented to him. Likewise, the mutual fund manager tries to select those securities that will provide superior returns, relative to the potential risks. Investment judgment is thus a critical quality in managing many financial businesses.

In certain financial sectors, success is highly dependent on performing simple tasks in an assembly-line fashion. A bank may process tens of thousands of checks in a single day, an insurance company may review thousands of claims, and a brokerage firm may clear thousands of trades. In the processing field, therefore, a financial firm's operating controls and cost efficiencies should rival those of an industrial manufacturer or distributor. The investment-decision-making culture is thus intertwined with the production environment, requiring the analyst to consider two sets of management skills.

SAVINGS AND LOANS

The savings and loan (S&L) industry is the last pure spread business. A spread business borrows money at one rate, and lends it out at a higher rate, to profit from the spread between the two rates. Finance companies, banks, and insurance firms have significant spread businesses, but their operations also include substantial fee services and securitization activities that sometimes overshadow the spread component. For this reason, it is easiest to begin a review of financial stocks with an S&L, which lacks such complications.

In its simplest form, a spread business's income statement has only a few line items, as indicated in Exhibit 20–2. The balance sheet of the spread business is straightforward (see Exhibit 20–3). Assets are almost 100 percent financial and leverage is high, reflecting the liquidity of the assets and the enabling regulatory environment. Additionally, the small spread on earning assets requires the business to have high leverage to produce a reasonable equity return.

As Exhibit 20–4 illustrates, the hypothetical business realizes a minuscule 1.0 percent after-tax return on assets (ROA), which is far lower than the return on assets achieved by the typical industrial operation. A spread business makes up for its tiny ROA by the heavy use of leverage. An S&L, for example, can have a liability-to-equity ratio of 12 to 1 or more. Compare this with the 1:1 ratio that is normal for an industrial company. (See Exhibit 20–5.) High leverage transforms the low ROA into an appropriate return on equity for the S&L stockholder.

Qualitative Issues

With equity comprising only 6 to 8 percent of assets, it is critical that S&Ls (and other spread businesses) select borrowers carefully. A write-off of only 2 percent of the portfolio, for example, decreases corporate equity by

EXHIBIT 20–2. Hypothetical Spread Business—Income Statement (in millions)

Interest income from loans	$100
Interest expense from borrowing	(65)
Net interest income (the "spread")	35
Provision for loan losses	(5)
	30
General and administrative expenses	(15)
Income before income taxes	15
Income taxes	(5)
Net income	$ 10

EXHIBIT 20–3. Hypothetical Spread Business—Balance Sheet (in millions)

Assets	
Loans receivable	$1,000
Accrued interest receivable	10
Offices and equipment	10
	$1,020
Liabilities and Shareholders' Equity	
Deposits and borrowings	$ 930
Accruals	10
	940
Shareholders' equity	80
	$1,020

EXHIBIT 20–4. Hypothetical Spread Business—Financial Ratios

After-tax return on assets	1.0%
Return on equity	12.5%
Liability to equity ratio ("leverage")	11.8 to 1

EXHIBIT 20–5. Capitalization Comparison

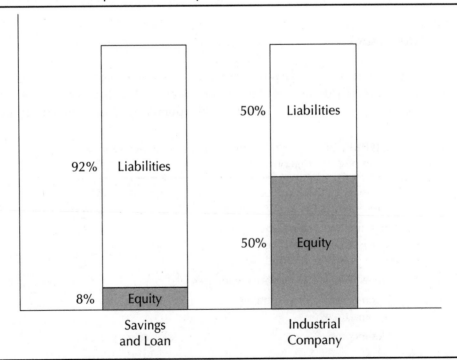

25 percent. For this reason, the credit culture of an S&L, bank, or finance company is the key to success.

This point is well illustrated by the experience of Lehman Brothers, where I worked in the late 1980s. Lehman, along with other New York investment banks, got into the lending business in 1987 as one means of drumming up new clients. The executives running Lehman's new lending operation were investment bankers, who focused on closing a deal, rather than putting a good asset on the firm's books. As a result, credit analysis and due diligence were cursory, and Lehman ran up huge loan losses within 18 months of the operation's start-up. Only the munificence of American Express, Lehman's parent, prevented the firm from going bankrupt under the weight of these bad loans. A similar billion-dollar bailout was performed by Credit Suisse on behalf of its affiliate, First Boston. This old-line investment banking firm was also saddled with massive bad loans from a new lending operation.

In part, a financial institution's credit culture can be surmised from its past record of loan losses in relation to loans booked. A high percentage of loan losses represents either an incompetent management or a risk-taking approach. Alternatively, it can indicate a loan portfolio concentrated in a region that has undergone tough times. In either case, the incidence of bad loans reflects the credit culture. If a management change is in the offing, the predictability of the past is suspect. Credit approvals are in the hands of top management, after all, and the introduction of a new chief executive, particularly an outsider, can mean change that does not correlate well with the past. This principle was demonstrated repeatedly in the early 1980s when conservative S&Ls were taken over by real estate developers who instituted aggressive lending programs that soured very quickly.

In addition to a solid credit culture, the principal intangible assets of an S&L consist of its reputation within the community, the prominence of its brand name, and the goodwill and contacts of its executives. All these qualities enable it to (1) attract the deposits (i.e., the borrowings) that support the institution's asset base; and (2) generate the leads that furnish new loans. For the analyst to measure such intangibles numerically is a difficult task. Nevertheless, the value of the "going concern" intangibles comes through, either in the analyst's financial projections, which show existing mortgages being gradually replaced by new loans, or in relative value comparisons, which show takeover prices around 250 percent of tangible book value in the 1990s.

Financial Statement Analysis of the Savings and Loan

The aim of financial statement analysis is the estimate of historical earnings power, from which a projection is constructed. The financial analysis of an S&L adopts the same methodical approach covered in Chapter 8. As reviewed in Exhibit 20–6, the three financial statements are evaluated

EXHIBIT 20-6. Financial Statement Analysis of an Established Business, Including S&L's

Raw Materials +	Primary Analytical Tools =	Results
The income statement	Absolute amount changes	Patterns and trends
The balance sheet	Percentage changes in growth	that have predictive
Statement of cash flows	Common sizes	ability.
Notes to financial statements	Financial ratios	

through the use of four tools, which enable the practitioner to discern trends and patterns in the subject's historical performance.

Because S&L assets are wholly financial, the ratios employed in the analysis and the vernacular used in the research report are different from that encountered previously in this book. Furthermore, the sensitivity of an S&L to bad loan problems requires a thorough study of loan loss experience, existing asset quality, and reserves for future losses. Finally, the extensive use of leverage requires the practitioner to assess carefully the S&L's asset/liability management. Long-term financial assets should optimally be matched with long-lived liabilities, and vice versa for short-term items.

Case Study: Maryland Federal Bancorp.   To illustrate S&L financial analysis, Exhibit 20-7 presents summary financial data of Maryland Federal Bancorp. for the three years ended February 29, 1996. Maryland Federal was a savings and loan that derived over 85 percent of its income from home mortgage loans. As of February 29, 1996, the company operated 25 branch offices in the Maryland suburbs of Washington, DC. On total assets of $1.1 billion, Maryland Federal realized net income of $8.7 million.

A quick glance at Exhibit 20-7 enables the reader to reach the following conclusions:

- *Profitability.* Maryland Federal was profitable, but the 1996 return on equity (9.7%) was low.
- *Growth.* The Company's assets were growing but net income was declining.
- *Normalized Results.* The decrease in net income was more significant if 1996's $8.8 million net income was normalized to $6.8 million (i.e., by eliminating the $2.0 million after-tax impact of the unusual $3.3 million securities gain).
- *Asset Composition.* Maryland Federal was a traditional S&L, gathering deposits to make loans. Investment securities and other assets represented a small portion of total assets.
- *Leverage.* The equity-to-total-assets ratio was 8.2 percent. The balance sheet had no intangible goodwill accounts.

EXHIBIT 20–7. Maryland Federal Bancorp.—Summary Financial Data (in millions except for share data)

	Fiscal Year Ended February		
	1994	1995	1996
Income Statement Data			
Interest income			
Mortgage and other loans	$ 56.5	$ 60.9	$ 72.2
Investment securities	6.8	8.2	7.9
Total interest income	63.3	69.1	80.1
Interest expense			
Deposits	27.9	30.3	39.9
Advance from Federal Home Loan Bank	4.5	8.7	13.0
Total interest expense	32.4	39.0	52.9
Net interest income	30.9	30.1	27.2
Provision for loan losses	0.7	0.3	0.1
Net interest income after provision for loan losses	30.2	29.8	27.1
Noninterest income			
Various fees and service charges	3.0	2.0	2.4
Gain on sale of investment securities	—	—	3.3
	3.0	2.0	5.7
Noninterest expense			
Compensation and benefits	7.2	8.4	8.8
Occupancy and equipment	2.4	2.8	3.2
Other	4.7	5.9	6.6
	14.3	17.1	18.6
Income before income taxes	18.8	14.7	14.3
Income tax expense	7.1	5.7	5.5
Net income	$ 11.7	$ 9.0	$ 8.8
Earnings per share	$ 3.55	$ 2.84	$ 2.76
Balance Sheet Data			
Assets			
Cash	$ 48.5	$ 15.8	$ 28.0
Investment securities	106.2	119.2	112.1
Mortgage loans	695.6	895.9	974.9
Other	21.9	27.9	28.3
	$872.2	$1,058.8	$1,143.3
Liabilities and Shareholders' Equity			
Deposits	$678.1	$ 763.8	$ 788.9
Borrowings from Federal Home Loan Bank	103.2	190.7	243.8
Other liabilities	13.2	18.4	16.7
Total liabilities	794.5	972.9	1,049.4
Shareholders' equity	77.7	85.9	93.9
	$872.2	$1,058.8	$1,143.3

SEC filings provide many disclosure items that supplement the financial statements, including information on asset composition, asset and liability management, and loan losses. The supplementary data enable the analyst to gauge the impact of changing interest rates on the profitability of the existing portfolio, along with a sense of management's risk-taking profile. These schedules extend for several years, but selected data for 1996 is shown for summary purposes. Exhibit 20–8, for example, shows the interest rates attached to the Company's loans and liabilities. Note that the net interest income/interest rate spread was a positive 2.07 percent. From this spread (i.e., $27 million), Maryland Federal financed operating expenses

EXHIBIT 20–8. Maryland Federal Bancorp.—Spread Summary

	Year Ended February 29, 1996		
	Average Balance	Interest	Yield/Rate
Interest-earning assets			
Loan receivable	$ 957	$73	7.54%
Mortgage-backed and related securities	71	4	6.77
Investment securities and other interest-earning assets	51	3	5.98
Total interest-earning assets	1,080	80	7.42
Noninterest-earning assets	15		
Total assets	$1,095		
Interest-bearing liabilities			
Deposits			
Certificates of deposit	$ 604	$35	5.80%
Noncertificate accounts	168	4	2.87
Total deposits	772	39	5.16
Advances from FHLB and other interest-bearing liabilities	216	13	6.06
Total interest-bearing liabilities	988	53	5.35
Noninterest-bearing liabilities	20		
Total liabilities	1,008		
Stockholders' equity	87		
Total liabilities and stockholders' equity	$1,095		
Net interest income/interest rate spread		$27	2.07%

and loan losses for 1996. Because many of its loans and liabilities have floating rates that change over time, Exhibit 20–8 is only a snapshot of the Company's performance.

Since the assets and liabilities of Maryland Federal are monetary in nature, changing interest rates have a significant impact on performance. As Exhibit 20–9 shows, $434 million (or 39%) of the thrift's interest-earning assets were long-term fixed-rate mortgages, even though $504 million of liabilities (49%) matured within one year. Thus, an upward movement in interest rates increases interest costs, without a commensurate jump in

EXHIBIT 20–9. Asset/Liability Management at February 29, 1996 (in millions)

	1 or Less	1–3	3–5	5–10	10–20	More Than 20	Total
Interest-earning assets							
Fixed-rate mortgage loans	$ 75	$ 106	$110	$ 92	$46	$ 5	$ 434
	8.01%	7.79%	8.40%	7.62%	7.56%	7.64%	7.92%
Floating rate mortgage loans	159	211	147	34	—	—	552
	7.24%	6.98%	7.12%	7.39%	—	—	7.12%
Other loans	1	2	1	—	—	—	4
	9.72%	9.72%	9.72%	—	—	—	9.72%
Mortgage-backed securities	16	13	7	18	11	—	66
	6.21%	6.95%	7.03%	6.94%	6.90%	—	6.78%
Investment securities	45	3	1	1	—	13	62
	5.03%	5.30%	4.76%	4.29%	—	7.25%	5.47%
Total interest-earning assets	298	335	266	145	58	18	1,119
	7.05%	7.24%	7.65%	7.46%	7.43%	7.35%	7.33%
Interest-bearing liabilities							
Deposits	504	193	50	32	6	4	789
	5.26%	5.09%	5.15%	2.98%	2.74%	2.94%	5.11%
Advances from FHLB	128	114	1	1	—	—	244
	6.04%	5.68%	4.90%	6.50%	—	—	5.87%
Total interest-bearing liabilities	632	307	51	32	6	4	1,033
	5.42%	5.31%	5.16%	3.05%	2.74%	2.94%	5.27%
Excess (deficiency) of interest-earning assets over interest-bearing liabilities	$(334)	$28	$214	$112	$52	$14	$86
Cumulative excess (deficiency) of interest-earning assets over interest-bearing liabilities	$(334)	$(307)	$(92)	$21	$72	$86	$86
Cumulative excess (deficiency) as a percentage of total assets	(29.28)%	(26.83)%	(8.04)%	1.80%	6.30%	7.54%	7.54%

income. To avoid this imbalance, many thrifts sell off a large portion of their fixed-rate mortgages, emphasize adjustable-rate loans, and seek long-term borrowings.

The firm's bad loan problems barely made a dent in loss reserves over the fiscal 1994 to 1996 period (see Exhibit 20–10). The favorable experience reflected a conservative credit culture and a stable regional economy, permitting management to reduce the annual provision for losses from $662,000 in fiscal 1994 to $120,000 in fiscal 1996. The $4.4 million allowance for loan losses equaled 0.5% of outstanding loans, which is slightly below the savings and loan average.

As is readily apparent, an S&L management may be tempted to manipulate the loss reserve account. Accruing a low loss provision (when a higher number is justified) inflates earnings; lending more money to a troubled borrower defers losses; and providing favorable seller financing to promote the sale of foreclosed real estate misleads investors. All these sins were repeated on a grand scale during the 1980s' S&L crisis.

Practitioners use a dazzling array of financial ratios to interpret the historical results and management efficiency of a thrift institution. An in-depth review of these ratios is beyond the scope of this book, but selected ratios are listed in Exhibit 20–11. They are segmented by nine categories: liquidity, deposit mix, asset mix, loan mix, asset quality, capital adequacy, profitability, interest analysis, and growth. Such ratios are calculated for a 3- to 5-year period, compared with similar firms' statistics and then applied to financial projections.

EXHIBIT 20–10.   Maryland Federal Bancorp. Loss Reserves (in thousands)

	Loans Receivable	Foreclosed Real Estate
Balance, February 28, 1993	$4,267	$ —
Provision for losses	662	—
Charge-offs	(3)	—
Transfer to allowance for losses on foreclosed real estate	(739)	739
Balance, February 28, 1994	4,187	739
Provision for losses	300	300
Charge-offs	(13)	(7)
Transfer to allowance for losses on foreclosed real estate	(50)	50
Balance, February 28, 1995	4,424	1,082
Provision for losses	120	200
Charge-offs	(70)	—
Balance, February 29, 1996	$4,474	$1,282

Note how the provision for loan losses declined over the period.

EXHIBIT 20–11. Savings and Loan Financial Ratios

Liquidity Ratios
Cash and investment securities to total assets
Total borrowings to total deposits

Deposit Mix
Fixed maturity deposits to total deposits
Passbook deposits to total deposits

Asset Mix
Mortgage loans to total assets
Consumer loans to total assets

Asset Quality
Nonaccrual loans to total loans
Allowance for loan losses to total loans
Allowance for loan losses to nonaccrual loans

Loan Mix
Mortgage loans to total loans
Federally guaranteed mortgages and mortgages on 1- to 4-family dwellings to total loans
Fixed-rate loans to total loans
Floating rate loans to total loans

Capital Adequacy
Shareholders' equity to total assets

Profitability Ratios
Return on average assets
Return on average equity

$$\text{Efficiency ratio} = \frac{\text{Noninterest Expense}}{\text{Net Interest Income Plus Fee Income}}$$

Interest Analysis
Interest income to total assets
Interest expense to total assets
Net interest margin to total assets

Annual Growth Statistics
Earnings per share
Net interest income
Deposits
Mortgage loans

VALUATION OF MARYLAND FEDERAL BANCORP.

Practitioners emphasize relative value techniques to price stocks such as Maryland Federal. Popular S&L valuation ratios are P/E and price/book, and most research reports include takeover premiums since the industry is consolidating. Their reliance on relative value notwithstanding, most analysts prepare financial projections and include DCF modeling as a backup to the relative value method. In May 1996, shortly after the publication of its fiscal 1996 results, Maryland Federal's shares were trading at $30, or 11× earnings and 1× book value; these multiples were in line with similar stocks.

FINANCE COMPANIES

Publicly traded finance companies are in the business of originating and servicing consumer loans. With the exception of credit card originations, a large proportion of their loans are made to individuals to whom traditional sources, such as banks, S&Ls and captive auto-finance companies, refuse to lend because of the applicant's poor credit history. Common loan categories include:

- Auto loans.
- Home equity loans (second mortgages).
- Credit card outstandings.
- Unsecured consumer loans.
- Nontraditional mortgage loans.
- Manufactured housing loans.

Due to the unique credit evaluation process and servicing requirement required for these subprime loans, it is not unusual for a publicly traded firm to specialize in only one or two categories. Thus, the Money Store emphasizes home equity loans, Olympic Financial is a subprime car lender, and Greentree Financial provides loans for manufactured homes.

Prior to the growth of the asset securitization market, consumer finance companies were spread businesses. The evaluation approach was similar to that of an S&L, although there were important differences. Without the ability to attract low-cost government-insured deposits, the finance company borrowed at higher rates in the capital markets. Correspondingly, its assets provided relatively higher interest rates. Creditworthy consumers gravitated to banks and S&Ls, leaving the riskier customers to the consumer finance industry. This situation changed completely in the 1990s as the asset securitization market advanced into the subprime arena.

In asset securitization, the finance company recruits the customer, performs the credit analysis, and makes the initial loan, just like a normal spread lender. However, once a sufficient number of loans have been originated, the company bundles them up into $50 million to $100 million lots, which are then sold to special purpose corporations. These corporations have no function other than to hold the loans, and they finance these loan purchases through the issuance of bonds backed only by the underlying loans. Thousands of consumer loans are thus transformed into large bond

EXHIBIT 20–12. The Consumer Loan Securitization Process

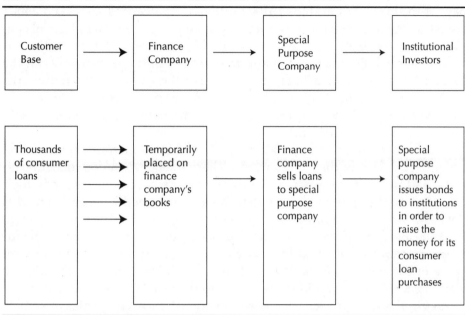

issues (i.e., "securitized"), which are purchased by pension funds and mutual funds. The process is illustrated in Exhibit 20–12.

As Exhibit 20–12 illustrates, the securitization market allows the finance company to quickly remove the loans from its balance sheet, which frees up the firm's capital. The capital is then redeployed to make additional loans and the process repeats itself. Loan growth, therefore, is not a captive of the finance company's own ability to raise more capital in the marketplace.

Securitization has a profound effect on the operation of finance companies. No longer must management patiently wait for the interest spread to roll in over a loan's maturity, as shown in Exhibit 20–13 for a five-year loan. Instead, by securitizing the loan shortly after its origination, the finance company can realize an immediate gain, because the consumer loans being

EXHIBIT 20–13. Consumer Finance Company—Interest Spread Earnings Forecast—Five-Year $10,000 Consumer Loan

	Year				
	1	2	3	4	5
Interest income at 14%	$1,400	$1,400	$1,400	$1,400	$1,400
Borrowing cost at 7%	– 700	– 700	– 700	– 700	– 700
Spread income before loan loss provisions	$ 700	$ 700	$ 700	$ 700	$ 700

sold have higher interest rates than the asset-backed bonds being issued to pay for the loans. For example, $100 million of 7 percent asset-backed bonds are issued by a special purpose corporation to purchase $100 million of consumer loans with an average interest rate of 14 percent. The loan seller has a gain, before adjustments, equal to the *present value difference* between the 14 percent loans and the 7 percent bonds. For the five-year illustration, the $700 annual spread ($3,500 over the 5-year term) provides the finance company with a $2,000 *present value* gain, assuming the $10,000 loan is sold shortly after its origination.

In practice, this gain calculation is affected by numerous expenses that occur over the life of the loan portfolio. These include defaults, collection efforts, and payment processing. Furthermore, many consumers repay their loans before the stated maturity date, so the presumed 7 percent spread is not available over the entire five-year period. As a result, when management (and the auditors) prepare the financial statements, estimates are made for prepayments, defaults, and loan servicing costs, and the resultant present value of these expenses is deducted from the initial gain. For the $10,000 loan, the $2,000 gain would likely be reduced to an $800 to $1,000 figure.

With the rise in securitization, many finance companies resemble "packagers" instead of "spread lenders." They derive the majority of their earnings by packaging the loan portfolios into large pools, selling them, and capturing the present value of the spread. A smaller portion of their income is derived from servicing the loans they have sold to others and from retaining loans that are not securitized. The Money Store's income statement (see Exhibit 20–14) is illustrative of the publicly traded finance company— 70 percent of its accounting revenues for 1996 were attributable to gains on sales of receivables. Only 30 percent came from spread income and servicing fees.

The accounting employed by The Money Store is perfectly legal under GAAP, but it presents certain problems for the security analyst:

- *Noncash Gains.* Although the firm recognizes gains in the year that loans are sold, the actual *cash* is received over the lives of the loans. Concurrent with the book gain, the company records a corresponding asset, "Excess Servicing Asset" on the balance sheet. As stated previously, the equity investor prefers cash-in-the-bank to noncash income.

- *Assumption-Dependent Income.* Although all GAAP accounting relies on management judgment, the proportion of finance company income calculated according to assumptions about future events is higher than in most other businesses. The analyst must research carefully the basis for these assumptions.

- *Continuing Obligations on Servicing Portfolio.* The Money Store had $1.4 billion of loans on its books and serviced another $12 billion for special purpose corporations. Although these serviced loans were "off the books," the firm facilitated the loan sales by agreeing to perform

EXHIBIT 20–14. The Money Store, Inc.—Income Statement Data for the Year Ended December 31, 1996

	Millions	**Percent**
Revenues		
Gain on sale of receivables	$544	70
Finance income, fees earned, and other	234	30
	778	100
Expenses		
Operating expenses	364	47
Provision for credit losses	146	19
Interest	124	16
	634	82
Income before income taxes	144	18
Income taxes	58	7
Net income	$ 86	11
Earnings per share	$1.41	

Note how the "gain on sale of receivables" far outstrips conventional "finance income."

certain remedial actions if the underlying loan portfolios performed badly. The accountants' estimates of these future liabilities is described as "allowance for credit losses on loans sold."

The importance of accurate estimates is highlighted by The Money Store's equity base, which at $582 million, is $224 million less than the intangible excess servicing asset. Exhibit 20–15 provides summary balance sheet data.

The Engine of Growth

Over the past five years, numerous finance companies have gone public and recorded compound annual earnings increases in excess of 30 percent. Their above-average growth is wholly dependent on bond investors continuing to buy asset-backed bonds collateralized by consumer debt. Bond investor confidence, in turn, rests on the foundation that the finance companies will bail them out of their bonds if rising consumer defaults threaten the bonds' principal values. At the time of this writing, AT&T, First Chicago, First Union, and other finance companies have supported securitizations over and above their respective legal obligations. Without these voluntary capital infusions, these firms presumed that the bond community would have "blackballed" them from further securitizations. In fact, one finance executive confided to me, "Forget the accounting treatment. In our eyes we retain the credit risk of all these securitized loans."

EXHIBIT 20–15. The Money Store Inc.—Summary Balance Sheet Data at December 31, 1996

	Millions	**Percent**
Assets		
Receivables, net of allowance for credit losses	$1,385	53
Excess servicing asset	806	30
Other assets	421	17
Total assets	$2,612	100
Liabilities and Shareholders' Equity		
Notes payable	$1,319	51
Other liabilities	471	18
Allowance for credit losses on loans sold	220	8
Subordinated debt	20	1
Shareholders' equity	582	22
	$2,612	100

Note how "excess servicing asset" exceeds shareholders' equity.

The implicit backstop of these deals negates the objective of securitization in the first place, but it showcases the need for a strong capital base if a finance company expects to weather a cyclical downturn in consumer credit worthiness. Without the securitization alternative, a firm's growth potential is unlikely to exceed that of a basic spread lender.

Finance Company Valuations

The P/E ratio is the primary yardstick by which finance company stocks are measured. Historical EPS trends and projected EPS growth contribute to relative value justifications.

COMMERCIAL BANKS

Commercial banks represent the third leg of this chapter. For several reasons, they are more difficult to evaluate than either S&Ls or finance companies:

1. *Asset Composition.* The asset composition of a bank is far more diversified than either the S&L or finance company, which focus on only one or two market segments. A bank's loan portfolio includes loans to consumers, small and large businesses, other financial institutions, real estate developers, import/export traders, and others. The importance of credit culture is doubly stressed.

2. *Liquidity Needs.* A good portion of a bank's liabilities are represented by checking accounts and large certificates of deposit. Accordingly, a high

proportion of a bank's assets must stay in liquid investments such as government bonds. Because of the unique nature of many bank loans, they are not as salable as mortgage loans or home equity loans, so a bank's loan-to-asset ratio (50% to 60%) is frequently lower than the comparable S&L or finance company ratio (70% to 90%).

3. *Fee Income.* A bank provides more services than the average S&L or finance company. As a result, its fee income is correspondingly higher as a percentage of revenues.

4. *Complexity of Business Lines.* As a bank grows in size, it usually offers numerous financial services, which sometimes overshadow its basic lending business. Many of the large ($75 billion + in assets) money-center banks are financial conglomerates, with separate line items for their trading, foreign exchange, trust and investment advisory, and corporate finance businesses. A thorough security analysis requires a top-down review of each segment.

5. *Regulatory Oversight.* Commercial banks draw more regulatory attention than their S&L counterparts. Adherence to liquidity, asset quality, and trading rules are watched more closely by the government.

Inefficiencies in Commercial Bank Valuations

The banking industry in the United States is slowly consolidating, but it remains highly fragmented. The largest participant has only a 3 percent market share, and an investor can choose from hundreds of publicly traded stocks. Given the limits of analyst horsepower, obvious pricing discrepancies appear from time to time, providing trading opportunities for the astute investor.

Regional Focus

Reflecting earlier prohibitions on multistate banking, most banks focus on a specific geographic region and their operating results trend against the regional economy. The recovery of the California economy and real estate market in the early 1990s helped numerous Western bank earnings results. Similarly, the drop in oil prices in the early 1980s weakened Texas-based banks. Consumer loan defaults went up as layoffs increased, while reduced oil prices hurt real estate values, which led to a jump in real estate loan losses.

When a bank starts loaning money outside its historical region, this presents a potential problem, since the credit officer is going to be less familiar with appraising transactions beyond his traditional area. Additionally, in my experience, a bank that attempts to increase loans more rapidly than the underlying growth of its regional economy is a risky investment. Inevitably, management boosts growth by making lower-quality loans, while assuming low default ratios.

Asset Quality

Like S&Ls, banks are highly leveraged. Equity-to-asset ratios of 7 to 8 percent are not uncommon, yet banks frequently have significant exposures to the riskier loan categories such as business loans, construction loans, and commercial real estate (see Exhibit 20–16). Obviously, a small error in estimated bad loans, say 2 percent of total loans outstanding, reduces equity by 20 percent or more. To instill more confidence in the investment community, publicly traded commercial banks are required to disclose numerous schedules on loan composition, loss reserves, and loan performance. Nevertheless, as noted earlier, past credit performance is only one indicator of future credit decisions.

Supplemental Disclosures

Important supplemental disclosures that help the bank analyst include:

- *Mark to Market.* On the balance sheet, banks record assets, including investment securities, at original cost. The fixed-income component of these assets changes in value with interest rate movements. In the footnotes, banks mark such assets to market. Increases in interest rates depress the economic values of fixed-income investments.
- *Asset and Liability Management.* In a manner similar to an S&L, a bank provides extensive information on the duration and interest rates of its related assets and liabilities.
- *Fee Income.* Bank fee income is segmented by business line to provide insight to the investor, creditor, and depositor.

Exhibit 20–17 summarizes financial results for Regions Financial Corporation, a sizable bank focusing on the southeastern United States. Note the diverse sources of noninterest income as well as the substantial leverage employed.

EXHIBIT 20–16. Loan Ranking by Risk of Default

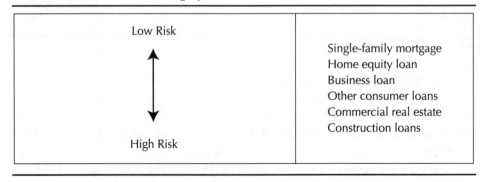

EXHIBIT 20–17. Regions Financial Corporation—Summary Financial Data

Income Statement Data (in millions)

Interest income	$1,386	
Interest expense	(685)	
Net interest income	701	
Provision for loan losses	(29)	
Net interest income after provision for loan losses	672[1]	Gross spread income is $672 million.
Noninterest income		
Trust department	28	
Service charges on checking accounts	88	Note the diverse sources of fee income.
Loan servicing and origination fees	51	
Securities gains	3	
Other fees and charges	51	
Total noninterest income	221[2]	
Operating expenses	(554)[3]	
Income before income taxes	339[1+2–3]	
Income taxes	(109)	
Net income	$ 220	
Earnings per share	$3.70	

Balance Sheet Data (in billions)

Total assets	$18.9	
Net loans	13.3	Shareholders' equity is only 8.5% of total assets.
Loan-loss reserves	0.2	
Deposits	15.0	
Shareholders' equity	1.6	

Other Data

Nonperforming loans (NPL)	$101 million	The bank's 1.3% return on assets is typical for the industry. Loss reserve coverage is adequate.
Loss reserves/NPL	194%	
Return on assets	1.3%	
Return on equity	15.2%	

Franchise Value

Like the accounting statements of an S&L or a finance company, a bank's financial statements only tell part of the story. The ability of the bank to maintain growth depends not only on its financial strength but also on its management, reputation, and transaction processing infrastructure. Banking is fundamentally a cyclical service industry, and some firms provide services and recruit clients better than others.

Bank Stock Valuation

The comparative historical analysis of bank stocks incorporates a dizzying array of ratios and statistical calculations that are beyond the scope of this book. It suffices to say that bank analysis is more involved than either an S&L or a finance company evaluation.

Banks are considered to be relatively homogeneous, particularly compared with industrial businesses. Valuation comparisons emphasize P/E and price/book multiples. Analysts do not use EBIT or EBITDA multiples for bank stocks. Loans, the principal assets of most banks, rarely have a market value in excess of historical cost, so the market price/book ratio is closely watched by practitioners. Too high a price/book ratio is a danger signal, and even growth-oriented bank stocks rarely break through the 2.0 barrier. As the industry consolidates, bank mergers are common and professional investors buy stocks on takeover potential. With takeover prices averaging around 2.5× book value, any well-regarded bank stock trading at less than 75 percent of this figure (i.e., 1.8×) is viewed as attractive.

SUMMARY

Due to the specialized nature of their assets and liabilities, financial businesses require valuation techniques using a new vocabulary and a different set of ratios. Nevertheless, the fundamental approach is identical to that for industrial stocks. The historical financial statement analysis of a financial company uses the same four tools to discern business behavior and performance. This process facilitates an understanding of the company and provides certain predictive factors. Financial projections incorporate the top-down method reviewed earlier, and valuation conclusions rest on relative value and DCF techniques.

S&Ls, finance companies, and commercial banks are fundamentally "spread lenders," taking in money at one rate and lending it out at a higher rate. Spread lending is a commodity business, and generating a reasonable profit depends on management's ability to sustain a conservative credit culture, exploit the institution's franchise, and keep transaction processing costs down. Reflecting the liquid nature of financial assets, leverage is high among these businesses and asset/liability administration becomes an important concern. As a supplement to lending, most firms offer consumers, businesses, and governments an array of ancillary services that provide an attractive source of fee income.

Banking stocks are both cyclical investments and consolidation plays. Loan growth parallels the economy's performance, and bad loans increase with a weakening economy. Over the past 10 years, changing conditions have prompted a wave of bank acquisitions as larger participants seek to buy rather than build market share. As a result, practitioners watch takeover values closely as indicators of bank stock prices.

QUESTIONS AND SHORT PROBLEMS

1. Why is evaluating a financial institution so different than the evaluation of a manufacturing firm? Select one answer.
   a. Financial assets are fundamentally pieces of paper, the value of which is supported by contracts and other assets.
   b. Financial institution ratios are far more difficult to calculate and the information is often undisclosed.
   c. Financial institution accounting is a separate class under GAAP categories.
   d. Financial institutions have highly leveraged balance sheets and questionable loss reserves.

2. Which of these industries is the last "pure" spread business?
   a. Savings and loans.
   b. Finance companies.
   c. Commercial banks.
   d. Brokerage firms.

3. How are the principal products of S&L's and banks similar to the principal products of natural resource firms:
   a. Both have substantial "hidden" value.
   b. Both have a commodity orientation.
   c. Both defy a conventional DCF analysis.
   d. None of the above.

4. Circle all of the non-price competitive elements that are relevant to a mutual fund management firm:
   a. Claims of above-average performance.
   b. Marketing ability.
   c. Management fees.
   d. Reputation.
   e. Convenience.

5. In your hand you have a contract that says Talbot Corp. will pay you (a) $100 per year at the end of three years, plus (b) interest annually at the market rate. List three reasons why the contract might be worth less than $100 in "present value" terms.

6. Which of the following are the two principal skills of a good commercial bank:
   a. Ability to recruit new borrowers.
   b. Selecting creditworthy clients.
   c. Managing transaction flows.
   d. Following regulatory mandates of the Comptroller of the Currency.

7. For the hypothetical spread business in Exhibits 20–2 and 20–3, calculate the following:
   a. Average interest rate on loans.
   b. Average interest rate on borrowings.

    c. Net interest rate "spread."

    d. Loan losses as a percentage of total loans.

8. Despite a low 0.8 percent after-tax return on assets, Maryland Federal Bancorp. had a 9.5 percent return on equity in 1996. How did the company achieve this return?

    a. High leverage.

    b. Cost controls that were effective.

    c. Very high interest spread.

    d. Low leverage ratio.

9. Why does an analyst "normalize" Maryland Federal's $8.8 million net income result in 1996 by reducing it to $6.8 million?

10. What comprised the bulk of Maryland Federal's liabilities?

11. Why should an S&L such as Maryland Federal consider developing an asset portfolio that emphasizes floating rate loans instead of long-term fixed-rate loans?

12. From Exhibit 20–9, describe the significance of the negative $334 million deficiency of "interest-earning assets over interest-bearing liabilities for maturities of one year or less." What would have happened to the company's earnings per share if short-term interest rates went up in 1997?

13. List four categories of S&L financial ratios.

14. Among other loans, finance companies make the following sorts of loans: credit card cash advances, unsecured consumer loans, and mobile home loans. Why are these loans considered more risky than traditional home mortgage loans?

15. Describe the consumer loan securitization process employed by many finance firms. How does it free up capital so the finance firm can make more loans?

16. A finance company makes a $5,000 unsecured consumer loan payable at maturity in 3 years. The interest rate is 13.5 percent. Estimated default loss and administrative expenses are each $100 per year (i.e., $200 on a combined basis). If the loan can be "securitized" at 6.5 percent annually, what is the finance company's hypothetical gain if securitized on day 1?

    If the borrower repays the loan at the end of year 2, how much of the hypothetical gain is reversed?

17. Compare the provisions for credit losses for the Money Store in Exhibit 20–14 with the loan loss provisions for Maryland Federal. As a percentage of total assets, why were the Money Store's losses so different from Maryland Federal?

18. What was the excess servicing asset on The Money Store's balance sheet?

19. The "excess servicing asset" calculation relies on which of the following assumptions? Circle all that apply:
    a. Hedging rate on future receivables.
    b. Collection rate on loans.
    c. Future repayments on loans.
    d. Default rate on loans.
    e. Administrative expenses on loans.

20. Several key differences between banks and S&L's affect the respective security analyses. Outline three differences.

21. Non-interest income as a percentage of total income was 25 percent for Regions Financial Corporation. Compare this statistic to other banks of a similar size.

22. Compare and contrast the loss experience of Regions Financial with the Money Store and Maryland Federal. What does your analysis tell you about the quality of the respective loan portfolios?

21

Insurance Companies

*Insurance companies are part of the financial industry, but they pro-
vide a service that differs from that of the spread lender. Chapter 21
examines how professionals evaluate insurance stocks.*

In Chapter 20, our survey of financial stocks covered spread lenders—savings and loans, finance companies, and commercial banks. In this chapter,
we continue with the financial industry by reviewing one more sector—
insurance.

Insurance companies seek to make a profit by providing a risk-taking
service. They contract to indemnify their customers against losses arising
from a specified contingency or peril that cannot be predicted at the time of
the contract. A subset of the industry, the life insurance sector, supplements
its risk-taking business by engaging in spread lending.

GENERAL BACKGROUND

In exchange for a designated payment (i.e., a "premium"), the insurance
company compensates its customer (i.e., the "policyholder") for the cost of
an expected loss. The event causing the loss, such as a fire, accident, or
flood, is well defined in the policy and its financial severity is large enough
for the customer to want to avoid it. Thus, even though the chances of someone's house burning down in any given year are remote, say 1 in 1,000, the
financial effects of such an event, possibly $150,000 or more, are so unthink-
able for the average homeowner that the annual premium, perhaps $200,
seems a small price to pay for the security of being protected against the
occurrence.

Insurance companies absorb the risks that others care to avoid. They
make money in the process by adhering to three basic principles:

EXHIBIT 21–1. Principal Components of an Insurance Premium

Cost of paying for losses	+65¢
+	
Cost of underwriting, claim processing and operations	+12¢
+	
Marketing costs	+10¢
+	
Reserves for unexpected losses	+9¢
+	
Investment income	−8¢
+	
Operating profits	+12¢
=	
Insurance premium	$1.00

Source. From *Introduction to Insurance* by Mark Dorfman (Englewood Cliffs, NJ: Prentice Hall, 1982).

1. *Predictable Events.* Insurers try to stick to absorbing risks where the history of occurrence and severity of loss are well known (e.g., fires, car accidents, mortality). The industry has encountered problems in untested areas such as hazardous material and product liability.

2. *Law of Large Numbers.* This mathematical principle states that the greater the number of observations of an event based on chance, the more likely the actual result approximates the expected result. Thus, a company insuring 100,000 houses against fire is able to predict its losses more accurately on an annual basis than one insuring 100 houses. Successful insurance firms spread risk among large client bases and failing this, they reinsure the risk with other insurers.

3. *Investment Returns.* Many policies protect against risks for long periods of time. As the premiums are paid in, the insurance company invests the cash, waits for losses to occur, and then waits further to pay them out. The resultant investment income is an important element of an insurer's finances.

Part of the pricing of an insurance policy thus represents an interesting combination of the laws of chance and the time value of money. The remaining components consist of (1) *marketing:* the cost of securing the policy; (2) *underwriting and claims processing:* selecting insured risks, setting rates, and processing claims; and (3) *profit.* These categories are set forth in Exhibit 21–1.

PRINCIPAL FUNCTIONS OF AN INSURANCE COMPANY

Insurance companies are divided into two categories: (1) property and casualty (P&C) insurance companies; and (2) life insurance companies. As this chapter illustrates, each type requires a different analysis; but the broad functions of both are reasonably similar (see Exhibit 21–2).

EXHIBIT 21–2. Functions of an Insurer

1. Ratemaking.
2. Sales and marketing.
3. Underwriting.
4. Loss adjustment and claims paying.
5. Investment management.

Source. From *Essentials of Insurance* by Emmett Vaughan and Therese Vaughan (New York: John Wiley & Sons, 1995).

Ratemaking

Ratemaking is determining the price at which an insurance company's policies are sold. Unlike the cost of producing a car, for example, where most of the expense is known prior to its sale, the bulk of an insurance policy's cost is based on educated predictions relating to loss occurrence, investment returns, and inflation. Insurance companies employ a specialized class of mathematician—an actuary—to (1) study the numerous statistical and financial variables involved in insurance; and (2) produce rates that cover losses, operating costs, and profit requirements.

Sales and Marketing

Insurance is sold principally through independent agents (or brokers) who represent one or more companies selling similar products. Compensation is provided on a commission basis.

Underwriting

An insurance company does not approve all customers who ask for coverage. Rather, it picks and chooses among applicants, looking for those whose probable loss experience fits into the actuary's ratemaking framework. For example, most auto insurers refuse to insure convicted drunk drivers because the presumed risk of loss falls outside the established parameters. Underwriters are asked to produce a pool of customers (i.e., insureds) whose actual loss experience will approximate the estimated losses of a hypothetical group, as outlined by the actuaries. Rates should thus conform to expected customer risks.

Underwriting involves a significant amount of judgment and requires gathering information about the applicant. For example, a worker's compensation policy might require an inspection of the applicant's production plant. A life insurance policy might involve a physical examination of the person to be insured. In instances where the policy is renewable, the firm may have the option of cancellation (or raising rates), which might happen if the customer's loss experience has been particularly unfavorable.

Loss Adjustment and Claims Paying

After a loss occurs, the insured notifies his insurance company. In life insurance, the claim is a set amount, agreed on at the beginning of the policy. In property and casualty, the insurer's obligation is to make the customer "whole" from a financial point of view (i.e., the policyholder isn't supposed to profit from a loss). Investigating the loss, determining whether the insurer is liable to pay the claim, and estimating the financial impact is the job of the "loss adjuster."

In many claims, there is a dispute over the size of the financial loss, while with others there is a dispute over whether the policy actually covers the event. Also, numerous insurance claims are fraudulent. The adjuster tries to resolve these issues.

Investment Management

Insurance companies employ full-time professional investment staffs. Since premiums are paid in advance and cash outlays for claims take place years afterward, insurance companies generate cash which is invested to produce a return. The predictability of fixed-income securities is preferred by insurance companies. Property and casualty (P&C) firms typically select short-to-intermediate term securities, reflecting the time horizon of their liabilities and the cyclical nature of the P&C business. Life insurers are more apt to select intermediate-to-long-term bonds. The life companies' insurance liabilities are easy to forecast, and they can take advantage of the higher yields available on longer maturities.

Case Study: Financial Statement Analysis—Property and Casualty Company. Of the industries presented in this book, the property and casualty insurance industry is the most complex to analyze. It involves bewildering arrays of schedules and statistics. Moreover, many of the GAAP reports rest on quicksand, as much of a P&C company's results are based on actuarial estimates reflecting uncertain outcomes. In fact, one insurance executive told me, "It's one of the few industries without a true bottom line." Many corporate financial statements include "guesstimates"; it's just that the P&C industry has an especially heavy reliance on them.

Exhibit 21–3 provides summary income statement data for the Progressive Corporation, a property-casualty company specializing in nonstandard auto insurance. "Nonstandard" means insurance for high-risk drivers such as those with DWI convictions, multiple speeding tickets, or expensive sports cars. Note how the category "premiums earned" substitutes for revenues in the income statement. About two thirds of Progressive's expenses reflect claims payments and loss adjustment expenses.

Income Statement Data

Premiums Earned

This item *does not* equal cash premium payments received during the year. Rather, under the accrual method of accounting, a $100 premium paid in advance (for a one-year policy) on June 30, 1996, is only 50 percent earned in 1996. The remaining $50 is "earned" for accrual purposes in the first six

EXHIBIT 21–3. The Progressive Corporation—Income Statement Data (in billions)

	Year Ended December 31		
	1994	**1995**	**1996**
Revenues			
Premiums earned	$2.2	$2.7	$3.2
Investment income	0.1	0.2	0.2
Other	0.1	0.1	0.1
Total revenues	2.4	3.0	3.5
Expenses			
Underwriting expenses			
Losses and loss adjustment expenses	1.4	1.9	2.2
Policy acquisition costs (marketing)	0.4	0.5	0.5
Other underwriting expenses	0.1	0.2	0.2
Total underwriting expenses	1.9	2.6	2.9
Service expenses	—	—	0.1
Interest expenses	0.1	0.1	0.1
Total expenses	2.0	2.7	3.1
Income before income taxes	0.4	0.3	0.4
Income taxes	0.1	0.1	0.1
Net income	$0.3	$0.2	$0.3
Earnings per share	$3.59	$3.24	$4.11

Note. A large boost in loss expense caused a dip in 1995 earnings, despite 25 percent higher revenues.

months of 1997. At December 31, 1996, the $50 cash is offset by a $50 unearned premium liability on the balance sheet.

LOSSES AND LOSS ADJUSTMENT EXPENSES

These items reflect the estimated cost of paying and handling (1) known claims plus (2) claims regarding events the firm believes have incurred but have not been reported. The estimates are made by experts, but uncertainty is present. As the reader knows, even the cost of a routine traffic accident can take years to unravel, particularly if pain and suffering is alleged. The ultimate matching of loss reserves to actual cash payments becomes more accurate as time passes, and the companies make reserve adjustments regularly. As a result, current earnings are regularly impacted by prior events.

An aggressive management may be tempted to lowball loss estimates and thereby inflate reported earnings temporarily. If the in-house actuaries are cooperative, there is little the analyst can do in the short term. Over the long term, however, deficiencies in reserves become obvious in financial statements and regulatory filings.

COMBINED RATIO

Insurance analysts use many standard financial ratios and several industry-specific ratios. The most popular P&C ratio is the combined ratio, which measures whether the company is actually making money in its pure insurance business, as divorced from the investment portfolio. When the combined ratio is less than 100 percent, the firm is supposedly making money from underwriting. A ratio in excess of 100 percent indicates an underwriting loss. Exhibit 21–4 shows the calculation for Progressive.

In reviewing a P&C company's income statement, remember that the P&C business in the United States (where most public firms do all of their business) is mature and reasonably fragmented. Price and distribution are key competitive elements. Furthermore, profitability in any given year should be evaluated in the context of the P&C business cycle, which is best described by Vaughan and Vaughan in *Essentials of Insurance* (New York: John Wiley & Sons, 1995):

> The property and liability industry is highly cyclical, and goes through periods of underwriting profit, followed by periods of losses; the insurance market is characterized as "hard" or "soft," depending on the phase of the cycle. During periods when insurers are earning underwriting profits, the market is said to be "soft," as insurers engage in price cutting to increase their market share. The price cutting includes not only reduction in the absolute level of rates, but the loosening of underwriting standards. This has the natural result of generating losses, resulting in a "hard" market, during which insurers increase prices and tighten underwriting standards.

As one example, over the past decade, Allstate's combined ratio peaked in 1992 at 121 percent, only to drop to 100 percent in 1996. Over time, the average P&C combined ratio is around 107 percent, indicating a consistent underwriting loss for the industry.

EXHIBIT 21–4. Combined Ratio Calculation for the Progressive Corporation—Year Ended December 31, 1996 (dollars in millions)

		Policy Acquisition Costs and
Combined Ratio =	$\dfrac{\text{Losses and Loss Adjustment Expenses}}{\text{Premiums Earned}}$ +	$\dfrac{\text{Other Underwriting Expenses}}{\text{Premiums Earned}}$
Combined Ratio =	$\dfrac{\$2,236}{\$3,199}$ +	$\dfrac{\$691}{\$3,199}$
Combined Ratio =	69.9% +	21.6%
Combined Ratio =	91.5%	

Note. Progressive's 91.5 percent combined ratio is relatively low. Many P&C companies have combined ratios of 100 percent or more, with a corresponding higher investment income.

BALANCE SHEET DATA

Exhibit 21–5 shows balance sheet data for the Progressive Corporation. Like all P&C companies, Progressive's assets are practically 100 percent financial in nature. Liabilities consist primarily of unearned premiums and loss reserves.

Investments

Over 75 percent of Progressive's investments resided in investment-grade corporate bonds with maturities under five years. The short maturities minimized interest-rate risk. Over 40 percent of equity securities represented fixed-dividend preferred stocks. The portfolio reflects the typical P&C firm's preference for fixed-income investments that can be sold easily if liquidity needs arise.

Unearned Premiums

Since Progressive's premiums were paid in advance, inevitably a portion was not earned during the fiscal year. This item was a contra account for the cash received, but not earned in an accounting sense.

EXHIBIT 21–5. The Progressive Corporation Summary Balance Sheet Data at December 31, 1996 (in billions)

Assets	
Investments	
Corporate bonds	$3.4
Equity securities	0.9
Money-market investments	0.2
Total investments	4.5
Premiums receivable	0.8
Other assets	0.7
Property and equipment, net	0.2
	$6.2
Liabilities and Shareholders' Equity	
Unearned premiums	$1.5
Loss and loss adjustment expense reserves	1.8
Payables and other	0.4
Long-term debt	0.8
Total liabilities	4.5
Shareholders' equity	1.7
	$6.2

Note that assets are almost 100 percent financial in nature for an insurance company.

Loss and Loss Adjustment Expense Reserves

Loss reserve adequacy is the most important consideration in evaluating a P&C stock. Reserve estimates are based on a combination of historical experience, known facts, and interpretation of circumstances. They are thus judgmental in nature and lack the exactness of many accounting entries. It's easy for a company to skimp on reserves because the associated claims usually aren't paid for several years (much like an aggressive lender books risky loans but keeps low loss reserves).

The independent accounting firm that audits a P&C company's books, as a matter of course, reviews reserve estimates, but the real examination is conducted by an independent actuarial consulting firm, which provides a written opinion on the reserves' sufficiency. This annual opinion is a requirement of state regulators, who are the primary governmental overseers of insurance companies. In addition to the actuarial opinion and financial statements, regulators examine supplemental data on P&C reserves and perform field audits every three to five years.

You can obtain this detailed information by visiting the relevant state insurance departments. Some firms send the data to individuals on request. The reserve information is located in Schedule P of these filings, and several such tables appear in SEC documents. For the beginner, these tables are hard to decipher. Exhibit 21–6 provides a portion of Progressive's consolidated analysis of loss and loss adjustment expenses (LAE) development.

Exhibit 21–6 indicates that Progressive has consistently overestimated its need for loss reserves. To illustrate, in 1992 the Company set aside $956 million of loss reserves for policies written in that year. One year later

EXHIBIT 21–6. The Progressive Corporation—Analysis of Loss and LAE Development (in millions)

	For the Year Ended December 31				
	1992	**1993**	**1994**	**1995**	**1996**
Loss and LAE reserves	$956	$1,012	$1,098	$1,314*	$1,533
Restimated reserves as of:					
One year later	858	870	1,042	1,209*	
Two years later	766	838	992		
Three years later	737	811			
Four years later	725				
Cumulative redundancy	231	201	106	105	
Percentage of original estimated reserves	24.2%	19.9%	9.7%	8.0%	

The table shows how the Company's loss estimates conformed to actual losses.
After one year's experience, Progressive decided 1995's original reserve estimate* could be lowered from $1,314 million to $1,209 million, producing an 8.0 percent redundancy.

(1993), after examining claim experience, the actuaries concluded that only $858 million of reserves were needed. In 1994, with two years of hindsight, the Company lowered 1992's reserves again, to $766 million. By 1996, four years later, most of 1992's claims had been settled and the reserve estimate (which included all paid claims) had dropped to $725 million, which was 24.2 percent lower than the original estimate. Similar redundancies occurred for the years 1993 to 1995. This history reflected both the firm's conservative approach to estimating loss reserves; and lower than expected inflation in health care costs, a contributing factor to the cost of automobile accidents.

Not all P&C companies have redundancies in their loss reserve development schedules. Allstate, for example, showed deficiencies ranging from 20.9 to 36.5 percent in the late 1980s. Redundancies only began to appear in 1992. Imagine if a manufacturer's cost of goods sold was in error by 20 to 30 percent! That company wouldn't last long!

FINANCIAL STATEMENT RATIOS

The uncertainty of insurance liabilities and the conservative bent of state regulators limit the debt incurrence ability of P&C companies. A debt-to-total-capitalization ratio of 30 percent or more is unusual, and many firms have ratios of 20 percent or less. To measure a firm's growth, profitability, activity, and leverage, practitioners calculate numerous ratios on prior results, evaluate trends, and compare performance to similar firms. Jack Berka and Lee Shepard, valuation experts at Houlihan Lokey Howard and Zukin, provided the key ratios feature in Exhibit 21–7.

PROPERTY AND INSURANCE STOCK VALUATION

Like the other practitioners we have discussed, P&C equity analysts rely on a combination of relative value and DCF techniques. As cyclical businesses, P&C firms have lower P/Es on average than manufacturing and service companies. Exhibit 21–8 compares property and casualty P/Es with selected manufacturing and service company P/Es. Note how property and casualty P/E ratios tend to be lower than manufacturing and service P/Es.

LIFE INSURANCE COMPANIES

Because life insurance policies have a fixed payment and mortality schedules change little, a life company's loss predictions are more accurate than those of a property and casualty insurer. Problems tend to occur in the investment portfolio or the policy acquisition expense area. Accordingly, a life company analyst pays more attention to investments and policy acquisition expenses than to loss reserves.

EXHIBIT 21–7. Property and Casualty Insurance Companies—Key Financial Ratios

Growth

- Growth in earned premiums.
- Growth in total revenues.
- Growth in total assets.

Profitability and Activity

- *Loss ratio* (including loss adjustment expenses) is loss and loss adjustment expenses divided by premiums earned. (1)
- *Underwriting expenses (including policy acquisition costs) to premiums earned* is a measure of overall operating costs. (2)
- *Combined ratio* 1 + 2 is a measure of underwriting profit before investment income.
- *Investment income to premiums earned* is an indicator both of profitability and capital adequacy.
- *Investment income to average investments* gauges both the performance of the investment portfolio and its risk.
- *Operating income (EBIT) to premiums earned* and *EBIT to total revenues* measures overall profitability on a debt-free basis.
- *Pretax income to premiums earned* and *pretax income to revenues* measure overall profitability after debt service.

Coverage and Capital Adequacy

- *Loss reserves to net worth* is a good measure of the overall level of capital adequacy.
- *Premiums earned to net worth* measure the amount of new business written to capital. If these ratios exceed 2.0, the company is considered to be capital short in terms of new business accepted.

Source. From "Insurance Underwriting Companies," by Jack Berka and Lee Shepard, *Financial Valuation: Business and Business Interests,* Warren, Gorham & Lamont, Boston, MA, 1997 (ed. James Zukin).

Life insurance companies have traditionally combined the insurance function with a savings component. Until the 1980s, the industry was heavily dependent on the whole-life policy, whereby a customer's premium payments built up a cash value over the policy's duration. The income earned through the cash value build-up was tax deferred, and made the policy's savings feature attractive relative to competing fixed-income investments. With the growth in retail-oriented money-market, bond, and equity mutual funds, many consumers substituted term life policies for the whole-life product. This change forced life companies to compete more vigorously for the investment dollar.

As a result of this development, the 1990s' life company has modernized its investment department to the point where it closely resembles a spread lending function. Depending on the company, the spread lending business receives more emphasis than selling insurance. Western National Life Insurance

EXHIBIT 21–8. P/E Ratio Comparison 1991–1996

	Five-Year Average P/E Ratio	
Property and Casualty		
Allstate	13.4	
Chubb	13.7	12.7 average
Ohio Casualty	12.2	
Progressive Corp.	11.6	
Industrial Manufacturing		
Crane	14.7	
Mark IV Industries	14.5	15.3 average
Pentair	15.2	
Tyco International	16.8	
Industrial Service		
Angelica	20.8	
Equifax	17.8	19.5 average
Kelly Services	19.9	
Rollins, Inc.	19.6	

Note the lower P/Es of the insurance firms.

Company, for example, generates practically all its income through spread lending. U.S. Life Corp., in contrast, primarily sells term life insurance.

Due to the special tax-deferred nature of its products and the oversight of state regulators, the life industry is loathe to refer to its spread business as such. Rather, the investment product is called an *annuity* and the customer's deposit is called a *premium*. Nevertheless, annuity providers openly advertise their rates of return, just as banks publicize their CD rates, and the companies disclose their respective spreads between the earned rate on investment assets and the promised rate on annuities. In 1996, for example, Western National's spread was 2.1 percent, which easily covered operating expenses, annuity payouts, and investment losses.

Given the predictability of mortality losses and the emphasis on spread income, life companies have a tendency to stretch for yield on the asset side of the balance sheet. Thus, in addition to studying the financial statements, the analyst must pay special attention to the life company's investment portfolio. Most of the holdings are in corporate bonds, so a knowledge of the firm's credit culture is helpful. Previous life company meltdowns, such as First Executive Life and Mutual Benefit Life, resulted from risky junk bonds and faulty real estate mortgages.

Exhibit 21–9 shows summary financial data for Western National Corporation, the parent company of Western Life. Note that net investment income represented 88 percent of revenues. Interest expense on annuities and financial products represented 59 percent of benefits and expenses. Equity was less than 10 percent of total liabilities. These statistics resemble a savings and loan's results more than those of a traditional life insurance company.

EXHIBIT 21–9. Western National Corporation—Summary Financial
Data (in millions)

Income Statement Data	Year Ended December 31, 1996	
Revenues		
Insurance policy income	$ 0.1	12%
Net investment income	0.7	88
Total revenues	0.8	100
Benefits and expenses		
Insurance policy benefits	0.1	14
Interest expense on annuities and other financial products	0.4	59
Other benefits and expenses	0.2	19
Income before income taxes	0.2	19
Income taxes	0.1	7
Net income	0.1	12%

Balance Sheet Data	At December 31, 1996	
Corporate bond investments	$ 8.8	88%
Other investments	0.8	6
Total assets	10.1	100
Insurance liabilities	8.7	87
Shareholders' equity	0.9	9

Note how Western National's income and expenses have little to do with
insurance. Investment income and interest expense dominate the income
statement.

SUMMARY

Insurance companies have a peculiar matching problem. They receive premium revenue when a policy is sold, but are unsure of the policy's ultimate
cost because the related losses occur in the future. The firm's cash flow
generating capability is thus subject to more uncertainty than that of many
industrial companies.

The accuracy of actuarial estimates of loss reserves is dependent on the
type of insurance underwritten. Life insurance expenses, for example, are
more easily predicted than property and casualty claims. A company's experience in gauging future losses is disclosed in public filings, but, as the
reader knows, the past is only a partial guide to forward results.

Like other financial sectors, the P&C insurance business is cyclical, and
this contributes to P&C stocks trading at a discount to the P/E multiples of
similar-size manufacturing companies. Life companies are beginning to resemble spread lenders, and the shares trade accordingly.

QUESTIONS AND SHORT PROBLEMS

1. Why does a typical insurer pay out substantially less than 100 percent of premium income in the form of loss compensation?

2. How might the time value of money affect the cost of an insurance premium?

3. How is the insurance business fundamentally different than a manufacturer? Circle one answer.
    a. The costs of providing insurance are mainly in the future, rather than the present.
    b. The cost of sales and marketing insurance are generally far higher than in a manufacturing business.
    c. Insurance firms are less regulated than most manufacturers.
    d. Manufacturers rarely employ independent sales agents.

4. How is the underwriting function of an insurance company similar to the credit evaluation function in a commercial bank?

5. Why has one insurance executive said, "Insurance companies don't have a true bottom line"?
    a. Because so many of the insurance company's income statement items are based on actuarial estimates.
    b. Because P&C premium levels tend to fluctuate wildly over the cycle.
    c. Because unexpected loss occurrences from natural disasters, such as earthquakes, are very difficult to forecast.
    d. Because the investment return on fixed-income securities is highly variable.

6. If prices for homes and office buildings increase faster than expected, a property insurer should:
    a. Increase investment income by acquiring more stocks.
    b. Lower its premiums for fire insurance.
    c. Increase its loss reserves.
    d. Tighten up its underwriting function.

7. Axel Property Insurance issues Tdel Corp. a two-year fire insurance policy. The up-front premium is $10,000 for the entire coverage. How much revenue does Axel accrue in the first year?

8. The assets of a property and casualty company are principally:
    a. The insurance policies.
    b. Stocks and bonds.
    c. Underwriting contracts.
    d. Reinsurance agreements.

9. Information regarding Standish Property Insurance Co is on page 398.

Standish Property Insurance Co.
Summary Balance Sheet Data at December 31, 1999
(in billions)

Assets

Investments	
Corporate bonds	$5.1
Equity securities	1.4
Money-market investments	0.3
Total investments	6.8
Premiums receivable	1.1
Other assets	1.0
Property and equipment, net	0.4
	$9.3

Liabilities and Shareholders' Equity

Unearned premiums	$2.3
Loss and loss adjustment expense reserves	2.7
Payables and other	0.6
Long-term debt	1.2
Total liabilities	6.8
Shareholders' equity	2.5
	$9.3

Income Statement Data
Year Ended December 31
(in billions)

	1998	1999
Revenues		
Premiums earned	$ 4.0	$ 4.8
Investment income	0.3	0.2
Other	0.2	0.2
Total revenues	4.5	5.2
Expenses		
Underwriting expenses		
Losses and loss adjustment expenses	2.9	3.2
Policy acquisition costs (marketing)	0.4	0.7
Other underwriting expenses	0.3	0.3
Total underwriting expenses	3.6	4.2
Service expenses	—	0.1
Interest expenses	0.1	0.1
Total expenses	3.7	4.4
Income before income taxes	0.8	0.8
Income taxes	0.3	0.3
Net income	$ 0.5	$ 0.5
Earnings per share	$5.00	$5.00

Analysis of Loss and LAE Development
For the Year Ended December 31
(in millions)

	1996	1997	1998	1999
Loss and LAE reserves	$1,580	$1,650	$2,000	$2,300
Reestimated reserves as of:				
One year later	1,390	1,500	1,850	
Two years later	1,340	1,490		
Three years later	1,330			
Four years later				
Cumulative redundancy	250	160	150	
Percentage of original estimated reserves	15.8%	9.7%	7.5%	

a. What does the unearned premium account signify? Why is it listed as a liability?

b. Why might Standish Property Insurance prefer bond investments rather than stocks?

c. Calculate the combined ratio in 1999.

d. What was the trend in the ratio of losses and loss adjustment expenses to premiums earned? List two reasons why the ratio might have changed.

e. Consider the trend evident in the Analysis of Loss and LAE Development. Does the company utilize aggressive or conservative loss assumptions?

f. If 1998's reestimated loss reserves were $2.2 billion in 1999 (instead of $1.85 billion), what would be the new percentage redundancy (or deficiency)?

g. For 1998 and 1999, calculate the following ratios: (1) EBIT to premiums earned; (2) investment income to premiums earned; and (3) premiums earned to net worth. Compare the trends in the ratios to those for the Progressive Corporation.

10. Two insurance companies seem similar in many ways. One has a history of redundancies in its Analysis of Loss and LAE Development, and the other has a history of deficiencies. Which stock would you prefer in your portfolio?

11. Assuming its actuaries cooperate, how can a property insurance company instantly increase net income:
   a. Reduce its LAE Development expense.
   b. Amortize policy acquisition expense faster.
   c. Lower loss reserves.
   d. Lower the assumed rate of return.

12. Why do life insurance companies purchase bonds with longer maturities than those purchased by P&C companies? Circle one answer.
    a. Life insurance losses are more predictable.
    b. Life companies have higher equity ratios.
    c. Life companies trade their portfolios less.
    d. None of the above.

13. Why should equity analysts examine the investment portfolios of insurance companies? Circle one answer.
    a. Investments represent most of the firms' assets.
    b. Expected rates of return are mostly overstated.
    c. Two large insurance company receiverships stemmed from bad investments.

14. Western National was a life insurance company, yet in 1996 investment income was 7 times the amount of insurance income. Explain how investments overshadowed the insurance business.

22

Highly Speculative Stocks

During hot stock markets, many speculative enterprises go public, despite dubious prospects and questionable histories. The rational evaluation of such investments is a significant challenge.

Probably everyone reading this book has received a cold call from a broker touting a "can't miss" stock. Typically, the broker is working at an obscure securities firm—a "bucket shop" in Street parlance—and is pushing the stock of an unknown company with no track record. The sales pitch lies in the "unlimited potential" of the offering and frequently coincides with a new technology, fad, or fashion. Being human, an investor sometimes lets greed and excitement cloud his better judgment, but over the long term it's better not to base decisions on hopes and dreams. Like the other equity categories profiled in this book, the valuation of highly speculative equities has a structure that lends method to the madness.

In this chapter, we cover the ways by which professionals value speculative growth stocks:

- *Discounted Cash Flow.* The analyst uses higher discount rates (25% to 30%) and fancier projections to set values.

- *Relative Value.* Without meaningful sales, cash flows or earnings statistics to compare, relative value techniques rely heavily on forecast performance.

- *Venture Capital Mark-Ups.* If venture capitalists paid $10 per share one year prior to the initial public offering, a $15 price to the public is a good starting point.

BACKGROUND

For the most part, companies with little or no historical track record of sales, cash flow, and earnings are unsuitable for the public market. The expected level of operating risk and price volatility is better handled by sophisticated private investors such as venture capitalists, mezzanine funds, and large corporations. From time to time, however, certain sectors of the public marketplace are gripped by an undue optimism, and these speculative enterprises receive a warm welcome. Such was the case with Internet stocks, for example, in 1998.

As the specific industry attracts more investor interest, initial public offerings of participating companies quickly enter the mainstream. No longer do regional firms and boutiques handle the underwritings. Instead, the deals go to the big-name firms such as Merrill Lynch and Goldman, Sachs, who invariably lend a high degree of credibility to their banking clientele. Furthermore, as valuations increase and transactions grow larger, sophisticated sponsors such as venture capitalists and Fortune 500 companies lay off the financial risk of their more speculative investments by foisting off a part of them to the public—usually at a price substantially in excess of the founders' cost.

For example, in October 1996, a small telecommunications company named Viatel sold $95 million in stock in its initial public offering. Introducing a new system of routing long-distance international calls through switches in the United States and England to take advantage of rate disparities, the young business was very shaky. In 1995, the business lost $28 million on $32 million in revenues. At the time of the IPO, estimated losses for 1996 were $39 million on revenues of just $51 million, and the company's burn rate indicated cash could run out in as little as six months' time, according to Irv DeGraw of *IPO Insider*, a newsletter. Nevertheless, Salomon Brothers, one of the Street's largest firms, acted as lead underwriter on the deal. Offering materials featured the prominent ownership positions of Comsat, the billion-dollar satellite conglomerate, and George Soros, the legendary hedge fund manager. Having bought in two years earlier at $3 per share, neither participated in the $12 per share new offering, which traded down to $8 within four months. Since so many investors are followers, the patina of respectability provided by the Soros name naturally attracted substantial institutional and individual interest.

A hot stock market is the best time to bring a large, speculative issue. Inevitably, the successful introduction of numerous quality stocks provides an umbrella shielding low quality shares from tough investor scrutiny. And, as mentioned in Chapter 3, IPO's carry commissions which are five to six times those of regular trades, so brokers have an extra incentive to push even the most dubious merchandise. They are thus reduced to "selling the sizzle, not the steak" and encourage clients to resort to wishful thinking. As the deals involve more esoteric businesses and technologies, the stockbroker is hard pressed to comprehend the issuer's business, and one becomes mindful of the old salesman's adage: "Don't tell me how it works, just give me something to sell!"

Inevitably, a certain percentage of these shaky investments are highly successful, and the investor makes 50x his initial commitment. Who doesn't want to get in on the ground floor of a company like Microsoft or Intel? But, the flip side of dicey IPO's is a short ride up, followed by a long ride down when the dreams go unrealized. Referring to investors in an upcoming offering of an untested business, Wolfgang Demisch, managing director of BT Securities, cautioned "They're pioneers, but pioneers get arrows in their backs."

Rather than discourage these investments totally, this chapter provides the reader with a rational framework for evaluating them. A businessman's risk can then be the basis for valuation, rather than a hyperbole spun by a smooth-talking salesman.

DISCOUNTED CASH FLOW

The DCF valuation for a nascent enterprise starts off with the same top-down procedure employed for a seasoned business. The analyst should understand the company's place in its industry and the economic indicators affecting the industry. The first significant departure in the process begins with the financial analysis. Since the subject firm has no established history, the analyst is heavily dependent on examining (1) management's pronouncements and (2) the early performance of other growth industries.

From this research, he cobbles together a future-looking financial model that makes sense, although certain assumptions require a leap of faith. In the typical case, the stock provides no cash dividends for the next three to five years because it incurs negative cash flow. At the end of five years, earnings are positive and it is presumed to sell at the same P/E multiple as an established growth vehicle, such as 20 times earnings. A discounted cash flow forecast for speculative stock uses the following equation:

	1999	2000	2001	2002	2003	2004

$$\frac{Stock}{Value} = \frac{0}{(1+k)^1} + \frac{0}{(1+k)^2} + \frac{0}{(1+k)^3} + \frac{0}{(1+k)^4} + \frac{0}{(1+k)^5} + \frac{P/E \times EPS}{(1+k)^5}$$

where P/E = Growth company P/E forecast for 2004
EPS = Subject company's earnings per share in 2004
k = Estimated discount rate

Setting up the financial projections is similar to the laborious procedure outlined earlier in this book, but the many guesstimates that the analyst attaches to fundamental items, such as sales, cost of goods sold, advertising, and research and development, lowers the already scant threshold of forecast believability. Compensating for the greater doubt of a new business, the analyst increases the discount factor, k, far above the numbers used for seasoned growth companies. If blue chip firms require a 15 percent k, the practitioner uses 30 percent for an untested operation.

The choice of k depends on the perception of risk. Certain growth stories have less inherent risk than others. For example, a low-tech newcomer to a mature industry is seen as having less risk than a hi-tech entrant in a pioneer industry. The latter is still working on its technology and proposes to offer a product whose consumer acceptance is questionable. Thus, at the time of this writing, Shells Seafood Restaurant, a start-up dining chain, appears safer than Triangle Pharmaceuticals, a developmental drug company. Neither company has much in the way of sales or earnings, but the restaurant concept has a higher comfort level given Shells approach.

To illustrate the means by which professionals place a value on such stocks, the next section includes case studies of two speculative investments. The first case, United States Satellite Broadcasting Company, Inc., fits the hot IPO model (see Exhibit 22–1). The second, Celgene, is an unpredictable biotech firm with a long trading history.

UNITED STATES SATELLITE BROADCASTING

Case Study: United States Satellite Broadcasting, Inc.   At the time of its 1996 IPO, United States Satellite Broadcasting, Inc. ("USSB" or the "Company"), had 18 months of commercial operations and $153 million of accrued losses. Security analysts, including those at the lead underwriters, forecasted two years of additional losses, yet the Company sold $200 million worth of common stock at $27 per share. At this price, the market placed a

EXHIBIT 22–1. Elements of Speculative Stocks That Gain Broad Acceptance

The issuer has little or no track record.

The issuer is unprofitable, with negative cash flow.

The offering appears during an optimistic stock market.

The issue is an initial public offering, so a broker's commissions are multiplied.

The company participates in a hot industry receiving lots of business media coverage.

The underwriting is handled by a big-name firm such as Merrill Lynch or Goldman Sachs.

The company is backed by high-octane investors, such as well-known Wall Streeters (e.g., George Soros), venture capitalists (e.g., Kleiner Perkins), or corporations (e.g., Walt Disney). The original investors, however, do *not* augment their existing ownership by buying more shares at the IPO price.

$2.5 billion value on a business barely out of the start-up phase. Insiders, in fact, had paid only $2.10 per share to capitalize the Company, so they reaped huge paper profits.

How did a rational analyst justify USSB's initial public offering?

Before proceeding to the discounted cash flow (DCF) analysis, it is necessary to review the key positive factors that prompted institutional investors to purchase USSB shares:

- *Hot Sector.* In 1996, Wall Street was infatuated with the entertainment industry. Movie, TV, and radio stocks reached new highs. USSB was unique in two ways: (1) it was one of only three providers of subscription television programming via direct broadcast satellite (DBS); and (2) of the three DBS participants, only USSB's signal covered the entire U.S. market.

- *High Technology.* Besides being an entertainment stock, USSB was a hi-tech play. Recent advances in digital compression and satellite technology were the linchpin of its operations. In 1996, Wall Street was in love with hi-tech stocks, and the resultant buying spree provided most of the increases in the broad indexes.

- *Better Mousetrap.* The new DBS technology offered consumers better reception, digital programming, and more channels, all at the same monthly price as cable TV (although this price was *after* the consumer installed an 18-inch reception dish). The Company's subscriber count was 600,000 and growing, but breakeven was far away.

- *Prominent Backers.* The principal USSB shareholder was the Hubbard family, which had been successful in TV and radio broadcasting. Other "Tiffany" investors included George Soros, Paul Allen (co-founder of Microsoft), and Dow Jones & Company. The founders bought in at $2.10 per share. Was their success going to rub off on the new shareholders? Apparently, investors believed so, because they bought the IPO at a lofty $27 per share.

- *Prestigious Underwriters.* Companies are known by their associations. The key underwriters were CS First Boston and Goldman Sachs, two of Wall Street's toniest firms. According to some practitioners, the better investment banks uphold their reputations by rejecting questionable financings. Presumably, this belief reinforced investors' notions that USSB was a better-than-average speculative deal.

USSB's stock had attractive aspects, but it involved the following substantial risks, which the company and its bankers successfully underplayed:

- *Uncertain Demand.* USSB's short history did not provide a sufficient basis for extrapolating a demand curve. Analysts looked at the product as a potential substitute for cable TV, and they compared the household penetration results of prior technologies such as color TV, VCR, and compact disc. The forecast subscriber base then had to be divided among USSB, Direct TV (its closest rival), and future DBS competitors.

- *Customer Acquisition Costs.* Besides the likely number of customers, the big question for the USSB investor was: How much will it cost to acquire (and retain) the average customer? Other media industries—magazine publishing, cable TV, and mail order—had customer acquisition histories, but not DBS. The 18 months of USSB operations provided a guide, but future profitability was dependent on marketing costs declining for each new customer. This assumption only made sense if consumer acceptance widened and word-of-mouth increased substantially.

FINANCIAL PROJECTIONS

Given this backdrop of positives and negatives, it is helpful to look straight-away at a composite USSB projection prepared by prominent sell-side analysts. The report follows the five steps outlined in Chapter 11:

1. *Potential Market.* Assess a global demand for the new product over the long term.
2. *Subject Company's Market Share.* Determine a likely market share for the subject company, once its new product achieves acceptance. Express share in terms of unit volume.
3. *Revenue.* Attach revenue estimates to the predicted unit sales (e.g., one customer month of DBS equals $25 of revenue).
4. *Income Statement.* Prepare income statements by offsetting revenue projections with sensible expense estimates. Working capital and financing needs are then derived from forecast balance sheet and cash flow data.
5. *Earnings per Share, EBITDA, and EBIT.* These calculations become part of the projected income statement.

Exhibit 22–2 shows the projection of the DBS and digital satellite system (DSS) markets. (DSS is a submarket of DBS and offers a digital signal with better picture resolution than DBS). Studying the increasing demand for the nascent industry and the introductions of prior entertainment technology, these analysts (and several other observers) concluded that DBS had a realistic chance of being in 14 percent of U.S. homes by the year 2000. This assumption was dicey, since it suggested that penetration could zoom from zero to 14 million homes in five short years. Of these new DBS households, 45 percent would subscribe to the high-quality DSS service.

Once the market for the new service was established, the next step was fixing a USSB share. Unlike many new industries, DSS only had two

EXHIBIT 22–2. Projecting the DSS Market (in millions)

	Actual	Estimated	Projected			
	1995	**1996**	**1997**	**1998**	**1999**	**2000**
U.S. television households[1]	95.9	97.2	98.6	100.0	101.4	102.8
Growth rate	1%	1%	1%	1%	1%	1%
Beginning DBS subscribers	0.1	1.2	2.9	5.4	8.5	11.2
New DBS subscribers	1.1	1.7	2.5	3.1	2.7	3.2
Ending DBS subscribers	1.2	2.9	5.4	8.5	11.2	14.4
Growth rate[2]	—	145%	86%	57%	31%	29%
Year-end penetration	1%	3%	6%	9%	11%	14%
Year-end DSS subscribers[3]	0.6	1.6	2.8	4.2	5.3	6.5
Growth rate	—	150%	78%	49%	25%	22%
DSS market share of DBS	54%	55%	53%	50%	48%	45%

[1] Any house with a TV is a potential customer.
[2] The aggressive growth is pushed by optimistic penetration levels.
[3] DSS is a submarket of DBS.

competitors in 1996 and many customers subscribed to one or more providers. As a result, analysts felt comfortable in increasing the Company's share of DSS customers from 50 percent in 1995 to 60 percent in 2000. As Exhibit 22–3 indicates, a growing market, combined with an increasing share, made USSB's customer count quadruple (to 3.9 million) by the year 2000. Average revenue per customer month started at $26.38 in 1995, but declined to $21.50 in 2000, as competition intensified in later

EXHIBIT 22–3. USSB Market Share and Revenue

	Actual	Estimated	Projected			
	1995	**1996**	**1997**	**1998**	**1999**	**2000**
Market Share						
DSS Subscribers (MM)	0.6	1.6	2.8	4.2	5.3	6.5
USSB Share	50%	56%	57%	58%	59%	60%
Year-end USSB Subs. (MM)	0.3	0.9	1.6	2.5	3.1	3.9
Growth Rate	—	350%	90%	60%	35%	25%
Revenue/Subscriber/Month	$26.40	$25.00	$23.50	$22.50	$22.00	$21.50
Annual Revenue (MM)	$42	$183	$356	$552	$738	$904
USSB Revenue Growth	—	330%	94%	55%	34%	23%

Note. The optimistic increases in customers and revenues are characteristic of speculative company projections.

years. Nevertheless, projected revenues grew 85 percent annually, resulting in assumed annual revenue of $904 million by 2000.

With revenue estimates in hand, analysts applied expense ratios. Cost of sales were totally variable. The largest expense, TV programming, was billed on a per customer basis, with discounts kicking in at prescribed subscriber volumes. Cost of sales thus began at 65 percent in 1996, and declined rapidly to 55 percent by 2000 as the customer count increased. Selling, general, and administrative expenses were harder to forecast. A high proportion of SG&A was attributable to the heavy advertising needed to attract customers to the new service. In 1996, these costs were running at $165 per new customer, although heightened consumer knowledge was expected to reduce this number to $100 by 2000. Exhibit 22–4 shows projected income statement data.

EXHIBIT 22–4. United States Satellite Broadcasting—Company Projected Income Statement Data (in millions except for percentages and per share data)

	Actual	Estimated	Projected			
	1995	1996	1997	1998	1999	2000
Percentages						
Revenue	100%	100%	100%	100%	100%	100%
Cost of sales	66	65	64	61	58	55
SG&A expense	137	68	43	30	25	20
EBITDA	(103)	(33)	(7)	9	17	25
Net income	(196)	(49)	(10)	8	17	20
Income Statement Data						
Revenue	$ 42	$ 183	$ 356	$ 552	$ 738	$ 904
Cost of sales	28	119	228	337	428	497
Gross margin	14	64	128	215	310	407
SG&A expense	58	125	153	166	184	181
EBITDA	(44)	(61)	(25)	50	125	226
Deprec. and amort.	23	22	22	17	15	13
EBIT	(67)	(83)	(47)	33	110	213
Interest income (expense)	(7)	(7)	11	12	16	27
Pre-tax income	(74)	(90)	(36)	45	126	240
Income taxes	—	—	—	—	—	60
Net income	$ (74)	$ (90)	$ (36)	$ 45	$ 126	$ 180
Shares outstanding	90	90	90	90	90	90
Earnings per share	$(0.82)	$(1.00)	$(0.40)	$0.50	$1.40	$2.00
Dividends per share	—	—	—	—	—	—

Note. Observe how sales and margins rapidly increase in the speculative company projection. The result is exponential EPS growth.

As Exhibit 22–4 illustrates, the Company was scheduled to go into the black by 1998, and deficits prior to that time would be covered by the $200 million of IPO proceeds. Steady-state growth was projected after 2000, and the research reports further assumed that an investor could sell his USSB stock in 1999 for 25× forward earnings, or $50 per share (i.e., 25 × $2.00 EPS = $50). Using a discount rate equal to the expected market return (government bond rate plus historical market premium) of 13 percent, one obtained a USSB present value of $34 per share:

$$\text{USSB Share Value} = \frac{D_1}{(1+k)} + \frac{D_2}{(1+k)^2} + \frac{D_3 + \text{Sales Price}}{(1+k)^3}$$

$$\text{USSB Share Value} = \frac{0}{1.13} + \frac{0}{1.28} + \frac{0 + \$50}{1.44}$$

$$\text{USSB Share Value} = \$34$$

where D = Cash dividend
$\quad\quad k$ = USSB's discount rate, which equaled the 13% market return.
$\quad\ \$50$ = Sales price in 1999.

Since the $34 DCF valuation exceeded the $27 IPO price, the typical analyst labeled USSB a buy. To support the recommendation, he supplied certain comparative industry valuation multiples, such as value/subscribers and value/revenues, which showed USSB to be reasonably priced compared with cable TV firms. At the cable TV industry benchmark of $1,900 per customer, for example, USSB's enterprise value in 2000 was $7.1 billion, about $78 per share (net of debt).

ALTERNATIVE CONCLUSION FOR USSB STOCK

Although these reports followed my step-by-step projection technique to the letter, this work demonstrated the irrational exuberance that sneaks into sell-side research, particularly when the practitioner's firm provides investment banking services to the company. I had the benefit of 20–20 hindsight at the time of this book's writing, but the reports contained a few obvious flaws among their positive attributes. Several items raise commonsense objections:

- *Market Share.* The researchers assumed a 60 percent market share for USSB, which was overly aggressive. Admittedly, many customers subscribed to both of the existing DSS channels, but MCI, the communications giant, had spent $700 million in 1996 for the rights to position a new DSS satellite. In light of the prospective competition, a 50 percent share by 2000 was a more reasonable assumption.

- *Terminal Multiple.* Even though seasoned growth stocks traded at 25× earnings in 1996's heated market, a better historical marker is a 20 P/E. The terminal value calculation should have used the lower multiple.
- *Discount Rate.* Including the 13 percent expected market return was an obvious mistake. USSB's business had many uncertainties and the stock was far more risky than buying a broad index. As noted in Chapter 12, a 20 to 25 percent return is appropriate for such speculative investments.

Modifying the assumptions on market share, terminal multiple, and discount rate produced a sharp decline in USSB's present value. As shown in Exhibit 22–5, these changes produced a share value of $17, versus the $34 conclusion. By February 1997, some months after the reports' publication, the stock price had collapsed, falling from $30 to $10 per share. A slower customer acceptance rate shaved Wall Street's earnings projections, and several analysts dropped the terminal multiple to 20× and bumped the discount rate to 15 percent. Even though the average stock price rose 20 percent over this time span, the sell-side analysts who derived the $34 value were not penalized for this disastrous recommendation. In true Wall Street fashion, they were gainfully employed at press time.

The lack of attention paid to realistic market studies is a key flaw in satellite-related issues, resulting in frequent overvaluations. According to one participant in satellite deals, "It's the stiff neck syndrome. Everybody's enamored with the in-the-sky technology. They don't focus on how the firms get on-the-ground customers!"

EXHIBIT 22–5. Modifying the USSB DCF Analysis (as of March 1996)

Assumptions	Original Projection Irrational Exuberance	Modified Data Common Sense
Market share	60%	50%
Terminal multiple[1]	25×	20×
Discount rate	13%	20%
Present value calculation	$34	$17
Margin of safety	26%	15%
Actual market price	$27	$27
Recommendation	Buy	Sell

[1] Terminal EPS equaled $2.00 under irrational exuberance and $1.50 under common sense.

CELGENE CORPORATION

Case Study: Discounted Cash Flow—Celgene Corporation. Celgene develops small molecule drugs to treat disease, and produces chiral intermediates, the building blocks of advanced drugs. The company was spun off from Hoechst Celanese Corporation in 1986, and went public in 1987. Laboratories and executive offices are in Warren, New Jersey. The company employs 45 people. Summary results appear as Exhibit 22–6.

Like many public biotech firms in 1997, Celgene had few revenues from the sale of proprietary products and a string of operating losses. Its $110 million market value was based totally on potential, since the Food and Drug Administration (FDA) had not approved the sale of most Celgene products.

In constructing a financial model for Celgene, the analyst has to remember that sales and earnings projections for drugs in development are highly uncertain. Factors to consider include: shifting demand criteria, the entry of competing products, dependence on the results of clinical trials in progress, the availability of research contracts for internal funding of operations, and a fair assessment of monthly expenses to measure the burn rate.

Celgene's valuation was heavily tied to the prospects for Synovir, a drug designed to relieve AIDS-related cachexia (i.e., diarrhea-induced

EXHIBIT 22–6. Celgene Corporation[1]—Summary of Financial and Market Data (in millions except per share data)

	Year Ended December 31		
	1995	**1996**	**1996**
Income Statement			
Revenues	$ 2.3	$ 1.2	$ 2.5
Research and development	6.5	8.2	16.3
Other expenses	4.2	4.1	5.0
Net loss	(7.9)	(10.5)	(17.8)
Net loss per share	(1.00)	(1.30)	(2.29)
Balance Sheet	At December 31, 1996		
Cash	$17.9		
Total assets	20.9		
Total debt	2.0		
Accumulated deficit	(92.6)		
Net stockholder's equity	16.1		
Market Data	At March 1, 1997		
Share price	$ 7.00		
Shares outstanding[2]	10.6		
Total market value	$74		

[1] Celgene develops small molecule drugs.

[2] Before conversion of preferred stock and options.

weight loss). Early trials showed promise, but the FDA process for drug approval was daunting. Total time to commercialization for the average new drug was 10 years, and cost over $100 million, with only 20 percent of new drug applications receiving approval. Synovir had two advantages: (1) it had several years of documentation on patient safety; and (2) AIDS drugs received highly expedited reviews because of the fatal nature of the disease. Nevertheless, FDA approval and subsequent commercial success of the drug were highly speculative.

In such cases, the analyst begins by assuming FDA approval, estimating the time to commercial production, and then forecasting global demand in a top-down manner, similar to the methodology used in the USSB example. As revenues grow, expenses decline on a relative basis, and by the end of the five- to seven-year forecast period, the company's sales to expense ratios resemble those of a seasoned drug manufacturer. At this point, the analyst assigns a terminal P/E multiple to the final year's earnings per share, and discounts the resulting price to the present.

Besides figuring the probability of FDA approval, the real trick in biotech stocks is the timing related to FDA approvals, commercial ramp-ups, and competitive introductions. Since the subject business is usually losing money quarter after quarter, a quick resolution of these matters saves tens of millions of dollars and avoids painfully dilutive follow-up financings. Anticipating a late 1997 approval for Celgene's Synovir (for AIDS cachexia) suggested a meaningful sales stream beginning in 1998. However, even the most dedicated FDA watcher knew there was much uncertainty attached to this prediction.

CELGENE SALES FORECAST

A good system for modeling the finances of a speculative biotech enterprise is outlined by Scott Weisman in the book, *Financial Valuation* (James Zukin, Ed., Financial Valuation: Businesses and Business Interests, Warren, Gorham & Lamont, Boston, MA., 1997). Weisman's approach is appropriate for biotech firms with multiple products as well as the one-product business. The six steps of his model are summarized in Exhibit 22–7 as well as in the following text.

POTENTIAL MARKET SIZES

Theoretical market sizes of proposed drugs are calculated as the product of the total number of patients, the estimated price per course of therapy, and the number of courses of therapy per patient per year. Patient numbers are determined from disease incidence data, generally available in standard medical references. Cost of therapy is derived from comparable drugs on the market. For breakthrough medicines, pharmaeconomic studies can be used to establish potential cost savings and reasonable market prices. When license agreements are in place or expected, a royalty rate is assumed.

EXHIBIT 22–7. Speculative Biotech Companies—Six Steps of the Discounted Cash Flow Model

1. *Potential Market Sizes.* The revenue potential for each product line is calculated by multiplying patients × therapy cost × therapies per year.
2. *Market Penetration.* Assess the company's market share in each potential product by examining probable competitive position.
3. *Probability of Market Entry.* The progress of the potential drugs through the testing and FDA pipeline assists the analyst in assigning FDA approval probabilities. Once FDA approval is achieved, the firm can start selling product.
4. *After-Tax Profit Margins.* Steady-state, after-tax margins of 20 percent are common among pharmaceutical companies. The resultant earnings forecast can be used in calculating the terminal value.
5. *Terminal Value.* Look at seasoned company multiples of sales/EBIT and P/E, as well as short-hand sales multiples. The terminal value is then discounted to the present.
6. *Discount Rate.* A 25 percent to 40 percent discount rate is appropriate for these risky stocks.

Celgene's Case. As indicated in Celgene's projection (Exhibit 22–8), the United States is expecting 200,000 AIDS patients by 1998, of whom 36 percent will have cachexia. Assuming that 22 percent of these individuals continue with Synovir, related revenues should total $41 million. Current drugs to fight cachexia cost $8,000 per year, so the projection's $3,500 per year Synovir cost seems reasonable.

EXHIBIT 22–8. Celgene Corporation—Projected Revenue from Synovir

	1998	1999	2000
Total AIDS population	200,000	180,000	160,000
Percent males	84	82	82
Male AIDS population	168,000	148,000	130,000
Percent cachexia	36	36	36
Potential Synovir customers	61,000	53,000	47,000
Percent use Synovir (or competition)	25	30	35
Total users	15,000	16,000	17,000
Percent Celgene (Synovir) customers	90	85	80
Synovir population	13,500	13,500	13,600
Price per year—Synovir	$3,500	$3,600	$3,700
Revenues	$47 mil.	$49 mil.	$50 mil.
Probability of approval	× 0.75	× 0.75	× 0.75
Probability-adjusted revenues	$35 mil.	$37 mil.	$38 mil.

MARKET PENETRATION

Market share is estimated from an assessment of the firm's competitive position, including product differentiation and advantages, competing products in development, patent strength, and corporate alliances. Different market shares can be tested in a valuation model by including a sensitivity analysis for optimistic, pessimistic, and expected scenarios.

> *Celgene's Case.* Because no competitors have an equivalent drug, Celgene maintains a near monopoly position over the projected period (i.e., 80% to 100% share).

PROBABILITY OF MARKET ENTRY

The likelihood of any given drug candidate making it to the market and generating revenues is a function of its stage of development. Products in the later stages of clinical trials (i.e., they've already been tested successfully in large numbers of patients) have a much greater chance of making it to the market than drug candidates that have not yet completed animal studies.

The highly regulated drug development and approval process provides a useful set of objective milestones for monitoring a drug's progress and for assigning incremental value. The stages of drug development are preclinical testing; Phases I, II, and III clinical testing; and filing of a New Drug Application (NDA) or Product License Application (PLA). These milestones also provide benchmarks for attaching probabilities to the successful commercialization of a drug candidate depending on its stage of development. By multiplying the estimated market share numbers by these probabilities, one calculates a probability-adjusted market size. These probabilities are approximated as follows:

Development	*Probability*
Preclinical testing to market	$P = 0.10$
Phase I to market	$P = 0.20$
Phase II to market	$P = 0.30$
Phase III to market	$P = 0.60$
NDA or PLA to market	$P = 0.75$

> *Celgene's Case.* As an AIDS drug, Synovir enjoyed expedited review procedures. Celgene targeted an early 1997 NDA filing for Synovir, and analysts predicted nine more months for FDA approval.

AFTER-TAX MARGINS

After-tax operating margins of 20 percent, comparable to those of the major pharmaceutical companies, can be assumed on sales of drugs.

Celgene's Case. A slightly higher margin is appropriate, given the Company's monopoly position.

TERMINAL VALUE

Once commercial sales have been established, the analyst forecasts terminal value as a multiple of revenues, after-tax earnings, earnings before interest and taxes (EBIT), cash flows, or EPS. P/E multiples of 16 to 20 are typical for large firms in the pharmaceutical industry.

Celgene's Case. A small growing firm such as Celgene merits a 25 P/E in 2000, if Synovir pans out.

DISCOUNT RATE

Identifying a discount rate in a quasi-scientific manner is difficult, because the Capital Asset Pricing Model $[k = R_f + B (R_m - R_f)]$ offers little guidance for a speculative business. Venture capital discount rates of 25 to 40 percent per annum are realistic for these stocks.

EXHIBIT 22–9. Celgene Corporation—Projected Income Statement (in millions except per share data)

	1998	1999	2000
Synovir revenues	$35.0	$37.0	$38.0
Other revenues	5.0	11.0	17.0
	40.0	48.0	55.0
Cost of Synovir	7.0	7.0	8.0
Research and development	20.0	21.0	22.0
Other operating expenses	4.0	8.0	12.0
Operating income	9.0	12.0	13.0
Interest income	1.0	1.0	1.0
Pretax income	10.0	13.0	14.0
Income taxes[1]	—	—	—
Net income	$10.0	$13.0	$14.0
Earnings per share	$0.74	$0.93	$0.97
Earnings per share normalized for income taxes	—	—	$0.58
Shares outstanding[2]	13.5	14.0	14.5

[1] Celgene's tax loss carryforwards cover tax liabilities through 2003.
[2] Assumes conversions.

Celgene's Case. Celgene is not a complete start-up and its primary product has a good chance of FDA approval in the near term. A 30 percent discount rate is justifiable.

Including Synovir revenues from Exhibit 22–8 with prospective expenses in the selling, general, and administrative (including research and development) category produces a projected income statement. This Exhibit 22–9, also includes non-Synovir revenues from chiral products and royalty payments. Earnings per share are forecast at $0.97 in 2000, and include the dilutive effects of a projected one-million-share offering in 1998.

VALUATION CONCLUSIONS

Valuation Conclusion 1: Completing Celgene's DCF Valuation

With no cash dividends forecasted, I generated the present value of Celgene stock by (1) taking a 25× multiple for earnings per share in the year 2000, and (2) discounting the resultant terminal price back to 1997 at a 30 percent rate. I normalized 2000 EPS by applying a theoretical 40 percent tax rate. The company had $70 million in tax loss carryforwards in 1997, but these would be extinguished by 2003, leaving the firm as a taxpayer thereafter. Curiously, none of the three professional research reports I consulted included this important adjustment.

$$\text{Celgene Share Value} = \frac{D_1}{(1+k)} + \frac{D_2}{(1+k)^2} + \frac{D_3 + \text{Sales Price}}{(1+k)^3}$$

$$\text{Celgene Share Value} = \frac{0}{(1+.30)} + \frac{0}{(1+.30)^2} + \frac{0 + \$14.50}{(1+.30)^3}$$

$$\text{Celgene Share Value} = \$6.60$$

where
$$D = \text{Cash dividend}$$
$$k = \text{Celgene's discount rate of 30\%}$$
$$\text{EPS in 2000} = \$0.97 \times (1 - \text{tax rate}) = \$0.58$$
$$\text{Sale Price} = \$0.58 \times 25 \text{ P/E} = \$14.50$$

The $6.60 present value per share was only 57 percent of the market price at March 1, 1997. Accordingly, the stock was overvalued. In my experience, DCF analysis provides similar conclusions for most speculative biotech (and hi-tech) growth stocks. Sensible people have a hard time justifying the superoptimistic assumptions needed to match DCF values and market prices. As a result, analytically inclined investors who participate in the biotech industry tend to deemphasize their stockpicking tendencies in favor of a portfolio approach. They purchase shares of ten companies, hoping that one or two big winners provide enough gains to offset the eight or nine losers. Other analysts throw away the financial models and take a "visionary approach," although there is no evidence to suggest this method is more effective.

Valuation Conclusion 2: Venture Capital Markups

In selling a speculative stock, brokers like to trumpet the presence of sophisticated investors in the company's ownership base. Well-known venture capital firms (and Fortune 500 companies) bring needed credibility to an untested firm. What brokers inevitably fail to highlight is what the big-name insiders paid for their shares, versus what the initial public offering price is. In 99 cases out of 100, the insider cost is less than the IPO price. Unless a substantial amount of time has elapsed between the founders' buy-in and the IPO, the analyst should consider the latest insider cost as one guide to valuation.

As Chapter 3 noted, institutional investors who invest in private placements have substantial advantages in the evaluation process as compared to public market investors. First, they have greater access to management, and ask many detailed questions. Second, they peruse corporate books and records that are unavailable to the public, including business plans and financial projections. Finally, their time horizon for a decision is longer, typically extending for several months; and, thus, their analysis is conducted in a methodical fashion, rather than in the hurried manner that accompanies the institutional consideration of an IPO. It follows that the venture capitalist has a good handle on a company's prospects when he commits to an investment. If the transaction occurred within 24 months of the public offering and nothing special affected the firm's business, the founder's price can be used as a jumping-off point for a public valuation.

The venture capital markup procedure covers four elements, none of which is scientifically determined: (1) timing; (2) rate of return; (3) illiquidity discount; and (4) the implicit assumption that venture capital firms are reasonably competent. As an illustration, suppose a venture capitalist paid $2 for his Hitech shares in June 1998 and you're analyzing the company's IPO in June 2000, two years later. Absent a huge change in the business, $11.43 per share is one reference point for the stock price. The valuation procedure is set forth in Exhibit 22–10.

Exhibit 22–11 reviews three initial public offerings of speculative companies. The VC markup value is compared with the IPO price.

Valuation Conclusion 3: Ratio of Current Market Value to Future Sales

Early-stage biotech companies lack the historical benchmarks such as sales, EBITDA, and net earnings that lend themselves to relative valuation

EXHIBIT 22–10. Hitech Corp.—Three Steps of Venture Capital Markup Procedure

1. *Establish Timing.* The venture capital (VC) investment was outstanding for two years. The VC firm paid $2 per share.
2. *Consider VC Rate of Return.* Venture capitalists attempt to achieve compound annual rates of return of 40 percent to 50 percent. Since Hitech Corp. has met its business plan targets (otherwise it wouldn't be going public), it is above average, so the public buyer can permit a 100 percent annual return to the VC firm. Thus, the "fair value" over a two-year period jumps from $2 per share to $8 per share.
3. *Illiquidity Discount.* There is value in the ability to sell a common stock in a liquid marketplace. A minority position in a publicly held business thus has more worth than a similar ownership stake in a privately traded firm. A reasonable private market discount is 30 percent off the public market value. In the case of Hitech Corp., the $8 per share value inflates to $11.43 [i.e., $8 ÷ (1 − discount)], thus providing one guidepost for the initial public offering price.

EXHIBIT 22–11. Speculative IPOs Using the Venture Capital Markup Method

	Puma Technology	Triangle Pharmaceuticals	Coulter Pharmaceutical
Business[1]	Mobile data exchange software	Research for potential new AIDS drug	Novel drugs for cancer treatment
Date of offering	December 96	November 96	January 97
Size of offering	$37 million	$42 million	$30 million
IPO price per share (A)	$9.50	$10.00	$12.00
Implied value of company	$110 million	$170 million	$120 million
Prior venture capital investment	December 94	June 96	April 96
VC price per share (B)	$1.50	$5.40	$6.75
IPO price/VC price ratio (A ÷ B)	6.3/1.0	1.9/1.0	1.8/1.0
Public price according to VC markup formula (C)	$8.60	$10.90	$16.10
IPO price/formula price[2] (A ÷ C)	110%	92%	75%

[1] All of the companies had operating losses and minimal revenues. Each underwriting was managed by a leading investment banking firm.
[2] Note how the formula prices are close to the IPO prices.

EXHIBIT 22–12. Market Value-to-Sales Ratios at March 1997

Company	Market Capitalization (in billions)	Annual Sales (in billions)	Market Cap to 1996 Sales
Amgen	$16.0	$2.0	8.0×
Biogen	2.3	0.2	11.5
Genzyme	2.0	0.4	5.0
Average multiple (which is used to value other biotech shares)			8.2

techniques. To compensate, practitioners divide current market values by future results, and compare the ratios. For each firm in a comparable group, the analyst computes future sales five years out. The projected sales are then multiplied by a group capitalization-to-sales ratio, such as the 8.2× ratio in Exhibit 22–12. The future market value is then discounted to the present at a 25 percent rate. If the resultant share value is low relative to the market price, the issue is considered a good buy.

Exhibit 22–12 provides market-cap ratios for three firms. The data indicate that Genzyme is an attractive investment relative to the other two companies because its 5.0 ratio is lower. Applying this technique to future results stretches credulity, but practitioners use it as a double-check for the DCF approach.

SUMMARY

Brokers tout the terrific future of speculative stocks, but the underlying companies have trouble generating sales and earnings in the present. These shares are better left to highly sophisticated investors who specialize in private placements, but from time to time the broad public market lays out the welcome mat to such offerings. The discounted cash flow method—with all its flaws—is the most appropriate vehicle for valuing a speculative stock. A popular double-check to the DCF approach is the VC markup technique. Lacking the financial markers of sales and earnings, speculative businesses are poor candidates for the relative valuation method. Practitioners, nevertheless, gauge fair pricing by comparing the ratio of current equity value to sales.

APPENDIX: HIGHLY SPECULATIVE STOCKS

The most remarkable phenomenon of recent years has been the meteoric rise in the popularity of Internet stocks. Occupying an obscure niche of the technology group when this book was written in 1996 and 1997, Internet shares took a commanding position in U.S. markets in 1998 and 1999. Mutual fund executives, on-line day traders, hedge fund managers, brokerage firms and media outlets jumped on the most highly touted investment bandwagon of modern times.

HISTORICAL PERSPECTIVE

The stock market's repeated infatuation with technology is nothing new, but it has led to mixed results for investors despite the eventual success of the scientific breakthroughs. In the late 1880s, railroad stocks were the rage and financiers furnished millions to crisscross the United States with thousands of miles of railroads, many of which failed to generate enough traffic to repay their backers. In the 1920s, radio stocks were hot, but the underlying technology didn't provide major corporate profits for another 20 years. The early 1980s produced the personal computer craze, and the related IPOs obtained 50 to 100 P/E multiples, yet only a handful of them survived into the 1990s. Biotech stocks were fashionable in 1991 and 1992, and they raised billions with no history of sales or profits. Few of the stocks exceeded their IPO prices in later years.

The booms were followed by busts, and many share prices collapsed. Inevitably, a handful of the stocks left standing yielded exceptional returns, but the overall impression was that fads demonstrated the need for careful study and selection of technology stocks.

INTERNET COMPANY VALUATIONS

Only a few years old, the Internet and its applications have made a significant impact on America. The ultimate influence on daily life and commerce is not well understood, but the new medium appears likely to have an impact rivaling the changes brought by the telephone, radio, and television. This potential for future use has not translated into meaningful sales and profits for most Web firms, and Exhibit A1 shows only three of the top 10 Internet companies (ranked by market value) made a profit in 1998.

The huge market values assigned to these money-losing companies, and the accompanying scramble by investors to buy into the stocks, has outstripped any previous Wall Street mania in terms of scale and breadth. The magnitude of the excess has reflected not only the acute optimism surrounding the Web, but also a market environment that de-emphasizes security analysis in favor of less scientific methods (see Exhibit 2.1 in Chapter 2). Magnifying these effects has been the rapid rise of individual day traders, who number in the tens of thousands and exhibit a marked preference for Internet stocks. Their lack of interest in security analysis was summarized by Mayer

EXHIBIT A1.   1998 Sales and Net Income of Top 10 Internet Companies

	June 1999 Market Value (in billions)	1998	
		Sales (in millions)	Net Income (in millions)
America Online	$114	$2,606	$ 92
Yahoo	29	203	25
eBay	18	47	2
Amazon.com	18	610	(124)
Priceline.com	13	35	(112)
@Home	6	48	(144)
E*Trade	6	245	(1)
CMGI	5	70	(22)
Ameritrade	4	164	—
Lycos	4	56	(96)

Offman, an executive at New York's Carlin Financial Group, "This is complete momentum style investing for day traders; valuation is meaningless."

Other technology-based run-ups have been fueled by money-losing firms, but the Internet craze developed the most pronounced disconnect between corporate financial results and equity valuation. To rationalize this phenomenon, many Web investors echo this mantra: Internet stocks are different than other stocks and conventional value rules (as set forth in this book) do not apply. How else could one appraise iVillage.com—a two-year-old company with $43 million in losses, $15 million in sales, and 48 employees—at $1.8 billion? Any attempt at a discounted cash flow valuation (explained in Chapters 5 to 12) for such a stock was futile, according to many Web investors, because the assumptions in the model would be too optimistic. Lisa Buyer, CS First Boston's Internet analyst, admitted, "I can't make the math correlate with the stock prices." Normal relative value measurements such as P/E and EV/EBIT (explained in Chapter 13) were also irrelevant because the firms had no "E" or "EBIT." Non-earnings based financial ratios like EV/Sales produced such high multiples that Internet stocks appeared totally overvalued in comparison to other growth industries (see Exhibit A2).

To remain active, a large number of investors threw up their hands at logically pricing Internet shares, and simply bought the firms they sensed were going to be winners. The absence of numerically derived justifications was explained by Alec Ellison of the Broadview investment banking firm, when he reviewed the iVillage IPO, "iVillage is a lesson that the (Internet) companies with the highest profile in the media earn the highest valuations. In the absence of any rational metric with which to value a company, investors are betting on the future, and that means image and brand."

EXHIBIT A2.   Growth Industries,
Enterprise Value to Sales Ratios

Internet	20 to 100x
Pharmaceutical	4 to 6x
Cable Television	4 to 5x
Telecommunications	2 to 3x

Note: On an EV/sales basis, Internet stocks
traded far higher than other growth industries.
Relative value indicates a potential overvalua-
tion for the Internet sector, even after accounting for the latter's early stage of development.

SECURITY ANALYSIS AND INTERNET STOCKS

Despite the insistence of many Web shareholders that security analysis is
irrelevant, the fact remains that a substantial minority of Internet investors
use discounted cash flow and relative value methods to establish pricing
benchmarks. The DCF evaluation process is identical to the methodology
outlined in this book, with carefully constructed projections and very high
discount rates, such as 35%, to reflect the risk of unproven enterprises. "The
challenge for analytically-inclined investors," says Andy Klingenstein,
principal at Fairfax Partners, a Northern Virginia-based merchant bank, "is
to study the underlying business plans carefully, narrow your focus, and
make an educated judgment about future profitability."

Relative value adherents, faced with pricing stocks that have no accounting earnings, resort to the non-earnings-based techniques described
in Chapter 14. Besides the popular EV/Sales multiple, analysts employ a
number of "shorthand multiples" derived from operating statistics, such as
EV divided by the firm's number of users, number of subscribers, or number of monthly ad views (i.e., hits). Steve Harmon, a Mecklermedia analyst
who is credited with inventing several shorthand multiples, said, "What if I
took the market value of an Internet company and divided it by page
views?" By comparing CNET and Yahoo on this basis, he saw CNET was
trading at a premium, suggesting Yahoo was undervalued. Bill Appleby,
partner at Columbia Financial Advisors, a Washington, DC-based investment firm, voices an opinion shared by many money managers. "We use
discounted cash flow and relative value to put a reasonableness factor on
these stocks, but pricing is ultimately a question of supply and demand."

In the end, the Internet stock boom will result in incredible returns for
investors in a few stocks, with most other issuers languishing behind as
their technology, product offerings, or marketing fail to keep up. Lester
Thurow, the noted economist who sits on E-Trade's board, likened Web

investing to a simple game of chance, "I think it's the lottery model. Americans buy millions of lottery tickets knowing they're going to lose money. But one in a million wins big—and that keeps everyone buying."

QUESTIONS AND SHORT PROBLEMS

1. Why should most individual investors avoid companies with little or no historical track record? Circle one answer.
   a. These companies usually provide poor returns.
   b. Most individuals are ill equipped to absorb the risk involved in such investments.
   c. Institutions underprice the initial private offerings.
   d. Investment banks don't provide adequate liquidity.

2. Why do speculative companies often realize equity valuations that seem out-of-line with their earnings prospects?
   a. The companies are often participating in an industry about which Wall Street is very optimistic.
   b. Analysts are unfairly judging the "g" and "k" factors in the DCF model.
   c. Analysts are reluctant to use value investing techniques with growth firms.
   d. None of the above.

3. If General Motors has a cost of equity (Ke) of 15 percent, what should be the (Ke) of a high-tech company with no track record of operating profit?
   a. 10 percent.
   b. 15 percent.
   c. 20 percent.
   d. 40 percent.

4. Why might investors buy the shares of a speculative company if George Soros has already invested in the company?

5. As an exercise, research recent initial public offerings. Select one offering that has at least four of the elements set forth in Exhibit 22–1. Extra credit is provided for students finding IPOs with all seven elements.

6. Why might an investor feel more confident about buying an IPO underwritten by Goldman Sachs as opposed to an IPO underwritten by Tucker Anthony?

7. In the United States Satellite Broadcasting IPO, the company's short operating history precluded the use of time series analysis for financial forecasts. What alternate methods did security analysts use to estimate future demand?

8. Assume the United States has 100 million households with a refrigerator penetration of 99 percent. The maker of a new kitchen appliance

that costs $300 predicts the device will have 50 percent penetration at the end of five years (10 percent in each year), and a 5 percent net margin to the manufacturer. If the manufacturer has a market share of 70 percent in the first two years and 40 percent thereafter, predict its sales and net income for each of the next 5 years.

9. In Exhibit 22–4, USSB selling general and administrative expense declined from a projected 43 percent of sales in 1997 to 20 percent in 2000. Explain the sharp decline.

10. How was USSB intending to finance its cash flow deficits prior to 1998?

11. In the USSB example, security analysts recommending the stock in 1996 used aggressive assumptions that were plainly wrong at the time they wrote their reports. These aggressive assumptions were:
   a. A discount rate for future cash flows that was unduly low.
   b. A terminal P/E multiple that was unduly high.
   c. A discount rate that was unduly high.
   d. A sales projection that was unduly pessimistic.
   e. Profit margins that were too high.

12. How did investors justify a $74 million equity market value for Celgene Corp. in March 1997, when company's revenues and net loss for the previous year were $2.5 million and $17.8 million, respectively?

13. What was the appropriate cost of equity capital for a speculative biotech firm such as Celgene?

14. Teldrug Inc. is developing a new drug to fight a specific allergy. A market review and financial forecast includes the following:
   a. To alleviate the allergy, the product must be taken by the user 5 times per year at a cost of $40 per use.
   b. The total U.S. population afflicted with the allergy is approximately one million.
   c. Research indicates that 30 percent of the affected population will use the drug.
   d. Teldrug will learn of the FDA's decision on December 31, 2000. The probability of approval is 60 percent. Commercial production and product roll-out will begin exactly one year later.
   e. Net profit margins of similar products are 20 percent.
   f. P/E ratios of large established pharmaceutical firms are 20 times.
   g. Teldrug has sufficient cash to finance all initial production and roll-out costs. It anticipates paying no cash dividend in the near term, as excess cash must be reinvested.
   h. Shares outstanding are 10 million.

Estimate Teldrug's per share value using the discounted cash flow method. Terminal value should be determined using a P/E multiple and 2005 as the "terminal year." What is Teldrug's present ratio of market value to 2005 sales?

15. What are fundamental problems with using the "market value to future sales" ratio as an indicator of relative value?

16. On June 30, 1997 two venture capital firms paid $4 per share of Ivtex Corp., a pioneer stage company. On June 30, 2000, Ivtex is preparing to go public. Using the "venture capital markup" procedure, what is a reasonable IPO price?

23

Distressed Securities and Turnarounds

Many novice investors wonder why companies with large operating losses have positive equity values. Why do the bonds of some bankrupt companies have substantial value? In this chapter, we'll answer these questions by exploring bankrupt companies and turnarounds.

OVERVIEW

A distressed security doesn't always belong to a bankrupt business. For highly leveraged companies, the continuation of operating problems prompts investors to anticipate debt service troubles, causing the bonds to sell off, their prices to decline, and their yields to increase. Thus, the *nondefaulted* bonds of troubled firms can yield 5 to 10 percentage points higher than U.S. Treasury bonds debt having similar maturities. Depending on seniority, collateral, and other factors, *defaulted* debt may trade from pennies on the dollar to a high percentage of par value. Of course, investors in defaulted debt don't count on being repaid at maturity. They're hoping these "fallen angels" will be transformed into higher value securities, once a workout or exchange offer is completed by the debtor.

The distressed bond sector is a subset of the larger junk bond market. A junk bond is strictly defined as a bond that is rated lower than *investment grade* (i.e., the category encompassing the top four rungs of the rating agency ladder). Any bond falling into one of the lower rating levels is referred to as non-investment-grade—a "junk bond" in Street jargon (see Exhibit 23–1). Despite the derogatory nickname, many issues falling below investment grade belong to healthy companies, but the bonds have heightened risk when compared with their investment-grade counterparts.

EXHIBIT 23–1. Bond Rating Categories

	Standard & Poor's	Moody's
	AAA	Aaa
Investment	AA	Aa
Grade	A	A
Ratings	BBB	Baa
Noninvestment-	BB, B	Ba, B
Grade Ratings	CCC, CC, C	Caa, Ca, C
("Junk")	D	D

Common shares falling into the distressed category belong to two kinds of firms: (1) bankruptcies; and (2) turnaround candidates (see Exhibit 23–2). A shareholder of a bankrupt firm derives value primarily from his ability to impede progress in the Chapter 11 proceedings. This value is primarily of the legal nuisance variety and has little to do with the company's economics. In this chapter, we will discuss only the shares of companies that fit the second category—a turnaround business. A turnaround is an established enterprise that is experiencing operating problems which *appear* to be temporary. After a year or two of substandard performance, investors anticipate the company's results will return to normal.

Until the mid-1980s, distressed securities were the backwater of the investment industry. Blue chip money managers and big-name institutions avoided acquiring defaulted bonds and money-losing stocks, and the business of buying and selling these instruments was relegated to a small group of obscure hedge funds and brokerage houses.

The rise of Michael Milken, the most famous student of distressed securities, thrust the business of low-grade stocks and bonds into a prominent position, and analysts with the requisite training became valuable commodities. Accompanying this new spotlight was a sharp increase in the number of such securities. The huge volume of leveraged buyouts resulted in many new

EXHIBIT 23–2. Comparing Problem Companies (in millions)

High Leverage Company		Turnaround Candidate	
Sales	$1,000	Sales	$1,000
EBIT	50	EBIT	(10)
Interest	(75)	Interest	(15)
Pretax income	(25)	Pretax income	(25)
The high-leverage problem company loses money after interest expense.		The company turnaround at the operating level.	

workout situations, which complemented the normal supply coming from reasonably capitalized firms with conventional operating problems.

Today, the distressed securities industry still falls outside the mainstream, but it is a strong niche that attracts billions from sophisticated individuals and institutions. This increased attention is a source of complaint to some of the sector's traditional investors, because they have a harder time finding pricing inefficiencies. Bill Heyman, who manages an $800 million special situation fund for Travelers Insurance, says, "There's no free lunch anymore in the distressed securities business." No matter. The volatility of the business world and the continuing popularity of high leverage guarantee a plethora of problem companies, and value discrepancies are inevitable. Furthermore, with the vast majority of pension funds, insurance companies, and mutual funds showing a marked preference for investment-grade bonds and dividend-paying stocks, the distressed securities investor is assured of an investment environment where detailed analysis pays off.

INVESTMENT OPPORTUNITIES

The companies falling into the distressed security investor's sights are troubled, weak or financially crippled enterprises. Since the securities of these firms trade far below normal valuation multiples, buyers of this merchandise are sometimes referred to as the ultimate "value investors." A more derogatory term relates to their search for bargains—"bottom fishers." A third nickname derives from the search for weakness—"vulture capitalists." Whatever term is used, this investor category focuses on companies fitting one of two principal profiles:

1. *High Leverage.* The company is operationally profitable *before* interest costs, but incurs net losses *after* interest expense is applied. This situation is unsustainable in the long run, and many LBOs face this problem. In numerous instances, the investment candidate is in Chapter 11 proceedings and is being reorganized under the Bankruptcy Court's jurisdiction.

2. *Turnaround.* The company's underlying business is in trouble. It is either losing money or is marginally profitable at the operating level. It needs new management, new product lines, or new capital. In certain cases, the new managers have just been installed, and the investor is betting on a reversal of the trend. Turnarounds don't fit the "distressed" category until they're close to bankruptcy.

SCREENING TECHNIQUE

Aware of the downside exposure inherent in troubled company investments, the distressed security buyer tries to manage the risk by focusing on safe businesses and sensible valuations. "Safe businesses" are low-tech manufacturers or service providers with a prior history of generating operating income from a stable revenue base. "Sensible valuations" are at sizable discounts to market averages. A common screening technique employs the bottoms-up approach for three ratios:

1. *Price to Book.* A low price-to-book ratio, such as 1.0× or less, acts as an insurance policy. If the subject company's business falls apart completely, the salvage value of its assets to a corporate acquirer should approach book value. Obviously, a P/E screen is irrelevant since "E" is small or nonexistent.

2. *Enterprise Value to Sales.* A marginal firm with a substantial sales base is doing something right, because customers are still buying its products. The investor pins his hopes on the ability of management (or new management) to restore profitability through cost cutting. A low value-to-sales ratio leverages the investor's chances of a positive return. Thus, Morgan Products, an ailing wood products manufacturer, was trading at 22 percent of sales in April 1997. Profitable comparable companies were trading at over 50 percent of sales.

3. *Enterprise Value to EBITDA.* Many companies that show accounting losses have positive cash flow, due to heavy depreciation and amortization charges. Assuming the firm's debt situation is manageable, a low EBITDA ratio, such as 3× to 4×, provides a safety net for the investor. Few public companies trade consistently at ratios below 5×. (Those that do become takeover targets, unless their legal defenses are unusually strong or they have a narrow ownership base.)

By screening troubled businesses carefully, the practitioner narrows the field to those firms with an underlying business that can survive. He then begins his financial analysis, and keeps his focus on the short-to-intermediate term. His first concern is whether the company can generate enough cash to stay afloat while its operations and finances are being straightened out. His second concern relates to time-adjusted rate of return. Will the recovery happen quickly enough to provide an acceptable profit, given the uncertainty of any turnaround? Exhibit 23–3 illustrates the investor's quandary. If he buys Problem Company's shares at $8 and the turnaround occurs in two years, his annual rate of return is a handsome 37 percent. A five-year turnaround time, in contrast, provides a mediocre 13 percent return. No turnaround, of course, means a substantial loss.

The troubled company evaluation process emphasizes four items:

1. *Sustainable Business.* The problem company has a base business that can sustain the vagaries of a turnaround/workout situation.

2. *Likely Reversal.* Management has the ability to reform the business and return it to normal profitability.

EXHIBIT 23–3. Turnaround Investing—Evaluating Time-Adjusted Return

Scenario 1: Success in Two Years

	Year		
	0	1	2
Problem Company			
Earnings per share	$(0.50)	$0.50	$1.00
Dividends per share	—	—	—
Share price	$8	$12	$15

The investor's two-year rate of return is an impressive 37 percent on a compound annual basis. He buys at $8 and sells at $15.

Scenario 2: Mediocrity over Five Years

	Year				
	0	1	2	3	5
Problem Company					
Earnings per share	$(0.50)	$(0.15)	$0.10	$0.60	$1.00
Dividends per share	—	—	—	—	—
Share price	$8	$9	$10	$12	$15

The investor's five-year annual rate of return is only 13 percent because the turnaround requires more time.

3. *Valuation.* The going-in price to the investor is relatively low. The risk of failure is thus well-balanced against the chance for success.

4. *Timing.* The rehabilitation of the business will occur within a time frame that produces a satisfactory risk-adjusted rate of return. Target annual internal rate of returns (IRRs) for the distressed security community are in the 20 to 30 percent range.

INVESTING IN HIGHLY LEVERAGED COMPANIES

Numerous highly leveraged companies, such as LBOs, issue bonds and stocks in the public markets. In many cases, the prices of these securities decline although the LBO's underlying business is healthy; it is just the balance sheet that is sickly. Saddled with debts that can never be repaid, the LBO's owners have three options: (1) do nothing and pray for a miraculous recovery; (2) work out a voluntary restructuring plan with the creditors; or (3) play brinkmanship with the creditors and look toward a Chapter 11 filing. Since unpaid creditors lose their patience after a couple of years, Option No. 1 has a short duration. Options No. 2 and 3 extend over months and years; they are dubbed "workouts" because the creditors and stockholders

EXHIBIT 23–4. Workout Company Options

Voluntary Restructuring	Investor Tactics
"Restructuring" is a fancy word for paying creditors less than 100 cents on the dollar. In the rare case where the company is sold in one piece to a corporate buyer, creditors split the proceeds according to an agreed-on formula. In most restructurings, the principal creditors receive a combination of new debt and equity securities, in exchange for their old loans. Even under the most optimistic scenario, the security package is worth less than the loans' face value. Shareholders resist debt restructurings because the proposed equity issuance dilutes their ownership by 90 percent to 95 percent.	The investor anticipates a restructuring and buys corporate obligations at large discounts to face value. Unhappy creditors that need cash incur a loss. Major creditors form committees to negotiate a restructuring that provides (1) the company with a solid balance sheet and (2) the creditors with a controlling equity stake.

Chapter 11 Reorganization	Investor Tactics
Unable to reach a compromise with creditors, the firm files for Chapter 11, which suspends payment obligations and prevents creditors from filing lawsuits or foreclosing on assets. Unless an asset liquidation provides the highest payout on claims, the company and its creditors pursue a reorganization under the auspices of the Bankruptcy Court. Eventually, the firm survives with a new balance sheet. Dominated by lawyers, the Chapter 11 process is time consuming and very expensive; creditors and debtors alike try to avoid it.	The investor purchases corporate obligations at large discounts to face value. The investor hopes that a reorganization of the debtor will provide him with an attractive package of securities, worth more than the original investment. Large investors play an active role in the reorganization process.

spend countless hours working out a plan to put the business back on its feet. Workouts follow two avenues: voluntary restructuring and Chapter 11 reorganization. Both options are reviewed in Exhibit 23–4.

FINANCIAL ANALYSIS OF A COMPANY WITH LEVERAGE PROBLEMS

By screening troubled, indebted businesses on industry and asset characteristics, the investor narrows the field substantially. With the remaining candidates, he performs a summary financial analysis, concentrating primarily on *cash flow, timing,* and *continuing operations.* The analytical emphasis takes on different elements, depending on whether the company is a restructuring candidate or a Chapter 11 bankruptcy (see Exhibit 23–5).

During his initial screen, the distressed security analyst determines normalized results for a leveraged target in an interesting fashion. Most security analysts start with a bottom line analysis and look at net income and EBIT trends, but the bargain hunter does his analysis backward. He looks at top-line results first—(i.e., sales). Over the expected sales data, he superimposes the income statement template of a successful firm in the candidate's industry. The investor reasons as follows: If my subject company wasn't burdened with leverage problems, it might perform as well as the next company. For example, in considering the normalized results of a processed foods manufacturer in bankruptcy, the practitioner might construct the

EXHIBIT 23–5. Financial Analysis of a Troubled Leveraged Business

Critical Issues	Voluntary Restructuring	Chapter 11
Cash	Does the firm have sufficient cash to keep creditors at bay until a restructuring is concluded? The investor carefully prepares quarter-to-quarter cash flow forecasts.	Does the firm need to borrow more money from court-approved debtor-in-possession (DIP) lenders to maintain operations? DIP lenders receive priority claims at a 100 percent repayment rate, thus reducing reorganization values.
Timing	What is the investor's expected holding period? Restructuring results are uncertain. A long holding period or an unforeseen Chapter 11 filing reduces the investors' rate of return. Poststructuring, how much time is needed for the business to recover fully? The investor's experience in similar situations provides a guide.	When will the company emerge from bankruptcy? Can the investor's intervention accelerate the process? A long holding period reduces the investor's rate of return. Post-reorganization, how much time is needed for the business to recover fully?
Continuing Operations	What are the company's normalized operating results?	Same.
Exit Price	Assuming eventual profitability at what future P/E ratio can the investor sell his stock?	Same.

EXHIBIT 23–6. The Analyst Normalizes the Operating Results of a Bankrupt Processed Foods Company (in millions)

	Annual Sales (in millions)	Gross Margin	Operating Margin
Bankrupt company—actual	$ 800	42.0%	3.0%
Other Processed Foods Companies			
Flowers Industries	$1,239	45.5%	5.3%
General Mills	5,416	58.6	15.9
H.J. Heinz	9,112	36.6	14.1
Lance Foods	475	51.0	8.0
	Average	47.9%	10.8%
Analyst Estimates			
Bankrupt company—normalized	$ 800	44%–46%	8%–10%

The normalized operating margins of 8 percent–10 percent represent a conservative combination of healthy company margins.

template in Exhibit 23–6 and conclude that the firm's normalized EBIT margin is in the 8 to 10 percent range.

With his projected margins in hand, the investor forecasts the firm's operating income going forward, using sensible sales estimates (see Exhibit 23–7). In this example, I assumed sales jump 10 percent in the first year out of bankruptcy. Sales growth then declines to a constant annual rate of 6 percent. Operating margins rebound to 5 percent in year 1, increasing steadily to 9 percent by year 5. Returning the company to industry profit margins provided a 300 percent gain in operating income from $24 million to $100 million! This is the ideal situation for the bottom fisher because there is the possibility of a large increase in value

The bargain hunter next determines the present value of the business, on a debt-free basis. The first step is estimating the firm's share price in three to five years, using the techniques described earlier in this book. This future value is discounted to the present at the estimated cost of capital,

EXHIBIT 23–7. The Investor Normalizes the Operating Results of the Bankrupt Processed Foods Company (in millions)

	Actual	Year Projected				
	0	1	2	3	4	5
Sales (from Exhibit 23–6)	$800	$880	$933	$989	$1,048	$1,110
Operating income	$ 24	$ 44	$ 56	$ 69	$ 84	$ 100
Operating margin (%)	3	5	6	7	8	9

including both debt and equity cost components. To determine this capital cost, the analyst makes a lot of assumptions on what the reorganization plan will look like. How much will each class of creditor receive on its claims? How much debt and how much equity will be outstanding after the plan's implementation? Constructing good answers to these questions goes to the heart of the analysis.

Although every distressed situation is unique, the reorganization plan is usually designed to reduce existing debts to an amount that the borrower can reasonably service in the future. Once the composition of the new debt securities is determined, the remaining enterprise value is allocated to newly issued common shares. Both the debt securities and common shares are distributed to creditors on the basis of complicated formulas, which are the product of long and trying negotiations. Usually, the shareholders end up with little in this process; the new owners are the former creditors which received the most shares in the distribution.

For our hypothetical food business, a reasonable enterprise value in year 5 is $1 billion (i.e., 10× EBIT). Using a capital structure with equal percentages of debt and equity, the reorganized company's assumed capital cost is approximately 20 percent (assuming debt costs 10% and equity costs 30%) annually. Given the uncertainties associated with projections in troubled investments, this high capital cost is justifiable.

Discounting the firm's $1 billion future value at 20 percent annually results in an initial "plan capitalization" value of $400 million, as shown in Exhibit 23–8. The investor has a reasonable analytical framework to assist in the investment decision.

As one illustration, Carson Pirie Scott, a bankrupt department store chain, had a reorganization plan that was confirmed in 1993; the company discharged $581 million of claims for $369 million, or 64 cents on the dollar. The new debt-to-equity ratio was 60:40. Federated Department Stores, one of the 1980s' largest LBOs, was reorganized in 1992. Prebankruptcy

EXHIBIT 23–8. Cost of Capital Calculation—Bankrupt Processed Foods Company

Capitalization	After Plan Implementation	Cost of Capital	Rationale
Debt	$200	10%	The 10% rate is equivalent to junk bond yields.
Equity	200	30	The equity investor target return of 30% is appropriate for the high risk.
Total	$400	20%	

claims were paid out 51 cents on the dollar. The revised debt-to-equity ratio was 69:31.

THE INVESTMENT DECISION

Distressed security investors participate in an active secondary market for troubled company claims. Buyers and sellers trade all sorts of obligations, ranging from secured loans to trade payables to subordinated debt. The participants set prices for these instruments based on their respective views of time-adjusted returns. In May 1997, for example, the bonds of Mobile Media traded at 19 percent of face value; Marvel Holding bonds traded at 16 percent of face value. The related equity securities traded for pennies.

In the example of the bankrupt processed foods company, $700 million of claims are outstanding. For the sake of argument, assume that each claim has the same priority in reorganization. According to our $400 million valuation model, the claims should trade at an average 57 percent of face value (see Exhibit 23–9).

This example is simplistic. In reality, bankrupt companies have a bewildering variety of claims, assigned to specific creditor classes. Each creditor class has a priority designation. Those with the higher priorities, such as IRS liens and secured loans, receive the higher percentage payouts in the reorganization.

In 1993, four large investors purchased claims from the pre-Chapter 11 secured bank lenders of Carson Pirie Scott. In the subsequent reorganization, these investors obtained significant ownership positions in the new equity: FMR Corp. (13.7%); New South Capital Management (10.4%), Dickstein Partners (7.9%), and Intermarket Corp. (7.8%). The new shares began trading publicly in October 1993 and climbed in price by 300 percent before the company was acquired.

EVALUATING TURNAROUNDS

A turnaround is not a bankruptcy candidate, but it has operating problems that cause it to lose money. Leverage is a secondary factor. The operating

EXHIBIT 23–9. Distressed Company Financial Analysis—Simple Pricing Calculation—Bankrupt Processed Foods Company (in millions)

Estimated enterprise value (1)	$400
Claims outstanding (2)	$700
Average claim trading value (1 ÷ 2)	57%

problems stem either from economic conditions beyond the control of management or from conditions that exist inside the firm. Principal causes for operating problems include:

- Management ineptitude.
- Economical cyclicality.
- Failure to foresee technology, fashion, or competitive challenges.
- Poor cost controls.
- Growing sales without adequate capital.
- Unsound acquisitions.
- Lawsuits.

Firms suffering from these deficiencies survive for years. Operating cash shortfalls are made up through borrowings and asset sales, deferring the day of reckoning.

If the cause of the failure is external to the company, a new approach is unlikely to reverse the situation. If the reason is found within the business, the problem is usually with the management. A new team of executives can theoretically replace old practices, find new capital, and kick-start the recovery. Assuming the underlying business is not the next buggy-whip manufacturer, a firm heading for oblivion can thus be "turned around" into a successful company.

Along with new management, many turnaround stories come with a prominent brand name. If consumers still accept the goodwill associated with the brand, that's one major item the new management doesn't have to rehabilitate. To illustrate, the next few pages cover five turnaround situations.

Case Study 1: Florsheim Group, Inc.   Florsheim Group, Inc., is a manufacturer, wholesaler, and retailer of quality men's footwear. Spun off from its parent company in November 1994, the company had poor operating results through 1995, prompting the majority shareholder, Apollo Capital Management, to overhaul management late in that year. The next twelve months were a transition period as the new managers cut inventories, repositioned the merchandise and refinanced a costly loan. In this case, the lead brand, "Florsheim," was highly recognizable, but it needed more push to reverse a flat sales trend.

The new management stopped the downward slide in 1996, and investors were optimistic about 1997. Indeed, two analysts projected 1997 earnings per share to more than double 1996's results. Florsheim's relative value was thus expressed as 15× *forward* earnings, as opposed to a multiple of *current* earnings. Summary results appear in Exhibit 23–10.

Case Study 2: Golden Books Family Entertainment, Inc.   Golden Books is a leading publisher of children's books. Despite a strong consumer franchise

EXHIBIT 23–10. Turnaround Candidate—Florsheim Group, Inc.—Summary of Financial and Market Data (in millions except per share and ratios)

Income Statement	Divisional Predecessor		Public Company		
	1993	1994	1995	1996	1997(E)
Revenues	$263	$266	$246	$238	$260
EBIT	30	20	7	11	17
Net income	12	6	(5)	2	5
EPS	—	—	(0.58)	0.23	0.60
Trend	Down	Down	Down	Up	Up

Comments. Florsheim's results were in a steady downward slide until 1996. By early 1997, analysts suggested the firm could reach normal retail margins by 1998.

Balance Sheet	At December 31, 1996	
Total assets	$185	*Comments.* The firm's leverage was high for a retailer.
Total debt	69	
Stockholders' equity	58	

Market Data	At April 30, 1997	
Share price	$9	*Comments.* By pricing the stock on 1997 forward earnings, an investor could justify the high P/E (39.1×) on 1996 historical earnings. Florsheim's shares traded at $5 only a few months earlier.
P/E multiple (96 EPS)	39.1×	
P/E multiple (97 EPS)	15.0×	
Price/book value	1.3×	
Enterprise value/EBIT	7.2×	
Dividend yield	None	

with the "Golden Books" brand, the company had been losing money and market share for years. In May 1996, new management, led by Richard Snyder, former CEO of Simon & Schuster, began a complete overhaul of the business. During that year, over $200 million in new equity was raised from sophisticated investors, including Warburg Pincus Ventures, Hallmark Cards, and Barry Diller. These funds financed the hopeful transition from specialty publishing house to family media company.

Among the first objectives of the new management was extending the Golden Books brand into other product lines. A family-oriented adults' book operation was expanded and the firm acquired a library of character-based family videos as a platform for promoting book videos. At the same time, management divested several noncore businesses and implemented numerous cost-cutting measures.

These major management changes boosted the stock price from $9 to $16, but the initial euphoria was dampened by the dilution of the new share issuance and the realization that a turnaround required two years or more. Given the firm's burn rate of $50 million per year, cash was forecast to run out in two-and-a-half years without a recovery. Exhibit 23–11 provides more information.

Case Study 3: Morgan Products Ltd. Morgan Products is a manufacturer and distributor of wooden door and window products. Its well-known "Morgan" and "Nicolai" brand names represent 27 percent of sales volume, and the company is a major distributor of premium "Andersen" windows (40% of sales). Despite this solid brand-name affiliation, Morgan had lost market share until 1996, the year *after* new management was installed. The new chief executive was Larry Robinette, who had earned a reputation as a turnaround specialist at Newell Corp., an important hardware manufacturer.

Assisted by an upturn in housing starts, Mr. Robinette stopped the bleeding, enabling Morgan to attract $9 million in fresh equity. The stock

EXHIBIT 23–11. Turnaround Candidate—Golden Books Family Entertainment, Inc.—Summary of Financial and Market Data (in millions except per share and ratios)

Income Statement[1]	1993	1994	1995	1996	1997(E)
Revenues	$616	$401	$371	$255	$305
EBIT	(20)	(21)	(39)	(53)	(10)
Net income	(35)	(37)	(48)	(62)	(25)
EPS	(1.70)	(1.85)	(2.31)	(2.75)	(0.40)
Trend	Down	Down	Down	Down	Up

[1] Normalized data. 1996 is 11 months.

Comments. After a string of increasing losses and declining sales, Wall Street projected a reversal by the end of 1997. Analysts anticipated a normal publishing margin of 3 percent after-tax by 1999, providing a $14 to $16 share price.

Balance Sheet	At December 31, 1996	
Cash	$140	*Comments.* The $200 million in new capital provided Golden Books with a cash cushion for the turnaround period.
Total assets	367	
Total debt	150	
Stockholders' equity	(20)	

Market Data	At April 30, 1997	
Share price	8\frac{1}{2}$	*Comments.* Golden Book's stock price was 40 percent lower than preceding twelve-month high. Even at 8\frac{1}{2}$ per share, the investment was risky.
P/E multiple	Not meaningful	
Price/book value	Not meaningful	
Enterprise value/EBIT	Not meaningful	
Dividend yield	None	

price, which hit a low of $4 in 1994, increased to $8 by April 1997. Analysts projected higher sales and forecast a 2.5 percent net margin, which was similar to the margin enjoyed by similar firms. These two assumptions implied $1.15 of earnings per share by 1998, a major reversal of earlier trends.

When I applied a 12× industry P/E ratio to the $1.15 1998 earnings, a $14 share price was the result. Thus, if one believed the turnaround story, Morgan Products stock offered the possibility of a 75 percent gain in just two years, (i.e., from $8 per share in 1997 to $14 in 1999). Exhibit 23–12 provides summary information.

Case Study 4: Reader's Digest.   One of the most prominent companies in publishing, Reader's Digest is a global direct mail marketer of magazines and books. *Reader's Digest* magazine supplies 24 percent of revenues. Revenues (adjusted for inflation) have been flat for five years, operating income

EXHIBIT 23–12. Turnaround Candidate—Morgan Products Ltd. (in millions except per share and ratios)

Income Statement	1994	1995	1996	1997(E)	1998(E)
Revenues	$358	$338	$373	$430	$470
EBIT	(6)	1	3	13	18
Net income	(9)	(3)	—	7	12
EPS	(1.10)	(0.30)	.03	0.65	1.15
Trend	Down	Up	Up	Up	Up

Comments. The new management began in 1995 and the reversed the downtrend. Whether earnings per share can advance to $1.15 by 1998 is another question.

Balance Sheet	At December 31, 1996	
Total assets	$142	*Comments.* The company sold $9 million of common stock in 1996.
Total debt	50	
Stockholders' equity	62	

Market Data	At April 30, 1997	
Share price	$8	*Comments.* The author's inquiries about this thinly traded issue caused a mini-rally, as the price advanced 20 percent in one week. Price-to-book was a conservative 1.3× and the firm's assets are almost all tangible items, such as receivables, inventory, and property.
P/E multiple (96 EPS)	Not meaningful	
P/E multiple (97 EPS)	12.3×	
Price/book value	1.3×	
Enterprise value/EBIT	Not meaningful	
Dividend yield	None	

has been declining, and the firm has incurred over $300 million in restructuring charges. A principal money-loser has been the European business, although the flagship operation, *Reader's Digest* magazine, has been experiencing difficulties.

Installed as CEO in August 1994 was James Schadt, who first joined Reader's Digest as Chief Operating Officer in 1991. In April 1995, he initiated several major changes, including:

- Developing new distribution channels, such as direct response television and the Internet.
- Reducing the frequency of direct mailings to cut costs.
- Moderating price increases to stimulate demand.
- Entering into new partnerships with Avon, Microsoft, Public Broadcasting, and Spiegel.
- Downsizing the staff to reduce expenses.

As the 1997 forecast in Exhibit 23–13 shows, analysts expected these actions to boost margins, but they forecasted sales to drop slightly. Assuming profit margins returned to industry norms, earnings per share in 2000 could exceed $3.00, giving an upward push to the $23 stock price.

Case Study 5: Sunbeam Corporation. In July 1996, Sunbeam Corporation, an established consumer products concern, became the "mother of all turnarounds" when Albert "Chainsaw" Dunlap, the hero of Scott Paper's reversal, was put in charge. Mr. Dunlap characterized the situation darkly:

> In July 1996 Sunbeam was flat on its back. Earnings had plunged 83 percent since July of 1994. Excluding acquisitions, sales were down 4 percent. The operating margin had shrunk to an almost invisible 2 percent. The stock price had plummeted 52 percent, to $12.50, since its $26 high in 1994. And even as this once great company headed towards possible bankruptcy, Sunbeam had no strategic plan.

What Sunbeam *did* have was a strong brand name, a $1 billion sales base and a conservative balance sheet.

Mr. Dunlap's rescue plan for Sunbeam was straightforward: "(1) Recruit a new management team; (2) Eliminate waste and make the company cost-competitive again; (3) Focus on core businesses, divesting everything else; and (4) Implement an aggressive strategy for global growth."

Sunbeam instituted cost-savings measures swiftly, designed to save, in management's opinion, over $200 million per year. For example, it consolidated six divisional headquarters into one, reduced 26 production facilities (some operating under 50% capacity) to 8, consolidated 61 warehouses to 18 and divested six noncore businesses. Excluding the divestitures, employee headcount was reduced 32 percent, from 8,800 to 6,000. With these actions,

EXHIBIT 23–13. Turnaround Candidate—Reader's Digest Association, Inc.—Summary of Financial and Market Data (in millions except per share and ratios)

Income Statement	1993	1994	1995	1996	1997(E)
Revenues	$2,869	$2,806	$3,069	$3,098	$3,020
EBIT	330	506	392	109	345
Net income	203	340	264	138	220
EPS	1.74	2.94	2.35	0.73	1.70–2.10
Trend	Down	Up	Down	Down	Up

Comments. Due to their recurring nature, restructuring charges are included in the results.

Balance Sheet	At December 31, 1996	
Cash	$ 258	*Comments.* Reader's Digest has no debt, so its balance sheet is very conservative.
Total assets	1,904	
Total debt	—	
Stockholders' equity	479	

Market Data	At April 30, 1997	
Share price	$23	*Comments.* On estimated 97 results, the stock appears cheap (11.0× EPS, 7.9× EBIT, and 0.7× sales) relative to other publishing firms. Voting control is held by a charitable foundation, which takes the long view on the turnaround. The 7.8 percent dividend yield is too generous and a reduction is likely.
P/E multiple (96 EPS)	31.5×	
P/E multiple (97 EPS)	11.0×	
Price/book value	5.1×	
Enterprise value/EBIT (96)	24.7	
Enterprise value/EBIT (97)	7.9×	
Dividend yield	7.8%	

the firm hoped to achieve the 9 percent net margins of other household product firms within three years.

After six months of Mr. Dunlap's changes, Sunbeam's stock price had doubled to $25. By April 1997, the shares traded at $31, supported by optimism regarding the makeover and speculation regarding a quick sellout. Exhibit 23–14 provides summary information.

LIQUIDATIONS

In the rare case, a publicly held company is viewed as a liquidation candidate. It has poor prospects as an operating business and shows a history of

EXHIBIT 23–14. Turnaround Candidate—Sunbeam Corporation—Summary of Financial and Market Data (in millions except per share and ratios)

Income Statement	1994	1995	1996	1997(E)	1998(E)
Revenues	$1,044	$1,016	$984	$1,150	$1,400
EBIT	151	70	(133)	150	235
Net income	85	38	(124)	85	130
EPS	1.03	0.45	(1.49)	1.00	1.50
Trend	Up	Down	Down	Up	Up

Comments. Analysts expected a significant upturn over a short period of time, indicating confidence in Mr. Dunlap's track record.

Balance Sheet	At December 31, 1996	
Total assets	$1,073	*Comments.* Sunbeam's balance sheet was solid.
Total debt	202	
Stockholders' equity	395	

Market Data	At April 30, 1997	
Share price	$31	*Comments.* Relative to similar firms, the company's value multiples were inflated. Investors were very optimistic about Dunlap's plans.
P/E multiple (97 EPS)	31.0×	
P/E multiple (98 EPS)	20.7×	
Price/book value	6.6×	

losses. Investors appraise the business not as a going concern, but rather as a collection of assets better off in the hands of others.

In performing a liquidation analysis, you examine the worth of each asset category in a quick sell-off, aggregate these liquidation values, and subtract from this sum the estimated cost of closing the business and paying off its liabilities. If this calculation provides a positive number, such as $10 per share, you have established a ceiling purchase price. From this $10 must then be subtracted your time-adjusted rate of return requirement.

Unless the business has substantial intangible assets such as well-respected brand-names, exclusive patents or quasi-monopoly operating rights, the first "back of the envelope" evaluation focuses on historical balance sheet financial data. For each balance sheet item, you determine an estimated range of "liquidated value" percentages, which are based on experiences for similar businesses. Later on, after further study, these percentages are adjusted to include the new information. Consider the hypothetical case of Siegel Corporation, a troubled manufacturer of construction materials, as presented in Exhibit 23–15.

EXHIBIT 23–15. Siegel Corporation—Summary Liquidation Analysis (in millions except per share)

	Historical Book Value	Estimated Liquidation Percentages	Estimated Liquidation Values
Assets			
Cash	$ 10	100%	$ 10
Accounts receivable	40	70	28
Inventory	40	50	20
	90		58
Plant & equipment	100	40	40
Goodwill	20	0	0
	$210		$ 98
Liabilities and Stockholders' Equity			
Short-term debt	$ 15	100	$(15)
Other current liabilities	25	100	(25)
	40		(40)
Stockholders' equity	170	Costs of shutdown	(8)
	$210	Net outflows	$(48)
		Net liquidation value (98 − 48 = 50)	$ 50
		Shares outstanding	÷ 5
		Value per share	$ 10

The $50 million liquidation value is far below Siegel's stockholders' equity of $170 million. This significant discount-to-book value is characteristic of most liquidation analyses and emphasizes an important point: Firms realize a better stock price when they are viewed as going concerns, whereby their respective values are based on future earnings power rather than on tangible asset compositions. To prove this assertion, one need only look at the November 1997 pricing for the Dow Jones Industrials, which were then trading at 5× historical book value.

Unless an analyst works for a firm that is considering a takeover of Siegel Corp., there is no way for him to unlock the liquidation value. Thus, his rate of return requirement must reflect not only the uncertainty of his liquidation estimates but also (1) Siegel's burn rate and (2) the likelihood of its acquisition by a third party interested in unlocking those values. Assuming a 30 percent IRR requirement and a two-year holding period, the $10 liquidation value translates into a $6 investment price (i.e., $10/(1.30)^2$).

SUMMARY

An increasing number of practitioners research the securities of troubled companies, believing such investments don't attract broader market interest. Their investment rationale suggests that problem situations can provide above-average returns, assuming the relevant opportunity is thoroughly investigated.

Analyzing the troubled company is more rigorous than the average security evaluation. Typically, the firm is undergoing severe operating, financial, or legal problems that prove difficult to interpret properly in a financial analysis. The uncertainty surrounding a turnaround or workout is therefore balanced by a high expected return.

The illiquidity of distressed securities, the instability of a turnaround, and the intensity of the research process combine to make troubled company investments an area best left to full-time professionals.

QUESTIONS AND SHORT PROBLEMS

1. Define a junk bond.

2. The definition of a distressed company includes which of the following firms? Circle all that apply:
   a. Companies showing consistent net losses on a GAAP basis.
   b. Companies showing consistent negative EBIT on a GAAP basis.
   c. Bankrupt companies.
   d. All of the above.

3. How can a company with positive EBIT over several years still be categorized as a distressed situation?

4. What's the difference between a hi-leverage distressed firm and a turnaround?

5. What are the most popular ratios for a distressed company "bottoms up" screen? Circle one answer:
   a. P/E, EV/EBITDA, Price/Book.
   b. Price/Book, EV/EBITDA, Price/Cash flow.
   c. Price/EBITDA, P/E, Price/Book.
   d. EV/EBITDA, EV/Sales, Price/Book.

6. Why do many distressed company investors avoid technology companies?

7. Why might a distressed company prefer a voluntary restructuring rather than a Chapter 11 reorganization? Circle one answer.
   a. The company doesn't need to negotiate with creditors in a restructuring.
   b. Chapter 11 requires a management turnover before closing.
   c. Voluntary restructurings often provide lower legal costs and shorter time horizons than a Chapter 11.
   d. The restructuring results in more ownership dilution for existing shareholders.

8. How does a distressed security analyst "normalize" a problem company's income statement results?

9. In April 1997, Florsheim Group—a low growth, low-tech firm—was trading at 39.1 times historical earnings per share. Why were investors paying this premium multiple?

10. With $140 million in cash at December 31, 1996, how long did analysts estimate that Golden Books Family Entertainment could operate without a new cash infusion?

11. For Golden Books, why was the price to sales ratio a better relative value measurement than the EV/EBIT or P/E ratio?

12. In April 1997, various analysts predicated a turnaround in the operating performance (Exhibit 23–12) of Morgan Products. What actually occurred in 1997 and 1998? Compare actual and forecast results.

13. Speculate on how the inquiries of the author stimulated a 20 percent increase in the price of Morgan Products stock.

14. Readers Digest Association Inc. had a number of attributes that made it an attractive turnaround candidate. List them.

15. Racket Co. will exit bankruptcy on January 1, 2000, with the following balance sheet and 10 million shares outstanding.

Racket Co.
Pro Forms Balance Sheet
"Fresh Start" Post-Bankruptcy Accounting
January 1, 2000
(in millions)

Assets	
Current assets	$200
Fixed assets	300
	$500
Liabilities and Stockholders' Equity	
Current liabilities	$100
Total debt (10% interest rate)	200
Shareholders' equity	200
	$500

For the prior three years, the company's operating results were as follows:

Year Ended December 31
(in millions)

	1997	1998	1999
Sales	$800	$810	$815
EBITDA	60	58	62
EBIT	45	42	46

Comparable companies have the following results:

	Sporting Co.	All Sports Co.	Tennis Inc.
Sales growth rate	8%	6%	5%
EBITDA margin	12	11	10
EBIT margin	9	8	7
EV/EBIT ratio	12 times	11 times	10 times

Assume that all Racket Co.'s excess cash over the near-term is reinvested in the business to reinvigorate the company's results. No new debt or stock is issued over the near-term. Project EBIT, net income, and EPS results, given the information provided. Remember that the company has now exited bankruptcy.

Provide an expected enterprise value at December 31, 2002, as well as an expected per share value.

What is your estimate of the value of a Racket Co. common share at January 1, 2000?

16. Office Supply Co., which will soon be liquidated, manufactures pens, pencils and stationery products. With 16 million shares outstanding, and a per share market price of $2, does the company's stock represent good value?

Office Supply Co.
Summary Balance Sheet
(in millions)

Assets	
Cash	$ 20
Accounts receivable	56
Inventory	43
	119
Plant and equipment	200
Goodwill	41
	$360
Liabilities and Stockholders' Equity	
Short-term debt	$ 62
Other current liabilities	35
	97
Stockholders' equity	263
	$360

24

International Stocks

In an attempt to diversify investment risk and boost returns, U.S. portfolio managers are buying more foreign stocks. This trend corresponds to the increasing globalization of the economy and foretells the internationalization of security analysis. Chapter 24 reviews the evaluation of foreign stocks.

THE MOTIVATION BEHIND INTERNATIONAL INVESTING

Investing in international stocks is becoming more popular, and foreign securities are now quite accessible to U.S. buyers. This situation mirrors the increasing globalization of the economy. It also reflects U.S. portfolio managers' desire to diversify a portion of their holdings out of the domestic market. As U.S. mutual funds and pension plans continue to pour money into domestic stocks, the dynamics of supply and demand ensure that the prices of many issues exceed historical markers. Some prudent managers hedge their bets and lay off a portion of their assets in foreign markets, where the risk/return tradeoff appears more favorable than that in the United States.

Besides the obvious diversification benefits, there is also the perception that foreign securities are not as efficiently priced as their U.S. counterparts. Regulatory barriers (such as Mexico forbidding insurance companies to invest in corporate securities) as well as the lack of local personnel with the requisite financial training contribute to this view. The presumed pricing inefficiencies leave opportunities for U.S.-schooled analysts who are willing to perform the extra work required of an international evaluation.

Also, many foreign economies, particularly in those developing countries known as "emerging markets," are expanding faster than the U.S.

economy. The implication is that rising GDP top lines translate into larger corporate bottom lines. Since earnings growth is the main engine behind higher stock prices, it is easy to see why U.S. investors look overseas.

THE ROLE OF SECURITY ANALYSIS

As investors go abroad in the search for profits, the demand for international security analysis increases, and mutual funds and investment banks now employ professionals to focus full-time on foreign stocks. These individuals apply U.S. techniques of top-down review, discounted cash flow, and relative value to the international marketplace. However, U.S.-style security analysis, like fine wine, does not always travel well, and the results of this technology transfer are decidedly mixed.

Problems with the Standard Approach

The security analysis process is heavily reliant on informed decisions. Not only must the data for a top-down analysis be available and reliable, but the prices of comparable securities must be based on open and honest trading. Such standards are usually met in the United States, assuming the analyst makes a determined research effort, but achieving the desired result in a foreign market is problematic. Only the stock markets in Canada and the United Kingdom approach domestic levels of full disclosure and transparent trading. The remainder have various degrees of shortcomings that are summarized in Exhibit 24–1 and outlined in the following text.

Less Information.   Foreign regulators and exchanges require less corporate disclosure than their U.S. counterparts. That information which is submitted by issuers faces little official scrutiny. Depending on the country, the availability and accuracy of macroeconomic, capital market, and industry data are also suspect. Moreover, much of the source material is not translated into English. For the security analyst, less information means more guesswork.

Questionable Trading Practices.   Insider trading remains a problem on the fringes of the U.S. market, but it is widespread on foreign exchanges. In most countries, insider trading is not illegal. Even those that have prohibitions rarely enforce them. For example, Germany, the world's third largest economy, only recently outlawed insider trading. Verifying the efficient floor execution of trades is a continuing concern for the international investor.

Unclear Accounting Standards.   Relative value analysis requires consistent accounting methods, but liberal rules on earnings management allow

EXHIBIT 24–1. Factors That Reduce the Effectiveness of U.S.-Style Security Analysis in Foreign Markets

Less Information. No countries match the United States in disclosure standards.

Questionable Trading Practices. While not perfect, the U.S. stock market is the most transparent in terms of fair and honest trading. Foreign markets lag behind the United States in this regard.

Unclear Accounting Standards. The clarity and consistency of foreign accounting standards are suspect.

Fewer Comparables. Smaller foreign markets mean fewer comparables to serve as relative value measurements.

Liquidity Concerns. Many listed stocks have small floats. As a result, investors can't easily obtain sizeable positions in the stocks they identify as undervalued. The profit objective of security analysis is undermined.

Reduced Emphasis on Share Price Enhancement. There is a preponderance of closely held, publicly traded firms in foreign markets. Majority shareholders take the long view on value creation, rather than the short-to-intermediate term favored by U.S. participants.

foreign firms to hide profits and losses. Japanese firms, for example, can retain huge reserves as a cushion against losses, and for many years Japanese commercial bank results were pure fantasy. Germany's Mercedes-Benz hesitated to list its shares on the New York Stock Exchange because conforming its financial statements to U.S. GAAP would have caused a $3 billion dent in the retained earnings account. On the positive side, Ericsson, the Swedish telecommunications giant, expends all development costs; these would be capitalized under U.S. GAAP, thereby increasing Ericsson's net income by 20 percent. The inconsistent application of such practices within a country (and across countries) diminishes the value of financial statement analysis.

Fewer Comparables. The U.S. market is so large that almost every public company has a few "comparables." As one proceeds to smaller economies, the number of comparables decreases rapidly. Practitioners compensate for this shortage by comparing similar firms across national boundaries. Given the different country environments and variable accounting systems, this approach has readily apparent weaknesses.

Reduced Emphasis on Share Price Enhancement. Except in the United States, Canada, and England, corporate managements are not under pressure to boost their share prices. Hostile takeovers are rare and shareholdings are dominated by founding families or associated banks, which hold the long view on value creation. In the average situation, U.S.-trained analysts are frustrated with management's apparent lack of interest in promoting the share price. As one example, Grupo Industrial Bimbo, one of Mexico's largest industrial concerns, refused to talk to security analysts until 1996, despite being a public company for the preceding 20 years.

Liquidity Concerns.   With the exception of the United States, United Kingdom, Japan, and a few other developed countries, most listed stocks have small floats. Even if the analyst sees a bargain, his clients may have difficulties profiting from his efforts, because anything more than a token buying effort sharply boosts the stock price.

Currency Movements

Overriding all these stockpicking concerns is the possibility of an adverse currency movement. U.S. investors determine their ultimate returns in U.S. dollars, though the earnings propping up a given foreign stock price are denominated in a foreign currency. If the U.S. dollar gains in value relative to the currency—perhaps independent of the foreign country's situation—the U.S. investor can lose money even if his stock selection advances sharply in local currency terms.

For example, in November 1996 a U.S. investor bought one million shares of a German company for 1.5 million German marks (i.e., 1.5 DM per share). One year later, the stock price had risen to 1.8 DM per share, a 20 percent gain. Before converting this result into US$, the investor was proud of his stockpicking abilities. Unfortunately, over the one-year period, the DM/US$ exchange rate shifted from 1.5:1 to 1.8:1. On a US$ basis, the investor's profit was nil, as the declining DM exchange rate wiped out the local share price increase. Exhibit 24–2 illustrates the investor's dilemma.

EXHIBIT 24–2. FX Movements Turn a German Mark Gain into a US$ Breakeven

Date	Action
November 1, 1996	1. Exchange US$1 million into DM 1.5 million.
	2. Buy 1 million German shares at DM 1.5 per share.
November 1, 1997	3. German shares rise to DM 1.8 per share, a 20 percent gain.
	4. Sell 1 million German shares at DM 1.8 per share, realizing DM 1.8 million in proceeds.
	5. Exchange DM 1.8 million into US$1 million at new 1.8:1 exchange rate.
	6. *Bottom line:* Invest US$1 million on November 1, 1996 and receive US$1 million on November 1, 1997. No US$ investment income on 20 percent German price gain.

On the flip side, if the German mark had *appreciated* against the U.S. dollar while the stock price *increased*, the U.S. investor would have achieved a "double dip." Not only would his stockpicking skills be rewarded, but his net returns (in US$) would be boosted due to the favorable foreign exchange movement.

In a few foreign markets, U.S. investors can eliminate the impact of unforeseen currency movements by buying insurance, which is readily available in the form of foreign exchange futures contracts. Such insurance is not cheap, and its practical use is limited to a handful of the most developed economies.

AMERICAN DEPOSITORY RECEIPTS

To facilitate the foreign investment process, international companies and U.S. stock exchanges promote the use of American Depository Receipts (ADRs). An ADR is nothing more than a legal certificate establishing the investor's ownership in a stated number of foreign shares, which are held on deposit in the vault of a respectable U.S. bank. Because ADRs are denominated in dollars and trade within U.S. borders, the unfamiliar legal, tax, and regulatory complications of trading "in country" are avoided.

TWO CATEGORIES OF FOREIGN STOCK MARKETS

Foreign stock markets are classified into two categories: (1) developed country and (2) emerging market. For the rest of this chapter, we'll consider developed country stocks. Chapter 25 reviews the second category.

DEVELOPED COUNTRY MARKETS

Developed countries are those nations that approach the United States in terms of wealth and economic development. Prominent examples include Japan, Germany, England, France, and Italy. Smaller developed nations include Denmark, Switzerland, and Sweden. These countries have stable economies with favorable prospects. Their capital markets are sophisticated, corporate disclosure is enforced, and trading is reasonably aboveboard. A strong currency and moderate inflationary outlook allow the issuance of long-term, fixed-rate corporate bonds that serve as a reference for equity market returns. In such markets, the principal analytical tools of discounted cash flow and relative value have a strong relevance to the stock pricing function.

As the financial markets become global, the stock markets of these countries are evolving into the U.S. model. At the same time, their local companies develop a greater appreciation for a favorable public profile. This means they disclose more information and interact with analysts regularly.

Hundreds of foreign "developed country" stocks trade in the United States. Well-known examples include:

- *BHP* (Australia). Global mining company.
- *British Airways* (United Kingdom). Top international airline.
- *Ericsson* (Sweden). One of the world's largest telecommunications equipment manufacturers.
- *NTT* (Japan). Japanese telephone monopoly.
- *Nestlé* (Switzerland). International consumer products company.
- *Polygram* (Netherlands). Global media company.

Security Analysis Approach—Developed Country

Assuming the analyst does a little digging, the evaluation of a developed country ADR is surprisingly similar to the methodology employed for a U.S. issue. All financial reports are printed in English, disclosure approximates U.S. standards and low inflation permits the use of U.S.-style historical accounting (also, U.S. GAAP conversion is shown in the corporate reports). The firm's finance officers speak English and respond readily to investor questions and correspondence. Besides the lack of comparables, the biggest complication for the U.S.-based ADR investor is referencing the local macroeconomic, capital market, and industry data. That's one reason large investment banks employ teams of analysts around the world, rather than just in the United States.

In terms of operating characteristics, the developed country multinationals resemble giant U.S. firms in many respects. Ericsson, for example, realizes only 8 percent of sales in Swedish kroner. About 65 percent of sales are denominated in U.S. dollar-linked currencies, representing products shipped to dozens of countries. Assuming that accounting differences are normalized, many practitioners feel comfortable in applying U.S.-type discount rates and valuation multiples across sovereign boundaries. Thus, Roche Industries, the large Swiss drug company, is frequently compared with Merck or Eli Lilly.

As the issuers get smaller and more localized in operation, practitioners tend to take a country-specific approach to discounted cash flow and relative value. Thus, a media analyst is likely to compare Associated Newspapers (United Kingdom) to United Newspapers (United Kingdom), rather than including a U.S. firm such as the Washington Post Company (United States) in the comparison.

In both the multinational drug case and the local publishing firm example, the analyst completes his financial projections in the issuer's local currency. He then translates projected dividend flow and the ultimate terminal value into US$ at the forecast exchange rate. A hypothetical example for Honda Motor Company appears as Exhibit 24–3.

EXHIBIT 24–3. Rate of Return Calculation—Honda Motor Company Share

Step 1. Determine Expected US$ Cash Flows

Honda Results	1998	1999	2000	2001	2002
Earnings per share (yen)	Y230	Y270	Y315	Y360	Y420
Dividends per share (yen)	15	15	20	20	25
Average Yen/US$ exchange rate	120	120	120	110	110
US$ Cash Flows					
Dividends	$0.13	$0.13	$0.17	$0.18	$ 0.23
Sale price	—	—	—	—	$61.10
US$ cash flows	$0.13	$0.13	$0.17	$0.18	$61.33
Discounted at 15%	$0.11	$0.10	$0.11	$0.10	$30.51

Where

Sale price = (EPS × 2002 P/E multiple) × 2002 exchange rate
Sale price = (Y420 × 16) × ($1/Y110)
Sale price = Y6720 × ($1/Y110)
Sale price = US$61.10

Step 2. Compare Present Value to Current Market Price

A. Present value per Honda Motor share = $0.11 + $0.10 + $0.11 + $0.10 + $30.51
    = US$30.93

B. Market price of Honda Motor share = Current market price × Current exchange
    rate
    = Y3000 × ($1/Y120)
    = US$25.00

Conclusion
Honda Motor shares are a good investment, since the US$30.93 estimated present
value exceeds the US$25.00 market price by the 15% margin of safety.

Discount Rates—Developed Country

As Chapter 12 described, the discount rate for determining the present
value of a U.S. stock is derived from the Capital Asset Pricing Model,
whereby:

$$K_{U.S.} = R_F + \beta\,(R_M - R_F)$$

where $K_{U.S.}$ = Expected rate of return on U.S. stock
    R_F = U.S. government bond rate (from newspaper)
    β = Beta of the stock (from financial publications)
    R_M = Assumed to be U.S. government bond rate plus a 6% to 8%
        equity market return premium

Applying the formula to a foreign stock creates some problems. First,
the foreign stock doesn't have a meaningful β because its ADRs don't have

a long trading history. Second, few data services calculate an adjusted β for a foreign stock's price behavior in its local market. Third, practitioners and academics are unsure whether (1) to use the local government bond rate and the local market return in the equation, or (2) to continue with the U.S.-derived variables and then add a foreign risk premium. Fourth, if the analyst wishes to work with the foreign risk premium concept, how large should the premium be?

One academic view is to calculate the foreign stock's k entirely with local variables: R_F is the local government bond rate, R_M is the expected return on the local market, and β is measured against the local index. The resultant present value of the stock's predicted cash flow is denominated in the foreign currency, which is then translated into U.S. dollars at the current exchange rate.

While this technique has some theoretical strengths, I have yet to see professionals use it. Two practical shortcomings inhibit its implementation. One, the calculation and publication of foreign stock betas (i.e., measured against the home market index) is very limited. Two, the resultant discount rate doesn't include the future risk of adverse currency movements against the U.S. dollar. This risk is foremost in the minds of U.S. investors.

More research needs to be done on foreign discount rates for the U.S. investor, but at this time there is no definitive technique. When I examine a foreign stock, I use the U.S.-derived R_F and R_M while guestimating the appropriate values for β and foreign risk premium. The formula, which is far from theoretically perfect, is stated:

$$K_{Foreign} = R_F + \beta \, (R_M - R_F) + FRP$$

where $K_{Foreign}$ = Expected rate of return on a foreign stock in U.S. dollars
 R_F = U.S. government bond rate (from newspaper)
 β = Average beta of comparable U.S. stocks
 R_M = Assumed to be U.S. government bond rate (R_F) plus 6% to 8%
 FRP = Foreign risk premium. Probably ranging from 1% to 5% for developed country stocks

FOREIGN RISK PREMIUM

Given two practically identical stocks—a U.S. stock and a foreign stock— the discount rate on the foreign stock is higher for the U.S. investor. The reduced information access, the less transparent trading environment, and the adverse currency issue combine to make the foreign stock a relatively riskier investment. Quantifying this extra risk into a single number is a subjective exercise, and people do it differently.

A starting point for many practitioners is examining the difference between the 10-year U.S. Treasury rate and the developed country's sovereign bond rate (denominated in US$). Thus, if this difference is 1 percent between

EXHIBIT 24–4. Higher Discount Rates for Foreign Stocks

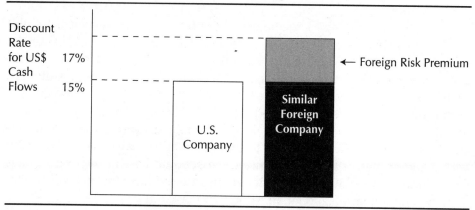

the United States and Italy, the FRP has a floor of 1 percent. Depending on the analyst's assessment of the overall risk of the foreign stock versus its U.S. comparables, he adds additional premium to this number (see Exhibit 24–4). For most developed country stocks, the FRP has a 1 to 5 percent range.

COMPARABLE COMPANY MULTIPLES

For large foreign multinationals that operate across national boundaries and have U.S.-listed ADRs, it's reasonable to compare their valuation multiples against similar U.S. multinationals, assuming the requisite U.S. GAAP accounting adjustments have been made and no particular political risks are in evidence. Indeed, the reader should take note of the foreign exposure included in prominent U.S. stocks. Coca-Cola, for example, derives 80 percent

EXHIBIT 24–5. Multinational Stock Comparisons—Consumer Companies

Multinational	Home Country	P/E Ratio	Enterprise Value/EBIT
Coca-Cola	United States	43×	30×
Procter & Gamble	United States	24	15
Sara Lee	United States	19	14
Cadbury-Schweppes	United Kingdom	14	10
Grand Metropolitan	United Kingdom	15	11
Kirin	Japan	35	14
Unilevèr	Netherlands	18	11
LVMH	France	25	15
Nestlé	Switzerland	18	10

of its income overseas. Exhibit 24–5 shows a comparison chart used by practitioners.

As noted in Chapter 13, the objective of preparing charts such as Exhibit 24–5 is to identify discrepancies in relative value. If Procter & Gamble, Grand Met, and Nestlé have similar businesses, historical results, and future prospects, then their respective shares should have similar valuation multiples. A lower-than-average multiple indicates a bargain, whereas a high multiple means an overpriced stock. Brokerage firm reports on multinational stocks are chockful of these comparisons. However, the myriad differences between the "comparables" signify that the analysts are comparing apples and oranges. No matter. Since the discounted cash flow technique is out of favor on Wall Street, practitioners need some rational basis for investment recommendations. Relative value fills the void.

SUMMARY

Practitioners have successfully transferred U.S. valuation techniques to international securities. Developed country markets are approaching the U.S. model, but significant differences exist. The risk of adverse currency movements is difficult to quantify, but it suggests a premium rate-of-return requirement.

QUESTIONS AND SHORT PROBLEMS

1. Circle the principal reasons why some U.S. investors purchase foreign stocks:
   a. Diversification away from U.S. stocks.
   b. Higher returns than U.S. stocks.
   c. Lower risk than U.S. stocks.
   d. More disclosure than U.S. stocks.
   e. Presumed pricing inefficiencies in foreign markets.
   f. Some foreign countries have higher economic growth rates than the United States.

2. Outline the six principal factors that make U.S.-style security analysis—as set forth in this book—less relevant in many foreign stock markets.

3. Which one of the following activities is commonplace in many foreign markets?
   a. In-depth top-down analysis.
   b. Insider trading.
   c. Underpricing management warrants.
   d. Overpricing initial public offerings.
   e. Institutional bias against small issuers.

4. Generally, a foreign stock market has fewer "comparables" for any given industry player, as compared to the U.S. stock market. Which valuation method becomes, as a result, less appropriate?
    a. Leveraged buyout.
    b. Liquidation.
    c. Relative value.
    d. Discounted cash flow.
    e. Technical analysis.

5. If a U.S. investor purchases shares of Karlstadt A.G., a German retailing firm, on the Frankfurt exchange, he faces (circle one answer):
    a. Higher beta than a U.S. retailer stock.
    b. Management that is unreceptive to increasing shareholder value.
    c. Currency risk.
    d. Insider trading in the stock.
    e. Liberal accounting.

6. Felix Raider was considering a hostile takeover of a French company. On July 1, 1999, he exchanged US$100 million into 600 million French Francs. On the same day he acquired 50 million shares of Rencoil, S.A., on the Paris Bourse for 12 French Francs per share. On January 2, 2000, his takeover attempt failed and he accepted "greenmail" from Rencoil in the form of a buyout of his position at 15 French Francs per share. Assuming he liquidated his French currency on January 2, 2000 at an exchange rate of 6.6FF per US$, what was his annualized rate of return?

7. What is the instrument whereby many U.S. investors acquire a direct economic interest in specific foreign stocks?
    a. American Depository Receipts.
    b. Global Trust Certificates.
    c. Securitized Share Receipts.
    d. Limited Partnership Interests.
    e. Exchangeable Common Shares.

8. Which of the following countries is not considered a "developed market"?
    a. Brazil.
    b. Japan.
    c. Denmark.
    d. Italy.

9. How does the presence of long-term fixed-rate bonds (denominated in the local currency) assist in the security analysis process of shares in a foreign stock market?

10. What is *not* a feature of a foreign company ADR?
    a. Financial statements conforming to U.S. generally accepted accounting principles.
    b. Financial reports written in English.

    c. Adequate disclosure of material facts.

    d. Footnotes including the impact of projections.

11. Recalculate the present value of a Honda Motor Company share (see Exhibit 24–3), using the following modified assumptions:

    a. Average yen/US$ exchange rate in 2002 is ¥ 100/US$.

    b. 18 percent discount rate.

12. The five-year sovereign US$-denominated bonds of Denmark trade at 150 basis points higher than five-year U.S. government bonds. What is the minimum FRP (foreign risk premium) that a U.S. investor should use in his discounted cash flow evaluation of a Danish stock?

25

Emerging Markets:
The Final Frontier

*In their search for value, U.S. equity investors travel far and wide.
They now appear regularly in exotic locales, where stock markets are
sometimes in their infancy. In this chapter, we'll look at applying
rational analysis to these speculative markets.*

Emerging market equity investment is one of the hottest areas on Wall
Street. From a base of practically zero only seven years ago, approximately
$100 billion of new portfolio money has flowed into these stocks. Amidst
this spectacular growth, the U.S. investment industry has rushed to develop
a research function that can capably appraise these dynamic, but risky,
opportunities.

Before proceeding, it is helpful to define an "emerging market." The International Finance Corporation, the private sector arm of the World Bank,
first coined the term in 1984 as a positive-sounding synonym for "developing country." A developing country has an economy that is poor relative to
the highly developed, rich economies represented by the United States,
Canada, Western European nations, Japan, Australia, and a few other countries. According to the World Bank, developing nations include all countries
with a per capita income of less than $9,000. Mexico, for example, has a per
capita income of $3,000. (By comparison, per capita income in the United
States is $30,000.) This designation covers countries encompassing 85 per-
cent of the world's population and includes those whose gross domestic
product (GDP) is rapidly growing (e.g., Indonesia + 6% annually) as well as
those whose economies are moving steadily backward (e.g., Zaire).

For people who haven't traveled extensively, it is difficult to visualize
the grinding poverty afflicting most developing countries. Things most of
us take for granted in the United States—a telephone, a decent home, and a

family car—are not within the means of the average breadwinner in developing nations. Well-paying jobs are scarce and economic advancement opportunities are limited, as wealth is concentrated in the hands of a small elite who promote a rigid class structure.

For years, the majority of these nations clung to statist or socialistic economic policies that tended to retard economic growth rather than foster it. The failure of these policies and, later, the fall of communism, brought about economic liberalization to many of them. Demonstrated successes in selected nations such as Chile, Taiwan, and Thailand (and corresponding increases in local share prices) convinced foreign investors of the potential for huge gains in equity values as certain countries "emerged" from a period of economic stagnation to one of rapid growth.

Today, over 60 developing countries have stock markets and the number of domestic companies listed on their exchanges approximates 20,000 (which is a healthy fraction of the developed country total). Of this amount, less than 10 percent trade actively, and an even smaller number represent the bulk of market capitalization. In India, the situation is typical; 10 stocks account for 30 percent of the market's total value. As a result, security analysts usually focus on just 20 to 30 large-cap stocks in a given market.

The stock markets are small compared with those of major industrial countries. Brazil, the largest emerging market, is only 3 percent the size of the U.S. market, as indicated in Exhibit 25–1. Considering the restricted liquidity of most Brazilian stocks, the base of investment opportunities for investors in Brazil is minuscule relative to that in the United States. This

EXHIBIT 25–1. Comparative Sizes of Market Capitalization

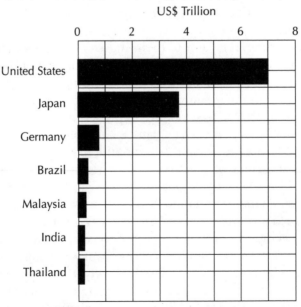

EXHIBIT 25–2. Typical Emerging Market

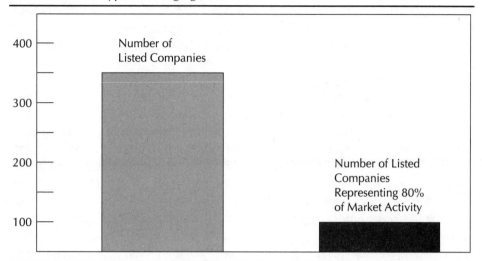

situation is identical in other prominent emerging markets including Argentina, China, Chile, India, Indonesia, Malaysia, Mexico, Philippines, Thailand, and Turkey (see Exhibit 25–2).

One only has to observe the stock exchanges of a few emerging markets to understand the vast differences between them and their developed country counterparts. As an investment executive for the International Finance Corporation (IFC), I visited several stock exchanges in Latin America. The Medellin Stock Exchange in Colombia, for example, is a far cry from the image of the modern exchange. Situated in a room that resembles an elementary school gymnasium, the Medellin exchange is positively tranquil. Trading happens only two hours per day from 10 A.M. to noon, and transactions are recorded in chalk on elevated blackboards. There is nary a computer in the place, and the few phones available are the old-fashioned rotary variety. After lunchtime, the building is virtually deserted, with a lone security guard standing by the entrance.

EMERGING MARKETS AND SECURITY ANALYSIS

Practitioners are gradually applying conventional security analysis to these exotic markets. They are writing research reports incorporating top-down reviews, financial projections, and relative values. Despite such attempts at rational analysis, the approach is valid only in a handful of the more advanced countries, and perhaps with just a few of the dominant stocks in the lesser markets. For the most part, share valuations remain the subject of speculation and momentum investing. Consider the remarks of Peter Alexander, who works for Direct Pacific Financial Services, a Shanghai-based brokerage firm. Commenting on the wild gyrations in China's stock market in 1997, he said, "Compare it to an OTB (off track betting) parlor at 42nd Street and Sixth Avenue (in New York). There are people staring at a huge screen; there's some guy crying in the corner that he just blew his daughter's college tuition, and the boss is in the back counting all the money. Exactly the same."

A gambling mentality prevails in these markets, and the serious investor who isn't willing to dedicate a full-time effort is better off participating in a country fund that more or less "indexes" a given market. Even savvy investors such as ING Emerging Markets Investors (EMI) are emphasizing the country approach, rather than picking individual stocks. According to Scott Gordon, an EMI portfolio manager, "We tend to express a broad view on a market rather than a view of the stock or company's performance." In a *Latin Finance* interview, he cited studies which "indicate that picking the right emerging market country has been a much more important criteria than picking the right stocks."

The five factors that inhibit effective security analysis in international markets (Chapter 24) come up in spades in the emerging market arena:

1. Less information.
2. Questionable trading practices.
3. Unclear accounting standards.
4. Few comparables.
5. Reduced emphasis on share price enhancement.

Less Information

Emerging markets have fewer disclosure requirements than the developed countries. Furthermore, emerging market companies are lax in reporting events affecting their respective businesses, and they release financial results in an untimely fashion. If the corporation is controlled by a founding family, the managers (who usually are family members) are reluctant to provide information to the public and meet with analysts, citing competitive reasons. Notable exceptions to this behavior are the emerging market companies which have American Depository Receipts (ADRs) listed in the United States; they must adhere to stock exchange standards.

Questionable Trading Practices

Insider trading, front-running, poor execution, and other unsavory practices are common on emerging market exchanges. To some, the situation is reminiscent of the U.S. market's lack of regulation in the early 1900s. Charles Randolph of KPMG Peat Marwick summarized the problem in the Czech Republic, "One of the biggest complaints of the Czech financial markets has been not that there's a lack of laws on the books, but rather there's a lack of enforcement." Although such practices are regrettable, for now foreign investors in these markets consider them a cost of doing business.

The phenomenal gains realized in certain markets overshadow the trading regime. Exhibit 25–3 provides summary data. In the first 10 months of 1997, Russia's stock market was up 250 percent. The Budapest market rose 98 percent.

Unclear Accounting Standards

The variety of accounting regimes in the developing world and the differing manner of application present the analyst with a daunting challenge in interpreting financial results and estimating a company's current earnings power. The difficulties increase as one goes down the corporate status chain (see Exhibit 25–4).

The large firms that list their ADRs in the United States adhere to the strictest accounting certification and presentation. Furthermore, they show their results in US$ equivalent and provide U.S. GAAP translations. The remaining blue chip firms, numbering from 20 to 30 companies in an emerging market, release financial statements that are usually a fair representation of the economic results of their respective businesses. Nevertheless, the practitioner needs to examine these statements with a great deal of care and must be prepared to ask management pointed questions that can uncover well-hidden deficiencies. One Mexican firm I visited papered over operating losses by buying small businesses at prices below book value. The

EXHIBIT 25–3. Performance of Emerging Market Stock Indices—Percentage Appreciation in Stock Market Index[1]

Emerging Markets	Five Years Ended October 1997
Argentina	92%
Brazil	252
Chile	56
India	(30)
Indonesia	(1)
Malaysia	(21)
Mexico	11
Thailand	(71)
Turkey	300
United States	118

[1] US$ appreciation.

EXHIBIT 25-4. Emerging Market Companies—Quality of Accounting Disclosure

Companies with ADRs listed in the United States	High-standard of disclosure. Accurate audits with supplementary presentation in U.S. GAAP.
Other first-tier emerging market companies	Financial statements provide a reasonably fair presentation of economic results. The analyst must still conduct a thorough study to estimate current earnings power.
Second-tier firms	Publicly disclosed accounting results are suspect. Income tax avoidance and family enrichment are normal practices. Foreign investors should seek an extra margin of safety.

company then wrote up the assets and realized a gain; all this was permitted by the firm's independent auditor.

As the investor proceeds to the second-tier firms that make up 40 to 50 percent of an emerging market's capitalization, the accounting shenanigans increase. At many such firms, an important objective is minimizing asset, value-added, and income taxes. As a result, perhaps 10 to 30 percent of sales go unreported and the tax burden is commensurately reduced. Furthermore, the majority of second-tier companies are family affairs, so there is little hesitation in placing personal charges on the books, obviously at the expense of outside shareholders. Also, transfer pricing between the family companies is frequently an undisclosed issue. If the publicly traded pulp producer purchases its lumber from the family's privately owned timber operation, the price of that timber should be a matter of public record. Although local regulations require that listed companies have their books audited by an independent accounting firm (or designated auditor), emerging market accountants often turn a blind eye to these practices or simply fail to perform the necessary investigations.

The majority of investment books and research reports on emerging markets fail to publicize these accounting problems. This deficiency highlights the need for more study of these frontier markets, before the average investor takes the plunge.

Few Comparables

Adherents of relative value include most professional investors, and they find the shortage of comparables for any given stock to be a real problem. The solution is to compare a telephone company stock in Thailand with one in another developing country, such as Indonesia, India, or Mexico. Since sovereign factors dominate the pricing of securities in each market, this approach has a critical weakness, yet professionals continue the practice.

Reduced Emphasis on Share Price Enhancement

The preponderance of emerging market companies are controlled by their respective founding families. Therein lies the fundamental conflict between listed firms and their outside shareholders. Families are not driven to maximize value for the benefit of outside shareholders. Rather, the emphasis is on keeping the family executives in power, so they can preserve their status and influence within the community. This represents an important philosophical difference with U.S.-style investors, who want to see an issuer pursue aggressive tactics that boost its share price.

The "family-first" attitude is manifested in several ways. One, the company may pass on promising growth opportunities if the resultant financing requirement means ownership dilution. Two, the firm may display a marked preference for family executives, as opposed to hiring skilled outside management. And three, it may permit the family's enrichment (through personal expenses or insider deals) at the expense of the passive outside shareholder. Exhibit 25–5 summarizes these issues.

As institutional shareholders play a larger role in the emerging markets, the family-first preoccupation is likely to diminish. In the meantime, investors who want to minimize the problem should focus on public privatizations and new technology businesses. Public privatizations are businesses that were formerly owned by the local government. As a result, there is no founding family and ownership is dispersed. Prominent shareholders of these privatizations often include multinationals that believe in creating value quickly. New technology businesses in the emerging markets such as cellular phones or cable TV, are frequently run by a combination of local investors and international companies. The latter share the U.S. portfolio manager's penchant for near-term gains.

Currency Risks

Emerging market stocks present the U.S. investor with considerable currency risks. Unexpected devaluations against the U.S. dollar are common

---

EXHIBIT 25–5. Family Influence in Emerging Market Stocks

The family-controlled firm often:
- Is not driven to maximize shareholder value.
- Is reluctant to meet with analysts and provide information.
- Prefers family executives to professional managers.
- Sacrifices growth opportunities to avoid shareholder dilution.
- Permits improper insider arrangements.
- Stresses income tax avoidance instead of complete financial reporting.

---

occurrences and contribute to stock price declines in both local and US$ terms. The most notable currency devaluation in an emerging market was the peso decline in Mexico in 1994. In a few days, the peso dropped 41 percent in value against the U.S. dollar, and the Mexican stock index plummeted 54 percent over the next three months. Similar events took place in Pakistan in 1996 and Thailand in 1997.

Unlike developed markets such as Japan and Germany, emerging markets don't have currency hedging mechanisms. Plenty of investors want to protect against devaluations in these countries, but no financial service provider wants to stand up and insure against the possibility. The risk of devaluation is simply too great.

STOCK-PRICING GUIDELINES

In the typical emerging market, the quasi-scientific investors who rely on the discounted cash flow and relative value techniques are greatly outnumbered by the speculators, country rotators, and momentum investors. As a result, the pricing of a stock often has little relation to its perceived economic value, as calculated using this book's methodology. These discrepancies present interesting investment opportunities (both on the long and short side), but the time it takes for the market to "correct" itself is sometimes prolonged, relative to the time needed for pricing inefficiencies in the United States to resolve themselves. Veteran emerging market professionals acknowledge the situation and urge investors to consider the long-term perspective.

Mark Mobius, director of the Templeton Funds' emerging market research effort, summarized the long-term philosophy, "Taking a long view of emerging markets will yield excellent results for the investor prepared to be patient and willing to apply sound and tested principles in a diligent and consistent manner. The approach we take in our reports is not to focus on the short-term since we invest the funds entrusted to us not for a three-month, six-month, or even one-year period, but for at least a five-year period. Over the many years that Templeton Funds have been investing, we have found that striving for short-term performance increases the risks to the shareholders and actually results in poorer returns. Only by taking the long view will we be able to do the best job for investors."

The speculative nature of these markets means they lurch from one valuation extreme to another. An investor can buy a Venezuelan stock at 500 bolivars per share, believing its intrinsic value is 700 bolivars. However, if market sentiment becomes negative, the stock price can easily drop 30 percent (to 350 bolivars) in a few weeks. Even though the margin of safety has widened to 50 percent, it takes an investor with a strong stomach to "double-up" at the lower price. He's never quite sure when the crash will bottom out. Exhibit 25–6 illustrates the volatility of emerging markets. A thorough review of stock selection in these markets is beyond the scope of

EXHIBIT 25–6. The Emerging Market Roller Coaster

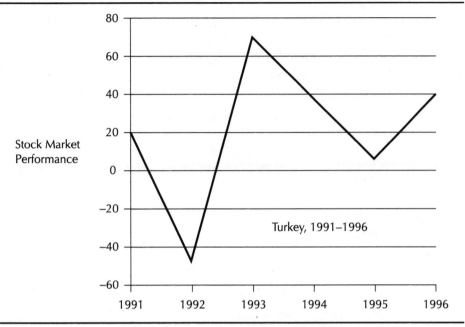

Stock Market Performance

Turkey, 1991–1996

Note the extreme volatility of Turkey's stock market.

this book, but a few principles can be applied to the individual segments of the top-down format (see Exhibit 25–7).

Country

Unlike the United States, most emerging markets lack an independent central bank. Economic stability is compromised by capricious government policies and legislators fail to appreciate the benefits of strong financial markets. In contrast, foreign investors seek a stable country in both a political and economic sense. (Exceptions are made for specific companies that deal primarily in export industries, such as gold mining or oil exploration, where revenues are generated in a hard currency like the U.S. dollar.) Besides macroeconomic matters, foreign investors assess the likelihood of government interference with their equity investment. Defined as political risk, these actions include foreign exchange blockage, legal discrimination, and expropriation. Just recently, the Hungarian government enticed Western investors into the electric utility industry by promising to raise electricity prices by 35 percent. When the time came to implement the tariff increase in 1996, the government reneged, fearing riots in the streets. After intense investor pressure, the government pushed through a 24 percent increase. Political action reduced investor returns.

EXHIBIT 25–7. Emerging Markets—Stock Selection Guidelines

A few guidelines to follow in buying an emerging market stock include:

Country
- Reasonably stable economic indicators.
- Moderate political risk.

Capital Markets
- Semblance of fair trading and honest disclosure.
- Degree of liquidity.

Industry
- Good growth prospects.
- Internationally competitive.
- Profits not reliant on
    Tariffs.
    Quotas.
    Other trade barriers.

Company
- Modern management techniques.
- Widely held ownership or influential multinational shareholder that promotes share price enhancement.
- Strong government connections through family or management.
- Good track record and solid balance sheet.
- Growth prospects are favorable.
- Share price meets margin-of-safety rule.

Capital Markets

Since few stocks move against the general trend in an emerging market, the investor needs to be confident of the market's upward direction (or downward move, in the case of a short sale). Additionally, a minimal standard of fair trading and honest disclosure is a strong plus for the foreign participant. With many countries suffering from high inflation, interest rates are unusually high by U.S. standards. Annual rates of 30 to 50 percent are not uncommon.

Industry

The primary focus of the foreign investor is finding local industries with good growth prospects. Surprisingly, many industries considered stodgy in the United States are considered hot in the emerging markets. One illustration is the electric utility industry. In the United States, this industry is mature; unit sales growth is only 2 to 3 percent annually. In contrast, electricity demand growth can be 2 to 3× this rate in a market such as Brazil, because advancing prosperity means more electronic conveniences and appliances. The same can be said for the old-fashioned wireline phone company. The United States, with 60 lines per 100 residents, is saturated for conventional phones, but in the emerging markets, the average family doesn't have a phone. Thus, Peru's phone company, with an average of 6 phones per 100 residents, can experience 10 years of 10 percent unit growth, and the country would still remain far below its saturation level.

To ensure long-term shareholder returns, the local industry has to be cost competitive, or substitute providers will enter the market. Determining the economic efficiency of a local industry, and the magnitude of this threat is a challenge. In many emerging markets, local industries are strongly protected against foreign competition by high tariffs, import quotas, or obtrusive regulations enforced by the government. Because of an artificial pricing environment, a local industry that is inefficient by international cost standards can generate consistent profits. The textile industry in Colombia, for example, survived for years using outdated methods; eventually, extensive smuggling from India and Bangladesh crippled local producers.

Alternatively, the artificial environment enables the local industry to charge oligopolistic prices, thus providing excess profits and the image of premium economic returns. In Mexico, 1996 cement prices averaged US$75 per ton, and the primary cement firms, Cemex and Apasco, were very profitable. Across the border, in south Texas, the price was US$40 per ton. With a $10 per ton transportation expense and a $5 tariff, imported U.S. cement had a landed cost of about $55 per ton in Mexico, but no one saw U.S. cement south of the border. The Mexican government halted U.S. cement at customs for "quality inspections" and Mexican unions refused to handle the product. The little U.S. cement that was used in Mexico arrived in border towns through smuggling.

Depending on the nature of the protections, the analyst must determine whether they represent a sustainable competitive advantage. Does the industry have enough influence with the government (and with future governments) to maintain the status quo? If the answer is no, the analyst must assess the likelihood and timing of a rollback of the protections. For example, the Mexican cement industry has enjoyed import protection through numerous administrations. The Mexican packaged food industry, however, has never enjoyed this benefit.

The practitioner must also consider the investment required by industry participants to fight off international competitors. More investment means fewer dividends and more share issuances, translating into lower share prices.

If the industry's international advantage is readily apparent—such as cheap labor—the analyst wants to be sure of the duration of that advantage. Relatively high wages in Singapore sent low-tech assembly industries to lower-wage Malaysia. Now, as Malaysian salaries increase, the jobs are shipped to Indonesia. Paul Ziegler, Asian CEO for Asea Brown Boveri, the Swedish power equipment manufacturer, said, "It's just common sense. You make these things where they are cheapest to make," noting that labor costing his company the equivalent of $10 in Singapore can be obtained for $3 in Malaysia and just $1.60 in Indonesia.

Company

The company selection process incorporates appraisal techniques that are similar to those discussed earlier in the book. Good growth prospects, a solid balance sheet, Western-style management, and enlightened owners are especially notable for emerging market investments. Furthermore, because of the heavy government influence and arbitrary regulation that characterize these economies, a firm with close ties to the ruling party is a good bet. Since governments come and go in these countries, political influence can wane, so it is important that the firm selected for investment have intrinsic competitive qualities. Helmut Paul, who administered the International Finance Corporation's vast Latin American portfolio, explains, "In today's global arena, it's not enough for an emerging market company to be excellent by country or by regional standards; it must be competitive by world standards. And a good distribution system or local brand name is not sufficient; these can be duplicated by international competition."

INFLATION ACCOUNTING

The existence of high rates of inflation in undeveloped countries is hardly new. Lacking the fiscal and monetary discipline of the developed nations, many of these countries suffer annual inflation rates of 30 percent or more. Severe inflation plays havoc with the ability of historical cost accounting to provide meaningful corporate performance measurements.

Exhibit 25–8 provides sales data for a Turkish company from 1994 through 1996. On the surface, the Turkish business looks like a tremendous growth company, but inflation rates of 88 percent and 80 percent in 1995 and 1996, respectively, distorted the firm's true progress. If we adjust the

EXHIBIT 25–8. Elbo Gaz Mamulleri ve Kontrol Cihazlari (in billions of lira)

	1994	1995	1996
Sales	1,427	3,046	5,998
Growth	—	+113%	+97%

The company is a Turkish manufacturer of valves.

EXHIBIT 25–9. Elbo Gaz Mamulleri ve
Kontrol Cihazlari (in billions of 1996 lira)

	1994	1995	1996
Sales	4,826	5,480	5,998
Growth	—	+14%	+9%

sales data for inflationary effects using 1996 as the base year, the company's growth is much different (see Exhibit 25–9).

Adjusted for inflation, the new results show the 1996 revenues increasing by 9 percent in *real terms*. This is a major departure from the 97 percent growth rate set forth earlier.

To improve financial reporting in inflationary economies, many developing nations require public companies to use inflation accounting, whereby the numbers in the financial statements are adjusted for changes in prices. Depending on the country, the emphasis is "constant currency" (i.e., adjusting for general inflation) or "current cost" (i.e., adjusting specific accounts for specific cost increases).

Income Statement under Inflation Accounting

On the income statement, the presentation is straightforward for an individual accustomed to GAAP. When the analyst reaches the interest expense line, however, it gets complicated. There, he encounters "comprehensive financing costs," as set forth for Grupo Minsa, a Mexican food producer (see Exhibit 25–10).

EXHIBIT 25–10. Grupo Minsa, S.A.—Comprehensive Financing Costs under Inflation Accounting (millions of 1996 Mexican pesos)

Sales	Ps. 2,219
Cost of sales	(1,757)
Gross margin	462
Operating expenses	(301)
Operating income	161
Comprehensive financing costs:	
Interest expenses, net	(81)
Foreign exchange (gain) loss	5
Gain (loss) on net monetary position	(82)
Net comprehensive financing income (cost)	6
Income before taxes	Ps. 167

"Interest expenses, net" is an item that bears close watching for a company like Grupo Minsa. Some firms keep large cash balances as a reserve for national liquidity crises, even if they must borrow to maintain the reserve. Interest income can thus be sizable in relation to interest expense. With good credit ratings, others play the arbitrage game. They borrow in the international markets at a low rate, and lend the money locally at a high rate. Cellulose Aracruz, a large Brazilian pulp and paper concern, derives 30 percent of its income in this manner.

Due to the small size of emerging economies and the limited availability of local borrowings, a sizable firm may have substantial foreign exchange dealings, perhaps through exporting abroad or by borrowing hard currencies. The volatility of the local currency (a soft currency) relative to the hard currencies (e.g., US$, Japanese yen, Deutsche mark) may result in significant gains and losses. When the peso devalued in 1994, Grupo Minsa incurred a Ps. 112 million loss in foreign exchange versus the Ps. 5 million gain in 1996.

The gain or loss on net monetary position is a confusing item. It attempts to measure the effect of inflation on monetary assets (cash and claims to receive a fixed amount of money, such as receivables) versus monetary liabilities (obligations to pay a fixed amount of money in the future, such as accounts payable and debt). Most companies have more monetary liabilities than assets, so this account usually shows a net gain (as a noncash income item).

To eliminate the arbitrage and noncash effects of these entries on the income statement, professionals use EBIT as a performance measure, rather than net earnings. EBITDA is also a popular statistic.

Balance Sheet

On the balance sheet, inflation accounting requires the restatement of multiple items on a frequent basis. Prior periods are also restated. Important fixed assets are sometimes reappraised each year, while other assets are revalued by the inflation index. The net result falls into an equity account called "revaluation." Companies with a large fixed asset component have significant revaluation accounts. Grupo Minsa's revaluation account represents 33 percent of stockholders' equity (see Exhibit 25–11).

With all the adjustments and revaluations, the balance sheet of the emerging market firm using inflation accounting is less understandable than its developed country counterpart. The analyst must pay special attention to the footnotes and historical comparisons.

For those firms operating in high-inflation countries and still using historical cost accounting, the common practice among sensible practitioners is to index the results. Once the results have been restated to constant currency, the analyst proceeds to exchange the results into US$ dollars. At the IFC, we translated the past statements at the average exchange rate of the

EXHIBIT 25–11. Grupo Minsa, SA de C.V.—Summary Balance Sheet Data (in millions of 1996 Mexican pesos)

Assets		
Current assets	Ps.	566
Property, plant and equipment, net		947
Other assets		344
	Ps.	1,857
Liabilities and Stockholders' Equity		
Current liabilities	Ps.	339
Long-term debt		340
Stockholders' equity:		
Revaluation	390	
Other equity	788	
Total stockholders' equity		1,178
	Ps.	1,857

Note. Revaluation represented 33 percent of stockholders' equity.

latest year's results. Others translate the data at separate rates over each year. Exhibit 25–12 provides an example using data for the Turkish firm.

PROJECTIONS AND DISCOUNT RATES

Practitioners complete corporate projections in constant currency and U.S. dollars. Obviously, the latter translation involves assumptions about future exchange rates, which are likely to be volatile in the emerging market.

There's no scientific way of selecting an appropriate discount rate for an emerging market stock. Given the degree of country, currency, and company-specific risk, the rate is substantially higher than its U.S. counterpart. As noted in Chapter 24, practitioners begin calculating the foreign risk premium included in such a discount rate by viewing the spread between the

EXHIBIT 25–12. Adjusting Historical Cost Accounting for High Inflation and US$ Exchange Rates (in billions of 1996 Turkish lira)

	Elbo Gaz Mamulleri ve Kontrol Cihazlari		
	1994	**1995**	**1996**
Reported sales	1,427	3,046	5,998
Real sales adjusted for inflation	4,826	5,480	5,998
Translated into US$ at 1996 average exchange rate (US$ millions)	$59.3	$67.3	$73.7

EXHIBIT 25–13. Yield Spread between Emerging Market Sovereign Debt and U.S. Treasury

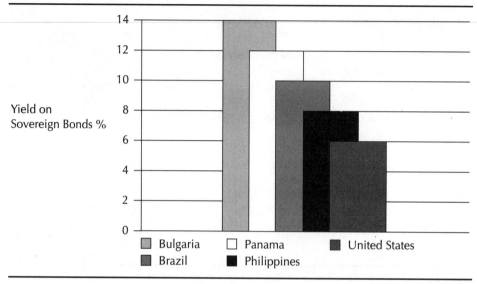

respective interest rates of the country's debt and U.S. Treasury bonds. Since 95 percent of all developing nations fall into the junk bond category, this spread starts at 2 percent and moves higher. Exhibit 25–13 provides examples of sovereign bond returns.

The cost of equity calculation incorporates the notion of risk premium set for in the sovereign bond yields. A practical formula appears below:

$$K_{\text{Emerging Markets}} = R_F + \beta\,(R_M - R_F) + FRP$$

where $K_{\text{Emerging Markets}}$ = Expected rate of return on a foreign stock in U.S. dollars

R_F = U.S. government bond rate (from newspaper)

β = Average beta of comparable U.S. stock

R_M = Assumed to be U.S. government bond rate (R_F) plus 6% to 8%

FRP = Foreign risk premium. Probably varying from 5% to 15%

The discount rate for an emerging market stock is likely to range from 18 to 28 percent. As a practical matter, the discount rate of an emerging market stock is at least 5 percent more than the discount rate of a comparable U.S. security. As the degree of risk grows, so does the premium. Because country and currency risks dominate company-specific factors in emerging markets, practitioners group risk premiums by countries. A low-risk country such as Chile stands in contrast to a high-risk country such as Russia. Prior to the Southeast Asian meltdown in late 1997, the Southeast Asian tigers—Indonesia, Malaysia, Philippines, and Thailand—were classified as low

EXHIBIT 25–14. Emerging Markets—Target Equity Returns by Country

	Recommended Rate of Return (%)
Low Risk	
Chile	
Poland	18–20
Czech Republic	
Medium Risk	
Brazil	
India	
Indonesia	20–25
Mexico	
Thailand	
Turkey	
High Risk	
China	
Peru	25–30
Russia	

risk, illustrating how wrong the consensus can be. They now fall into the medium risk category. Exhibit 25–14 provides a brief listing alongside recommended rates of return.

Given the high targeted returns, many newcomers to the emerging markets expect the stocks to trade at low P/E and EV/EBIT ratios relative to the developed country markets. After all, the larger one makes k in the dividend discount models, the smaller P becomes, as illustrated below:

"Steady-state" or "constant" growth model

$$P = \frac{D_1}{k - g}$$

"Two-step" growth model

$$P = \frac{D_1}{1+k} + \frac{D_2}{(1+k)^2} + \cdots \frac{\dfrac{D_{n+1}}{(k-g)}}{(1+k)^n}$$

where P = Price of stock

D = Annual cash dividend

k = Investor's annual required rate of return in percentage terms
   (k_n may be lower than k in the "two-step" model)

g = Annual dividend growth rate in percentage terms

n = Year in which dividend growth becomes constant

EXHIBIT 25–15. Comparative P/E Ratios—Selected Emerging Markets

	October 1997 P/E Ratio
Low Risk	
Chile	18.0
Poland	12.7
Czech Republic	24.6
Medium Risk	
Brazil	16.4
India	15.2
Indonesia	15.9
Mexico	23.1
Thailand	11.2
Turkey	17.4
High Risk	
China	39.9
Peru	14.5
Russia	Not meaningful
United States	18.5

Source. International Finance Corporation. Note that the P/Es are not normalized for GAAP accounting.

Despite this fact, emerging markets frequently trade at premium P/Es (see Exhibit 25–15). Counterbalancing the higher k is a higher growth rate g, according to emerging market professionals. Furthermore, as the countries' economies mature, investors expect k to decline, which also supports a high P/E. Finally, as noted earlier, for tax reasons many firms understate earnings. Savvy investors include the understatement in their calculations.

RELATIVE VALUE IN THE EMERGING MARKETS

Despite the logical foundations of the dividend discount models, research analysts give them short shrift. As the reader knows, exact projections of dividends are inherently uncertain, and few analysts care to calculate—or even mention—an estimate of k, the discount factor, in research reports. Instead of an intrinsic value estimate based on discounted cash flows, investors are offered relative value analysis, where the positive and negative aspects of a stock are evaluated against those characteristics of similar stocks in the same industry category. The stocks' valuation parameters are then compared and contrasted.

For emerging market stocks, dividend discounting poses problems that are identical to these confronted in developed market analysis, but relative value benchmarks are even more complicated. In any emerging market, the analyst has a small or nonexistent pool of comparable stocks from which to

EXHIBIT 25–16. Latin American Telecom Comparables

Company	Country	Company's Market Capitalization (US$ billions)	P/E	Enterprise Value/ EBITDA
Telebras	Brazil	20	24×	3.4×
Telesp	Brazil	12	33	5.5
CTC	Chile	6	18	6.6
Telefonica de Argentina	Argentina	8	15	5.4
Telecom Argentina	Argentina	6	15	4.4
Telefonica de Peru	Peru	5	15	7.1
Telmex	Mexico	17	14	4.6

Note. A shortage of comparables forces the emerging market telecom analyst to make comparisons across borders.

derive P/E and other ratios. He is forced to evaluate the relative merits of similar companies located in different countries. Thus, Telmex is compared with Telebras, Telefonica de Argentina, and CTC (see Exhibit 25–16). There is an obvious problem here. The "top" of the top-down chain of projections for each to these firms is dramatically different. Accordingly, the analyst should adjust the statistics used in comparing the relative value, but typically they do not, at least not in any quantifiable terms. Growth and risk factors for these stocks are mixed into the valuation ratios, with little discussion of trade-offs. Maybe Telebras was a better growth story than CTC in 1997, but did it deserve a 24 P/E ratio versus CTC's 18 P/E? What differences in P/E ratio should we assign to the country risk of Brazil relative to that of Chile? Should we reduce a Brazilian stock's multiple by four relative to a Chilean company? No one wants to define these numbers.

SUMMARY

Emerging markets represent the final frontier for the security analyst. Situated in exotic locales and dominated by speculative elements, these volatile markets provide good investment opportunities, but the bottom line is that U.S.-style research doesn't travel well. The lack of information, poor regulatory environment, and illiquidity conspire to frustrate investors using the techniques in this book.

Furthermore, the pattern of actual trading suggests that traditional stock picking takes a backseat to sovereign concerns. Investors ignore the important distinctions among individual stocks, focusing instead on countries as a whole. This behavior makes for inefficient pricing, but the investor relying on fundamental analysis to earn premium returns must be prepared to ride out the speculative waves. As a result, only investors with a strong stomach should pursue these markets.

QUESTIONS AND SHORT PROBLEMS

1. An "emerging market" is a country with an annual per capita income of:
   a. Less than $9,000.
   b. More than $3,000.
   c. Between $10,000 and $30,000.
   d. More than $30,000.

2. Which of the following does not characterize an emerging market:
   a. Wealth is concentrated in a small portion of the population.
   b. Most residents have phones, but lack automobiles.
   c. Well paying jobs are scarce.
   d. Society is governed by a rigid class structure.

3. Emerging markets began to attract U.S. portfolio investors in large numbers in:
   a. 1980.
   b. 1990.
   c. 1987.
   d. 1977.

4. In the typical emerging market, what percentage of stocks represent the preponderance of market capitalization?
   a. Less than 10 percent.
   b. 20 percent.
   c. 1 percent.
   d. Generally 20 percent to 30 percent.

5. Brazil's population is 80 percent of the U.S. population, yet Brazil's stock market capitalization is only _____ percent of the U.S. market capitalization?
   a. 10 percent.
   b. 3 percent.
   c. 12 percent.
   d. 20 percent.

6. Explain why U.S.-style security analysis is less valid in the emerging markets than in foreign "developed countries" such as England, Germany, and France.

7. Discuss two accounting shenanigans often used by second-tier emerging market companies.

8. How is the worth of the "relative value" method diminished in the emerging markets?

9. Families control many emerging market companies, and family members are often in the executive ranks. In many situations, the families take actions that fail to enhance shareholder value, despite the fact that the families are major shareholders. Explain the apparent contradiction.

10. To avoid the "family first" problem outlined in Exhibit 25–5, the author suggests U.S. investors interested in the emerging markets consider companies associated with:
    a. Multinationals.
    b. Privatizations.
    c. New technologies.
    d. All of the above.

11. A portfolio manager of Fidelity Emerging Markets Fund recommends the purchase of Delbras, S.A., a small publicly-traded Brazilian auto parts manufacturer. He describes Delbras as follows:

    > Delbras S.A. is a small, publicly-traded auto parts manufacturer that is 63 percent owned by the Bilbao family, whose other interests include a metal refinishing company and auto parts distribution firm (the latter is a major Delbras customer). José Bilbao, son of Delbras' founder, Vincente Bilbao, is the chief executive officer and he has over 15 years experience in the business. Vincente Bilbao, the Chairman, was previously a minister in the Fernando administration until President Fernando lost his reelection bid last year. The Brazilian auto market is growing and Delbras has a stable 12 percent market share, as local tariffs and shadow quotas restrict imports to under a 20 percent market share. With a conservative balance sheet and good five-year track record, Delbras is an attractive investment. 16 million shares are outstanding, and the current share price is the equivalent of US$11 per share. Other major stockholders include Banco Guarantia (9%) and Fundo Investimo S.A. (6%).

    Consult the author's "Emerging Markets—Stock Selection Guidelines." Which guidelines is the portfolio manager violating with this stock recommendation?

12. U.S. imported cement is cheaper than Mexican cement made in Mexico. Mexico does not prohibit the importation of inexpensive U.S. cement, but very little U.S. cement is imported into Mexico. Explain.

13. Terez S.A. is a Columbian paper manufacturer with the following historical sales profile:

Terez S.A.
(millions of Columbian pesos)

1997	1998	1999
3,698	5,231	7,890

Over the 1997 to 1999 period, inflation averaged 30 percent annually in Columbia. Provide the "real" sales growth record for Terez S.A.

14. Why do so many emerging markets have high inflation rates?
    a. Strong unions cause rapid price increases.
    b. The shrinking money supply drives up interest rates, leading to higher prices.

c. Their commodity-oriented economies are subject to rapid price fluctuations.

d. The central banks lack independence and discipline in managing the money supply.

15. The bond credit ratings of most emerging market countries fall into which category:

a. AAA to AA.

b. AA to A.

c. A to Baa.

d. Below Baa.

16. If the estimated return on the U.S. stock market index is 15 percent, what expected return should a U.S. investor demand from a basket of emerging market stocks? Explain your answer.

17. Referring to Exhibit 25–13, which country would likely have the highest expected rate of return on equity investment for a U.S. investor?

18. Why must emerging market stocks have higher expected growth rates than U.S. stocks in order to compete for U.S. investors' attention?

19. Examine the author's characterization (Exhibit 25–14) of various emerging markets' relative risks in 1997. Given the passage of time, how accurate were his assessments?

20. The chapter exposes several inadequacies of the relative value method for emerging market stocks. Why should you still use this method in a security analysis for such stocks?

PART V

Summary

26

Closing Thoughts on Security Analysis

Over the past 20 years, the United States has enjoyed a rising stock market and interest in equities has surged among professional money managers, corporate executives and business students. This enthusiasm has spread to the average American. Forty percent of households have a portion of their savings tied directly into individual shares or mutual funds.

The effectiveness of the U.S. stock market in providing stable investor returns, promoting efficient corporate funding, and fostering economic growth has spawned many imitators. In fact, numerous formerly Communist countries are copying the U.S. model.

Accompanying the growing popularity of stock markets has been a marked change in the way in which professionals value common stocks. Compared with the 1970's model, far less attention is being paid to historical financial analysis and discounted cash flow techniques. Most of today's research emphasis rests on forward projections and relative values. Another difference is the complicated analytical landscape of the 1990s. The increasing number of mergers and acquisitions, leveraged buyouts, international offerings, hi-tech stocks, and special situations require the practitioner to apply multiple methodologies in appraising a stock, all of which we covered in this book. Given the uncertainty attached to any valuation, double-checking one pricing approach against another is a sound investment practice.

This book has presented a comprehensive guide to security analysis. It has described the process of evaluating a specific security in a step-by-step fashion and noted the likely pitfalls one is likely to encounter along the way. The careful reader now has the tools to appraise every kind of stock—just as the pros do!

Although the equity market is in the midst of a long upward move, many individual share prices have gone down as well as up, and I ask the reader to venture into the appraisal process with a skeptical eye. Caveat emptor reigns supreme on Wall Street, and both issuers and brokers are prone to exaggerations and half-truths. Professional analysts, meanwhile, are frequently compromised by the investment banking relationships of their employers. Even those practitioners who don't have a conflict-of-interest problem are loathe to stick their necks out on investment recommendations; they fear the ridicule from their colleagues at being caught in a wrong prediction.

When perusing an equity research report, the favorite remark of the hard-bitten floor trader is, "This is B.S. A stock is only worth what someone will pay for it." In a narrow sense, this statement is true, but the same could be said for the value of any asset. A four-bedroom house in my town, Chevy Chase, Maryland, is only worth what someone will pay for it. Yet, the reasonable asking price for this asset isn't a mystery. A history of transactions and an expectation of future real estate values combine to set a price for the house within a relatively narrow range on a year-to-year basis. The same can be said for the stock market. A set of past experiences, shared expectations, similar practitioner training, academic logic, and common sense combine to establish rational prices for most stocks. From time to time, emotional forces overwhelm the conventional pricing process, but these tend to exhaust themselves over an intermediate time period.

Past experiences
Shared expectations
Similar practitioner training   } Tendency for rational equity values
Academic logic
Common sense

The goal of security analysis is to generate investment ideas that provide superior *absolute* and *relative* returns. Why do I stress absolute returns? Because an investor shouldn't be satisfied when his portfolio value drops 10 percent, even as the market declines by a greater number, such as 20 percent. Losing 10 percent is still *losing*. Only the large money managers declare victory when their portfolios *lose* less than the market. On a *relative* basis, I believe the time and expense dedicated to researching equities properly suggests that this effort provides more profit than a passively managed index fund.

To balance the risks of equity investment against the potential rewards, the key to success is the disciplined approach outlined in this book. A critical part of this approach is the preparation of a written research report, which includes a thorough top-down review along with detailed financial projections and comparative studies:

Model Research Report

1. Introduction.
2. Macroeconomic review.

3. Relevant stock market prospects.
4. Review of the company and its business.
5. Financial analysis.
6. Financial projections.
7. Application of valuation methodologies.
8. Recommendation.

It is important to mention that a complete research report doesn't rely entirely on published information and management interviews. The intelligent practitioner supplements this data with hands-on fieldwork that includes discussions with the firm's customers, suppliers, competitors, line employees, and government agencies. The research report and its recommendation are the culmination of an investigative effort. Instead of accepting management's rosy forecasts, the experienced analyst uses independent sources to determine whether corporate expectations are realistic.

Modern security analysis rests on four valuation techniques:

1. *Intrinsic Value.* A business is worth the net present value of its dividends.
2. *Relative Value.* Determine a company's value by comparing it with the values of similar companies.
3. *Acquisition Value.* Calculate a company's share price by determining its worth to a third-party acquirer, such as another operating business, a leveraged buyout firm, or a liquidator. Then apply a 25 percent discount for a passive minority investment.
4. *Breakup Analysis.* One values a multiline business by segmenting its components and valuing each separately. The whole is thus the sum of its parts.

Most of the time, the analyst applying these four techniques is frustrated. The resulting estimates usually fall within the ±15 percent margin of safety, indicating no buy-or-sell decision is recommended. In other words, the analyst spends a lot of time and has nothing concrete to show for his efforts, except further demonstration of the market's efficiency. He shouldn't be discouraged. In perhaps 10 percent of the company-specific reviews, he'll find a meaningful price discrepancy, which may reverse itself and provide an above-average profit. Even in this small universe of recommendations, however, the analyst doesn't have to be 100 percent right. Just being correct 60 to 70 percent of the time makes you a Wall Street superstar.

Furthermore, to make a difference, an investor needn't beat the market by leaps and bounds. Just exceeding the popular averages by 2 to 3 percent per year is sufficient. If the market returns 10 percent annually from 1999 to 2009, $1,000 invested in an index fund returns $2,594. At 13 percent annually (instead of 10%), the return is $3,394, a substantial $800 difference on a $1,000 investment.

By necessity, the professional adhering to the principles of security analysis often takes a contrarian approach, and may be selling a stock when the market is buying. This requires the courage to maintain a view at odds with conventional wisdom. It also suggests a long-term investment horizon since the market may take a while to accept the analyst's investment rationale. During this period, the investor following such advice may underperform the market on a quarter-to-quarter basis.

The traditional value approach in use today tells the stock picker to select issues with below-average P/E and price-to-book ratios. This strategy results in a portfolio of low-tech industrial, service, and cyclical businesses with a limited downside. Many practitioners place security analysis within the value style, but, as we have discussed, the principles covered in this book cannot be defined in such black-and-white terms. Indeed, the methodology set forth herein can uncover opportunity in any number of investment categories—be they out-of-fashion industries, deep cyclicals, speculative ventures, or international stocks. The common thread running through all these situations is the analyst's commitment to discipline and hard work.

Equity valuation plays a major role in today's business world. Fortunes can be made or lost by the manner in which a company's future is interpreted by the stock market, and crucial corporate decisions may hinge on whether institutions will provide financial backing. On the investment side, millions of people and organizations commit a substantial portion of their savings to equities, with the hope of achieving satisfactory returns within a sensible risk framework. With so much at stake, it is essential that those who are active in business, finance, or investments develop an understanding of security analysis, particularly as it is practiced on Wall Street, where the actual money changes hands.

As noted earlier, consider the applications of security analysis for the following four categories of users:

1. The *corporate executive* must be sensitive to valuation issues when he draws up his company's strategic plan, as well as when he conveys the corporate growth story to potential investors.

2. The *investment professional* regularly encounters the full variety of evaluative techniques described in this book. Many fail to appreciate the practical and theoretical underpinnings of the methodologies they employ on a daily basis. A sequential review of the building blocks of security analysis can only contribute to better job performance.

3. The *business student* learns about the 1990s' emphasis on enhancing shareholder value, but graduates with only a superficial knowledge of how the real world translates corporate results into P/E ratios. An appreciation of security analysis is necessary equipment when confronting the harsh realities of business and finance.

4. The *individual investor* who seriously follows common stocks benefits from studying security analysis. His first reward is a reduced susceptibility to "torpedo stocks," those overpriced speculative issues whose prospects have been hyped by others and whose disastrous price plunges can sink a portfolio's performance. Later, as he gains experience and sticks to this book's methodology, he'll be comfortable in making stock selections based on his own research and judgment. A strong adherence to the disciplined approach should provide superior returns, assuming the investor has a reasonable knowledge of business, accounting, and finance.

The reader is now armed with the requisite tools to evaluate individual securities and the broader markets in a rational way. He knows that stock prices represent a jumble of academic theories, practical applications, economic expectations, and emotional factors. Underlying this morass of conflicting forces is a series of time-tested valuation techniques that instill a fundamental order to the pricing process. Notwithstanding the wide acceptance of current valuation approaches, the key elements comprising a specific security appraisal are subject to frequent change, and financial projections, which play an important role in valuation, are inherently uncertain. This dynamic environment—along with the big money involved—contribute to making security analysis an interesting and vibrant occupation. It also ensures that the financial markets will continue to attract some of the brightest minds in American business.

Index